Dear Eddie,
We all hope
you feel better
soon! Hopefully these
goodies will make recovery
time fly by speedily.
Feel better soon!
The Rowdies Parents
and their Parents

Michael Bowler

Get well soon!!!
COACH Keeble

Chris Mulloy

Pat DiLiego

Joe Nicholson

Ian Volm
good luck Ed.

Scott Keeble

Kevin DeLuca

Steve Schwartz

Kevin Miller

Tim Washam
good luck

Mike Mitchell
good luck

Get well soon!
Coach Veg

James Rhoads
get better
soon.

Jake Veg (J-money)
Good Luck!

Rich Segaline
Hope you feel
better
we just
won 4-0

Get better soon
Dan R
(Doc)

Good Luck!
Chris Killian

THE OLYMPICS

ATHENS TO ATHENS 1896-2004

THE OLYMPICS

ATHENS TO ATHENS 1896-2004

WEIDENFELD & NICOLSON

4

CONTENTS

1896-2004

Forewords

BY **Jacques Rogge**
(PRESIDENT OF THE INTERNATIONAL OLYMPIC COMMITTEE) 6

BY **Michael Johnson**
(AMERICAN 200M AND 400M SPRINTER AND OLYMPIC GOLD MEDALIST) 7

Contents

Foreword

IN AUGUST 2004, THE WORLD'S GAZE WILL FALL ON ATHENS as the Olympic Games, a festival of tolerance, solidarity, peace and friendship, returns to Greece, their land of origin. To mark the occasion, this epic work, compiled with the assistance of the Olympic Museum in Lausanne, traces the summer Olympic Games, from the first Games of the modern era, in 1896 in Athens, to the 2004 celebration of the XXVIII Olympiad in the same city.

The Olympic Games are and will remain a meeting of the world's youth, where all participants share the same goal and enthusiasm. They represent the hopes and aspirations of the younger generation and the wider public across the globe. The Games are the only competition to bring together men and women represented by 200 National Olympic Committees. They transcend cultural, religious and political differences. This is symbolised magnificently by the Olympic Village, a place of solidarity and integration.

Having existed for just over a century, the Olympics have survived two World Wars, boycotts, the Munich tragedy and doping scandals. Sport, after all, can hardly avoid the impact of the wider world in which it exists. On each occasion, the IOC and the Olympic movement have managed to overcome these difficulties.

What is the secret of the success of the Olympic Games? It lies in the system of alternating between winter and summer Games, which generates real passion. The IOC has also kept the strengths of the ancient Olympic Games: their periodic nature, their duration and their location, which is confined to a single city. The universality of the Games themselves is reflected by the participation of the best athletes of the most popular sports. Taking part in the Games is the realisation of any athlete's dream. The IOC sees to it that these dreams become a reality through Olympic Solidarity.

Athletes are at the core of the Olympic movement and motivate young people through the image they portray. Our task is to inspire young people to take part in sport and to educate them through sport. Sport can teach them to respect rules and their opponents, allowing them to integrate into society and to develop a sense of team work. It also brings them hope, health and happiness.

Inevitably, the future of the Olympic Games and their success relies upon the defence of the intrinsic values of sport and through an unending battle against the dangers confronting it, such as drugs, corruption and violence.

The IOC, apart from organising the Games, is also responsible for supporting the practice of sport throughout the world. It will continue to invest in the increased participation of women in sport, the promotion of culture and education, the protection of the environment and humanitarian activities. Reducing the divide between rich and poor nations, in terms of sport, remains more than ever the IOC's priority and duty. The excellence, emotion, passion, triumph, sacrifice and adventure embodied in each Olympic Games appear in pictures in this wonderful history. The story is told through drawing on the archive of the French sports daily *L'Équipe* and its predecessor *L'Auto*. The power of this work lies in its ability to throw out the light of the eternal flame of the Olympics, bearer of all dreams.

Jacques Rogge

JACQUES ROGGE. PRESIDENT OF THE INTERNATIONAL OLYMPIC COMMITTEE

Foreword

THE OLYMPICS ARE A VERY SPECIAL EVENT FOR ME. I won five Olympic Gold Medals, my first in the 4x400m relay in Barcelona in 1992. But the pinnacle of my career was at the Olympics in Atlanta in 1996 when I won both the 200m and 400m titles and set a new 200m world record.

The Olympic Games in Sydney in 2000 were unbelievable. The facilities were first rate, the organisation, hospitality and entertainment from the city superb and the crowds really friendly and the added bonus was there was also fierce competition between some superbly trained athletes. Nobody wanted to leave! There will be great pressure on other Olympic venues after the success of Sydney.

I was fortunate to achieve all of my goals during my career so I don't miss competing but I look forward very much to attending each of the Games now that I am retired and watching the athletes compete. I am an even bigger fan of the sport now that I have the opportunity to take part as a spectator. I have been very fortunate in being able to make a living in doing what I loved to do, to run as fast as possible. It all started at Baylor University, Texas, where I began my relationship with my Coach Clyde Hart, who helped me to reach all of my goals. I'm often asked if I will be sad when my records fall but I will not feel sad even if any of my records are broken in these games because I don't spend any time thinking how long they are going to last. Records are meant to be broken and I actually hope I will be there to witness it when they do go because it will be a fantastic athletic performance. In the 400m in particular there is a pain barrier as you hit the last 7-8 seconds of the race and the body's systems begin to overload. You have to train and train to run in an even, fluid style, relaxed and with as much economy of effort as possible. I had been chasing the 400m record for nearly ten years and it all came right in Seville. I went out at a steady pace and covered the first 200m in 21.22. I knew I had to just keep going at the same pace no matter what my body told me and I managed 21.96. over the last 200m to beat Harry Butch Reynold's 1988 record by .11. I know what it takes to win and break records and the Olympic Games are the high point for every athlete. It is a fantastic occasion for spectators, both at the event and at home, watching athletes at the peak of their physical and mental powers compete against each other – and themselves.

This book is a really fascinating record of the dramas and achievements of successive Games since the first modern Olympic Games in Athens. Enjoy it, and the Games themselves.

MICHAEL JOHNSON. AMERICAN 200M AND 400M SPRINTER AND OLYMPIC GOLD MEDALIST

The Ancient Games

by Françoise Inizan

Imagine Olympia as a tourist would find it today: a peaceful land of fragrant pines under the heat of the sun, a silent valley at the foot of the gently rolling hills of the Peloponnese. Now imagine it as it would have been in ancient times when the Hellenic world met there every four years to celebrate its games: the vast, hectic agora, the large multicoloured forum packed with a crowd of 300,000 people, a considerable number at that time. Throughout Greece, from the coasts of the Mediterranean to those of the Black Sea, visitors converged on Altis, the sacred wood, the sanctuary dedicated to Zeus. Of course, some of the mainly male visitors were young athletes, but there were also pilgrims who flocked for religious ceremonies, merchants who set up stalls there, political orators who harangued the crowd, poets and philosophers who recited verses and speeches. The 'agon' or competition was never exclusively about sport.

Such were the games. Nobody has precisely dated their origin, but the creation of a ranking system in 776 BC marks the official beginning of the Olympic chronology. These celebrations of athletics took place in all Greek cities, but the four most significant pan-Hellenic Games were those of Delphi, organised around Apollo's sanctuary, the Isthmus of Corinth, held in honour of Poseidon, the Nemean Games and the Olympic Games, both dedicated to Zeus. A century after their creation, the Olympic Games had conquered the entire Greek world and, two centuries later, in 576 BC, their prestige and renown were at their peak. So it is here, in Olympia, that the Games' development can best be followed.

The Games as described by Homer were closely linked to the worship of a divinity or hero. Therefore, only champions judged worthy of competing under the eyes of the Gods took part. Olympia represented moral and physical development, the symbiosis of mind and body. The Games were neither entertainment for the masses (which they were to become later under the Romans), nor

were they a pastime for the privileged, since the pubic and nobility both attended. They encapsulated key ideas in Greek life, and the cult of the body and physical training were pushed to extremes never equalled by other nations. The Games exemplified the twin ideologies of aestheticism, which demanded the perfect beauty of the athletes, who mostly competed naked, and an aristocratic taste for excellence. In this sense, the Games' function was to designate the best of the Greeks. Therefore, only one champion was honoured. The Games took place every four years, probably at the first moon after the summer solstice, which fell between the last week of July and the first half of August. They rapidly gained in importance in the life of the ancient Greeks and became the basis for their calendar, which was divided into Olympiads. A year before the ceremonies began, the dignitaries responsible for their organisation dispatched heralds to inform the Greek world of the date of opening and, consequently, the date the sacred truce came into force. The truce principally denoted the inviolability of the land where the sanctuary was situated; it did not entail the suspension of ongoing conflicts.

The competition and training grounds were situated outside the sacred enclosure that protected the temples of Zeus and Hera. Here, in the palaestra, a square building arranged around a peristyle courtyard, wrestlers, pugilists and pankrationists trained. To the south, in the gymnasium, an outdoor area surrounded by porticos, runners and pentathletes made their preparations. In the bouleuterion, seat of the Olympic council, the competitors swore an oath to abide by the rules, on pain of a fine. Then there was the famous stadium, the greatest and most renowned of the time.

Through an arched, covered crypt – and the ruins of the long walls still exist today – the athletes gained access to the 192.27m-long track. According to legend, this distance represented six hundred times the length of Heracles' foot. Grooved stone slabs marked the

starting line on which the runners stood. At the end was a marker (terma) which the runner circled before returning to the starting line. Forty-five thousand spectators could gather there, seated on the embankment or on the white marble seats reserved for dignitaries. Finally, further to the south of the stadium, was the hippodrome, the length of three stadia (around 780m).

The first Games lasted one day; later, the Games extended over five days, with competitions taking place on three days before being closed by a final sacrifice and a procession and banquet celebrating the champions. The jury was made up of ten members (the Hellanodikes) who were elected from among the most important families for their impartiality. They were organisers and arbitrators; they kept order using whips, and issued penalties to those who broke the rules. They were strict and impervious to appeal from the athletes and their trainers. Corruption was considered an odious crime.

Law, regulation, order: the athletes had to abide by these precepts through self-discipline. But who were these champions? In the Greek world, they were so-called amateurs, people from good families who, rather than dedicating themselves to philosophy, devoted themselves to athleticism (among the Romans, they were workers or slaves, who were always paid and competed voluntarily – and this included the gladiators). In order to participate in the Games, the athlete had to prove his Hellenic quality and be 'neither slave nor metic' and have committed 'neither crime nor piety, nor sacrilege.' He then had to train for ten months - months of suffering and complete chastity, to purify the soul and gain courage. Thirty days before the Games, he would go to Elis where collective training would begin and the final competitors were chosen.

The Games were opened by the procession of the Hellanodikes. The dignitaries followed, and then the priests, who would sacrifice oxen on the altar of Zeus,. Finally, the athletes arrived. Pindar recorded thirteen or fifteen disciplines. Over the centuries this figure multiplied. Team sports never featured. No records were kept. Until 728BC (the thirteenth Olympiad), the Games consisted of one running event: the stade race, over the length of the stadium (*dromos*), which measured 197.27m. In 724BC, the double stadium (*diaulos*) of a little under 400m appeared. Then came a long race (*dolichos*) competed over seven, twelve or twenty stadia, or nearly 4km. But the dromos remained the most prestigious event, with the winner giving his name to the Olympiad. Koroibos – only his surname is known – was the first stade race champion in 776BC. Leonidas of Rhodes was the greatest Olympic running champion, winning four times between 164 and 152BC.

The pentathlon first appeared in 708 BC, with its five trials: the discus; the long jump, which was performed with a reduced run-up and carrying a weight in each hand; the javelin; the stade race and wrestling (*pale*), for which the competitors' bodies were coated in oil. Later, pugilism, the precursor of boxing, was added. It was fought with the hands, wrists and forearms wrapped in leather straps, which were sometimes inlaid with lead and iron, and the head protected by a bronze skullcap. The fights, which had no time limit, were never interrupted.

The pankration, a combination of wrestling and pugilism, was even more violent: any kind of blow was permitted, apart from biting or blinding. However, with its single rule, the pankration represented more than just a sport. It was a metaphor for the battle of life, battle without weapons. It was one of the essential aspects of Greek athletic education.

In 689 BC, during the twenty-fifth Olympiad, chariot racing began in the hippodrome. Dangerous and spectacular, these races became extremely popular in subsequent ancient games, like the mounted horse races. The races took place on a vast rectangle, with teams of two or four horses circling twelve times, a distance of around 9km. The difficulty lay in the very sharp turn at the boundary of each side. The riders were masters of

spirit and balance, and were honoured as such.

There was no glory sweeter than victory, and no hero greater than the champion, the Olympian, crowned with a wreath cut from a sacred olive tree with a golden sickle and celebrated during banquets where the wine flowed. His statue was erected in the Altis next to those of the gods and he became a hero, representing his city, celebrated, sculpted and sung about. This is how the great Olympic names have reached us: Milon of Kroton, a pupil of Pythagoras, a true reincarnation of Heracles, who won the pankration in five consecutive Olympic Games and six times in the Isthmian Games; Xenophon of Corinth, whose pentathlon exploits were praised in Pindar's odes.

However, it was the very mythical status of the Games that brought about their downfall. The champions were soon no longer winners of a simple olive wreath; they were honoured with privileges offered by the cities: free food, exemption from

taxes, and gifts. Some athletes became professionals, giving themselves to the highest bidder. The cost of training was so high that only the aristocracy was able to participate. Chariot races and the bloody gladiatorial competitions supplanted athletic competitions. Cheating and threats were used to secure victory. The Emperor Nero was declared a champion before he had even crossed the line, his opponents having withdrawn in fear for their lives. The Games descended into violence. Facing such perils, chariot owners began to send slaves in their place, offering freedom if they were victorious. Pankration confrontations ended in death. Fights between wild cats became fashionable. Even the sacred truce began to be violated.

The ancient Greek ideal died, taking its religious ideals with it. However, the public still wanted its *panem et circenses* – food and the games of the circus – and so the bedlam of the Roman games was born. They had enslaved the Greeks;

had they not every right to take over the Games? But to the Romans, the spectacle became everything. There were special effects which required sophisticated machinery. The crowd was sprayed with water perfumed with saffron, and showered with coins and jewels. Occasionally, riots broke out. One overthrew the emperor and caused the death of 30,000 spectators.

The Games became an instrument of government. They were ruinous to organise, and were surrounded by embezzlement and corruption. Under the denunciation of philosophers, the ancient Games disappeared forever in 394 AD when the Christian Emperor Theodosius I, fearing that they were reverting to a pagan Bacchanalia, abolished them. A year later, the Olympic site was destroyed by the Gothic invasion. Thirty-one years later, Theodosius II razed the temple of Zeus. Two earthquakes and a flood obliterated Olympia. In 1829, French and German archaeologists re-discovered Olympia's ruins.

23 June 1894 – The Games are reborn

by Serge Laget and Alain Lunzenfichter

'My listeners thought of the Olympic Games in the way they think of dead things that are only brought back to life at the opera,' protested Baron de Coubertin after a speech on 25 November 1892 that closed the celebrations of the fifth anniversary of the Union of French Athletic Sports Associations (USFSA) at the Sorbonne, and announced 'the revival of the Olympic Games'.

The audience had applauded his words, he suspected, without fully understanding them. To overcome their incomprehension and prove that the modern obsession with the Olympics could have a practical application, de Coubertin needed time to pursue his ideas. Adolphe de Pallissaux, the head of the USFSA, of which the passionate Baron had been made general secretary at the age of 29, immediately set about organising the assembly he needed, and at the beginning of 1893, the USFSA scheduled the next Paris International Athletics Congress for the Sorbonne between 16 and 23 June 1894.

The first issue on the agenda was the standardisation of the amateur-professional divide. The second was the revival of the Olympic Games. However, if the Congress was to be a success, de Coubertin would have to identify suitable and willing delegates from France and the rest of the world. It was no easy task, yet as de Coubertin busied himself with the Congressional invitations, he proved himself a bureaucrat of genius. In the autumn of 1893, he travelled to the United Kingdom and the United States in search of candidates. Charles Herbert, the honorary secretary of the Amateur Athletic Association, was appointed 'Commissioner for England and the British Colonies'. William Milligan Sloane, president of the Ivy Collegiate Faculty Committee on Athletic Sports, was appointed to represent the United States.

As chairman of the Congress, de Coubertin chose the Baron Alphonse de Courcel, a distinguished diplomat and former French ambassador to Berlin. Now he was a senator, shortly to fill the post of ambassador to London. Well disposed towards the sporting movement, which was only then emerging as an international force, de Courcel, like de Coubertin, believed that sport's social dimension had an important role to play in the pacification of national life, in which industrialisation was wreaking social havoc, and in stabilising relations between nations. Traditional diplomacy was, after all, beginning to prove limited in a Europe in which deep-seated enmities divided countries which were arming themselves to the teeth. Only a completely new counterweight, one for which the fundamental requirement was respect between members and nations, could present any hope of securing future peace. This force was to be Coubertin's renewed Olympics.

The Games were to be a novel compromise between the blood sports of the English, the gymnastics of the Swedes and quasi-military German gymnastics. The Baron de Courcel encouraged de Coubertin with words and actions, seeing in de Coubertin's dreams a new international vocation for France, something it had been lacking since its humiliating defeat by Prussia in 1870, when Emperor Napoleon III was captured with most of the French Army, and the provinces of Alsace and Lorraine were annexed.

The opening ceremony of the 'Paris International Congress for the Study and Propagation of Amateur Exercises' took place in the great amphitheatre of the new Sorbonne on Saturday 16 June 1894. Two thousand visitors, as well as seventy-nine representatives from the world of sport, heard the Baron de Courcel proclaim sport 'a modern necessity'. A new sphere of diplomacy was created among the representatives of forty-nine associations from thirteen different countries, from the Belgian Velocipede League to the New York Athletic Club and the Paris Polo Club. The participating countries were the United Kingdom, the USA, Russia, Greece, Australia, Italy, Holland, Bohemia, Spain, Hungary, Sweden, Belgium and France.

Over the following week, the framework for the Olympic revival was laid. On Monday they created two commissions: one to decide the definition of amateur status, presided over by Michel Gondinet, of the Racing Club de Paris; the other to work on the Games: the 'Comité International des Jeux Olympiques,' chaired by Demetrios Vikelas, the Greek delegate, a wealthy businessman and man of letters, connected to the King of Greece. Its first meeting decided against the incentive of cash prizes. On Tuesday, the 're-establishment of the Olympic Games in line with the requirements of modern life' was agreed by unanimous vote. The requirements of modern life, it was resolved, were four-yearly Games and federated national associations, as the Baron de Courcel proposed. Only amateurs would be permitted to take part in the first Games, an exception being made for fencers, to which professional instructors would be admitted. The first Games were to be held in 1896, in a capital city to be decided: the 1900 Games, however, would be held in Paris during the Universal Exposition. On Wednesday and Thursday, gambling was banned and the list of sports that were to be on the Olympic programme were selected: cycling, gymnastics, shooting, track and field athletics, rowing, sailing, swimming, fencing and equestrian sports.

On Friday, the Congress discussed sailing, shooting and equestrianism, without mentioning links to amateurism. Saturday 23 June 1894 was de Coubertin's day of triumph. It was a little after nine o'clock when the reports already drawn up were presented by the secretaries of the two committees. They were adopted by all members present. The Olympic Games were re-established, with one important provision: Athens, home of the ancient Games, would host the first reconstituted Games. Vikelas and King George I of Greece could not pass up such a wonderful opportunity to bring together a dynasty weakened by its Danish origins and to re-establish its international credibility.

Finally, the International Olympic Committee (IOC) was formed. It consisted of thirteen members, some extremely well connected. Vikelas took over the presidency with de Coubertin's blessing. Sloane represented the USA; Herbert and Lord Ampthil, grandson of the British Minister for Foreign Affairs, the UK; General Alexei Dimitrievic Butovski, responsible for sport in Russian schools, Russia and the Ukraine; Dr Jiri Guth-Jarkovski, well connected with the Austrian aristocracy, Bohemia; Viktor Balck, the founder of the Stockholm Gymnastics Association, represented Sweden; Leonard Cuff, a founder member of the New Zealand Amateur Athletics Association, New Zealand; José Benjamin Zubiaur (Uruguay), Mario Lucchesi Palli (Italy), Ferenc Kemeny (Hungary), France's Felix Ernest Callot, the president of French gymnastics, was treasurer. It was an able piece of engineering by de Coubertin: the vast majority of the newly elected members were absent.

After the closing dinner, the Baron thanked the Congress for 'bringing about what he had been working towards for the first ten years of his adult life'. He added for posterity: 'Greek Olympism has re-entered the world after lying eclipsed for several centuries. This bringer of joyous hope will light up the twentieth century.' Professor Michel Bréal, a French classical scholar, made another toast dwelling on the adoption of 'Citius, Fortius, Altis' as the Olympic motto: faster, stronger, higher. The motto had been adopted by de Coubertin's Committee for the Propagation of Physical Exercise in 1891, at the suggestion of de Coubertin's mentor and spiritual guide, the Dominican Father Henri Didon, a wise adviser to the emerging sporting movement.

Athens, 1877: the sack race during an early attempt to revive the Olympic tradition.

A priceless document: the invitation de Coubertin sent the diplomat Baron de Courcel, who supported de Coubertin and chaired the congress that revived the Games.

ALSO IN 1894...

The modern Olympics, were born in France, which had adopted modern sport later than Britain, and at the same time as Germany. In a world trying to establish rules, sport was joyously anarchic - folklore in short trousers. Only one thing counted: the game. The spectacle was a secondary consideration.

The powerful French union of French athletic sports associations (USFSA) devoted its efforts to the promotion of rugby, and was pressured into organising the first French association football championship in 1894. This came two years after French rugby had won a first international victory over Rosslyn Park (9-8), thanks to twice champions of French Stade Français. The USFSA had the competence to suspend the amateur status of a certain Désiré Delamare, of SA Montrouge, a cycling champion over a kilometre, for leading out the professional Gallott in his slipstream as Gallott attempted to break the record for the 1000 km - an adventure that lasted eleven days. In that first French football association championship, between six teams, Standard AC beating the White Rovers 2-0, although of the 22 players on the pitch, just one, Leguillard, was French. In the pole-vault, the head to head between Torchboeuf and Gustave Duchamps took French national record over 2.77m.

It was common to read in the newspapers: 'M. P Duchamps, Cours Gay-Lussac 28, Limoges, informs us that he challenges the Truffy brothers to a race in teams of two, over a distance of ten to fifty kilometres, for a stake of 100 to 500 francs.' Everything was a pretext for placing a bet, even the Paris-Le Havre-Paris walk, for which, we read, Ramogé and Péguet were joint favourites at 3/1; Bougé at 5/1; Vacher at 8/1 and Dufour at 10/1. Péguet was triumphant, with a time of 76 hours 55 minutes.

The most popular sport was cycling. Crowds packed the Buffalo Velodrome in Paris to see record attempts at every distance from 100m to 1,000 km, and every duration from an hour to six days. Sports advertising covered entire pages. Coming after solid tyres, pneumatic tyres began adding flexibility and comfort. Riders queued up to race from Paris-Dinan, Paris-Biarritz, Bordeaux-Paris, Lyon-Paris-Lyon, Paris-Saint-Malo, Paris-Bar-le-Duc, Paris-Trouville.

The winner of the first car race, Paris-Rouen, on 22 July 1894, achieved the dizzying average of 21km/h.

THE OLYMPIC RESURGENCE...

The modern Olympic Games came into being in 1896 in Athens. However, the idea of a meeting of the world's greatest sportsmen was already over a century old. As early as 1792, the French Revolutionaries contemplated bringing the Games back to life on the Champ-de-Mars in Paris.

In 1835, the Greek poet Panagiotis Soutsos wrote to his government requesting the revival of the Olympic Games. King Otto proposed a festival of art, industry, athleticism and agriculture, but nothing came of it. At Wenlock in England, Dr William Penny Brookes formed an Olympic committee in 1840, and from 1849 held 'Olympic festivals' including equestrian sports, running, swimming, cricket, and dancing.

Gustav Johann Schartau organised the Scandinavian Olympic Games between 1834 and 1836 in Ramlösa, Sweden. In 1834, these included wrestling, high jump, pole-vault, rope climbing, tug of war, speed race and even jumping onto a moving horse. In 1836, gymnastics replaced the jumps.

Evanghelis Zappas, a wealthy Greek patriot, founded the first Panhellenic Games in 1859. He obtained the support of his government, the royal couple and 20,000 spectators. The trials included a 200m race, a discus throw and a triple jump, and became farcical with the participation of old men, children, and even a blind man who had come to beg.

Regional Olympic Games were organised in Shropshire in England between 1860 and 1864. In 1860, the British National Olympic Society was formed and, in 1866, the British Olympic Games were organised in London. In 1880, the indefatigable Dr Brookes proposed an international Olympic Games and a fusion of his movement with the Greeks.

In France, the Schoolboy Olympic Games in Rondeau and Bosfleury, near Grenoble, had been keeping the pupils (including the youthful Henri Didon) happy for thirty years when in 1885, Ferdinand de Lesseps suggested the idea of a revival of the Olympic Games in Paris. Georges de Saint-Clair developed the idea in 1888, and the writer, journalist and Communard Paschal Grousset popularised it. A year later, at the Universal Exposition in Paris, national and international sporting competitions were set up. In 1890, Baron Pierre de Coubertin met with Brookes in Wenlock. The idea took shape and soon resounded around the world.

AMPHITHÉATRE DU PALAIS DE LA SORBONNE

Samedi 16 Juin 1894 à 4 heures

Séance d'Ouverture du Congrès International
pour le Rétablissement des Jeux Olympiques

Discours de M. le Bᵐ de Courcel, Sénateur, Président du Congrès.
Causerie de M. Jean Aicard, Président de la Société des Gens de Lettres.
Audition de l'Hymne à Apollon, (1ʳᵉ audition avec chœurs) sous la direction
de M. Gabriel Fauré. — Commentaire par M. Théodore Reinach.

AMPHITHÉATRE

Prière de présenter cette carte à l'entrée.

Pierre de Frédi, Baron de Coubertin

by Olivier Margot

Aged 24, Pierre de Frédi, Baron de Coubertin, leaves the mansion in which he was born at 20 rue Oudinot in the prestigious seventh arrondissement, and walks past the home of the Racing Club de France in rue Eblé. Sport is in its infancy in France: four years from now, the Racing Club will beat Stade Français 4-3 and become rugby champions of France. As he passes 'on his right' what is now the Victor-Duruy College and the Hôtel des Invalides, he has already embarked on his life's work. This bourgeois figure, as full of contradictions as life itself, is among the first to campaign for the right of sport for all, to promote the idea of free municipal gymnasiums and the necessity of workers' universities. Education will be his passion – he has launched himself into a reform of secondary education with vehemence and enthusiasm – until his death in Geneva on 2 September 1937. Within four years, on 25 November 1892, he will give an extraordinary speech at the Sorbonne. His theme: 'Physical exercise in the modern world'. His conclusion will centre on what he called 'This grandiose and virtuous work: the re-establishment of the Olympic Games.' Polite applause will greet him, a shade less enthusiastic than that received by the musicians of L'Harmonie de la Belle Jardinière who will have preceded him.

Now he is heading for the Seine. He skirts the École militaire before reaching the Champs de Mars in front of an immense building site: the four faces and the first floor of the Eiffel Tower have just been assembled. The Tower, the work of Gustave Eiffel, architect of modernity, is widely regarded as an insult to good taste, and has raised protests from an exclusive group of men of letters and arts, including the writer Guy de Maupassant, who has written: 'I left Paris, not to say France, because the Eiffel Tower was too upsetting.'

We can only imagine how Pierre de Coubertin felt in front of this prodigious opus, this feat of engineering which had until then been unimaginable. It was utopian, yet it was being made real. Coubertin was another of those rare beings who live their dreams and bring their ambitions about. He would make the Olympic utopia a reality. It would be his own Eiffel tower, the most respected and visited monument to sport.

The pompous style of Coubertin's thirty or so works, covering more than six thousand pages, has often been mocked. Referring to sport rather than the infernal tower that was growing in front of his eyes, he extolled 'the freedom of excess. That is its essence, its raison d'être, the secret of its moral worth…' In his work, 'Sports Pedagogy', he further developed this audacious proposition: 'Sport's tendency towards excess (…) is its psychological characteristic par excellence. It demands more speed, more height, more strength – always more. This is its disadvantage – from a human perspective that is! But it is also nobility, even poetry.' Pierre de Coubertin was a man of his time, but he was well ahead of this time, to the point of prefiguring the words of the great Tour de France champion Jacques Anquetil, a bronze medalist at the Helsinki Olympics in 1952: 'I am not in the same time as others.' Coubertin thought long-term and acted quickly. He was a visionary, at once generous, ambitious and naïve, blessed with a real sense for politics, a network of useful contacts, a capacity to unite others and a family fortune, which he was to deplete partially to achieve his dreams. He was a force in motion.

He was an aristocrat who came from a rich, very Catholic and strongly monarchist family. Pierre de Coubertin was the son of a religious painter, the majority of whose works are housed in the cellars of the Vatican. His mother, Marie-Marcelle Gigault de Crisenoy de Mirville – whose name alone tells a history of France – was descended from the first companions of William the Conqueror. Pierre de Coubertin was the product of a social class horrified by the defeat by Prussia at Sedan in September 1870, and the revolutionary fervour of the Commune of Paris – brutally put down in an orgy of revenge subsequently known as la semaine sanglante, 'the week of blood'. Yet de Coubertin demonstrated a wonderful spirit of rebellion. He avoided the temptation of the religious orders and their ceremonies, renounced the military school at Saint-Cyr, and grew tired of law. Pierre de Coubertin preferred following his own route.

Again, the scene can almost be imagined. In Normandy, not far from Bolbec, in a small renaissance manor house belonging to his mother's family, he read, or rather devoured 'Tom Brown's Schooldays' by Thomas Hughes, set at Rugby School when Thomas Arnold taught there. Arnold had the good sense to allow the pupils to develop by making their own rules – the key, perhaps, to a more responsible, more autonomous, more audacious and more courageous society. He also leafed repeatedly through Hyppolyte Taine's scenes of English life, where he would continue to focus on the description of the celebration following an Oxford-Cambridge boat race: 'In the evening there are speeches, applause, toasts, choirs singing, a joyous and glorious commotion. It is clear that such a triumph must be nearly as desirable as a palm wreath at the Olympic Games.'

It was in the Normandy beach resort of Étretat, in front of the needle in which the fictional gentleman-burglar Arsène Lupin – France's Sherlock Holmes – made his den in 'The Hollow Needle', that Pierre de Coubertin's thoughts first turned to a modern Olympics. And like the fictional Lupin, de Coubertin possessed the same intellectual audacity and mastery of situations. Indeed, de Coubertin was familiar with the correspondence of his contemporary Maurice Leblanc, the author behind Lupin, and could have read a letter Leblanc addressed to an old friend from his school in Rouen:

'For me, school signified large sombre walls pierced by a low door through which we went to recite lessons we did not understand, to complete homework we never had the time to do and to listen to the infinitely slow ticking of a clock that seemed to have invented extra-long

1896

Athens

THE INTERNATIONAL OLYMPIC COMMITTEE had just two years to organise the first Games in the face of opposition from an alliance of hostile Greek politicians. The Crown Prince of Greece brought his influence to the cause but Baron Pierre de Coubertin still had a diplomatic mountain to climb.

At the start of 1895, a public subscription fund in Greece raised 13,000 drachma in just two months and Alexandrian billionaire, Gheorghios Averoff, donated one million drachma towards the restoration of the stadium. The stands, marble throughout, could hold 60,000 and during the Games, it was often full to capacity.

American athletes dominated the Games and only the British offered resistance. The host country consoled itself by winning the marathon with more than 100,000 spectators lining the 40-km route. The Olympic Stadium was full to bursting as a passionate crowd roared the winner, Spiridon Louis, to victory like a mythical hero.

The Games were held in a fairground atmosphere. All-night street celebrations, processions, banquets, fanfares and fireworks celebrated a festival of sport rather than a solemn revival.

And when it was over, the very Greek ministers who had conspired to make the Games fail proclaimed their success and attempted, with the King's backing, to overthrow the International Olympic Committee and keep the Games in perpetuity. Baron Pierre de Coubertin brushed off their manoeuvring and it would be 108 years before the Games would return to Athens.

The fencing tournament took place before the King and Athenian high society in the magnificent open-air Zappeion Stadium.

Victory over the doubters

Works are being carried out in Athens in order to give the first modern Games a fitting welcome. Enthusiasm fills the air.

BY PIERRE DE COUBERTIN

It took two years of work to restore the Panathenic Stadium, keeping to its original design.

Spring came to Athens twice in 1896, warming the air and stirring the soul of the city. Sweet-smelling flowers sprout between the stones of the Parthenon, and the Palikares, the Greek soldiers, wear contented smiles. The sun shines and the Olympic Games are near. The anxieties of the past year are over. Spring has silenced the doubters.

Stalls on the sidewalks are selling the flags of France, Russia, Germany, Sweden and England. The Attic breeze lifts the lightest of them, to the delight of the Greek men who stroll before the picturesque façades in knee-length fustanellas. The world will soon flock to their city and they approve.

All over Athens, marble is being scraped, plaster and paint applied, paving stones laid. The great arch and Venetian masts before the stadium are the objects of a massive cleaning operation; the resultant whiteness has become almost blinding. However, the real interest is on the once-scorned banks of the Ilissus. Every evening a long procession of Athenians arrives to view the progress of the stadium. The Ilissus is dry, as usual, but the

monumental bridge that straddles it leads to the platform beneath the restored stadium.

Here, King George will proclaim the rebirth of the Olympic Games on Easter Monday, 6 April 1896, 1,502 years after Emperor Theodosius declared them abolished forever!

The stadium enclosure is deeply impressive. The ancestors of 19th century Greeks would have gazed on this very tableau. Yet, although the silhouettes of Greek temples never disappeared – their porticos and columns have seen 20 renaissances – they are surprising and disconcerting. Although the stadium died with the ancient Games, their architectural features were known, but never restored.

No ancient stadium has been seen in use for centuries but, in a matter of hours, the ceremony that will celebrate its revival will see multitudes flow up its steps and throng its terraces.

The modern crowds will be very different from the last to fill the stadium, but the same emotions will move them – the same love of youth, the same desire for human harmony.

There is space for approximately 60,000 spectators. A section of the terraces is fashioned in wood as there was not time to shape and install sufficient marble slabs. The construction will be completed only after the Games, thanks to the generosity of Georgios Averoff, who will have given his homeland a monument truly worthy of it.

The ancient dust track has been replaced by a modern cinder surface using the latest techniques, thanks to the expertise of the English. It will be jealously guarded by the Greeks.

Before the Games became a reality, physical exercise had few practitioners in Greece and the fencing and gymnastic societies had difficulty finding new members.

The revival of the Olympic Games has convinced the entire nation of the virtues of sport, and reminded the Greeks of the vigour and suppleness of their race.

So great is their passion, so rigorous their training, that visiting athletes are likely to encounter new opponents as formidable as the best-known athletics' stars of the day.

Early arrivals are Hungary's delegation, led by the IOC's amiable Hungarian representative, Mr Kemeny, director of the Royal School of Budapest. They were received with warmth and enthusiasm, to a musical accompaniment. Over the coming days the Russians are expected, followed by the Americans, the British and the Swedes.

They will be in for a shock. Instead of encountering the anticipated very paradigm of dilapidation, they will be confronted by extraordinary vitality engendering by the Games – a pulsing with life and energy. What an education awaits them at the foot of the Acropolis!

They will wonder at the vigor of an Athens reborn around the Parthenon, equal to its majestic beauty, enhanced by its ancient tranquillity.

Two revelations await them. First, they will be compelled to review their ideas of ancient Greece; second, they will come to a new appreciation of modern Greece.

The revived Olympic Games will teach them that the ancient order is united to contemporary reality by the most intimate possible links of resemblance and heredity. World history will gain new meaning through the Games, which will prove that a nation entombed by the passage of time, can be reborn.

At the entrance to the stadium, the statue of Georgios Averoff, the generous donor who financed the reconstruction work.

In the realm of dreams

Athens hosts a range of competitions in wonderful settings, bringing modernity and history together.

BY PIERRE DE COUBERTIN

The programme for the 'Great Week' has been finalised. The inauguration of the Stadium and the Opening Ceremony will take place on Easter Monday. The King, George I of Greece, will preside, accompanied by his ministers, deputies and diplomats. The Games will begin immediately and in the evening, the city will be illuminated. On Tuesday 7 April, the Zappeion Palace will host the fencing tournament followed, at nightfall, by a sunset vigil as the

sunlight falls on the Acropolis. On Wednesday 8 April, the shooting range and the velodrome will be officially inaugurated. The range has been constructed in Kallithea, on the road between Athens and Phalere. The shooting commission, headed by HRH Prince Nicolas, wanted a grand structure and have erected a magnificent edifice containing vast halls and luxurious changing facilities. A terrace serves as a rostrum, the view from which extends beyond Salamine

The members of the Organising Committee (Pierre de Coubertin, second on the left) have drawn up an exciting timetable for the 'Great Week'.

Athènes 1896-Le programme et règlement des Jeux olympiques de 1896.

to the steep shores of the Peloponnese.

The velodrome is based on the facilities at Copenhagen. The royal box, an elevated platform with a balustrade and mosaic paving, looks out over the Parnes, the Pentelic and the Hymettus, with the Acropolis behind the Phalere villas. A classic setting for this most up-to-date of sports – cycling. This symbol of modernity is played out at the foot of the venerable Parthenon.

The clash between old and new was the principal argument against the Olympic revival. With some justification: lawn tennis before the Coliseum or cycling beneath the arch of Titus might make a comic spectacle, but that is because the Roman monuments have aged. Not the Parthenon though; it is timeless. It belongs to all ages and modernity cannot detract from it. A protest led by the Belgian Federation against the inclusion of gymnastics in the Olympic programme came to nothing and the gymnastic events will take place on Easter Thursday, between Swedes, Germans, Greeks and a few British competitors.

The following Saturday, the charming and tiny bay of Zea will host the swimming competitions.

The modern residences of Piraeus crowd down towards the bay, their tiered balconies and terraces decorated with pampas grass. Below them,

temporary stands look out over the blue water. Never have swimmers enjoyed a more hospitable location to practise their sport. The regatta is scheduled for the final two days of the Games. An elegant, purpose-built pavilion, in wood of different hues and surrounded by the ruins of an ancient temple, provide all the luxury of a sumptuous English club.

Behind the hill, the ancient fortifications between Athens and Piraeus subsists, half-buried in the sand. All the millennial history of the Greek people is laid out in the folds of these shores.

If athleticism cannot but assume a historical dimension, the effect is surprising only to foreigners.

The 1896 Olympic Games will close on Tuesday, 14 April. The King will conduct the awards ceremony and prizes will comprise a certificate and a medal, the work of the French sculptor Jules Chaplain.

On one side Chaplain has engraved the outline of the rock of the Acropolis, with the Propylenes and the Parthenon, and on the other side the head of the Olympian Jupiter. The medals represent more than the symbolic laurel branch of ancient winners and less than the cash coveted by modern sportsmen. It is a simple souvenir uniting art and athleticism, consonant with the surroundings and the pure ideal on which sport itself is founded.

Spiridon Louis saves the honour of Greece

By winning the first Olympic marathon, the Greek has also restored his nation's pride after the damage it has suffered at the hands of the Americans.

BY PIERRE DE COUBERTIN

In general, the Greek crowd has accepted the victory of 'barbarians' in Olympic events with good sportsmanship.

At the entrance of the Stadium, in clear view, is a huge mast. After each event, the winner's number is posted at its foot and the relevant national flag is raised aloft.

It is an inspired rite, and it epitomises the international mission of the Games. One by one as the Games progressed, the colours of the great nations of Europe have been flown over the crowds but the most frequent has been the star-spangled banner of the Americans.

It is fitting that this should be so: the Americans were among the first to be enthused with the idea of re-establishing the Olympic Games and they were alone in never harbouring doubts.

The Games are not the first meeting between the American and Greek nations. Perhaps more than the Europeans, America has identified itself with the lofty ideals of the ancient democracy of Greece, to which their own political organisation bears more than a passing resemblance.

This sympathy led to the foundation of a fine School of Archaeology in Athens. It has remained little known outside Greece, and under-appreciated even within the country.

The school – a focal point of the American community in the Greek capital – sits on the slopes of Mount Lycabettus, where it devotes itself to the furthering of knowledge, well supported by voluntary donations by private citizens.

Its missionary zeal tells of the high cultural values of the United States. The Greek crowds, whose fondness for the Americans is reciprocated, have celebrated their Olympic Games successes with warm applause.

They even managed to smile when a student from Princeton University won the Games discus competition, one of the Olympic events which the Greeks felt was traditionally part of their cultural birthright.

However, Greek generosity might have been stretched to breaking point if the cup donated by Professor Michel Bréal to the winner of the marathon had

Spiridon Louis, resplendent in traditional Greek costume. No wonder the Greek public identified themselves with his marathon win.

The day after his victory, Spiridon Louis receives his trophy from the King. The public receives him like an ancient hero.

mounted like an unstoppable wave before this celebratory scene that joined past and future.

Calm returned but, bursting national pride, a woman unclasped her jewelled watch and threw it at the young hero's feet and a hotelier presented him with a certificate entitling him to 365 meals.

Even a shoeshine boy on the street corner offered him his services for free.

If these tributes had a comical air, they also captured the unaffected sincerity of the emotions the Games could inspire in the individuals moved to offer such gifts.

Even the poet Charles Maurras, who had so resolutely opposed the internationalisation of sport inherent in the Olympic ideal, declared: 'I can see that this internationalism will never kill national sentiment. It will make it stronger still!'

SPIRIDON LOUIS

According to popular legend, Spiridon Louis, 25, first heard of the revived Olympic Games while tending his sheep in the Amaroussion countryside but the reality is more prosaic. Enrolled in the first Greek regiment, the new marathon champion was serving under the orders of a Colonel Papadiamantopoulos, whose ambition was to see his men distinguish themselves at the Olympic Games. Several took part in the selection trials to decide which would be eligible to compete in this race on 9 April.

Seventeen athletes disputed the first Olympic marathon. The fifth of thirty-eight participants during the second round of selection, Louis, wearing the number 17, won the event in 2:58:50 before a delirious crowd. As the small figure of Spiridon Louis appeared in the stadium, Crown Prince Constantin and Prince George hastened to his side to urge him on, running the last few metres beside him. At the finish line, King George waited to congratulate the champion.

Louis explained: 'It was a moment I could never have imagined. The crowds were calling my name. Flowers and bouquets were raining down on me and hats were flying into the air.'

The following day, he shyly appeared at the presentation ceremony, then returned in triumph to his village.

gone abroad. When, after running the 40km separating Marathon from Athens in 2hours, 58 minutes, the first to enter the stadium was a Greek, they were at least spared this distress. It was an emotional arrival.

The stadium was full and the picturesque hill above it was also crowded – an estimated 60,000 spectators. The King of Greece was already in the amphitheatre, beside the King of Serbia, the Princess Royal of Greece and an international range of ministers and diplomats.

The moment the winner's approach was announced, the Greek spectators rose to their feet; it was as if an electric current had been passed through them. The thunder of their cheers must have carried across the plain to the foot of Mount Parnes, stirring the spirits of their ancestors.

The action taking place in the present mystically connected with collective memories passed down from antiquity. To protect the winner from the delirious crowd, the Crown Prince and his brother, Prince George, took him in their arms and carried him to the changing room. Mass enthusiasm

1896
OLYMPIC ROUND-UP

AUSTRIA'S SCHMAL FINALLY REWARDED FOR HIS EFFORTS.

The 12-hour track race was held in the open-air velodrome at Phalere on 13 April. The crowds were enormous, despite the conditions. The race went ahead in torrential rain driven by a gale which uprooted trees and caused the regatta, planned for the same day, to be postponed until the following day. It was eventually cancelled altogether.

The possibility of any sport taking place at all that day was in serious doubt. Many assumed the day's programme would be postponed, including the 12-hour cycling event, which had been included in the Olympic programme despite widespread misgivings. No-one, it was feared, would turn up to watch. Cycling, it was believed, would be the Games' weak point.

Instead, the event was a huge succes. Seven contestants set off at ten past seven in the morning. Only three finished the event and the first two had covered the modest distances of 314.997 km and 314.664 km, respectively.

The winner, Adolf Schmal, Austrian correspondent of the journal Paris-Vélo and a member of the Vienna Velocipede Club (see photo 2) defeated Briton Frank Keeping, chief steward to the British ambassador in Athens.

Through the raging storm these two fine athletes demonstrated great endurance and a huge physical effort was required each time they crossed the line.

Schmal's victory was reward for his Olympian efforts; two days earlier he had been bitterly disappointed to finish third in both the 10km track race and the one-lap sprint.

Four contestants, including Germany's Josef Weizenbacher, were not placed. Although most of the participants upheld the seriousness of Olympic competition, the same cannot be said for the two Greek entrants: Mr A Tryfiatis-Tripiaris abandoned the race only minutes after it had begun while his compatriot Mr Georgios Paraskevopoulos stopped halfway through the race to take lunch at Piraeus, before resuming his efforts later.

1 At the shooting range in Kallithea, the Greek marksmen triumph despite poor equipment. Left to right: Georgios Orfandiss (free rifle, 300m), Ioannis Frangoudis (rapid fire, 25m) and Pantelis Karasevdas (military rifle, 200m).

2 After finishing third in two events, Austria's Adolf Schmal wins the day in the 12-hour track event with drafting, despite the conditions. The champion was later to be suspected of professionalism.

3 In the Bay of Zea, Hungarian swimmer Alfréd Hajós (real name Arnold Guttmann, 1878–1955) adds two medals to his collection. He easily won the 100m freestyle in 1:22.2 and the 1,200m in 18:22.2.

4 and 7 The long horse vault goes to Germany's multiple champion Carl Schuhmann, 26, who also triumphs in the team parallel bar event and in Greco-Roman wrestling, defeating the Greek giant Georgios Tsiatis, whose hand he is shaking.

5 On the parallel bars, Alfred Flatow (GER) beats Louis Zutter (SWI), who wins the side horse.

6 The American students from Princeton return home with an impressive haul of titles. Placed athletes include (from left to right): Herbert Jamison (second, 400m, 55:2), Robert Garret (first, shot put, 11.22m and discus, 29.15m; second, long jump, 6m and high jump, 1.65m), Albert Tyler (second, pole vault, 3.25m) and (sitting) Francis Lane (third, 100m, 12.6).

8 Already champion in the long jump with 6.35m, the versatile American Ellery Clark adds victory in the high jump with a leap of 1.81m.

AMERICA'S BURKE ASTOUNDS ATHENS

Ancient tradition demanded the Games begin with the running events, so the modern Olympic Games began with the 100m heats. The first two in each heat qualified to compete in the final on 10 April. Frank Lane of Princeton University won the first heat. The victors of the subsequent heats, Thomas Curtis and Thomas Burke, both of the Boston Athletic Association, used a 'crouch' start, considered suspect by the Greek spectators. Curtis took no further part in the competition, preferring to save his energy for the 110m hurdles, the next event in the programme. Thomas Burke (second from left) recorded the best time in his heat – 12 seconds – a performance he repeated in the final when beating Fritz Hofmann (GER). It was Burke's second triumph of the Games: three days earlier he had won the 400m.

The first modern champion

By winning the triple jump, America's James Connolly became the first Olympic champion of the modern era.

On 6 April 1896, James Brendan Connolly became the first Olympic champion since the Armenian boxer Prince Varasdates in AD396. The first modern Olympics consecrated their first victor when Connolly, born in 1870 into a poor Irish-American family in south Boston, Massachusetts, outdistanced France's Alexandre Tuffère.

It was not a popular result, for the Americans are poorly regarded here. If the Frenchman had defeated Connolly, his victory would have been celebrated; if Ioannis Persakis, the Greek who finished third, had done so, the delirium that would have ensued could only be imagined. Instead, the superlative Americans demonstrated their superiority over the athletes of every other nation from the very beginning.

In the qualifying heats of the 100m, held before the triple jump, the American sprinters were astonishing. Not only did they win, but they did so by huge margins. The Greek public, once it had recovered from its state of shock, cooled to the US athletes for humbling their own men. In any case, even if the Games would be less compelling without them, the Americans' unremitting success and marked lack of modesty won them few admirers.

This background sentiment should not blind us to the fascinating story of Connolly's path to victory. The 27-year-old, self-educated undergraduate at Harvard, read about the Olympic revival and, as US triple-jump champion, asked the university for permission for leave to attend. When the university refused, Connolly gave up his studies to pursue his sporting ambitions. With no family wealth to fund his Olympic campaign, he paid for the journey with the support of the Suffolk Athletic Club and a bake sale organised in his home town.

Having raised the funding for his journey, the ordeal began. Ten US athletes and one coach endured the 16-day crossing from America to Naples in Italy, followed by an interminable onward train journey.

They reached Athens at 9pm on 5 April with Connolly's luggage and wallet having been stolen *en route*. At 4am the following morning, Connolly was woken by the strains of a brass band. He learned that he was due to compete that day and not 12 days later as he believed. He and his team-mates had been blissfully unaware of the discrepancies between the Western and the Orthodox calendars.

The Games were officially opened at 2pm on the afternoon of 6 April. In the triple-jump competition Connolly was the last to go. He marked his run-up by placing a red woollen sweater beside the runway. Prince George of Greece took exception to this, considering that it gave him an unfair advantage over other competitors because it allowed him to regulate his approach.

The Prince promptly removed the sweater, only to be challenged by another American athlete who tapped him on the shoulder and demanded to know why he was taking the sweater.

The Prince, with unwavering good humour and his constant, beaming smile, delivered a long, detailed explanation, and refused to replace the offending article.

Connolly's next setback was questions surrounding his technique. Every other competitor performed a hop and a step before the final jump; Connolly's sequence consisted of two successive hops. A scrutiny of the rule book confirmed this method was permissible.

As the competition progressed, the length of the jumps was known only to the officials. Connolly turned to the official responsible for raking the sandpit – an Englishman – and commented that the competitors ought to be informed. 'Then a fellow won't be breaking his back when there's no need of it,' the American complained.

'Don't worry – there's no-one within a yard of you,' was the reply he received.

After all his trials, Connolly had finally emerged victorious. Later in the Games, he finished second in the high jump and third in the long jump.

After his triple-jump win, Connolly telegraphed home, in characteristically emphatic terms: 'The Greeks only conquered Europe. I have conquered the world.'

RESULTS

Triple jump
1 James Connolly (USA), 13.71 m
2 Alexandre Tuffère (FRA), 12.70 m
3 Ioannis Persakis (GRE), 12.52 m
4 Alajos Szokolyi (HUN), 11.26 m
5 Carl Schuhmann (GER), –

Long after the Games in Athens, James Connolly became a celebrated journalist and writer, winning a Pulitzer Prize.

1896

ATHENS I OLYMPIAD

Pierre de Coubertin's attempt to revive the Olympic Games succeeds. Despite modest performances, even by the standards of the time, huge crowds witnessed the historical events.

THE GAMES IN BRIEF

Opening Date
6 April 1896

Closing Date
15 April 1896

Host Nation
Greece (GRE)

Candidate Towns
Athens was chosen as the host town for the Games of the first Olympiad at the first session of the International Olympic Committee (IOC) between 23–24 June 1894 in Paris.

14 Nations Represented
Australia, Austria-Hungary, Bulgaria, Chile, Denmark, Egypt, United States of America, France, Germany, Great Britain, Greece, Italy, Sweden and Switzerland.

245 Athletes
(0 women, 245 men)

9 Sports
Track and field, cycling, fencing, gymnastics, weightlifting, wrestling, swimming, tennis and shooting.

Demonstration Sports
None

43 Events
(none open to women)

Games officially opened by
King George I of Greece

Olympic flame lit by
The Olympic flame was first lit during the Opening Ceremony of the Amsterdam Games in 1928.

Olympic oath read by
The Olympic oath was first delivered during the Opening Ceremony before the Antwerp Games in 1920.

IOC President
Demetrius Vikelas (GRE)

DID YOU KNOW?

An Olympic hymn composed by Spyros Samaras (music) and Kostis Palamas (lyrics) was performed for the first time.

Subsequent Opening Ceremonies featured other musical compositions, until the Rome Games in 1960, when the Samaras / Palamas composition became the official Olympic hymn.

Olympic postal stamps were the first to celebrate sport. Of the 75,000 stamps released in Athens in 1896, 10,000 were Olympic issues. In 1895, the stamps helped the organising committee balance its budget and build the final five sites destined to host events.

Every winner received a silver medal and an olive branch. Runners-up received a medal alone. Third-placed participants were not rewarded.

The Hungarian swimmer Alfred Hajos won the 1200m event in which the nine competitors were taken out to sea by boat and left to swim back to shore.

1900

Paris

IN ORDER TO PROVIDE THE GREATEST possible stage for the second Olympic Games, the IOC had what at the time seemed the inspired idea of holding them in Paris during the Universal Exposition. In 1898, a committee drew up an ambitious programme centred on a vast stadium to be built in Courbevoie with athletes to be housed in a château. Reality fell far short of these grandiose but unrealistic dreams. On 14 July 1900, the Games opened in the presence of Pierre de Coubertin and French Minister of Trade Alexandre Millerand.

There was no new stadium and the participants stayed in hotels. The athletes enjoyed reasonable accommodation apart from the Germans – they had been forgotten.

Overshadowed by the Universal Exposition, the Games went almost unnoticed. The word 'Olympic' was nowhere to be seen and the Games were referred to as the 'Paris Championships' or 'The Great Exhibition meeting'.

The events were held between May and November, and many winners were unaware until years later that they were Olympic champions.

Only tiny handfuls of spectators attended, in an atmosphere of tedious formality, and there was additional controversy over Sunday competition which further blighted the spirit of the Games.

France's Filleul Brohy and Marie Ohnier had the honour of being the first women to compete – in a game of croquet – but the final balance was negative. Pierre de Coubertin told a friend later: 'It's a miracle the Olympic movement survived Paris.'

Many non-Olympic events took place alongside the official, amateur programme. Left, the professional 110m hurdles is won by the Frenchman Triyens in a time of 21 seconds, ahead of Belgium's Charbonnel.

Kraenzlein, King of the Games

America's Alvin Kraenzlein is the first to win four gold medals: one as a sprinter, two as a hurdler and one as a jumper.

Alvin Kraenzlein, an elegant 23-year-old American, arrived in Paris with a solid reputation. For some time, he has been unbeatable: truly the prototype of the athlete of the future. The versatile Kraenzlein, at six feet and 165 pounds, is a handsome, relaxed young man with dense, curly hair. He is equally at home in the sprint, hurdles, long jump and high jump. A virtuoso of speed and spring, Kraenzlein, whose father originated from Vienna, Austria, was born in Milwaukee, Wisconsin.

He brought a magnificent record to the Games. Two years before in Chicago, he became the US 120-yard hurdles champion in a world-best time of 15.2 seconds. In 1899, he won the US titles in the high and low hurdles and long jump, and finished second in the high jump and the 100-yard dash, the latter of which he completed in 10 seconds. The same year he also beat the world long-jump record four times with 7.29m, 7.40m, 7.42m and 7.43m.

In Paris he has contested eight events in just three days, culminating in the long jump on 15 July, and won four gold medals. Kraenzlein is truly the King of the Games!

In the 60m, he achieved a world record time of 7 seconds and in the heats of the 110m hurdles, on turf,

Untouchable in the hurdles, thanks to his superb technique, Kraenzlein took the 110m and 200m double.

he set a new world record of 15.6 seconds, reducing it to 15.4 in the final. The 200m hurdles were a formality and Kraenzlein's time of 25.4 seconds brought him victory ahead of Pritchard, Tewksbury and Choisel.

The long jump final should have seen Kraenzlein's eagerly-awaited duel with Meyer Prinstein, who robbed him of the world record by jumping 7.50m at the Penn Relays in Philadelphia, on

8 April the previous year. A dramatic turn of events marred the encounter, leaving American officials seething. Long before the Games, they had requested the French organisers to reschedule the finals planned for Sundays, in order to respect the religious convictions of some athletes. Their request was denied and Meyer Prinstein, to the amazement of the French, carried out his threat after a

jump of 7.17m in qualifying and not showing up for the final.

Kraenzlein had also hinted that he too would refuse to compete on a Sunday but changed his mind. He jumped 7.18m. His decision infuriated the American officials but Kraenzlein became the Olympic long jump champion, a quadruple gold medal winner and the phenomenon of the 1900 Games.

RESULTS

KRAENZLEIN'S FOUR WINS

60m
1 Alvin Kraenzlein (USA), 7.0
2 John Walter Tewksbury (USA) 7.1
3 Stanley Rowley (AUS) 7.2

110m hurdles
1 Alvin Kraenzlein (USA), 15.4
2 John McLean (USA), 15.6
3 Frederic Moloney (USA), 15.6

200m hurdles
1 Alvin Kraenzlein (USA), 25.4
2 Norman Pritchard (GBR), 26.0
3 John Walter Tewksbury (USA), 26.1

Long jump
1 Alvin Kraenzlein (USA), 7.18m
2 Meyer Prinstein (USA), 7.17m
3 Patrick Leahy (GBR), 6.95m

Ayat and Fonst, master and pupil

The fencing tournament during the Exposition brings together competitors from 19 nations. The French perform particularly well.

Ramon Fonst CUB (left), amateur, and his instructor Albert Ayat (FRA), professional, duel for Olympic supremacy in the épée. The instructor has the last word.

The foil tournament at the 1900 Exposition took place in the ballroom while the épée contests were in the open air on a terrace in the Jardins des Tuileries.

A number of spacious pergolas were erected, one as a changing room for the competitors, others to accommodate the buffet and to allow the events some protection from the elements.

This was great foresight since the skies opened regularly, drenching contestants who eventually had to continue under canvas.

Throughout the fortnight of competition, the terrace hosted a fair crowd. On the final day there were 165 paying spectators, a considerable number bearing in mind that committee members, the judges and all the Olympic competitors had free-entry cards, of which the Exposition had distributed more than 600.

Also all the official Exposition tickets gave free access to the tournament. The épée clearly has ardent and numerous followers and

the quality of the bouts, especially in the closing stages, was remarkable, and provided a fascinating spectacle.

The amateur tournament, with 154 swordsmen, opened proceedings with 17 qualifying rounds. The results mostly met expectations with the better-known, seeded competitors winning through.

The top two from each round progressed to the semi-finals and after 36 bouts, the top three from each of the three semi-finals competed in a league system involving nine fencers. Ramon Fonst and Louis Perrée were the first with two touchés.

In the barrage Fonst touched Perrée and was declared champion. The prizes consisted of objets d'art worth from 1,500 francs down to 50 francs.

Ramon Fonst is a slim and tall fencer, not yet 17. With his épée always perfectly aligned, he has a sharp riposte and an accurate advance attack. His patience and tenacity in the face of adversity are exceptional, and he possesses genuine skill, which he

owes to the excellent lessons of his master Ayat. He won the Dunkirk championship the previous summer.

Ninety signed up to the masters' event, raising the total number of entrants to an impressive 244. An incident similar to what had happened among the amateurs took place.

Dufraisse, a firm favourite among the event's followers, was eliminated in the first round, perhaps due to the unfamiliarity of competing in the open, and perhaps his lack of concentration.

The final brought together famous names. The champion was Albert Ayat, the son of master Ayat, who teaches with him at the Anjou fencing club, as does Bougnol who came second. Both are exciting to watch, with very strong attacks and confident parries

Laurent came third and no less would have been expected of his methods of attack using his legs, arms and head.

In line with the regulations, a grand final round was contested between the

top four amateurs and top four masters. On the whole, this confirmed the previous placings, with Albert Ayat and Fonst, the first professional and amateur, respectively.

Finally, it was Ayat who walked away with the 3000 franc prize, without sustaining a single touch.

RESULTS

Amateur épée
1 Ramon Fonst (CUB)
2 Louis Perrée (FRA)
3 Léon Sée (FRA)

Masters' épée
1 Albert Ayat (FRA)
2 Emile Bougnol (FRA)
3 Henri Laurent (FRA)

Épée
(amateurs and masters)
1 Albert Ayat (FRA)
2 Ramon Fonst (CUB)
3 Lieutenant Léon Sée (FRA)

1900
OLYMPIC ROUND-UP

SUPERB ATHLETES FROM THE NEW WORLD.

By the end of the year, we will have a wonderful collection of world champions. I have attempted to compile a list of the different titles on offer at the Exposition's great events – I reached forty-three.

Of all these great sporting heroes, none will be more deserving than those who emerged victorious at the amateur tournaments of 14 and 15 July. They were more exciting than the professional versions of the same events a fortnight earlier and the amateurs' individual performances surpassed those of the pros.

The United States of America sent the cream of their universities and the performances of Kraenzlein, Tewksbury, Jarvis, Long, Orton, Baxter, Sheldon and Flanagan were long remembered. Great Britain sent an incomparable squad of distance runners and although France was the host, none of its athletes was victorious.

The athletes of the other continental European nations also fared badly, with the exception of Hungarian discus thrower Bauer, who triumphed in a competition enlivened by the setting. The landing area was a narrow lane lined by trees and inaccurate throws which struck the trees were discounted.

Rather than feeling discouraged, the European athletes must strive to improve, even if there is certainly a long way to go before achieving the muscular strength, rich blood, methodical training techniques and sporting courage of the young, proud race that has developed in the New World.

With few exceptions, we should not expect to see Europeans beating American students in our lifetimes.

It must also be said that these young Americans generally have a superior moral life and, from an athletic point of view, morals have a significant impact on the physique. These reasons explained Europe's defeats; they do not excuse them.

1. Britain's Len Hurst, winner of the professional marathon, completes his second circuit of the Parc des Princes velodrome. He covered the 40km in 2:26:47.8.
2. Belgium's Léon de Lunden, the finest marksman in the live pigeon shooting event.
3. Three individual victories for Hubert Van Innis in archery events that have now disappeared.
4. Among the non-Olympic events, a line fishing competition was held from 5 to 8 August on the Île des Cygnes on the River Seine. 600 competitors, representing six nations, caught 881 fish, with Frenchman Emile Lesueur the winner.
5. The unknown Olympic champion. No-one knows the identity of the French boy who acted as coxswain for François Brandt and Relof Klein, the Dutch coxed-pairs champions of Team Minerva Amsterdam.
6. A crowd gathers to watch Hungary's Rudolf Bauer as he wins the discus with a throw of 36.04m
7. New Yorker John Flanagan begins his run of victories in the hammer with a throw of 51.01m. He also retains his title in 1904 and 1908.
8. With a 14.10m throw, America's Richard Sheldon is shot putt champion. His compatriot McCracken was second, a long way behind with 12.85m.
9. High-flying Irvine Baxter takes the high-jump title for America, with 1.90m, 12cm higher than the second-placed competitor. Baxter also won the pole vault at 3.30m.
10. The non-Olympic 75 cannon firing event in the Vincennes polygon. The Paris cannon club won the three events, ahead of teams from Poitiers and Lille.

TENNIS

Women compete for first time

Lawn tennis paradise, the Île de Puteaux, hosted the Olympic events characterised by the appearance of female competitors.

Women made their Olympic debuts at the Paris Games in the gentile atmosphere of the Île de Puteaux club, located near Paris.

With the backing of the club president, the Vicompte de Janzé, the Île de Puteaux had become the Mecca of lawn tennis and, as an Olympic venue, the eyes of the world were also upon it.

The foundation of the Île de Puteaux sports club (SSIP) was in 1886 when the racquet sport was still unknown by the majority of France. It has been in the vanguard of spreading the popularity of lawn tennis throughout France.

During the 1900 Games, this is the club that hosted the world lawn tennis championships.

First-rate competitors, ideal weather and perfect organisation characterised this meeting.

The sport was of superior quality, making worthy champions of brothers Hugh and Reginald Doherty, Mr Harold Mahony, Miss Charlotte Cooper and Mlle Hélene Prévost – and they are not even professionals.

The first three are famous in the world of English tennis. Their game is as varied as it is intelligent, especially that of Mr Hugh Doherty.

The highest compliment that can be given to Miss Cooper, who won the women's championship, is that she

Playing in a long dress under the heat of the sun is no easy matter. Miss Gillou does so with aplomb.

plays as well as a man – a man who plays well.

Her French rival, Mlle Prévost, is a slightly less intelligent player but so much more graceful.

The prizes were also highly tasteful and what a delightful drinks table Mr H.L. Doherty took away as winner of his championship!

This sets the Île de Puteaux club apart from the customs of some other clubs, which do not have the slightest concern for encouraging the arts.

The prize-giving ceremony was exquisite. The elegance of the summer outfits, scattered among which the red jackets in the club's colours stood out, enhanced the beauty of the setting. The beauty of the women, and the exhibition of prizes, formed a scene

worthy of a great artist. Everyone left the Île de Puteaux enchanted by the reception they received.

In truth, the club did not have the most auspicious of starts. The first tennis players were accommodated on an ordinary lawn and the first court constructed was not even.

Today the SSIP has more than 1,300 members and the club has spread so much on the Île de Rothschild that it now covers four hectares.

The attractive, elegant women of Paris meet at Puteaux. Moreover, the time spent here is made even more pleasant by the first-class buffet. Not to mention the fact that an electric boat powered by a trolley provided transport to the island.

The buildings, all made of wood

from the islands, have been erected next to each other, forming a sort of colony.

There could have been no better compromise than these facilities, which appear rustic, but are actually very comfortable inside.

English and American players have settled in Paris because of of the excellent facilities that can be found at Puteaux.

The surroundings are enchanting and the shade of the island provides a respite from the extreme heat that would be hard to find in remote locations.

The two arms of the Seine surround the island and if the tennis players want some variety, they leave behind their racquets and take up oars instead.

The management board is structured as follows: Vicompte de Janzé, president; Baron de Carayon-Latour, vice-president; Mr Alfred Gaillard, secretary, and Mr James Gordon-Bennett, administrator.

The members included the Duke of Uzès and the Count of Chasseloup-Laubat.

RESULTS

Women's Singles Final
Miss Charlotte 'Chattie' Cooper (GBR) beat Miss Hélène Prévost (FRA), 6-1, 6-4.

Mixed Doubles Final:
R.F. Doherty-Miss Cooper (GBR) beat H.S. Mahony (GBR)-Miss Prévost (FRA), 6-2, 6-4.

Men's Singles Final:
Hugh Lawrence Doherty (GBR) beat Harold S. Mahony (IRL/GBR), 6-4, 6-2, 6-3.

Men's Doubles Final:
Reginald Frank Doherty-Hugh Lawrence Doherty (GBR) beat Spalding de Garmendia-Max Decugis (USA/FRA), 6-2, 6-3, 7-5.

Beaten by Miss Cooper in the singles final, Miss Hélène Prévost takes revenge in the handicap, without removing her hat.

PARIS II OLYMPIAD

Swamped in the programme of the Exposition Universelle International,
the Olympic trials included the most diverse range of competitions
and were even open to scholars and professionals.

THE GAMES IN BRIEF

Opening Date

Closing Date

Host Nation
France (FRA)

Candidate Towns
None

24 Nations Represented

1,225 Athletes
(19 women, 1,206 men)

20 Sports
(4 open to women)
Track and field, rowing, cricket, croquet,
cycling, equestrian, fencing, football, golf,
gymnastics, pelote basque, wrestling,
swimming, tennis, shooting, water polo.

Demonstration Sports
None.

88 Events
(13 open to women)

Games officially opened by
No official opening

Olympic flame lit by
The Olympic flame first lit during the
Opening Ceremony of the Amsterdam
Games in 1928.

Olympic oath read by
The Olympic oath first delivered during
Opening Ceremony before the Antwerp
Games in 1920.

IOC President
Baron Pierre de Coubertin (FRA)

DID YOU KNOW?

Women competed at the Games, in spite of
the fact that Baron de Coubertin didn't want
them to.

The first female Olympic Champion was
British tennis player Charlotte Cooper, taking
the singles title. In men's singles tennis, two
British brothers, Reginald and Hugh Doherty
faced each other in the semi-finals. Reginald
withdrew from the competition and his
younger brother went on to win the final.
The athletics were disrupted by the refusal
of certain Americans to compete on a
Sunday for religious reasons. In the long
jump, the American Jewish athlete Meyer
Prinstein, a top performer in the qualifying
rounds, was ordered by his Christian coach
not to compete in the final, which took place
on a Sunday. His performance in the
qualifying rounds, carried over for the final
ranking, was beaten by another American,
Alvin Kraenzlein, by one centimetre.

In rowing, the Dutch coxed pairs team
suddenly found themselves without a
coxswain. A young French boy was drafted
in to fill the position. After the Dutch team
claimed victory, the young French boy
participated in the medals ceremony and had
his photograph taken. However, in spite of
years of research, the name and age of this
young boy, who would have been between
seven and twelve years old in 1900 and who
could be the youngest champion in Olympic
history is still unknown. These Games, which
were organised in the framework of the
Exposition Universelle International, (the
Paris World's Fair) gave rise to a great
many excesses. Some unusual events
were organised (swimming, obstacle race,
equestrian, high jump and long jump among
others) and most winners did not receive
medals, but cups or trophies, and the Games
even finished without a closing ceremony.

1904

Saint Louis

WHEN THE GAMES CROSSED THE ATLANTIC Ocean for the first time to be staged in Saint Louis in the American state of Missouri, it was the first step to becoming truly global. But the Games' first appearance on a new continent saw the organisers repeat the mistakes of four years before in Paris and again spread them over more than four months, losing them in the hubbub of a much larger event: the Louisiana Purchase Exposition.

The long, costly journey prevented many European nations from participating. Of the 89 events now generally considered as making up the Olympic programme only 42 included athletes from outside the United States. France had just one representative, the marathon runner Albert Coray, who lived in Chicago. Despite these problems, the Games spawned many popular and sporting success stories. Gold, silver and bronze medals were systematically awarded for the first time and boxing and freestyle wrestling made their debuts in the programme.

Marathon runners Len Tau and Jan Mashiani of the Tswana tribe were in Saint Louis for the Exposition as part of a Boer War show, and became the first African athletes to compete at an Olympic Games.

A shocking and inappropriate addition to the programme was an attraction entitled 'Anthropological Day' during which white segregationist America tested the capabilities of the so-called 'inferior' races. The Saint Louis Games will always be tainted by this.

Already taken hostage by the Louisiana Purchase Exposition, the Games were then hijacked by the lamentable 'Anthropological Days', on 12 and 13 August, when African and Native American tribes, such as the Pawnees (pictured), were forced to make a humiliating exhibition of their links with sport.

Archie Hahn, the Milwaukee Meteor

A little-known sprinter wins three finals and earns the sobriquet 'the Milwaukee Meteor.'

Archie Hahn, far left, has an unorthodox style, but it does not prevent him winning at 60m (above), 100m and 200m.

Between 29 August and 3 September, the track and field tournaments saw national and regional contests take place beside the official Olympic events.

The organiser, James E. Sullivan, intended them to demonstrate the superiority of US athletes even more categorically than in previous Games. Sullivan began the events with the

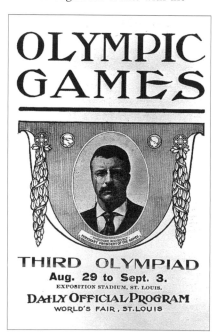

60m, a distance the United States has no rivals over.

The event brought the tiny Archie Hahn of the Milwaukee Athletic Club to the attention of the world. The sprinter, 24, from Dodgeville, Wisconsin, competed for the University of Michigan in the western states but was little-known in the East and few regarded him as a potential champion in Saint Louis.

He had won the 100 yards in the 1903 American Championships and, right from the Olympic heats, Hahn showed his mettle, moving from unknown to Olympic favourite in a matter of metres.

In the final, Hahn faced the best of American sprinting talent – William Hogenson and Clyde Blair of the Chicago Athletic Association; Fay Moulton from the Kansas City Athletic Club; and Franck Castelman and Meyer Prinstein, both of the Greater New York Irish-American Athletic Club. Hogenson, Blair and Moulton were considered a class above Castelman and Prinstein. Hahn was considered in a class of his own and he did not disappoint.

As a result there was considerable interest in the battle between Moulton

and Hogenson for second place.

Hahn covered the distance in 7 seconds, equalling the world and Olympic records of his compatriot Alvin Kraenzlein and finishing metres ahead of Hogenson and Moulton, who were neck and neck.

However, Hahn's style troubled attentive athletics 'purists'. Hahn's pace seemed to depend on that of his rivals: after a fast start, he appeared to be playing with them, allowing them to catch up, before accelerating away again, clearly tailoring his effort to the occasion.

'It is perfectly clear that he could have beaten the world record if he had been pushed,' commented US official Charles Lucas.

Two days later, still basking in the glory of the 60m victory, Hahn was among the favourites for the 200m, in which he faced Nathaniel Cartmell, a real thoroughbred, sporting the colours of the Louisville YMCA in Kentucky.

The fans from Chicago hoped Hogenson would triumph over Hahn and those from Missouri were cheering for a Moulton victory.

On the starting line, with the finalists crouched down in readiness,

Hahn laid a trap for his rivals. With an almost imperceptible sway, he panicked Cartmell, Hogenson and Moulton into jumping the gun.

His three greatest rivals now incurred penalties for their joint false starts – their distances being extended by one yard. Hahn's movement had escaped notice, and he received no penalty.

It was no more than an insurance policy, for when the starting pistol fired, Hahn's reaction was so rapid that his rivals appeared to be anchored to the starting line.

After 20m Cartmell was already 7m behind Hahn and two strides behind the others. He then accelerated with such vigour that by 75m he was level with the three stragglers, then darted past Hogenson and Moulton who finished third and fourth.

Hahn was uncatchable and finished two metres ahead for a new Olympic record time of 21.6 seconds.

His starting line strategy had worked perfectly – although it seems that the man now relishing the name the 'Milwaukee Meteor' did not really need it.

On Saturday 3 September, with two gold medals already under his

Two years after his victory in Saint Louis, Archie Hahn wins the 100m at the 1906 Intercalated Games in Athens.

belt, Hahn lined up for the 100m against Cartmell, Hogenson and Moulton, as well as local hope Fred Heckwolf of the Missouri Athletic Club and Lawson Robertson of the Greater New York Irish-American Club.

Once again, Hahn was off his mark in a flash and the race was decided almost before it had even begun. After 20m, the three-metre advantage he had opened on his rivals was too great for them to bridge.

Cartmell, after a start that was as laborious as ever, struggled to catch up. He picked off his rivals one by one and bravely finished two tenths of a second behind Hahn, who equalled the Olympic record of 11 seconds.

As in the 200m, Hogenson had to be content with bronze and Moulton with fourth.

Archie Hahn is the first sprinter to win the double of the 100m and 200m in the Olympic Games – a double made all the sweeter by the addition of a third gold medal in the 60m. These victories justified the sobriquet the 'Milwaukee Meteor.'

Hahn's hat-trick places him among a select group of triple medal winners at these Games. These include Harry Hillman (USA), the winner of the 200m and 400m hurdles, and the 400m flat; and fellow countryman James Lightbody, the 18-year-old who has won the 800m, 1500m (in world record time) and the steeplechase.

Ray Ewry (USA) repeated his Paris performance by winning all three standing jumps with Prinstein taking the conventional long and high jump titles, albeit in the absence of the world record holder, Peter O'Connor (IRL). Prinstein also finished fifth in the 60m and the 400m.

RESULTS

100 metres
1 Charles 'Archie' Hahn (USA), 11.0
2 Nathaniel Cartmell (USA), 11.2
3 William Hogenson (USA), 11.2
4 Fay Moulton (USA), 11.4
5 Frederick Heckwolf (USA) -
6 Lawson Robertson (USA) -

ATHLETICS

A test of courage

The 25 miles of the marathon saw an astounding race produce two winners: a real one and an impostor.

On the starting line, Thomas Hicks (number 20, first) stands beside Fred Lorz (31, disqualified). Cuba's Félix Carvajal (30, fourth) and France's Albert Coray (7, second) are also in the front row.

If the marathon had taken place on a good surface, in the coolness of the morning over a flat course, it would still have been an ordeal.

It is never easy to cover 40.2km (25 miles), the distance chosen by the Saint Louis organisers. Instead, and with no real experience of this type of competition, they seemed to be trying to complicate the competitors' task.

After five circuits of the track, the course meandered over pot-holed paths and sand, climbed a series of seven hills (each of which, for the tired runners, must have resembled Everest) before another circuit of the stadium.

Only one water station was provided – a well 12 miles from the stadium and the pack of 32 runners

RESULTS

Marathon
1. Thomas Hicks (USA), 3:28:53
2. Albert Coray (FRA), 3:34:52
3. Arthur Newton (USA), 3:47:33
4. Félix Carvajal de Soto (CUB) -
5. Demetrios Velouis (GRE) -
6. David Kneeland (USA) -
7. Henry Brawley (USA) -
8. Sidney Hatch (USA) -

began the race at three o'clock with the temperature 32°C in the shade. A fleet of vehicles carrying judges, officials, doctors and journalists surrounded them, no doubt making the dusty atmosphere even more stifling.

Only 14 competitors made it to the finish line and the only one who did not seem totally overwhelmed by these circumstances was Cuba's Félix Carvajal, one of the most colourful competitors to have competed in an Olympic Games.

This tiny postman, barely 5ft tall, decided to compete in Saint Louis two years ago. Convinced he would win and return in glory to his country, newly freed from Spanish colonisation, Carvajal funded his entry by staging running exhibitions in city squares.

Untiringly, he circled the town hall for days, then climbed up onto a soapbox to ask astounded passers-by for their charity. Some say Carvajal raised enough money to reach Saint Louis; others that the mayor paid for his journey.

All agree that once he arrived in New Orleans, Carvajal squandered his savings playing dice.

He maintained his dream of

Olympic victory, much to the generosity of those he encountered *en route*, hungry and destitute, up the Mississippi to Saint Louis. The American throwers fed him and looked after him until the day of the race, which Carvajal started in long trousers

and heavy shoes.

One of the US discus throwers held up the start of the race to cut down the Cuban's trouser legs. Carvajal finished an excellent fourth, despite having no experience of marathon running and suffering severe stomach cramps. In order to slake his thirst during the race he had stolen peaches from an official and apples from a roadside orchard.

He may have not even won a medal, but in the hearts of the American spectators he was the moral victor.

Saint Louis saw the first competitors from the African continent to take part in the Games. They were Len Tauw and Jan Mashiani, two members of the Tswana tribe from Zululand, and Bob Harris, a white man from the Transvaal in South Africa.

Tauw and Mashiani were in Missouri as part of a group of South Africans at the Louisiana Purchase Exposition where they performed a daily reconstruction of the Boer War's two famous battles.

They entered the marathon as a joke but ran remarkably well. Tauw was ninth and Mashiani, who lost time thanks to a considerable detour through a wheat field to avoid ending up in the jaws of two enormous dogs, finished 12th.

Mashiani was not the only person to court disaster during the race. Two of the officials policing the race route were seriously injured when their vehicle swerved to avoid one of the participants and careered off the road and down an embankment.

In the stadium, the spectators were oblivious to the difficulties faced by the runners and were beginning to wonder why none of them had yet finished. Then with three hours and 13 minutes gone, the New Yorker Fred Lorz appeared.

His victory was no surprise. This 24-year-old builder was one of the best American specialists in this event, having finished fourth in the Boston marathon in 1903 and fifth in the same event last April.

He received a champion's welcome, was photographed with US President's daughter Alice Roosevelt and was about to receive his gold medal when it was discovered that he had cheated.

After nine miles, he had collapsed with cramp beside the road when he was offered a lift in one of the accompanying cars. As the car overtook the runners he applauded them and cheered them on, glad not to be suffering like them.

Eleven miles on, the car broke down and, as Lorz's cramp had passed, he trotted towards the stadium to get

The poor quality of the roads meant that the winning performance was the slowest in Olympic history.

changed. That, at least, was his version of events.

When he entered the stadium, the crowd roared for America's first Olympic marathon champion and officials prepared the laurel crown. Lorz smiled broadly, raised his arms in victory and crossed the finish line like a national hero.

He had certainly enjoyed the moment, but it was just a piece of fun.

The AAU officials had a less-developed sense of humour: they

immediately announced a lifetime ban on him.

The true champion of the Saint Louis marathon finished 15 minutes later. Thomas Hicks was an English-born metal worker from Cambridge, Massachusetts, and his victory was something of a miracle. He found himself in the lead after the collapse of Sam Mellor, but 10 miles from the finish, he was growing extremely weak himself.

Although a mile and a half ahead of his closest follower, his coaches would not allow him to rest and made him swallow a mixture of strychnine sulphate mixed with raw egg white.

They also gave him strychnine, mixed with brandy, and sprayed him with water warmed in the boiler of a steam-driven automobile accompanying him.

Hicks staggered, walked and ran until the last steep hill, two miles from the finish.

On several occasions, only the support of his handlers prevented him from collapsing and he won the race with a six-minute lead.

Runner-up Albert Coray lost 10 pounds and a good deal of his sense, but none of his spirit. He immediately

announced his retirement: 'I have always wanted a marathon trophy. I can leave the way open to others.'

Hicks staggers towards the finish line, thanks to the support of his coaches.

ALBERT CORAY, THE UNKNOWN FRENCHMAN

France sent no representatives to Saint Louis, yet a Frenchman appears on the list of medalists. The marathon line-up featured Albert Coray, registered under the name of the Chicago Athletic Association, yet he is a Frenchman through and through. In July 1902, he won the 155km Paramé-Rennes-Paraméin in 16 hours and 32 minutes when he was running for the US Paris club. It was only in 1903, that Coray left France for Chicago where he worked as a professional strikebreaker.

Four days after finishing second in the Olympic marathon, Coray demonstrated his ability to recover by competing in a new event: the four-mile team race. Finishing ninth individually, he played a big part in winning second place for the Chicago AA, behind the New York Athletic Club.

1904
OLYMPIC ROUND-UP

A BATTLE FOR REGIONAL SUPREMACY.

The vast majority of the 9,000 athletes competing in the sporting festival organised by James E. Sullivan were American. Great Britain, Germany, Greece, Austria, Hungary, Ireland, Switzerland, Canada, Australia, South Africa (Zululand and Transvaal), Cuba and France were all represented but not necessarily by their best athletes.

In fact, many of those present were not chosen for their athletic prowess but for being resident in the US.

University participation was no more representative. The Harvard team remained at Cambridge and Yale, Columbia, Dartmouth, Georgetown and Amherst also refused to travel to Saint Louis, as did the private universities of Pennsylvania, Illinois and Michigan.

As a result, the Games were not so much the Olympic Games as a tournament between the eastern and the western states, or even the Chicago Athletic Association versus the New York Athletic Club.

Pierre de Coubertin's grand Olympic vision became an American athletics meeting, or less. For James E. Sullivan and his supporters, it was of no importance that the best European athletes had stayed at home.

According to one of the organisers, Charles Lucas: 'It is doubtful that a single Frenchman would manage to finish above fourth place in any of our events.'

As it turned out, the events were not contested between nations and the fact that the major universities were absent was also of no significance in the eyes of the organising coimmittee. They seemed to take the view: 'Why should the Games be a battle between students when they could see the triumphant struggle of workers pursuing the American dream common to all immigrants?'

As a result the festival, spread over months in Saint Louis, had only remote links to the Olympic ideal.

1 and 7 New Yorker Meyer Prinstein sails through the long jump and triple jump events with leaps of 7.34m and 14.35m.

2 With a 51.23m throw, John Flanagan (USA) exceeds his Paris performance by 1.50m to retain his Olympic hammer title.

3 In the heavyweight division, Greek weightlifter Perikles Kakousis lifts 111.70kg with two hands – and the gold medal in one.

4 The American runners take the first six places in the 400m. Harry Hillman is first in 49.2 seconds, ahead of Frank Waller (49.9) and Herman Groman (50).

5 In the 50 yards freestyle, the judges are unable to separate J. Scott Leary (USA) and Zoltan Halmay (HUN). The final was repeated, and this time the Hungarian was faster, leaving his rival trailing.

6 America's lone cavalier races over the hurdles. In the 200m and 400m, Harry Hillman, on the outside, is unstoppable. These races also see the first black Olympic medalist. George Poage (right) finishes third over both distances.

7 Indefatigable American weightlifter Oscar Paul Osthoff of Milwaukee AC, triumphs in the one-handed lift and comes second in the two-handed event with 83.36kg.

9 Ralph Rose of Chicago can be satisfied. He wins a medal of each colour in the throwing events: gold in the shot put (14.81m), silver in the discus (39.28m) and bronze in the hammer (45.73m).

10 On 4 and 5 August, American cycling champion Marcus Hurley takes four of the seven titles up for grabs: the quarter-mile, third of a mile, half-mile and the mile.

11 With only American entrants, like many other events, the water polo allows the New York Athletic Club to get the better of Missouri AC (5-0) and Chicago AC (6-0).

12 In the dumbbell competition, America's Frederick Winters finishes second in the one-hand lift.

ATHLETICS

Ray Ewry, the rubber man

In a confused Olympic programme that includes standing jumps, America's Ray Ewry leaps into history.

In the standing high jump, the first of his three events, Ewry achieves 1.50m – easily enough to take the gold medal.

Sport sometimes finds it hard to recognise its own boundaries, and the lines that divide athletics and equestrianism from the world of the circus act are sometimes unclear.

At Saint Louis we see runners – amateur and professional – in jockeys' clothes and using horses' names, and jumpers taking inspiration from circus

and cabaret. It's fashionable, practical and spectacular and, according to the advertisements, which are excessive, England's John Darby and America's John Higgins, the star attractions at this new Olympic circus, can achieve jumps of over two metres without a run-up.

Professional jumpers have claimed huge leaps. Darby is alleged to have cleared 12 feet 1.5 inches as long ago as 1890 and, more recently, a Mr W. Barker claims to have jumped 12 feet 6.5 inches in May this year. These claims, which far exceed the distances achieved by the extraordinary American Ray Ewry, should be treated with scepticism.

The standing high jump, long jump and triple jump have been part of the Olympic programme since 1900, and have been dominated by the amazing Ewry.

He was not yet 25 when, in July 1900 in Paris, he won all three standing titles.

His exceptional spring earned him the title of 'the human frog' at the Universal Exposition.

Ewry always followed the same procedure at the base of the jumping pit before miraculously springing 1.65m in the high jump, 3.30m in the long jump and 10.58m in the triple jump.

The competition from his omnipresent compatriot Irving Baxter, already winner of the pole vault and the running high jump titles the previous day, seemed to spur Ewry on.

Irving, lacking Ewry's incomparable spring, finished second to the uncontested master of this peculiar discipline in all three Paris events.

An expert designer of naval constructions, Ray was able to escape the limits of strength and balance that imprison the average athlete.

In Saint Louis, four years later, this jumping phenomenon has performed again.

In the standing high jump he performed slightly less well than he did in Paris, with a jump of 1.50m but it mattered little.

Ewry may be inconsistent, but Joseph Stadler, the number two, does not have Baxter's talent to push him to his limits. With this title safely under his belt, Ray prepared for 3 September, a day on which his other two specialities – the high and triple jumps – were scheduled.

Ewry dines on stamina-building buffalo meat, which the local chefs use in all of their dishes, to the great consternation of the few Europeans present, who have to make do with a diet of boiled potatoes.

In the long jump, perhaps benefiting from some unexpected side-effect of his buffalo diet, he jumped 3.47m – and it is a new world record!

Ewry then won the standing triple jump with a distance of 10.54m, leaving Charles King thirty-eight centimetres behind.

It was not the last that the Olympic Games was to hear of Ewry, who was destined to win two more gold medals in London in 1908, bringing his total to eight.

Perfectly proportioned, Ray Ewry has one set of wings on his jersey and another on his feet.

RESULTS STANDING JUMPS

High jump
1 Ray Ewry (USA), 1.50m
2 Joseph Stadler (USA), 1.45m
3 Lawson Robertson (USA), 1.45m

Long jump
1 Ray Ewry (USA), 3.47m(WR)
2 Charles King (USA), 3.28m
3 John Biller (USA), 3.26m

Triple jump
1 Ray Ewry (USA), 10.54m
2 Charles King (USA), 10.16m
3 Joseph Stadler (USA), 9.60m

SAINT LOUIS III OLYMPIAD

Just like the Paris event, these Games were organised as part of a world fair.
However, by moving away from the Old Continent for the first time, the Games
deprived themselves of having the maximum number of European participants.

THE GAMES IN BRIEF

Opening Date
1 July 1904

Closing Date
23 November 1904

Host Nation
United States of America (USA)

Candidate Towns
Chicago (USA)

12 Nations Represented

617 Athletes
(8 women, 609 men)

16 Sports
(1 open to women)
Track and field, rowing, boxing, cycling,
fencing, football, golf, gymnastics,
weightlifting, lacrosse, wrestling,
swimming (including diving and water-
polo), croquet, tennis and shooting.

Demonstration Sports
Basketball and women's boxing.

89 Events
(2 open to women)

Games officially opened by
David R. Francis, President of the
1904 World Fair.

Olympic flame lit by
The Olympic flame first lit during the
Opening Ceremony of the Amsterdam
Games in1928.

Olympic oath read by
The Olympic oath first delivered during
Opening Ceremony before the Antwerp
Games in 1920.

IOC President
Baron Pierre de Coubertin (FRA)

DID YOU KNOW?

For the first time, gold, silver and bronze
medals were awarded to the top three
contestants in each discipline. American
George Eyser got six medals and the
gymnast had one unusual feature: a
wooden leg.
   At discus, Martin Sheridan of the
USA threw the exact same length
as his team-mate Ralph Rose (39.28m).
The judges gave them an extra throw
in order to separate them, and
Sheridan won.
   In team sports, the Canadians, winners
at lacrosse and football, were the only
ones to draw level with the Americans,
who were champions in basketball and
water-polo. Among the very rare victories
which escaped the American clubs and
universities were individual golf, which
smiled on the Canadian Lyon, and fencing,
which allowed the Cubans, and in
particular Ramón Fonst Segundo, to win
three times out of five.

1908

London

AFTER THE ERUPTION OF MOUNT VESUVIUS in April 1906, Italy asked the IOC to re-allocate the Games of the IV Olympiad, initially awarded to Rome. A bid from London was accepted, and the British Olympic Association hastily erected the 68,000-seater White City stadium, which incorporated cycling and running tracks, a swimming pool and football pitch.

This magnificent setting hosted the wettest Games in history. The weather, and overpriced tickets, resulted in poor attendances.

They were not the happiest Games with the controversies dogging them matching the showers in frequency and intensity.

After noticing there was no American flag flying over the stadium during the Opening Ceremony, US discus thrower Martin Sheridan refused to dip the stars and stripes before the Royal Box during the procession.

Also missing was the Swedish flag, leading some Swedes to boycott the Games and athletes from Russian-ruled Finland were obliged to march behind the Russian flag.

The Americans abandoned the tug-of-war when one of the British team members were found to be wearing spiked shoes to prevent them slipping.

The Americans then boycotted a re-run of the 400m final, and a British athlete ran alone to victory. The disqualification of marathon runner Dorando Pietri (ITA) added to the trouble.

These were the last Games in which the host country had full jurisdiction over all the sports.

Huge crowds took the train from London to watch the rowing events at Henley-on-Thames.

Dorando Pietri: a lap too far

Before a hundred thousand spectators, the Italian is the first to the tape in the marathon, only to be disqualified after receiving illegal assistance.

At precisely 2.33pm on the east terrace of Windsor Castle, Queen Alexandra starts the marathon. The seventy-five participants leave the sumptuous grounds and begin their grueling ordeal.

On the eleventh day of the Games, the rain which has marred the first days of this Olympiad, finally relented. In its place, a temporary heatwave, much to the discomfort of the runners, coincided with the marathon.

By 2pm, more than 100,000 spectators – unprecedented for a purely athletic occasion – packed the stadium to see the marathon finish. Outside, eager fans offered great sums to be allowed to enter. When the race leader entered the stadium he was greeted to indescribable and unforgettable applause.

This Olympiad's route measured 26 miles and 385 yards; the additional 385 yards was added to place the finish line directly in front of Queen Alexandra's royal box.

Seventy-five starters represented Austria, South Africa, Greece, Finland, Russia, the Netherlands, Belgium, Italy, the United States, Australia, Germany, Sweden, Bohemia, Denmark, Hungary, Great Britain and Ireland. The favourites included Dorando Pietri (ITA), Svanberg and Laundquist (SWE), Duncan and Appleby (GBR) and the Onondaga Indian Tom

Longboat from Canada, who had prepared in Ireland and arrived in London four days before the race.

Immediately after the start by The Queen from the east terrace of Windsor Castle, separate bunches of runners formed. The British runners, under pressure to run well, set off too fast and after four miles, Scotland's Thomas Jack had a 40m lead over Jack Price (GBR).

After nine miles, Fred Lord (GBR) led, followed by Price and Charles Hefferon (SAF). Shortly after completing 12 miles in one hour and

three minutes, Hefferon took the lead and after 20 miles, his lead was over three minutes. Then Pietri caught him.

For three miles, Hefferon and Pietri ran shoulder to shoulder with John Hayes (USA) hovering just behind in third place.

A glass of champagne accepted from the roadside gave Hefferon stomach cramps, allowing Pietri to open a small gap on the South African.

This soon stretched into a considerable lead and over the final three miles, Pietri ran strongly. As he

entered the stadium gates, he was told that a runner was very close behind and it appears that between the outside door and the entrance to the track, he ran too quickly. All the time, the Americans John Hayes, Joseph Forshaw and Alton Welton were closing in.

Informed that he still had to complete two-thirds of a lap, the Italian ground to a halt and if he had not been held up, he would have collapsed.

Recovering, he set off again, only to fall again 50m further on. Forty metres from the finish line, it seemed that he was about to fall a third time just as

With the finish line tantalisingly close, Dorando Pietri collapses five times on the track. Each time, officials help him to his feet.

Pietri crosses the finish line; his closest pursuer, John Hayes (USA), has already entered the stadium.

Pietri is stretchered out of the stadium, physically exhausted but believing he is the new Olympic marathon champion.

Hefferon made the mistake of drinking champagne during the race, giving Pietri the chance to break away.

Hayes entered the stadium in second place. For a moment, it seemed Pietri would not finish.

After a few words of encouragement from an Italian journalist, he recovered and passed the finish line an exhausted, but victorious, man.

The event could scarcely have been more moving and, when Pietri finished, there were tears around the stadium.

An eye witness reported that three miles before the finish, Pietri had believed that there were only one and a half miles left to cover, the distance at which he had planned to launch his final sprint.

He ran too quickly and this sprint was the main cause of his breakdown, increased by his dismay when he learned there was another lap to go.

Pietri's victory had been telegraphed to the whole world and the Italian flag had been raised before anyone knew that the second-placed runner had lodged a complaint.

Second-placed Hayes, just 22, stands to win if his protest is upheld. A clerk paid to train by the Bloomingdale department store in New York City, Hayes has finished fifth in the 1906 Boston Marathon and third in 1907, the year he also won the Yonkers Marathon.

Hayes' preparation included storing energy for the race by remaining in bed for the two days prior to the race.

So gruelling was the event that a number of drop-outs thinned the field.

John Hayes (USA) prepared for the marathon by spending two days in bed: a radical form of tapering and an effective one.

Wyatt (GBR), abandoned the race at four miles; Buff (HOL) at 12 miles, Duncan, the English favourite, at 13 miles, Vosbergen (HOL) at 14 miles, Celis (BEL) at 14.5 miles, Lindquist (SWE) at 15 miles, Coutoulakis (GRE) at 16 miles, Couloumberdos (GRE) at 20 miles, and Appleby (GBR) at 20.5 miles.

Longboat, who had been the pre-race favourite, decided to drop out at 21 miles and arrived in a motor car.

One of the more gutsy performances was fellow Canadian Lister who suffered a twisted ankle after a mile. He refused to give up and covered the distance in 4:22:25.

LATEST NEWS

Dorando Pietri is disqualified

London, 24 July, 10:30pm (by telegram). At the last moment, after long deliberation, the track committee has disqualified Dorando Pietri after John Hayes lodged a protest that assistance allowed Pietri to recover after he had collapsed in the stadium. Hayes has been awarded first place, with Charles Hefferon second and Joseph Forsham third.

The Italian runner had been mistaken, on arriving in the stadium, to believe that he had finished as soon as he entered. Because of this, he mistimed his final sprint. Informed that he still had to do a lap of the track, he no longer felt capable of continuing. Those who saw him enter the tunnel to the stadium say that he arrived there still energetic and in good form and that he gave too much between the entry tunnel and the entrance to the stadium.

It is certain that from the moment Hayes entered the stadium, Pietri was supported on each side for 50m. The committee had to do what it felt was just. Public opinion is largely in favour of the Italian, who will, despite this decision, be fondly remembered.

Archery was one of just three events open to women competitors at the 1908 Games – the others were tennis and, uniquely for the Summer Games, figure skating. The women's archery tournament produced the oldest female medalist in Olympic history: 53-year-old Sybil 'Queenie' Newall. Newall trailed Charlotte 'Lottie' Dod (winner of five Wimbledon tennis championships and one of the first women to attempt the Cresta Run at St Moritz) by 10 points at the end of day one, but was irresistible on day two and eventually won by 688 points to 642. The competition was diminished by the absence of the greatest women's archer of the day, Alice Legh, who defeated Newall a week after the Olympic Games.

The loser becomes the hero

The Queen congratulates the disqualified Dorando Pietri. Sir Arthur Conan Doyle announces a public subscription in his honour.

The day after, Dorando Pietri's remarkable marathon is still on everyone's lips. is unjust disqualification has been greeted with widespread outrage.

Pietri's misfortune was that two track officials helped him up when he fell for the third time, just 10 yards from the finish line. One even held his arm until he reached the tape.

After the American protest the judges then showed a complete lack of imagination in interpreting the rules.

Should he have been disqualified on a technicality after such a valiant performance? If rules are to be adhered to blindly, the answer is yes.

However, those with any discretion are bound to disagree on the grounds that the Italian did not seek the assistance of the officials. This is the nub of the affair.

It can be argued that Pietri was not helped by friends but by officials who thereby pushed him beyond the rules.

LIST OF WINNERS

Since the beginning of the first Modern Olympic Games, the marathon won by Pietri is the fifth to have been contested. Below are the names of the winners:

1896, Athens (40km).
S. Louis (Greece) 2:55:20
1900, Paris (40.260 km).
Théato (France) 2:59:45
1904, St. Louis (40km).
T.J. Hicks (USA) 2:28:53
1906, Athens (41.860km).
W. Sherring (Canada) 2:51:23
1908, London (42.195km).
Pietri (Italy) 2:54:46

The marathon held in Athens was over excessively hard mountainous terrain, which makes any comparison of times impossible. The marathon in Paris in 1900 was run in scorching temperatures.

The best time for the marathon was set in Europe by professional Englishman Leonard Hurst in 1900 in Paris, in a time of 2:26:47. Longboat of Canada however, won a marathon in Chicago in 2:24:00, a time considered the world's best.

The future looks bright for Dorando Pietri. In 1908 and 1909 he defeats John Hayes in widely-publicised races in New York.

Pietri reached the stadium at midday, after rising at 7am. He continues to protest against his disqualification, blaming his collapse on the overwhelming welcome that greeted him in the stadium.

Hefferon, promoted to second place, expressed the view that Pietri was the best man and deserved to win, because from the moment he broke away, he could not have been caught.

His rivals, having not run at such a pace before the finish line, arrived at the stadium in better condition.

Given the injustice of the decision, the Queen's personal gesture of offering Pietri a cup to reward him for his performance has been met with public approval.

In addition, the celebrated author

Sir Arthur Conan Doyle has announced the creation of a public subscription fund for Pietri. This will allow the unfortunate runner to receive a bronze replica of the winner's trophy.

Lord and Lady Desborough sent a bouquet of roses and a letter of admiration to Dorando, who replied with typical grace and informed them that their charming letter would be one of his most treasured souvenirs.

After the events surrounding the marathon, the meeting the following day seemed insignificant.

THE QUEEN'S CUP OFFERED IN CONSOLATION

At the end of the meeting, during the presentation of medals and trophies, a remarkable incident took place. The Queen summoned Pietri, who made his way to the Royal Box amid rapturous applause. There, the Queen presented him with a magnificent gold cup. Pietri, deeply moved, paraded with his cup around the track, followed by an Italian flag.

The entire stadium rose to salute the Italian, who is without doubt the hero of London. The Queen watched him until he had completed his lap of honour, then resumed the official presentation ceremony.

The French fencing team was also given a warm welcome as they received their trophy.

After the presentation, the British National Anthem was played, bringing to a close a remarkable festival of sport that will leave a lasting memory in everyone's mind.

As the Queen prepared to leave, the traditional three cheers in her honour rang out from the 60,000 spectators in the stadium.

It was a fitting celebration of the effect her presence has had on these Games and on her decision to honour Dorando Pietri.

Silver medals were presented by the Duchess of Rutland and bronze medals handed over by the Duchess Dowager of Westminster.

Diplomas of merit were provided by the Duchess of Westminster, and commemorative medals by Lady Desborough.

Halswelle wins by default

The British athlete wins the 400m final – running alone!

The final of the 400m included what was to be a controversial mix of three Americans – John Carpenter, William Robbins and John Taylor – and a Briton.

Lieutenant Wyndham Halswelle was a 26-year-old London-born Scot who had set an Olympic record of 48.4 seconds in the semi-finals.

From the start of the final Carpenter, on the inside, took the lead followed by Robbins and Halswelle. At 200m Halswelle was in front by half a second.

Then in an amazing scene Carpenter, with an extraordinary sprint, reached him and elbowed him on to the grass.

This opened the way for Robbins and Taylor to follow Carpenter home but stewards reported the manoeuvre and the race was declared void.

The committee disqualified Carpenter and ordered Halswelle, Taylor and Robbins to re-run the final two days later. Refusing to accept the disqualification, the two US representatives boycotted the re-run so Halswelle ran a solo lap in the comparatively modest time of 50 seconds and won the gold medal.

The Briton Wyndham Halswelle (right) could hardly have dreamed of an easier victory, unchallenged in the re-run of the 400m final. John Carpenter (above), winner of the first final, was disqualified for elbowing him off the track. The measure provoked an American boycott of the repeat final.

1908
OLYMPIC ROUND-UP

LAPIZE IS NARROWLY BEATEN.

The Olympic Games have been plagued by bad luck. There has not been a rain-free day and revenues will suffer. Some results have also been affected by the conditions. The 100km bicycle track race was one that started in torrential rain.

Two elimination rounds had selected the 17 starters. Coeckelberg (BEL) took the lead from the gun, setting a blistering pace while the rest slipstreamed him in single file to bide their time. Within minutes, everyone was drenched and covered in mud.

On lap 20, Billy Pett (GBR) led, followed by Frenchmen Lutz and Lapize. After half an hour, 20.115km into the race, Sydney Bailey (GBR) led. On lap 47, a fall involved two Britons, Meredith and Robertson, and Andrews (CAN).

Lapize and Coeckelberg increased the pace, forcing Meredith to drop out. Then the speed relented. After covering 30.920km, in the first hour, Lapize still led, in front of fellow countryman Pierre Texier.

After 50km, covered in 1 hour, 16 minutes and 47 seconds, Bailey led, followed by Charles Bartlett (GBR), Texier and Lapize. Lutz had to stop to change bicycles but caught up with the leading group within two laps.

Three hours and 93.422km into the race, Texier was leading but Bartlett, Lapize, Pett and Charles Denny (GBR) remained in contention.

At this stage only these five – three Britons and two French – who could win the race; every other rider had been overtaken at least once.

In clearing weather, three laps from the finishing line, a puncture ended Texier's chances.

On the last bend Lapize was boxed in and unable to pass while Bartlett made four lengths on Denny before the start of the final straight. Lapize began his sprint hopelessly late, and could only finish third behind the two British riders. The Frenchman, although beaten, had provided a terrific race.

1 The stands are sold out for the 100km bicycle track race, despite awful weather.

2 Uniquely, figure skating appears on the programme of the Summer Games. The elegant Florence 'Madge' Syers and her brother Edgar (GBR) finish third in the pairs competition.

3 The celebrated cricketer, John Douglas, wins the middleweight boxing title. In the 1920s he heads for Hollywood to become a fitness coach to the stars.

4 Aged 23, Frederick Holman (GBR) already has a fine swimming record, including the gold medal for the 200m breaststroke.

5 Like his compatriot James Lightbody at St Louis, Melvin Sheppard (USA) wins gold in the 800m and 1500m in London.

6 Melvin Sheppard beats Harold Wilson (GBR) in the 1500m in a time of 4 minutes 34 seconds, the first of four gold medals. Because of a supposedly weak heart, the New York City police department had turned down Sheppard's job application.

7 Polo: an all-British affair, with three home teams taking a clean sweep of the medals.

8 Italy's Alberto Braglia, later a popular circus performer, dominates the overall gymnastics competition, as he would four years later at Stockholm.

9 The American Charles Bacon (left) triumphs over the St Louis Olympic champion, his compatriot Harry Hillman, in the final of the 400m hurdles.

10 Ray Ewry continues his winning streak. Since 1900, he has won every standing jump title – three high jumps, three long jumps and two triple jumps. He is shown winning the standing high jump with 1.575m.

11 Winner of the discus in 1904, the American Martin Sheridan repeats his performance in 1908. He also wins the Greek-style discus competition.

12 This shot of Forrest Wilson, winner of the 110m hurdles, running with a Bible in his hand, is believed to be an out-of-competition image made in protest against Sunday competition.

13 Born in Enniskillen, Ireland, Robert Kerr moved to Canada aged seven. He is carried on his team-mates' shoulders after winning the 200m.

Triple gold for Taylor

The British swimmer thrills the home crowd with wins in two endurance events and the relay.

Aged 23, Taylor deserves his congratulatory handshake. Victorious in the 400m and 1500m, he also made a decisive contribution to the British 4x200m win.

Henry Taylor is like a Dickens character. Orphaned, then raised by his older brother, he now works in a cotton mill, training at lunchtime and after work in any stretch of water available – canals, rivers or the public baths at Chadderdon.

At the Intercalated Games two years ago, he won the mile and finished second in both the individual 400m and as part of the British 4x250m team.

He has clearly made the most of the intervening two years, and has been in winning form at the Games, winning three gold medals and proving that he is the finest middle-distance swimmer around.

Taylor won gold in the 400m, easily beating the Australian Francis Beaurepaire and the Austrian Otto Scheff, who won in the Intercalated Games at Athens in 1906.

Then Taylor won the 1500m,

establishing the first internationally recognised world record for the distance with a swim of 22:48:4.

Taylor's record is partly due to the fast start of his team-mate Thomas Battersby. Taylor surged into the lead with less than 200m to go. As well as two individual victories, Taylor

also came away with gold in the 4x200m relay.

When he took to the water for the anchor leg, the Hungarian sprinter Zoltán Halmay had a huge lead. With just 20m to go, Taylor caught him, pushing the Hungarians into second.

Taylor, already six-times British

champion in his short career, was born in Oldham in 1885.

Observers say he has yet to reach physical maturity promising, despite his already remarkable successes, a long career ahead of him.

RESULTS **TAYLOR'S TRIPLE**

400m
1 Henry Taylor (GBR), 5:36:8
2 Francis Beaurepaire (AUS), 5:44:2
3 Otto Scheff (AUT), 5:46:0

1500m
1 Henry Taylor (GBR), 22:48:4
2 Thomas Battersby (GBR), 22:51:2
3 Francis Beaurepaire (AUS), 22:56:2

4x200m
1 Great Britain (John Henry Derbyshire, Paul Radmilovic, William Foster, Henry Taylor), 10:55:6
2 Hungary, 10:59:0
3 United States, 11:02:8

1908

LONDON IV OLYMPIAD

For the first time, the competitors were put into national teams,
each team marching into the stadium in line behind their
national flag during the opening ceremony.

THE GAMES IN BRIEF

Opening Date
27 April 1908

Closing Date
31 October 1908

Host Nation
Great Britain (GBR)

Candidate Towns
Berlin (GER), Milan and Rome (ITA)

22 Nations Represented

2,035 Athletes
(36 women, 1,999 men)

23 Sports
(3 open to women)
Track and field, rowing, boxing,
cycling, fencing, football, gymnastics,
field hockey, jeu de paume, lacrosse,
wrestling, motor boating, shooting,
archery swimming, figure skating, polo,
rackets, rugby, tennis, sailing and
water polo.

Demonstration Sports
No demonstration sport

109 Events
(5 open to women)

Games officially opened by
King Edward VII of England

Olympic flame lit by
The Olympic flame first lit during the
Opening Ceremony of the Amsterdam
Games in 1928.

Olympic oath read by
The Olympic oath first delivered during
Opening Ceremony before the Antwerp
Games in 1920.

IOC President
Baron Pierre de Coubertin (FRA)

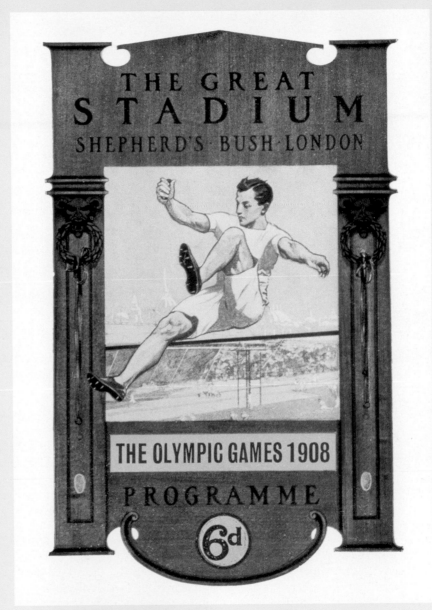

THE GREAT STADIUM SHEPHERD'S BUSH LONDON
THE OLYMPIC GAMES 1908 PROGRAMME 6d

DID YOU KNOW?

During the opening ceremony, the athletes
filed into the stadium country by country,
behind their flags. It was a first. The
Games took place in two parts: the
summer Games (for individual sports) and
the autumn Games (for figure skating,
boxing and team sports). The three sports
open to women were still very middle-class
disciplines: tennis, figure skating and
archery. In a remarkable sporting gesture,
the final of the middleweight division in
Greco-Roman wrestling between the
Swedes Martensson and Andersson was
pushed back by one day to allow
Martensson to recover from a minor injury.
In the end, Martensson won. British
archers William (winner in the York Round
discipline) and Charlotte Dod (second in
the national trials) became the first brother
and sister medalists in their sport. Swede
Oscar Swahn was already sixty years old
when he won his first Olympic gold medal
in the individual event of the single shot
running deer shooting event. The following
day, he got a second gold medal, in the
team event.

Frenchman Géo André finished second
in the high jump with a jump of 1.88m,
as it appeared that, on his third attempt
at 1.90 metres, his shorts, which were too
baggy, made the bar fall.

The Organisation Committee for the
Games had fixed the length of the
marathon at 42.195 kilometres – the last
195m were added so that the course could
stretch from Windsor Castle to the finish
line directly in front of the royal box. This
distance became the official distance for
the marathon from the 1924 Games.

In athletics, an unofficial 'Olympic relay'
was also held. The four successive
courses were 200m, 200m, 400m and
800m. Australia and New Zealand were
together represented by just one delegate,
under the name of Australasia.

It was at London that the bishop of
Pennsylvania declared: 'The important thing
about these Olympic Games is less the
winning than the taking part.' This quote
was later taken up by Baron de Coubertin.

1912

Stockholm

THE ORGANISATION OF THE STOCKHOLM Games was exemplary and innovative. For the first time electronic timing devices for the track events and a public address system were introduced. New events included the modern pentathlon and women's swimming and diving. However, Sweden's refusal to host the boxing tournament led the IOC to limit the powers of host nations.

Despite their friendly atmosphere, the leitmotifs of these Games were endurance and suffering. At 320km, the cycling road race was the longest in Olympic history. The light-heavyweight Greco-Roman wrestling final was stopped and both wrestlers declared equal second place after nine hours of tussling. The middleweight semi-final lasted two hours longer.

Hannes Kolehmainen of Finland set himself an incredibly difficult task. On 8 July he won the 10,000m and just two days later he won the 5,000m, breaking the world record. Three days after his initial triumph he set a new world record in a heat of the 3,000m team race, then on 15 July he won the 12km cross-country event.

Kolehmainen's achievements were equalled, even surpassed, by the remarkable Jim Thorpe. In the space of week, he won the five-event pentathlon, finished fifth in the high jump and seventh in the long jump.

He then capped all that by breaking the world record for the decathlon, setting a mark so far ahead of its time that it would have earned him silver in the 1948 Olympics!

Women's swimming appeared at the Games, and saw British swimmers Isabella Moore, Jennie Fletcher, Annie Speirs and Irene Steer win the first 4x100m freestyle relay.

ATHLETICS

The 17 trials of Hercules Thorpe

In eight days Jim Thorpe made his rivals in both the pentathlon and decathlon look ridiculous. He also competed in two other finals.

A force of nature: Jim Thorpe is capable of repeated exertions and seems to require little time to recover. He is also an excellent technician, especially in the discus.

Sport, like life, is full of contrasts. Yesterday, in the picturesque Olympic Stadium at Stockholm it was an American Indian who occupied centre stage.

Beneath a clear, sunlit sky, 30,000 spectators saw a meeting of kings. King Gustav V of Sweden was particularly happy to share the limelight with a king among competitors, a somewhat emotional American, James Thorpe.

The athlete's head is crowned with a laurel wreath as he received his second gold medal and two trophies engraved to celebrate his overall achievements.

The Olympic decathlon champion had won the pentathlon a week before and two imposing *objets d'art* had been placed on the royal podium near King Gustav especially for Thorpe

The athlete bowed before Sweden's monarch in order to receive a bronze

bust portraying the Swedish sovereign, as well as a silver replica of a Viking longboat, a gift from Czar Nicholas II of Russia.

Gustav told Thorpe: 'Sir, you are the greatest athlete in the world!'

It was a royal and spontaneous expression of admiration for a man who had, in truly Herculean fashion, taken part in no less than 17 events during the Games.

In answer to the King, Thorpe could only mumble two words: 'Thanks, King'.

On 7 July, Thorpe completed the five events of the pentathlon; on 13, 14 and 15 July, he then took part in the 10 events of the decathlon.

In addition, he contested two individual events: the high jump, in which he came fourth with a height of 1.87m, and the long jump, in which he came seventh with a leap of 6.89m.

Only the event schedule prevented

RESULTS **THORPE'S RECORD**

Pentathlon
First with 7 points
7.07m (long jump), First
46.71m (javelin), Third
22:9 (200m), First
35.75m (discus), First
4:44:8 (1500m), First

High jump
Fourth with 1.87m

Long jump
Seventh with 6.89m

Decathlon
First with 8412 points (6564 points adjusted to the 1985 table)
11:2 (100m); 6.79m (long jump)
12.89m (shot put); 1.87m (high jump)
52:2 (400m)
15:6 (110m hurdles)
36.98m (discus)
3.25m (pole vault)
45.70m (javelin)
4:40:1 (1500m)

him from competing in his strongest event, the 110m hurdles.

Even before the ceremony, Jim Thorpe had been informed that he and the other US Olympic champions would be rewarded with a welcome parade along Fifth Avenue in New York on their return across the Atlantic Ocean.

He was naturally proud, and relieved to have fulfilled his almost impossible task.

Everything had started straightforwardly enough in the pentathlon, which Thorpe dominated despite the efforts of two US compatriots, James Donahue (third) and Avery Brundage (sixth), and the Norwegian, Ferdinand Bie (second).

In the first official decathlon of the Olympic Games, Sweden was represented by three capable competitors, Hugo Wieslander, Charles Lomberg and Goesta Holmer.

The duel between Thorpe and Wieslander, the world record holder with 7,244,10 points, was one of the most anticipated contests of the Games.

Given the 21 competitors, the organisers had arranged to spread the decathlon events over three days.

On 13 July, Thorpe, who, at 1.84m and 80kg, brought a fearsome reputation to Scandinavia, stated his intent at the outset with 11.2 seconds in the 100m; 6.79m in the long jump; and 12.89m in the shot-put.

Wieslander lost by 0.6 of a second in the 100m, 37cm in the long jump and 75cm in the shot.

With his fourth high jump of 1.87m, Jim Thorpe missed out on a medal by two centimetres.

King Gustav V places Thorpe's laurel wreath with the words, 'Sir, you are the greatest athlete in the world.'

Thorpe competed in three separate long jump events in one week. His best performance was 7.07m.

In the second day's events Thorpe extended his lead, winning the high jump, 400m, discus and 110m hurdles competitions, and gaining further ground on Wieslander with 1.87m against 1.75m, 52.2sec against 53.6sec, 36.98m against 36.29m and 15.6sec against 17.2sec. Only injury could have spoiled his party.

On the third day Thorpe allowed his rival small comfort in the javelin event, in which the Scandinavian threw 50.4m compared with Thorpe's 45.70m.

But it was not to be in the pole vault in which Thorpe cleared the bar at 3.25m, compared with Wieslander's 3.10m, before beating him by 4.9 seconds in the 1500m with a time of 4.40.1 seconds.

Thorpe's points total of 8,412,955 points left Hugo Wieslander far behind with 7,724,495 points and fellow Swede Charles Lomberg with 7,414.

It smashed the world record by 1,000 points – a mind-boggling performance by a man who not only represented America, but also its decimated indigenous people.

Born on 22 May 1887, Thorpe had Irish ancestry through his paternal grandfather, a blacksmith named Thorpe who married a young woman from the Sac and Fox tribe in Kansas, then moved to Oklahoma.

Their son, Hiram P. Thorpe, married Charlotte Vieux, the daughter of a French colonist and an Indian.

At the Carlisle Indian School, Jim Thorpe was spotted by Glen Scobie 'Pop' Warner, a celebrated football and athletics coach and natural leader of men who wanted his football team to rival the best American colleges.

In 1911, Carlisle beat Harvard by 18-15 and it was Jim Thorpe who scored all 18 points.

He was also a gifted baseball player and played in minor leagues in the US.

Thorpe's sporting prowess went even further as he also excelled in every athletic discipline he turned his hand to. He started to practise them regularly from 1907 at the age of 20 and in five years he was displaying them to an incredulous world through the Stockholm Olympic Games.

While his clan name is Thunder, Thorpe's tribal name is the highly appropriate Wa-Tho-Huck, which means Bright Path.

AFTER THE GAMES, THORPE'S FORTUNES VARY

After the Stockholm Games, Jim Thorpe was a national hero. But in January 1913, it emerged that in 1909 and 1910, Thorpe had earned $25 a week playing minor league baseball for North Carolina. Thorpe confessed and apologised, arguing in his defence that he had merely been a schoolboy, unaware of the rules regarding professionalism, and had since turned down offers of thousands of dollars to safeguard his amateur status. On 27 January, the Olympic Committee stripped him of his titles, records and medals.

Offers from professional clubs came in abundance. Thorpe signed his first football contract with the New York Giants; his professional career lasted from 1915 to 1928. He played baseball for the Cincinnati Reds until 1919.

In 1943, a movement to reinstate him took place, but Thorpe did not live to see the outcome: he died of a heart attack on 28 March 1953 in Lomita, California. On 13 October 1982, the IOC abolished the ban on professionals and reinstated Thorpe. On 18 January 1983, his medals were returned to his children.

1912
OLYMPIC
ROUND-UP

SOUTH AFRICAN WINS
THE MARATHON.

Traditionally, the most important day of the Olympic Games is the day of the marathon. This year is no different. From 10am, the stadium doors were under siege. There was not a cloud in the sky and, unfortunately for the competitors, the temperature was stifling.

Seventy one competitors set off along roads that were extremely poor. The competitors were aiming for Sollentuna; 20.2km from the start and the organisation was flawless. Soldiers controlled the traffic, Boy Scouts indicated the route and ambulances and doctors followed in motorcars.

At the halfway point, Christian Gitsham (SAF) and Tatu Kolehmainen (FIN), the brother of Hannes, led. On the return route, the order did not change very much, until 5km from the finish, when Gitsham and fellow South African Kenneth McArthur led together, followed by Gaston Strobino (USA), Sigfrid Jacobson (SWE), James Duffy (CAN) and the Italian Speroni. The surprise was that Tatu Kolehmainen had dropped out.

In the final kilometre, the South African McArthur left compatriot Gitsham behind. He ran the final lap with a laurel wreath woven with yellow and blue ribbons, slung across his shoulder, crossed the finish line and collapsed. Gitsham, who was still in excellent condition, finished second, 200m behind him. Then Strobino, the first American, finished.

The Frenchman Boissière also finished in good shape, complaining that he had been misinformed of his place and could have finished three or four places higher than the 13th spot he achieved.

The high temperature for such a gruelling race did take its toll and cast a shadow over the event.

Francisco Lazaro, a 21-year-old from Portugal, collapsed with sunstroke 7km from the finish line and had to be rushed to hospital for treatment. Sadly he died there the next morning.

1 Eric Lemming (SWE), the winner in London in 1908, retained the javelin title.

2 After 11 hours of fighting, Martin Klein (RUS/EST) beats Alfred Asikainen (FIN) in the semi-final of the Greco-Roman wrestling middleweight division.

3 After seven false starts, three caused by the eventual winner, the 100m final is won by Ralph Craig (USA) in 10.8sec.

4 South Africa wins two medals in the marathon. Kenneth McArthur, who finished ahead of Christopher Gitsham, is seen here being carried by his supporters.

5 The Germans win the coxed four-oared shell, ahead of the British and Danish.

6 Charles Winslow and Harold Kitson (SAF) beat Felix Pipes and Arthur Zborzil (AUT) in the tennis doubles' final.

7 Carl Bonde (SWE) takes first place in an all-Swedish individual dressage podium.

8 Greta Johansson from Sweden becomes the first Olympic champion in women's platform diving.

9 The final of the football tournament is a replay of the 1908 final in London, with Great Britain beating Denmark 4-2.

10 In front of their home crowd, Sweden's athletes celebrate their second place in the 3,000m team race.

11 The American Patrick McDonald puts an end to his compatriot Ralph Rose's series of wins in the shot put (1904 and 1908).

12 After John Flanagan's three victories from 1900 to 1908, the hammer throw remains an all-American affair with Matthew McGrath winning.

13 At the age of 64, Oscar Swahn from Sweden wins the gold in the team running deer shooting, single-shot. It is the third and last of his titles.

14 The Swede Moren, the favourite in the road time trial, cannot beat the South African Lewis, who wins in 10hr 42min 39sec.

15 In his last appearance at the Games, Konstantinos Tsiklitiras from Greece wins gold in the standing long jump, becoming Ewry's successor.

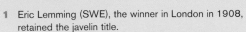

Kolehmainen's incredible record

After unbearable tension, the unrelenting Hannes Kolehmainen (FIN) wins an epic duel in the 5,000m.

The tension mounts as the tape approaches, and with inches to go, Hannes Kolehmainen edges out Jean Bouin.

There are four Kolehmainen brothers and all are excellent runners. Tatu, 27, will run the marathon at these Games; Guillaume, 25, is a professional runner in France; while Rodolph, 19, is already preparing for the Olympic Games planned for Berlin in 1916.

Then there is Hannes, a 23-year-old bricklayer with a vegetarian regime whose achievements over the past four days of these Games have been remarkable.

He won the 10,000m, then in his fourth distance race in four days he beat the French favourite Jean Bouin by a fraction of a second to take gold in the 5,000m. Both men beat the previous world record.

Bouin had been the great French hope of these Games, especially after beating the world record comfortably in the qualifying heat. In the final he seemed invincible – until Hannes Kolehmainen passed him on the line.

From the start of the final of the 5,000m Kolehmainen darted to the front of the 15 competitors. Bouin was

in fifth place and during the third lap found himself boxed in by two Americans.

Squeezing between them, Bouin then joined Kolehmainen to break

Smiling in defeat. The valiant runner-up, Jean Bouin, looks delighted with his silver medal.

away from the pack. Bouin followed his rival for several laps before taking the lead at about the 2,500m mark, apparently in complete control.

His pace was perfectly even, covering each 380.50m lap in 67-68 seconds. At the start of the bend with 500m to go, Kolehmainen tried to pass but Bouin, in the inside lane, responded by forcing the Finn to run wider. Kolehmainen had to retreat briefly – until the bell for the last lap.

Bouin lengthened his stride and pulled away slightly until, at the start of the final straight, the Frenchman's advantage was 3m.

Both men were calling on their last resources of strength and Kolehmainen, especially, looked on the point of collapse.

The colour had drained from Bouin's face but with 10m left, victory and the gold medal still seemed destined to be heading back with him to France.

Everyone in the stadium believed the Frenchman had won when Kolehmainen, incredibly, found an

irresistible acceleration and drew level with the Frenchman. Elbow to elbow over the last few metres, they seemed to lean on each other but with one last stride Kolehmainen literally threw himself at the tape.

He had won, and at last, those watching were able to draw breath. The tension of the runners' titanic struggle had been unbearable.

Kolehmainen was naturally ecstatic. He had set a new world record and beaten the Frenchman who had been the outstanding favourite in the event.

An amazing ovation rang out from all sides of the stadium. The many Finns in the crowd enthusiastically waved their little red flags with Finland's coat of arms, a flag forbidden by Russia – and one that could not appear officially inside the Olympic stadium.

The Swedes waved their blue flags with a yellow cross just as frantically. The three guttural hoorays boomed out from the Swedish and Finnish spectators in every corner of the stadium. It was almost a national victory for Sweden as well. The French tricolours, meanwhile, were still. French spectators applauded Bouin's valiant efforts but were rueing Kolehmainen's winning lurch for the tape.

Nobody seemed to take much interest in the other runners, although the battle for third between Hutson of England and Bonhag (USA) was extremely exciting, with the bronze medal going to the Englishman.

Henry Scott, America's former record holder with a time of 15:06, and Karlsson, the Swedish record holder, finished far behind.

RESULTS

5,000m
1 Johan 'Hannes' Kolehmainen (FIN), 14:36.6
2 Jean Bouin (FRA), 14:36.7
3 George Hutson (GBR), 15:07.6
4 George Bonhag (USA), 15:09.8
5 Tel Berna (USA), 15:10.0
6 Mauritz Karlsson (SWE), 15:18.6
7 Henry Scott (USA), -
8 Alex Decoteau (CAN), -

STOCKHOLM V OLYMPIAD

The sound of boots began to be heard throughout the world, but the Olympic Games didn't suffer because of this. In fact, they became truly universal, as for the first time, all five continents were represented.

THE GAMES IN BRIEF

Opening Date
5 May 1912

Closing Date
27 July 1912

Host Nation
Sweden (SWE)

Candidate Towns
None

28 Nations Represented

2,547 Athletes
(57 women, 2,490 men)

15 Sports
(5 open to women)
Track and field, football, modern pentathlon, sailing, gymnastics, swimming, diving, fencing, wrestling, rowing, shooting, tennis, cycling and equestrian.

Demonstration Sports
No demonstration sports

43 Events
(15 open to women)

Games officially opened by
King Gustav V of Sweden

Olympic flame lit by
The Olympic flame first lit during the Opening Ceremony of the Amsterdam Games in 1928.

Olympic oath read by
The Olympic oath was first delivered during Opening Ceremony before the Antwerp Games in 1920.

IOC President
Baron Pierre de Coubertin (FRA)

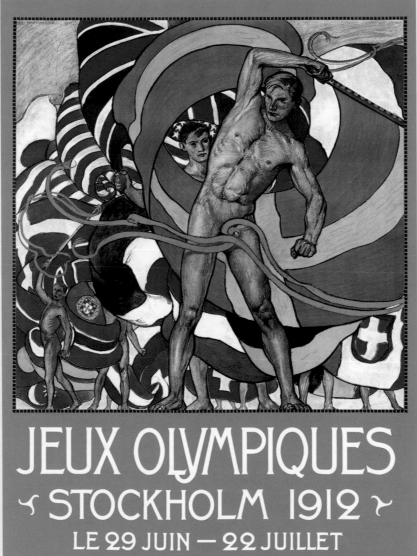

DID YOU KNOW?

The swimming competition was opened to women for the first time.

There was also new technology at Stockholm: electronic timing devices (used unofficially in the athletics competition), photo finish and the public announcement system using loudspeakers.

An art and literature competition was held outside the Games. Baron de Coubertin wrote under the pseudonyms of Georges Hohrod and Monsieur Eschbach, and was made Laureate as a reward for his 'Ode to Sport'.

The competitor who won the most medals in these Olympic Games was a Swiss man, Louis Richardet, winning six medals (four gold and two silver) in shooting.

The football tournament saw many goals, not least in the match between Russia and Germany, where German forward Gottfried Fuchs scored ten goals. Another footballing figure, Harold Walden, who was the United Kingdom's best goal-scorer, scored 15 goals for his country. Some years later he went on to become a very popular music hall figure.

1920

Antwerp

THE 1916 GAMES, AWARDED TO BERLIN, TOOK place in Antwerp. Germany, like the other aggressor nations – Austria, Hungary, Bulgaria and Turkey – was excluded from the 1920 Games. Russia, too, was absent: its troops were still fighting their civil war.

Among the 10 million who had lost their lives in the Great War were many Olympians. The 5,000m champion, Hannes Kolehmainen, would not be facing the men who had finished second and third in 1912. Jean Bouin (FRA) and George Hutson (GBR) perished in action in September 1914.

The 1920 Games were given to Antwerp to commemorate the suffering inflicted on Belgium during the conflict. The opening ceremony saw two historic innovations – the Olympic flag and the oath. The flag's five rings, adapted by Pierre de Coubertin from the altar at Delphi, signified the unity of the five continents, and the first oath was delivered by Belgian fencer Victor Boin.

In a clear voice he declared: 'In the name of all competitors, I promise that we shall take part in these Olympic Games, respecting and abiding by the rules that govern them, in the true spirit of sportsmanship, for the glory of sport and the honour of our teams.'

Of the 22 nations that participated in the depleted Antwerp Games – 28 had competed at Stockholm – Finland dominated. In celebration of independence in 1917, despite having been practically destroyed by the Great War and then the Russian Revolution, Finnish athletes achieved 15 track and field gold medals, equalling the mighty United States.

The women's platform dive. The swimming and diving events took place in a 100m pool excavated for the occasion from Antwerp's ancient system of fortified moats.

The human fish

The Hawaiian Kahanamoku retains the 100m title he won before the War – once again proving his exceptional abilities.

Paoa Kahinu Mokoe Hulikohola Kahanamoku, born in Hawaii in 1890, is a curious marine animal, equally gifted in swimming and surfing. He did not invent the crawl, but he has adapted it so effectively that his competitors acknowledge that this stroke will surpass all the others.

Nicknamed 'The Duke' after Britain's Duke of Edinburgh, who visited his home islands in 1869, what the human fish has achieved goes far beyond all expectations.

He first appeared on the Olympic stage in Stockholm in 1912 and became the star attraction. Equal to the colossal Jim Thorpe from Pennsylvania, who triumphed in the pentathlon and the decathlon, Kahanamoku forced the sporting community to accept that white athletes were not the only ones who could hope to shine.

The insular, Polynesian origins of the man in question turned out to be the very reasons for his success.

Having grown up just yards from Waikiki beach, the future hero was as much at home on the water as on dry land. At the age of eight he was already daring to take on the ancestral activity of surfing, defying the Calvinist rulers of the islands, who had banned it at least three generations before. Author Jack London had dedicated a few articles to it but London's literary efforts failed to compare the collective acrobatic skills of members of the Hui Nalu Club, the 'wave club,' in which the Kahanamoku tribe played the leading role.

First among them was the intrepid Duke, who during this same period created the hitherto unknown sport of windsurfing and another innovative discipline, body-surfing.

He dived from a barge anchored in the port of Honolulu to beat his first 100 yards world record, clocking 55.4 seconds.

The performance threw the press into disbelief, and they rushed to question it. The distance had to be measured four times before it was acknowledged that current holder Charles Daniels had been outstripped by 4.6 seconds and that the islands' record holder was worthy of national selection.

It was an honour that he did not fail to live up to. Already the 100m winner at Stockholm, the Duke repeated the performance at Antwerp, and led the American team to the 4x200m title.

If the war had not intervened, how many Olympic titles would he have today?

The Duke was a force of nature. He described his own style as a 'sophisticated crawl performed with flexibility'.

Kahanamoku, who had set a world record in the semi-finals and broke it in the first final, was untouchable in his events.

Nedo Nadi, gold on five fronts

Of the six fencing events, the Italian won five: two individuals and team foil, sabre and épée!

The hero of the Olympic Games in Antwerp is a 26-year-old Italian with dark eyes and wavy, brilliantined hair. Nedo Nadi won five gold medals in fencing. There is nothing unusual these days in being expert in the whole range of fencing blades – foil, sabre and épée – but Nedo Nadi achieved new heights. Olympic champion at 18 in the individual foil at Stockholm, he constitutes a unique case in international fencing.

A native of Livorno, he was born into the sport. His father, Beppe, was a fencing master and naturally Nedo and his brother Aldo, five years younger, quickly found themselves on the piste.

Beppe Nadi was a traditionalist, rejecting the épée as undisciplined. Nedo thought otherwise and, brimming with talent, fought expertly to help Italy take the team épée gold medal.

Nedo Nadi was 14 when he achieved his first victory, the Emperor's Trophy in Vienna. His style, tactical sense and physique, caused a sensation. The war interrupted his meteoric rise in the world of fencing but Nadi approached the battleground with the same bravery he showed on the piste, ending the war as a decorated captain.

At Antwerp, Nadi was destined for his lifetime's achievement. In the individual foil he nearly saw his hopes dashed after being beaten by the Frenchman Roger Ducret. Nedo sat alone in his corner, weeping, and the Frenchman had only one opponent

A Captain in the Italian army, Nedo Nadi (far right) arrived in Antwerp wearing military dress, as did his brother Aldo, seen here on Nedo's right.

left to beat, the Italian Pietro Speciale, last in the pool with no match wins to his credit. In his memoirs Ducret recalls: 'I was walking on air, seeing myself as Olympic champion. I could beat this man Speciale with my eyes closed.

'And then, I rushed at it, the other man delivered his riposte. I was trailing 2-0 and couldn't come back from that.'

Nedo emerged victorious almost by a miracle while his other great rival,

Lucien Gaudin, withdrew with a sprained toe.

In the sabre tournament, the Nadi brothers took gold and silver, in the absence of the Hungarians. But for Nadi's 1920 victory, the Hungarians would have held the Olympic individual sabre title continuously for 56 years until 1964. Nadi built on his two individual victories with three Italian team victories in foil, sabre and épée.

In the épée competition, the Italians

pushed the French, who had achieved a clean-sweep of the individual medals, into third place.

RESULTS

NADI'S FIVE TITLES

Foil
1 Nedo Nadi (ITA)
2 Philippe Cattiau (FRA)
3 Roger Ducret (FRA)

Foil, Team
1 Italy
2 France
3 United States

Sabre
1 Nedo Nati (ITA)
2 Aldo Nadi (ITA)
3 Andrianus De Jong (HOL)

Sabre, Team
1 Italy
2 France
3 Holland.

Épée, Team
1 Italy
2 Belgium
3 France.

Five titles for the Italian fencing team, seen here. And the same number for Nedo Nadi himself, posing among his team-mates in a grey cardigan.

Only the French, with a clean-sweep of the individual épée medals, resisted the total domination of the Italians.

Suzanne Lenglen's winning tale

The great French champion tells the story of her achievements in Antwerp where she won two gold medals in the tennis events.

As so often before, Suzanne Lenglen denied her opponents every chance in the singles on the courts of Beerschot: the Wimbledon champion lost only four games in the course of the tournament.

'Sometimes it is suggested that champions should let themselves be beaten in one or two games to please their opponent. I had no reason to act in this way, especially as these approaches succeed in doing nothing but giving the rival confidence and leading you often to an undeserved defeat. That's why I had made up my mind to assert myself in the qualifying heats.

The tactic worked well. Crushing the players who are playing against you gives you a sort of air of invincibility which, dare I say, weakens the morale of those you meet later. What's more, I didn't feel on top form, and so this tactic suited me all the more. Therefore, I had to go at full pelt and not prolong the game, to win as quickly as possible.

My father had given me advice which I followed slavishly and I reached the final having lost just one game in the preliminary games of the semi-final. Beforehand, I had won successively by 6-0 6-0 against my three opponents. Thank goodness! The rain prevented the deciding match from being played on Saturday 21 August. If the sun had been shining, I don't know if I would have achieved the same result. I was very poorly and I wouldn't have been able to do any rigorous exertions. The next day, I felt better and, when the solemn moment arrived, I was, if not quite at ease, at the very least ready to battle with all my energy. For the first time in the tournament, the first set went to my advantage and I won it 6-3. But would my opponent, Miss Holman, become a danger to me? I was confident: I returned to my game plan

The youth of 21-year-old Suzanne Lenglen combined with the experience of 37-year-old Max Decugis meant the French pair was perfectly equipped to win the mixed doubles tournament.

of the great days and I went on to smash my opponent in six games to love. I was Olympic Champion for the Women's Singles. The Mixed Doubles allowed my old team-mate Max Decugis and myself to secure a fresh victory for France. I really can't even begin to describe how brilliant my partner was. Max Decugis defended the

French colours with his customary skill. In the final, we beat Miss McKane and Mr Woosnam in 6-4, 6-2. This was no mean feat when you consider that Kitty McKane won the Ladies' Doubles with Miss McNair and that Max Woosnam won in the Men's Doubles with Turnbull. Shall I express my gratitude for the cheers which rewarded my

efforts very well? Shall I talk of the deep emotion I felt when the sport-loving Belgian king came to congratulate me? These are intimate impressions that will remain in the depths of my heart which I must not ruin by flaunting them on this great day.'

THE OLYMPIC VETERAN IS MAX DECUGIS

The most senior competitor in the tennis tournament at Antwerp was the Frenchman Max Decugis. He has participated in international trials since the age of 16, and had his victories embroidered, in miniature, on his team jersey. They were as follows:

1904 Davis Cup.
1905 Davis Cup.
1906 Victory at Athens Intercalated Games.
1910 National Champion at the Brussels Tournament.
France-Belgium (winner).
First French victory at Wimbledon in the Doubles Championships with Gobert;
Participated in the French victory in the Paris-London match.
1910 Paris-London (match won).
France-Belgium (match won);
World Champion on clay court.
1911 Paris-London (match won);
World Champion on clay court and covered court.
1912 World Champion on clay court.
1920 Paris-London (match won)
World Champion on clay court;
World Champion on covered court;
Olympic victory in Antwerp.

FOSS ACHIEVES RECORD VAULT OF OVER FOUR METRES

The Americans have demonstrated the effectiveness of their new technique in the pole vault. By bending the body at the waist when level with the bar, then making a two-stage recovery, world record holder Frank Foss staggered the spectators by clearing the bar several times at over four metres. He first beat Babrock's Olympic record with a 3.95-metre vault, before twice clearing 4.09 metres, only to see the pole fall back against the bar. Finally, at the third attempt, he cleared the bar without difficulty, achieving a remarkable feat that will go down in athletics history. Foss is a true vaulting phenomenon and looks as though he might be capable of clearing the bar at even higher levels.

1920
OLYMPIC ROUND-UP

ETHELDA BLEIBTREY AND AILEEN RIGGIN, SWIMMING SENSATIONS.

Ethelda Bleibtrey (photo 11) and the diminutive diver Aileen Riggin (photo 9) were among the most impressive Americans in the pool events swimmers at Antwerp. Miss Riggin at aged just 13 finished fifth in the platform diving and first in the springboard event. She dived splendidly with her slight, supple frame – she is just 140cm (4ft 9ins) tall and weighs just 30kg (65lb) – soaring skywards before cleanly parting the water.

With her blue eyes, light blonde hair and tanned complexion, Aileen is a true water baby. Aged three, she sailed the Pacific Ocean with her father, a US naval officer, and learned to swim in Manila Bay at the age of four years and three months. When she was eight, she travelled round the world with her parents, spending six months in China, where she swam every morning and evening. An act of carelessness in shark-infested waters once very nearly cost Riggin her life. She escaped thanks to her quick-wittedness and swimming ability. Back in America, her swimming talents were further developed at the Brooklyn Women's Swimming Association. Curiously, taking up dancing improved her swimming techniques.

Powerful Ethelda Bleibtrey has made her own waves, taking world and Olympic record victories in the 100m and 300m freestyle, and in the 4x100m relay backed by a strong American team.

Generously, her French rival Suzanne Wurtz attributes Ethelda's success to the fact that she is 'a true female athlete and trains every day' beneath the skyscrapers of New York.

Her times show just what a swimming phenomenon she is. In the 100m freestyle, she shaved almost three seconds off the world record set by the surly Australian Fanny Durack at the Stockholm Games in 1912.

In the 4x100m relay, Ethelda and team-mates Woobridge, Schroth and Guest beat the Great Britain team by a massive 30 seconds.

1 A police team from Great Britain (right) wins the tug of war. Its members had already won medals at previous Olympics.

2 Rough play mars the final of the men's football tournament between Belgium and Czechoslovakia. The Czechs, trailing 2-0, walking off the pitch in protest.

3 In the Figure Riding competition, held only at the Antwerp Games, the Frenchman Field (pictured here) takes silver in both the individual event and the team event, with teammates Salins and Cauchy.

4 On the Willebroeck canal, the Americans rediscover their supremacy in the eight-oared shell and the skull events. Pictured here is American oarsman John Kelly beating Beresford, of Great Britain.

5 The American rugby team, all former football players, win the championship by beating France 8-0, in spite of strong performances by French players Chilo, Bordes and Crabos.

6 Italian and Swedish riders steal the show in the equestrian event. The Italians take gold and silver in the individual three-day event, while the Swedes win the team tournament.

7 General Cubra congratulates the Belgian cyclist Henry George, winner of the 50km track race.

8 The Americans lose to the Finns in the 7.25kg shot put event but take their revenge in the 25.4kg weight throw, where McDonald takes gold and Pat Ryan (pictured here) wins silver with a throw of 10.965m.

9 Aileen Riggin with 15-year-old Swedish athlete Nils Skoglund, silver medalist in the high jump. These young athletes epitomise the Olympic Games' renaissance.

10 At 42.75km, the Antwerp marathon was the longest Olympic marathon course ever run. The Finn Kolehmainen wins by thirteen seconds from the Estonian Lossmann takes silver.

11 American swimmer Ethelda Bleibtrey's world record-breaking performances in the 100m, 400m and 4x100m freestyle events wipe out those formerly set by the Australian Fanny Durack.

12 The water polo again sees Great Britain face Belgium, as in 1900 and 1908, and the British, pictured scoring, made it a hat-trick of wins in 1920.

ATHLETICS

Three views of victory

Three champions and medal holders on the track at Antwerp recall their Olympic experiences in their own words.

Paddock had been a sickly child, yet became a strong athlete.

Loomis enchanted the crowds with his Olympic title and world record.

World War I veteran Albert Hill wears Great Britain's colours with pride.

CHARLES PADDOCK (USA): THE SUPERSTITIOUS SPRINTER

I came with every hope of winning after my success last year at the Inter-Allied Games in Paris, although I was aware of the progress made by athletes from other nations. Fortunately, I won. The best part about this win was that it ended a recent series of defeats for me in the United States. Some said my career was waning, and losing here would have caused many to forget my personal bests of 10.6secs in the 100m in New York and 21.6secs in the 200m in Paris. The crowd may have been surprised at the ritual I follow conscientiously before each race. I sprint up to the 400m mark to warm up, then I knock on the wooden post with both hands, crossing them alternately. After that, I go quietly back to the start and stand expressionless, waiting for the race to start. Up to now, this ritual has brought me good luck. I must admit that in the 200m, my pilgrimage to the 400m mark did not work out as well. As I had gone up to the 400m mark for the 100m race, I should really have touched the 800m mark for the 200m event – but there was no such mark. If you have to multiply the distance by four each time for my ritual to work, the marathon runners could be in trouble!

FRANK LOOMIS (USA): 400M HURDLES TACTICIAN

I'm an insurance broker in Chicago. I am 29 and I've been an athlete for 10 years. To be honest, I was expecting to win as my form has never been better.

Although I had some doubts about my ability and the results I'd been achieving before I left Chicago, the change of air helped me to achieve astonishing results in final training.

In my opinion, it was the great French champion Géo André who should have won the race.

He is a magnificent athlete who so impressed me that I could have become disheartened – had I been prone to such feelings.

He had already allowed Desch to beat him in the semi-final, when the race was in his hands, and he repeated the same unfortunate mistake in the final.

With a clear lead at the penultimate hurdle, he mistimed his take-off and never recovered his rhythm.

From that point, all I needed to do was finish the race without doing anything wrong. Desch did the same.

It goes to show how you can slip from winner down to fourth place very quickly and over a very short distance.

ALBERT HILL (GBR): 800M AND 1500M PATRIOT

The oldies are hanging in there! I am 32 and I have been running for 10 years. I made my debut at Newcastle, and have never stopped running there.

The best part about winning the 800m and 1500m events was gaining 14 points for my country in the important classification of nations. My countryman Baker, who took silver in the 1500m, also collected five points for dear old England. The 19 points we gathered between us fulfilled our most cherished desire – to see our individual victories contribute to our country's glory. In the 800m, I feared the South African Rudd and Eby of the USA. I managed to shake off Rudd just 80m from the finish line; Eby could not have been more than 1.5m behind me.

To give you an idea of the effort it took to win, remember that Rudd collapsed as soon as he arrived at the finish line and Campbell fell with 50m to go, overcome by an attack of nerves. It all shows that the biggest danger is overtraining.

In the 1500m, the men I feared the most were Lundgren of Sweden, who finished fifth, and the American Ray who was seventh. I decided to pace myself, rather than go all out against the clock.

With 450m to go, I lengthened my stride. At the bell for the final lap, I had a lead of 10m but I was saving my energy to respond to possible attacks.

Baker tried to catch up but I was not worried and picked up my pace again for one last effort, crossing the finish line just 5m ahead of my fellow Englishman.

Paddock leaps to the tape with his famous 'flying finish', which carries him past Kirksey (to his left) to victory in the 100m.

ANTWERP VII OLYMPIAD

Having emerged from the Great War, the world was ready to hold a true demonstration of peace. The Olympic flag, with its five rings representing the union of the five continents, flew for the first time.

THE GAMES IN BRIEF

Opening Date
20 April 1920

Closing Date
12 September 1920

Host Nation
Belgium (BEL)

Candidate Towns
Amsterdam (HOL) and Lyon (FRA).

29 Nations Represented

2,669 Athletes
(78 women, 2,591 men)

22 Sports
(4 open to women)
Track and field, rowing, boxing, cycling, fencing, football, gymnastics, weightlifting, wrestling, swimming, modern pentathlon, rugby, equestrian tennis, shooting and sailing.

Demonstration Sports
No demonstration sport

154 Events
(10 open to women)

Games officially opened by
King Albert of Belgium

Olympic flame lit by
The Olympic flame first lit during the Opening Ceremony of the Amsterdam Games in 1928.

Olympic oath read by
An Athletes' Oath was read by the Belgian water-polo player and fencer Victor Boin: 'In the name of all competitors, I promise that we shall take part in these Olympic Games, respecting and abiding by the rules that govern them, in the true spirit of sportsmanship, for the glory of sport and the honour of our teams.'

IOC President
Baron Pierre de Coubertin (FRA)

DID YOU KNOW?

The aggressor nations from World War I (Germany, Austria, Hungary, Bulgaria and Turkey) were not invited to take part in the Games. The opening ceremony was the first to feature the Olympic flag designed by Baron de Coubertin, with its five rings signifying the union of the five continents. It was also the first time that a competitor was called upon to say the Athletes' Oath. Doves were released as a symbol of peace for the first time.

At the age of 72, Swedish shooter Oscar Swahn won the gold medal in the team event for the double-shot running deer event, to become the oldest medalist in Olympic history.

The 1920 12-foot dinghy yachting event was the only event in Olympic history to be held in two different countries.The first race took place in Belgium, but the final two races were held in the Netherlands, because the two competitors were Dutch.

Dorothy Wright was part of the victorious British 7-metre sailing team, even though this event was ordinarily reserved for men.

1924

Paris

TWENTY-FOUR YEARS ON, THE OLYMPIC
Games returned to Paris. For Pierre de Coubertin,
who had announced his retirement, it was a final
opportunity to redeem France after the disastrous
events of 1900.

In a quarter of a century, the event had changed
completely. Participating nations had grown from 28
to 44, with more than 3,000 athletes – accommodated
for the first time in an Olympic village – competing.
The Games were also free-standing, no longer part of
a larger exhibition.

Spectators flocked to the purpose-built Colombes
Stadium, designed to hold 60,000, but there were still
peculiar sideshows such as the 'Pentathlon of Muses',
an art competition included at de Coubertin's request.

But all was not international harmony in 1924, and
the true 'spirit' of the Games became diluted. An
unwelcome side effect of the Games' success were the
first examples of extreme nationalism, if not
xenophobia.

After the US annihilation of the French in the
final of the rugby tournament, insults and blows were
exchanged and the American flag was torn down.

Four years earlier the Germans had been denied an
invitation to the Games and despite Coubertin's
efforts, Germany was absent once again in 1924.

The Games have become too important for haphazard preparation.
The Americans, pictured here at the Château de Rocquencourt, understand
this only too well.

Paavo Nurmi's four incredible days

Not content with winning the 1500m and the 5,000m in the space of an hour, the flying Finn went on to claim three more gold medals.

The Frenchman Dolquès leads Nurmi and Ritola in the 5,000m. The battle between the two Finns is later won by Nurmi.

It has become almost traditional to see the 5,000m race fought right up to the finish line. There had been compelling duels between Jean Bouin and Hannes Kolehmainen at Stockholm and Paavo Nurmi and Joseph Guillemot at Antwerp.

This year's contest between Nurmi and his compatriot Ville Ritola was no less spectacular.

However, the day belonged to Nurmi and not just thanks to victory at 5,000m. Under gathering storm clouds, the 'Phantom Finn' saw a brilliant solo run rewarded with victory in the 1500m; scarcely an hour before the 5,000m final started.

Nurmi's times destroyed the Olympic records for both distances – the 5,000m in 14:31.2 after winning the 1500m in 3:53.6; and this, after coasting to victory in order to save his strength.

Nurmi would certainly have been capable of setting a new world record – but since the record was already his, why try to better it, especially with another race minutes away?

The 1500m may have been easy for Nurmi but his task was much more delicate in the 5,000m, where he had

to dig deep to beat Ville Ritola, who trailed two metres behind him for much of the final eight laps, then came back courageously in the final stages to threaten his rival.

Nurmi had won three titles at the Antwerp Games. In Paris, he did even better.

Nurmi had only to accelerate just before the line to win by a couple of metres. 'It was a shame', he said, 'the two races were run on the same day. I had to save my strength in the 1500m, as I feared Ritola in the 5,000m!'

10 JULY – 1500M FINAL

At the start line Schärer (SWI) stands next to Nurmi who has a stopwatch in hand. Wiriath is in the outside lane. Lowe (GBR) causes a false start, but streaks into the lead at the second start.

Nurmi passes him on the bend and takes the lead coming into the straight, with Lowe, Schärer and Wiriath close on his heels.

Nurmi glances at his stopwatch and lengthens his stride. Half a lap back, Lowe is the only runner to remain within reach of the Finn after the first 200m.

Lowe comes back strongly, but cannot catch the leader. Nurmi's three compatriots are trailing at the rear, making no apparent effort to earn any points for their country. Their

performance is disappointing.

At the bell, Nurmi drops Lowe and by the 1200m mark leads by 60m and Schärer and Wiriath have both been dropped. Stallard attacks, drawing level with Schärer and Lowe, but he cannot catch Nurmi, who wins easily. Though he could have beaten the world record, he prefers instead to focus on saving his energy for the 5,000m.

Schärer and Stallard fight bitterly for the silver medal but it is the Swiss athlete who takes it on the line, and Stallard, who collapses, has to be carried from the arena.

Nurmi has proved his extraordinary superiority, winning at his own pace and commanding the race from start to finish. Wiriath is left far behind at the finish, but Schärer runs a marvellous race to beat the Swiss record by some margin.

10 JULY – 5,000M FINAL

At the gun, Dolquès takes the lead, followed by Wide. As they go into the bend, Wide moves ahead, with Ritola close behind. Dolquès moves into fifth position with Nurmi sixth.

By the end of lap one, Wide and Ritola lead Dolquès by over 10m. On lap two, Nurmi lengthens his stride to rejoin the leaders. As they pass the 1000m mark in 2:46.4, the four leaders have a clear lead over the rest of the pack. Mascaux is tenth, 100m further back.

At the 1200m mark, the three Scandinavian runners have a 20m lead on Dolquès. Wide quickens his pace and Nurmi, in third place, checks his stopwatch.

With two kilometres gone, the leaders have increased their lead over Dolquès to 80m. Romig, Clibon and Seppälä are 100m behind. For Mascaux, in last place, the race is over.

At the halfway point, the situation is unchanged. Wide still has a clear lead over Ritola and Nurmi but once they pass the halfway marker, Nurmi takes the lead.

Seppälä follows, passing Dolquès, who defends his position courageously. Nurmi raises the pace, but it is Ritola who moves into the lead with Wide struggling to keep up

After winning the cross-country event at the Antwerp Games in 1920, Paavo Nurmi again takes gold in Paris, beating his fellow countryman Ville Ritola by almost a minute and a half.

with the leaders. With the pace easing slightly after 3,000m, Wide gets his second wind and is back at the front. All but these three have been left far behind.

The indomitable Nurmi regains the lead at the 3,500m mark and picks up the pace.

Wide is clearly struggling and drops back 50m in the space of one lap leaving Ritola to maintain the challenge on Nurmi but he struggles to hang on.

With 4km gone, Nurmi has 10m on his fellow countryman and an 80m lead over Wide. At the bell, Ritola stages a recovery – but will he pass his team-mate? The question is answered half a lap further on when there is no change. Nurmi remains in the lead with Ritola in pursuit.

Going into the final bend, they remain in the same positions. The spectators are on the edge of their seats as the runners enter the final straight.

Ritola still cannot pass Nurmi. 'The Phantom Finn' is invincible and maintains a lead over Ritola, gaining victory in a finish reminiscent of the 1912 Stockholm Games, where the

unfortunate Bouin was beaten by Nurmi's Finnish predecessor, Hannes Kolehmainen. This time it is Nurmi who receives a standing ovation for his victory, won only one hour after his first. This performance confirms what everybody already knows: that Nurmi is a phenomenon, in all senses of the word.

12 JULY – CROSS-COUNTRY
Nurmi said that his individual victories mattered little to him and that his sole ambition was to see the Finnish flag flying over the stadium.

Under today's stormy skies, he again realised his ambition with a third victory, a win that brings him two Olympic titles: one in the individual cross-country event and one in the team race.

As usual, the lithe and elegant Wide, whose running style is undoubtedly the most appealing of all the runners and who is the Finns' accredited trainer, set off at a blistering pace with Ritola and Nurmi close behind.

The other runners, already far behind him, were unable to react as a gap opened between the leaders and the pack and ominously

continued to widen.

Nurmi waited, then suddenly accelerated to join his two Finnish team mates. And through the stadium's great blue 'marathon' door, one man appeared. It was Nurmi, the human machine.

Effortlessly, with that relaxed, almost mechanical stride, he crossed the finish line with his followers nowhere to be seen.

And as he sat, calmly contemplating yet another stunning victory, Ritola entered the arena alone, and the crowd cheered and cheered for the two famous Finns.

The American Johnson, who was to claim bronze, was still far behind.

13 JULY – 3,000M TEAM RACE
The last day in this great week of athletic events was hot, though not oppressively so.

The day belonged to the marathon, the American relay runners, and to Paavo Nurmi, competing in his final race of the Games.

As a farewell gesture, the flying Finn claimed his fourth victory and fifth Olympic title, and a new

Olympic record for the 3,000m, set effortlessly as he beat his rival Ritola by some 70m.

This means that over the course of the heats and finals run at Colombes, Nurmi has had the pleasure of being first to cross the finish line a total of seven times.

Always first – and with such style, such speed!

RESULTS

NURMI'S GLORIOUS VICTORIES:

1500m
Nurmi 3:53.6

5,000m
Nurmi 14:31.2

3,000m team race
FIN 8 points
(Nurmi 8:32.0, Ritola, Katz).

10,000m cross-country
Nurmi 32:54.8

Cross-country team race
FIN 11 points
(Nurmi 32:54.8, Ritola, Liimatainen).

1924

OLYMPIC ROUND-UP

AMERICAN SPRINTERS DEFEATED.

The second day of track and field dawned not too warm and without a hint of a breeze – a perfect day for breaking records before 10,000 spectators.

Their cheers are becoming an Olympic tradition, as is the raising of the three flags of the victors.

Twice, the American flag flew above the stadium thanks to Morgan Taylor, the record-breaking gold medalist in the 400m hurdles, and Harold Osborne, the high jump winner.

The star-spangled banner was destined not to fly after the 100m sprint final which contrived to stage the day's big upset – an American defeat.

This was despite the fact that four of their runners competing in the final could boast personal bests of 10.8 seconds.

A deafening silence filled the stadium as the some of the world's fastest men lined up for the start. Even the starter's orders could be heard.

On the first crack of the starter's pistol, the runners got off to a flying start and, for the first time in a major final, without a false start.

The Briton Harold Abrahams dominated the race from the outset, his admirable style stirring the enthusiasm of the crowd and ensuring him a decisive victory over America's four powerhouses, Bowman, Paddock, Murchison and the graceful Scholz.

For Abrahams, it is the third time he had run the 100m in 10.6 seconds, making him the best and most consistent sprinter in the world.

Is he just a freak phenomenon, like that of fellow Briton Stallard, who led much of the 800m and would have won, but for an injured toe? Or is British athletics, hitherto silent in Olympic events, beginning to make its voice heard?

In any case, the British champion's victory is warmly welcomed. Abraham's victory was indisputable and he was by far the best athlete on the track, something certainly not disputed by the disappointed Americans.

1 Paddock, who had taken gold in 1920, can only finish fifth in the 100m final. This time, victory goes to the Englishman Harold Abrahams (left, wearing number 419), in a time of 10.6 seconds.

2 The Americans triumph once again in the pole vault, with Barnes (3.95m) taking gold, and four of the first six places going to his fellow countrymen. Spearow, pictured here, finishes sixth.

3 After gaining automatic qualification in the first round, the French Olympic football team beat Latvia 7-0 in the second round. The tables are turned in the third round when they meet Uruguay, who cruise to a 5-1 victory despite good defending by Bonnardel (left) and Domergue to keep Uruguay's Petrone out of the game. The South Americans' fancy footwork delights the crowd and they go on to beat Switzerland 3-0 in the final.

4 Switzerland's rowers consolidate their victory by taking another gold in the four-oared shell with coxswain. This time, the French take silver to push the Americans into third spot.

5 Americans of Hawaiian, Black or Native Indian origin are progressively integrated into Olympic athletics, swimming and boxing, as this picture of Native American Indian Lester Magle shows.

6 First in the team event and fourth in the individual competition, the Italian Fernando Mandrini is the Lord of the (Olympic) Rings.

7 In the last-ever clay pigeon shooting tournament, the American foursome Hughes, Sharman, Silkworth and Etchen are as invincible in Paris as they had been in Stockholm and Antwerp.

8 Protected from the heat by a curious head garment, Albin Stenroos of Finland completes the marathon in 2:41:22.6, beating second-placed Romeo Bertini (ITA) by almost six minutes.

9 The 800m saw a titanic struggle between Douglas Lowe (USA, left) and Paul Martin (SWI, right). The American finally won in 1:54.4, 1.8 seconds ahead of his rival.

10 In the long jump, the American William DeHart Hubbard jumps 7.44m to take Olympic gold.

11 Now a maturing adolescent, Aileen Riggin has lost some of the sprightliness she displayed in Antwerp, but nevertheless wins a silver medal in the springboard diving.

12 American Harold Osborn, who sometimes gives the impression he is holding the bar, clears 1.98m to establish a new Olympic record.

13 With the Olympic ladies' doubles title at stake, Americans Helen Wills (pictured, with visor) and Hazel Wightman beat the English pairing Phyllis Covell and Kitty McKane 7-5, 8-6 in a hard-fought match.

14 The Hawaiians Kahanamoku and the Kealoha brothers stage a revolution in swimming. Pua Kela Kealoha had won gold and silver medals in the freestyle at Antwerp; his brother Warren Paoa (pictured here) takes gold in the 100m backstroke at Paris to keep the family name in the record books.

SWIMMING

Weissmuller shows his mastery

This consummate American swimmer, aged just 20, wins a thrilling 400m freestyle final.

The atmosphere was electric at the Tourelles swimming pool, where the 400m final stood out among the day's top events. Many believed Johnny Weissmuller of the USA would win comfortably but, instead, the event produced a memorable duel.

Sweden's Arne Borg, holder of the world record for the 1500m, led by six inches after 100m. At 200m, Weissmuller led by nine inches. At 300m, Borg was back in the lead, by just three inches. At that point Australian Andrew 'Boy' Charlton, whose stroke rate was distinctly slower than the leaders, closed the gap.

With 50m to go, as Weissmuller and Arne Borg fought at the front, the powerful Charlton accelerated irresistibly to within touching distance.

If the race had been 20m longer, Charlton would surely have won. For while Weissmuller and Borg showed clear signs of exhaustion after the race, the young Australian climbed out of the water with a broad smile, looking for all the world like he had just completed a successful dive, rather than a gruelling distance swim.

Weissmuller, this smiling, waterborne Adonis, is generous and unaffected, despite his all-round talent.

Nonetheless, he began his life in

The American coach Bachrasch (right), Weissmuller's discoverer and backer.

The strongest. Even in the 100m, the 34-year-old hero of the 1912 and 1920 Games, 'Duke' Kahanamoku (behind him), could only finish second, left trailing by the champion.

destitution. Weissmuller was born in 1904 in Freidorf, Germany and his family emigrated to the United States four years later. Weissmuller's father, a miner who became manager of a Chicago bar, indulged in frequent bouts of drinking and enjoyed beating his wife and children, before developing asbestosis and dying of tuberculosis when the boy was just 10.

Weissmuller was soon forced to work to help his mother and look after his younger brother. He left school at the age of 12, never to discover the torments of trigonometry.

Working as bellboy at the Chicago Plaza Hotel provided him in particular with a glimpse into the world of luxury, in which he no doubt took pleasure in being a part, though it eluded him just as surely as female companionship.

For the moment, his sole luxury was swimming, an activity he had practised since the age of eight on the advice of his family's doctor, who was keen to strengthen the boy's weak chest.

By the time he reached 16, swimming had already given him an enviably large physique and a friend introduced him to 'Big' Bill Bachrasch, who would become his mentor. His first encounter with the larger-than-life

Illinois Athletic Club coach, who tipped the scales at over 150kg, was a harsh one.

'First of all, you have to forget all you've learned and swear you'll work with me without asking questions and searching for excuses.

'You will be a slave and you will hate me, but in the end, you will break all the records you want,' said Bachrasch.

His understanding of swimming was flawless, and he had undeniable insight. Asked to describe Weissmuller's success, Bachrasch once said: 'His style was awful, but I felt as though an incredible talent was lurking behind it.'

Without a word of complaint, the teenager obeyed all his coach's commands. After months of swimming without being allowed to use his legs, however, Weissmuller did sometimes wonder whether he wouldn't be better off selling newspapers in the street.

His gruelling training schedule had the effect of positioning him very high in the water. Bachrasch's technique relied on the head commanding the body's supply of oxygen.

In the absence of lanes marked out in the water, the trainer would sometimes place his hat on top of the water, and ask the champion to swim straight over it.

On 9 July 1922, Weissmuller became the first human to swim the 100m freestyle in under a minute. On 17 February 1924 he improved this record to 57.4 seconds. The great attraction at Paris, Weissmuller is entirely capable of taking gold in the 100m and the 4x200m relay.

RESULTS

400m Freestyle
1. John (Johnny) Weissmuller (USA), 5:04.2
2. Arne Borg (SWE), 5:05.6
3. Andrew Charlton (AUS), 5:06.6
4. Ake Borg (SWE), 5:26.0
5. John Gatenby Hatfield (GBR), 5:32.0
6. Lester Smith (USA), highest-placed loser in the semi-finals

1924

PARIS VIII OLYMPIAD

This was the second time that Paris held the Games and they were a lot more successful than twenty-four years earlier. It was a double success for France as they also held the Winter Games that same year in Chamonix.

THE GAMES IN BRIEF

Opening Date
4 May 1924

Closing Date
27 July 1924

Host Nation
France

Candidate Towns
Amsterdam (HOL), Barcelona (ESP), Los Angeles (USA), Prague (CZE) and Rome (ITA).

44 Nations Represented

3,092 Athletes
(136 women, 2,956 men)

19 Sports
(6 open to women)
Track and field, football, polo, modern pentathlon, sailing, gymnastics, rugby, swimming, diving, fencing, rowing, shooting, wrestling, tennis, cycling, weightlifting, boxing, equestrian and water polo.

Demonstration Sports
None

126 Events
(20 open to women)

Games officially opened by
The President of France, Gaston Doumergue

Olympic flame lit by
The Olympic flame first lit during the Opening Ceremony of the Amsterdam Games in 1928.

Olympic oath read by
Georges André (athletics)

IOC President
Baron Pierre de Coubertin (FRA)

DID YOU KNOW?

William DeHart Hubbard of the USA was the first black athlete to win an individual event, the long jump. But his performance was overshadowed by the achievement of another American, Robert Legendre, who beat the long jump world record, in the pentathlon, with a jump of 7.76m. Gertrude Ederle (USA) won a bronze medal in swimming in the 100m freestyle. Two years later she went on to become the first woman to swim the English Channel. Hugh Hudson, star of the 1981 film 'Chariots of Fire', is a big reason for the 1924 Games' notoriety. The film follows the fortunes of two British heroes, Harold Abrahams, who won gold over 100m, silver over 4x100m and Eric Liddel, who won bronze over 200m, gold over 400 metres.

Many symbols associated with the Olympics took on an official form in 1924. The Olympic motto 'Citius, Altius, Fortius' (Swifter, Higher, Stronger) was used for the first time. At the Closing Ceremony, the ritual of raising three flags was introduced – the flag of the IOC, the flag of the host nation and the flag of the next host nation. Another first was the Olympic village, which housed all the athletes.

1928

Amsterdam

AMSTERDAM WAS A PICTURE OF PEACE AND harmony and Germany's return to the Games seemed to offer further proof that, 10 years after the Great War, the world was unified in peace. As the ninth Games took place in the carefree atmosphere of a country that had not even taken part in the 1914–18 war, how could anyone have imagined the Wall Street crash to come the following year with its disastrous effects on the world economy? How could the rise of Adolf Hitler's National Socialists have been anticipated, when elections for the German legislature had seen his party win barely 2.6 per cent of the vote?

The general atmosphere was one conducive to globalisation, ahead of its time. Athletes from 28 nations, including Asia for the first time, won gold medals, a record that would not be surpassed for another 40 years.

Athletics and gymnastics were finally opened to women and although tennis was withdrawn, female participation in Amsterdam was double that of the 1924 Games.

Pierre de Coubertin, by now a sick man, never saw the Olympic flame burn in Amsterdam. He did not even attend the Dutch-hosted Games, instead sending an official farewell message to the participants.

The passing of the 'Father of the Olympic Games' went by almost unnoticed and it signified the end of an era – never again would the Games be reliant upon the will and personality of one man.

The Olympic movement was here to stay.

A 1500m qualifying heat gets underway on cinder athletics track, framed by the banked cycling track – a common solution in stadiums of the time.

ATHLETICS

Four medals shared between Finnish friends

The Finns keep it all in the family, taking Olympic gold in the four middle-distance events.

On the penultimate day of the Amsterdam Games, the rain, wind and cold cast a gloom over the 3,000-metre steeplechase final. It was a subdued affair which, after a big build-up, saw a straightforward victory for yet another Finnish distance runner.

Early on, Finland's Toivo Loukola was in front with fellow countryman Paavo Nurmi. On the fourth lap, Loukola lengthened his stride and, by the end of the fifth, the increased pace saw him with a 60m lead – 80m on lap six. It was an easy victory for Loukola but how did he manage to gain such a lead over the great Nurmi?

Nurmi, leading Duquesne and French team-mate Henri Dartigues, held them up by slowing imperceptibly, allowing Loukola to extend his lead. The two Frenchmen seemed so pleased still to be on Nurmi's heels that they did not notice the Finnish game plan.

Nurmi surrendered to fatigue, allowing Loukola to win without the fight the Olympic ethic demands. Probably to avoid any suggestion that he had faked exhaustion he lay flat on a blanket as the race ended.

Eyebrows had already been raised in the 5,000m race. The Swedish runner Wide had been battling hard against habitual rivals, Nurmi and Ritola, until forced to capitulate after

Ritola should not have won the 5,000m but the Finnish camp's 'designated' champion drops out. Nurmi and Ritola then engage in a staged duel from which Ritola eventually emerges victorious.

Ritola leads Nurmi in the 10,000m, although this time it is Nurmi's turn to win the race – in Olympic record time.

RESULTS

FINLAND'S TRACK MEDALS

1500m
1 Harri Larva 3:53.2
3 Eino Purje-Borg 3:56.4

5,000m
1 Ville Ritola 14:38.0
2 Paavo Nurmi 14:40.0

10,000m
1 Paavo Nurmi 30:18.8
2 Ville Ritola 30:19.4

3,000m steeplechase
1 Toivo Loukola 9:21.8
2 Paavo Nurmi 9:31.2
3 Ove Andersen 9:35.6

3km. The ultimate winner was Ritola, with Nurmi right on his heels for a Finnish 1-2.

A repeat Finnish performance followed in the 10,000m which saw Nurmi home followed by Ritola. This time the Finns were visibly tired from the steeplechase heats the night before.

Under the Finnish tactics to dominate the middle-distance races it had been 'arranged' that Purje-Borg, who had assisted Larva in the 1,500m,

should take the 5,000m. When he dropped out, Ritola and Nurmi, still tired from the steeplechase, were forced to continue their efforts to the end. If there had been any doubts about Finnish physical superiority, their tactical nous certainly secured Nurmi his second 10,000m title, Ritola his first 5,000m gold and wins for Larva in the 1,500m and Loukola in the steeplechase. It was a triumph of teamwork.

FINLAND SHARES SPOILS

Finland's fourth track gold medal won by the blond powerhouse Loukola and the all-round prowess shown by Yrjölä in the decathlon have focused still more attention on Finland. This little Baltic Republic is a breeding ground for Olympic champions. So when the three blue and white Finnish flags were raised up above the stadium, representing Finland's clean sweep in the 3,000m steeplechase, everybody cheered for this tiny nation and the great example it has set.

And inevitably, alongside these new successes came endless debates. 'Racial superiority', said Ferretti, a member of the Italian legislature and President of the Italian Olympic Committee. 'Latin people are just not as powerful.'

'No, no', said his compatriot Count Bonacossa. 'Superiority of way of life and training methods. In Italy, for example, we make the mistake of entrusting all of our athletic events to one trainer, whereas specialists are needed for each event.'

'Yes, but that is very expensive and will mean that from now on, only rich and powerful nations will win at the Olympics,' came the reply.

Perhaps little Finland, where athletics is king, everybody enjoys a healthy life in the fresh air and distractions and excesses are unknown, will be the exception.

Percy Williams strikes again

The young Canadian fulfils his promise by taking gold in the 100m and 200m sprints.

100m final, l-r: Wykcoff, McAllister, London (2nd), Williams (1st), Lammers (3rd) and Legg.

200m final, l-r: Fitzpatrick (CAN, fifth), Scholz (USA, fourth) and Körnig (GER, third), Rangeley (GBR, second), Schüller (GER, sixth) and Williams (CAN, first).

No single country dominated the 100m and five different nations were represented by the six finalists. Germany expected several of its athletes to qualify for the final but only Georg Lammers started, and he finished third.

The Guyana-born black British runner, Jack London, was the surprise of the final. None of his achievements to date suggested that he would rank among the best sprinters in the world. Britain was acquiring a reputation for expert Olympic preparation and London was the first to use starting blocks.

The final was won decisively by Canada's Percy Williams. This unassuming young man at 5 feet 6 inches and 126 pounds, was dwarfed by the muscular London at 6 feet 2 inches and 200 pounds.

In the qualifying rounds Williams was the first sprinter in the tournament to run 100m in 10.6 seconds, and in the final, he demonstrated his unquestionable superiority.

For 50m, there was nothing between the finalists, but as the line approached, Williams pulled away into a winning lead.

Criticism had been voiced over the quality of the track, and as long as the heats failed to produce times of under 11 seconds, they seemed justified.

Two semi-finals won in 10.6 seconds silenced the critics and although the final was won in of 10.8 seconds, this may have been due to nerves and fatigue.

Williams became the third runner to win the Olympic 100m and 200m double.

The 200m final featured two Germans, Helmuth Körnig and Jakob Schüller; two Canadians, Williams and

With holes instead of starting-blocks, the equipment is still rudimentary.

John Fitzpatrick; an Englishman, Walter Rangeley; and the sole American, Jackson Scholz. In qualifying, Körnig had equalled the Olympic record of 21.6 seconds but the final was a very different matter, and would bitterly disappoint the Germans.

Williams' 200m victory was one of the great spectacles of the tournament. Körnig took an early lead and even 20m from the finishing tape, the Germans were already preparing their victory chants for their first gold medal in an athletic event. Their champion

had at least a metre's lead over the pack, and showed no signs of slowing down. Suddenly, Williams put in an electrifying late surge, leaving Körnig trailing. At the line the German had fallen back to third place.

Williams finished the race in 21.8 seconds and the admiration for this noble character of a thoroughbred athlete was even higher.

Wearing a toga made of the Canadian flag his team-mates had hung about his shoulder, he calmly returned to the starting line to look for his sweater.

Returning to his hotel, Williams encountered a huge crowd that had gathered to greet him.

With his face not yet published in the newspapers, Williams mingled anonymously with his fans, without revealing his identity.

'It was,' he recounted afterwards with typical modesty, 'much more fun.'

Williams, the outstanding sprinter of the Games, is carried in triumph.

1928
OLYMPIC ROUND-UP

HENRY PEARCE, ROWING GIANT.

The rowing delighted thousands of its most ardent fans, with splendid contests on the peaceful Sloten Canal.

The most impressive spectacle was the mastery, power and graceful technique of the great Australian Henry Pearce.

He beat Kenneth Myers (USA) with ease in the single sculls and was all smiles as he received the customary flowers and congratulations.

Myers tried to assuage his bitter disappointment by attempting to scale the flag pole to steal the Olympic standard.

A vigorous counter-offensive was co-ordinated by the police, who interpreted his offence akin to an act of high treason, despite the fact that close scrutiny of the Olympic regulations reveal no mention of any such offence.

As for 29-year-old Australian rower Pearce, he has proved himself to be a giant in his discipline, in stature and also in athletic prowess.

In his quarter-final heat against the Frenchman Victor Saurin, he interrupted his effort to allow a family of ducks to pass ahead of him. Then he still powered his way to victory!

The Sloten Canal regatta certainly brought together the world's rowing élite, including the German Flinsch, the Dane Schwarz plus Saurin and Myers.

The Australian outclassed the entire group, who in all truth never challenged him sufficiently to stretch him to the limits of his prodigious talents, which are truly exceptional, both in quality and quantity.

Pearce is physically impressive, too. This Australian giant is a towering 6 feet 2 inches tall and weighs 209 pounds.

He rows with remarkable ease and his stroke is the paradigm of grace.

Avid followers of the rowing sport firmly believe that the invincible Pearce would surely demolish the English professional rower Bert Barry, the current world record holder. Pearce is in a league of his own!

1 The first four finishers in the 110m hurdles cross the line in the space of a 10th of a second. Sydney Atkinson (RSA) is the winner.

2 At Sloten, the oarsman Henry Pearce attracts a crowd of young admirers.

3 Douglas Lowe (GBR) retains the 800m title he had won at Paris in 1924.

4 Canada's James Ball led the 400m when he turned to check on his rivals, and Raymond Barbuti (USA, pictured) crept past him to win.

5 Hungarians and Italians share the first five places in the individual sabre. Here, Sandor Gombos (HUN) takes on Bino Bini (ITA).

6 The Dutch pair Bernard Leene and Daniel Van Dijk succeed the French title holders Lucien Choury and Jean Cugnot in the tandem competition. In the final, here, they defeat the British pair John Sibbit and Ernest Chambers.

7 It takes two matches to separate Uruguay and Argentine in the soccer tournament. After a 1-1 draw, the Uruguayans win 2-1.

8 The Canadian victors and world record breakers in the women's 4x100m.

9 The tiny Canadian-born American Pete Desjardins wins both the Springboard and the Platform diving competitions.

10 Since 1896, US pole vaulters have won every title. In 1928, Sabin Carr adds his name to the list with a jump of 4.20m.

11 Second in the 400m freestyle, Maria Braun (HOL), 17, wins the 100m backstroke. She set a world record in qualifying.

12 Ethel Catherwood (CAN) competed for the first time a year earlier. She wins the women's high jump and the title of Miss Olympic Games.

13 Hungary begins its run of success in the sabre. It relinquishes the title only in 1964

ATHLETICS

El Ouafi, marathon man

The diminutive Mohamed Boughera El Ouafi, had the strongest legs in the marathon but it was, above all, his tactics that sealed victory.

Mohamed Boughera El Ouafi began the marathon with a relaxed pace, allowing his less-talented French team-mate, Guillaume Tell, to keep him company over the first third of the course.

Their gentle rhythm left them some way behind the leading group of 11. When the gap between them and the two Japanese front runners, Yamada and Tsuda, reached two minutes, 30 seconds, El Ouafi's chances of winning seemed remote.

With the Finns Marttelin and Korholin-Koski sharing the work at the front with the Japanese pair, the leading group finally began to fragment at around the fifteen mile mark. The race was about to be turned upside down.

The catalyst for this was, above all, the work of the extraordinary Yamada, who runs with surprising ease, appearing to jog rather than run yet giving the impression of bounding along the road. Such is the lightness of his stride.

Even in the final few kilometres, where defeat stared him in the face, Yamada's style remained impeccable: he is truly an expert in the long-distance contest.

His great mistake, which eventually cost him victory, was to break away alone. He was still a long way from the finish and he tried to break from team mate Tsuda, the American runner Ray, Marttelin and Laaksonen and Canada's Bricker, some of the most accomplished marathon runners in the world.

El Ouafi paces himself intelligently over the first fifteen miles.

Yamada's error in breaking up the leading group played into El Ouafi's hands. The French Algerian closed in on the remnants of the group, passing at speed.

Instead of a compact group able to mount a co-ordinated counter-attack, El Ouafi found a string of rapidly-tiring athletes struggling to recover after countering Yamada's previous surge.

With no hint of a struggle, El Ouafi passed all the other runners who had led him not long before at the two-hour mark.

Witnesses said it was a heart-rending moment as the Japanese runner glanced over at the Frenchman and saw his chance of victory disappear.

But the drama was not over yet! As El Ouafi maintained his pace, Chilean Miguel Plaza, very similar in style to El Ouafi, launched his own counter-attack.

After two hours, 20 minutes and fast approaching the finish line, Plaza moved to within 40m of El Ouafi. However, a mile from the finish line, Plaza's challenge petered out and El Ouafi was assured of victory.

French supporters exploded with joy when the French-Algerian entered the stadium. Having been ill informed about the race's progress, they expected to see an American, Finnish

El Ouafi takes gold in the marathon after battling to the finish to counter a move by Chile's Miguel Plaza, who almost stole the race a mile from the finish line.

or Japanese runner streak into the stadium to take gold.

Instead, it was their own brave countryman who strode so confidently into the arena, a man who had battled so calmly, run so elegantly and deployed his tactics with such precision.

El Ouafi is a real marathon-running legend. His victory at this arena brought him a success that he will remember for a long time to come.

EL OUAFI TO COMPETE IN AMERICA

Success can take you a long way! Since his marathon victory in Amsterdam, El Ouafi has accepted an invitation to run another marathon in America, and to make several professional appearances in other races. El Ouafi will leave France on 1 September, and his American tour is set to last around four months. He will, of course, shed his status as amateur runner, though one does wonder if this rather unexpected outcome is really an appropriate next step for an Olympic gold medal holder.

In sport, however, anything is possible.

RESULTS

Marathon
1. Mohamed Boughera El Ouafi (FRA/ALG), 2:32:57
2. Miguel Plaza Reyes (CHI), 2:33:23
3. Martii Marttelin (FIN), 2:35:02
4. Kanematsu Yamada (JPN), 2:35:29
5. Joie Ray (USA), 2:36:04
6. Seiichiro Tsuda (JPN), 2:36:20
7. Yrjo Korholin-Koski (FIN), 2:36:40
8. Samuel Ferris (GBR), 2:37:41

AMSTERDAM IX OLYMPIAD

His work was done, so Pierre de Coubertin left. He didn't take
part in the Amsterdam Games, which marked the passage of
the Olympic Games to adulthood.

THE GAMES IN BRIEF

Opening Date
17 May 1928

Closing Date
12 August 1928

Host Nation
Netherlands (NED)

Candidate Towns
Los Angeles (USA)

46 Nations Represented

3,014 Athletes
(290 women, 2,724 men)

9 Sports
(7 open to women)
Track and field, rowing, boxing, cycling,
equestrian, fencing, field hockey, football,
gymnastics, weightlifting, wrestling, modern
pentathlon, diving and sailing.

Demonstration Sports
None

109 Events
(23 open to women)

Games officially opened by
Prince Hendrik of Holland

Olympic flame
The Olympic flame was first lit during the
Opening Ceremony of these Games.

Olympic oath read by
Henry Denis (football)

IOC President
Henri de Baillet-Latour (BEL)

DID YOU KNOW?

The number of participants was double that
of 1924, mainly due to the introduction of
women's athletics. The first women's event to
be contested in athletics was the 100m.
Elizabeth Robinson of the USA won the final
by half a metre, even though it was only her
fourth time competing in an athletics meet.
She also won a silver medal in the 4x100m.

But the fact that several competitors in the
800m collapsed at the end of the race led to
a lively debate about the participation of
women in this type of event.

During the rowing, Australian Henry
Pearce stopped in the quarter finals to let
a family of ducks pass. That didn't stop him
from winning that race, nor indeed the
Olympic title.

Gold medals were won by 28 different
nations, a record which remained unequalled
for almost forty years. Germany participated
in the Games again, after an absence of
sixteen years, linked to the First World War.
For the first time, a gold medal was won by
an Asian athlete, with Japan's Mikio Oda
winning the triple jump.

1932

Los Angeles

BY MID-1932, SOME 13 MILLION PEOPLE – a quarter of the workforce – were unemployed in the United States alone, and many millions more in the wider world. Japan, Spain, Italy and Germany were soon to succumb to extremism.

The Los Angeles Olympic Games were deeply affected by the Great Depression that followed the Wall Street crash of 25 October 1929. Only 1,400 athletes from 37 nations made the costly journey to California – not since 1904 had participation been so low. Some events had scarcely a handful of entrants and the soccer tournament was cancelled because of a lack of participants.

However, even lacking basic necessities, the Americans threw themselves into the Games. More than 100,000 people attended the Opening Ceremony in the expanded LA Coliseum – the largest sporting attendance in history at the time – and 70,000 attended the athletic events, including Hollywood stars.

From 1900–1928, no Summer Olympics had lasted less than 79 days but the 14-day Los Angeles events programme was adopted as standard for the future.

The level of competition was extremely high. Many records were broken, notably those of France's Jules Ladoumègue and Finland's Paavo Nurmi, later both banned on grounds of professionalism.

Amid a worldwide financial crisis, the 1932 Los Angeles Games were the first to make a profit – about $1 million – and the last until the next Los Angeles Games in 1984.

Lauri Lehtinen heads for victory in the 5,000m. Behind the runners rises the imposing structure of the Memorial Coliseum; beneath their feet, the best track of its day anywhere in the world.

ATHLETICS

Didrikson's finest hour

A remarkable athlete, the 19-year-old American shines in many different disciplines. She chooses her events well and wins three medals.

When Mildred 'Babe' Didrikson is asked what her favourite sport is she replies: 'There isn't only one...' Not a surprising answer from one of the most accomplished all-round sportswomen in history.

American Didrikson represents the meaning of sport in its most complete and multi-faceted sense.

The gold medal winner in the 10th Olympiad in both the javelin and the 80m hurdles and the silver medal winner in controversial circumstances in the high jump, Didrikson believes in action, not specialisation.

It has been reported that she has scored more than 100 points in a basketball match, single-handed. Her incredible strength enables to her train with male American football players, and her skill at billiards allows her to compete against the best players in the country.

She is a competent swimmer and horsewoman and her talent in bowling is equalled only by her dexterity in lacrosse.

The morning she was scheduled to learn the basics of downhill skiing, she was granted a licence to join the amateur golf circuit.

Texan Mildred is the second youngest of seven children with a marine carpenter father who considered physical exercise an essential virtue.

RESULTS

80m hurdles
1. Mildred Didrikson (USA), 11"7
2. Evelyne Hall (USA), 11"7
3. Marjorie Clark (SAF), 11"8

High jump
1. Jean Shiley (USA), 1,65m
2. Mildred Didrikson (USA),1,65m
3. Eva Dawes (CAN), 1,60m

Javelin
1. Mildred Didrikson (USA),43,68m
2. Ellen Braumüller (GER), 43,49m
3. Tilly Fleischer (GER), 43m

Didrikson's first throw assures her of victory. Later, she would turn her hand to golf and win three US Opens in 1948, 1950 and 1954.

Instead of playing with dolls, his most indefatigable daughter improvised a dumbbell with two irons and a broomstick. Her stamina and long legs combined with a stubborn personality have marked her out as a true athletic phenomenon. As an adolescent she was unbeatable in any track and field event.

So impressive was she that she entered a women's athletic team championships – as the sole team member. The championships took place at Evanston, Illinois and served, incidentally, as trials for the Los Angeles Olympic Games.

Registered for eight events, Mildred won six: the 80m hurdles, the javelin and the high jump, the shot put, long jump and baseball throw.

When the points were tallied, Mildred had single-handedly won the team title with a score of 30 points. She had scored eight points more than the 22 competitors who made up the second-placed University of Illinois team.

During this period, Mildred also turned her hand to baseball. As her hits frequently exceeded 100m she earned her nickname 'Babe', after the great Babe Ruth.

He was the most famous baseball player of the time and a huge favourite throughout the US but Didrikson struck him out in front of a crowd of 72,000.

Embarrassed at the rare sight of this young girl taking on professionals, Olympic officials quibbled over her right to compete in multiple events at the Los Angeles Games.

Despite the fact that she had legitimately qualified for five events, officials finally authorised 19-year-old Didrikson to compete in just three disciplines.

Didrikson chose the javelin, the 80m hurdles and the high jump and promptly won the javelin event on her first throw of 43.68m, beating the German favourites.

She went on to win the 80m hurdles, after trying in a time of 11.8 seconds in the opening heats and setting a new world record of 11.7 in the final.

In the high jump, she tied again with fellow American Jean Shiley, clearing 1.65m to set another world record, but was robbed of gold by a technicality.

The judges ordered a jump-off and raised the bar to 1.67m. Again both athletes cleared it but officials deemed Didrikson's style illegal as her head appeared to clear the bar before her body.

Why this had not been noticed earlier is a mystery but the ruling meant that Shiley won gold and Didrikson had to be content with a share in the world record and the silver medal.

There is no doubt however that she would have been in contention for more medals in the discus, long jump and relay if she had been allowed to compete in these three further events.

Babe Didrikson (centre) only tasted defeat at Los Angeles in the high jump, where she was beaten on a technicality by Jean Shiley (left).

Didrikson's hurdling technique (right) was unpolished in comparison to her opponents, but she compensated for this with superior athleticism.

The first two cross the finishing line within a tenth of a second of each other, and the third trails closely behind. Didrikson had to fight for gold in the 80m hurdles.

1932

OLYMPIC ROUND-UP

TOLAN AND METCALFE – 100M KINGS.

International 100m sprint results are sometimes a lottery. Yet over the past two days we have seen seven heats, four quarter-finals, two semi-finals and a six-man final in which the same athletes have competed with extraordinary consistency.

The final, in particular, was as precise as a set of postal scales. Two African-Americans, Thomas 'Eddie' Tolan and Ralph Metcalfe, finished neck and neck, with Germany's Arthur Jonath a metre behind them.

This final could be re-run ten times and the results would never vary. In every one of his events, the magnificent Metcalfe keeps his supporters in a state of anxiety by running well within himself until the halfway point.

Only then does he unleash his full power and drive irresistibly to the finish line! His finishing spurt can be predicted, but not countered. Over 101m, Metcalfe is unbeatable.

Metcalfe, a well-built, powerful, strapping athlete, is perfectly proportioned. His style is preferable to that of Tolan, although Tolan is the more consistent of the two.

Tolan is slightly too round and almost gives the impression that he rolls rather than runs, even if he rolls very effectively.

If the final had been run over 101m, Metcalfe would have been the clear winner, as the finish-line photos show. But it is precisely because Metcalfe outstrips the other contenders only in the final metres of a race that his finish with Tolan was so difficult to judge.

The moving pictures of the race give an exact view of the position of the two sprinters, and specifically, of the evolution of the angle their bodies form with finish line traced on the ground.

It is on this basis that the result must be judged, and the film clearly and distinctly shows that although Metcalfe reached the ribbon first; Tolan crossed it first by a hair's breadth. According to the rules, which are quite clear on this point, Tolan was judged the winner.

1 While Jacques Lebrun (FRA) triumphed in sailing's Finn class, the Swedish team of Holm, Hindorff, Akerlund and Bergqvist enjoyed a spectacular win in the Six-Metre class. Sadly, as the regatta drew to a close. the world learned of the death of Virginie Heriot, who had lit up the Eight-Metre event in Amsterdam.

2 With a jump of 1.97m Duncan McNaughton (CAN) took a surprising victory in the high jump.

3 A relaxed Henry Pearce (AUS) after rowing the perfect race to retain his Olympic single sculls title.

4 The Finns had dominated the 3,000m steeplechase since the Paris Olympics in 1924. At Amsterdam, Loukola, Nurmi and Andersen took a clean sweep of the medals. At LA, Volmari Iso-Hollo wins a race with an extra lap added, thanks to confused race officials.

5 A bespectacled Thomas 'Eddie' Tolan (USA) shows winning form in the 100m, snatching gold from his friend, rival and compatriot Ralph Metcalfe.

6 Two Americans, George Saling (14.6 secs) and Percy Beard (14.7 secs), head for the tape in the 110m hurdles, on their way to gold and silver, respectively.

7 The Scandinavian monopoly on the javelin competition is extended as the Finn Matti Järvinen throws 72.71m. Here, he rehearses a throw.

8 American rowers, who had dominated the eight-oared shell since 1896 with the exception of 1908 and 1912, reigned supreme again, despite the challenge of a formidable Italian team.

9 Following his success in 1938, Ireland's Patrick O'Callaghan once again takes gold in the hammer throw, improving on his winning throw in Amsterdam by more than 2.50m.

10 Only second in the all-around gymnastics competition, Hungary's Istvan Pelle takes sweet revenge by winning both the floor exercise and the side horse, seen here.

11 Argentina's Juan Carlos Zabala collapses on the grass after winning the marathon in a new Olympic record of 2:31:26.

12 After dominating the 1500m freestyle, Kitamura (right) and Makino congratulate each other after Japanese swimmers win the relay and finish first and second in four out of five individual events.

13 With the French Greco-Roman wrestler Emile Poilvé absent due to injury, the way is clear for Finnish middleweight Väinö Kokkinen, seen here defeating Germany's Jean Földeak.

14 The Japanese retain the triple jump title, won in 1928 by Mikio Oda, thanks to Chuhei Nambu, who, already the world long jump record holder, sets a new world triple jump record of 15.72m on his way to victory.

SWIMMING

Madison goes to the ball…

The American swimmer, barely 19, wins three freestyle gold medals and an evening with Clark Gable. She is dubbed 'Queen Helene'.

On the 100m podium, Helene Madison looks like a veteran beside 14-year-old Willemijntje den Ouden (HOL).

Japan has dominated the men's swimming tournament, but the United States reigns supreme in the women's events.

There are US victories in the 100m and 400m freestyle, the 100m backstroke, the 400m relay plus the springboard and platform diving and the star, as expected, was Helene Madison.

She broke 16 world records for the distances between 100 yards and a mile in 16 months in 1930–31. Her 100m world record, in particular, made her the darling of the American public.

After a fine performance at the US national championships, Madison's form dipped, when she was beaten over 50 yards by Eleanor Saville, who had not even achieved Olympic selection at the time.

The defeat spurred Madison into action. She worked especially hard on her starts, repeatedly perfecting her dive

Her performance in the 100m

Olympic semi-finals raised serious doubts over her chances in the final.

The first semi-final was won by the tiny 14-year-old from Holland, Willemijntje den Ouden, in 1:07.6. In the second semi-final, Helen Madison had to be content with a far more modest time of 1:09.9, which would have placed her no better than fifth in the earlier race.

The explanation lay in a tactical decision to start very quickly, with the result that Madison slowed markedly in the second part of the race.

The US team coaches seem to have given her sound advice between then

A smile from the three medalists after a fierce battle in the 400m freestyle.

Led by the irrepressible Helene Madison, the US women won all but the 200m breaststroke.

and in the 8 August final, when Madison beat den Ouden in a new Olympic record of 1:06.8, she was just two-tenths of a second outside Madison's own world record time of 1:06.6.

Even more impressive was that this was a 100m time that only a small elite of male international swimmers could complete any quicker.

The 1928 women's 100m final was won by Albina Osipowich (USA) in 1:11.0 – which means women's swimming has progressed by an

average of a second a year over the previous four years.

Four days earlier, Madison had helped the US team to clear victory in the 4x100m freestyle relay. The following day, however, the 400m was less straightforward: Lenore Knight (USA) led at 325m, only to see Madison draw level at the final turn and win by a tenth of a second in 5:28.5.

This impressive late surge meant Madison had beaten her own world record by 2.5 seconds.

At 5 feet 11 inches tall and weighing 126 pounds, Helen Madison has an almost stretched appearance with huge hands and feet.

Born in Seattle beside the Pacific, Madison's Scandinavian descent was forgotten and the stars and stripes were raised over the Los Angeles stadium. She celebrated her third gold medal by dancing the night away at the famous Coconut Grove club with actor Clark Gable. American patriotic pride could hardly have been better expressed!

RESULTS

Swimming

100m
1. Helene Madison (USA), 1:06.8
2. Willemijntje den Ouden (HOL), 1:07.8
3. Eleanor Saville (USA), 1:09.3

400m
1. Helene Madison (USA), 5:28.5
2. Lenore Knight (USA), 5:28.6
3. Jennie Maakal (SAF), 5:47.3

4x100m
1. USA, 4:38.0
2. HOL, 4:47.5
3. GBR, 4:52.4

Crabbe saves America's honour

The Japanese win every men's swimming title except the 400m freestyle, which sees Buster Crabbe (USA) and Jean Taris (FRA) duel for victory.

Three Japanese started the 400m final, but victory was disputed between an American (Crabbe, nearest the camera) and a Frenchman (Taris). Both broke the Olympic record.

By winning 11 of the 28 track and field events in the programme, the United States demonstrated its supremacy in the competitions of these 'home' Olympic Games.

It was Japan which has shown even greater dominance in men's swimming, winning the 100m freestyle, 100m backstroke, 200m breaststroke and 800m relay.

Virtually unknown in the 1920 Games in Antwerp, where the primitive style of Kavekichi and Masayoschi provoked mirth, the Japanese have now won the battle for global pre-eminence.

This amazing advance owed as much to intense training as to the use of performance-enhancing drugs, which the Japanese would later admit.

Never in Olympic history has one nation's swimmers monopolised the pool so completely. Three Japanese representatives qualified for every final, except the 1500m, in which Ishiharada was knocked out in the

semi-finals. Japan won five out of six men's swimming events.

Only the 400m freestyle and two diving events – the springboard and platform – escaped them. Largely uninterested in diving, they were a major force in the 400m, with three swimmers in the final. Unfortunately for them, they faced two superior rivals and had to be content with third, fourth and fifth place.

Their twin nemeses were an American student from Honolulu, Clarence 'Buster' Crabbe, and the French world record holder, Jean Taris. The pair were meeting for the second time in Olympic competition. At Amsterdam four years ago, Crabbe finished fourth in the 400m and third in the 1500m. Taris, who had over-trained, did not swim well. This time, both men were competitive.

The event caused consternation among the Japanese but was the race of Crabbe's life. He showed hunger, courage and sportsmanship.

The Japanese swimmers had been

duped in the elimination heats and semi-final, during which they were repeatedly caught, then outstripped.

Taris, who was normally stronger during the first half of the race led for most of this swim, completing 100m in 1:04.6; 200m in 2:18.0; and 300m in 3:33.5. Crabbe caught him at the final turn just as the Japanese lost

After an end-of-race comeback that took him past Taris, Buster Crabbe is congratulated by his coach. American swimming had not completely foundered.

contact and played no further role in the final battle.

The American opened a slight lead, before Taris fought back, only for Crabbe to beat him by a hand. Crabbe's winning time was 4:48.4; Taris was a 10th of a second slower.

The Olympic record had fallen, although Taris retained his world record of 4:47.0. Andrew 'Boy' Charlton's time of 4:58.6 placed him last in the final but in the previous two Games, his time would have won gold.

The French were left speculating on Taris's narrow defeat, in the light of the Japanese dominance.

As a world-class swimmer, some suggested Taris was too isolated in France and, lacking real adversaries, had to contend with tackling records instead.

Accordingly, he developed a rhythmical and precise swimming method better suited to competing against the clock than racing. In the final, Taris had provided Crabbe with a focal point.

LOS ANGELES X OLYMPIAD

Due to the Great Depression taking place at the time, and the outlying position of the city in which they were held, the 1932 Games had fewer participants than the 1928 Games. But the level of competition was still excellent.

THE GAMES IN BRIEF

Opening Date
30 July 1932

Closing Date
14 August 1932

Host Nation
United States of America

Candidate Towns
None

37 Nations Represented

1,503 Athletes
(35 women, 1,468 men)

15 Sports
(7 open to women)
Track and field, rowing, boxing, cycling, fencing, field hockey, gymnastics, weightlifting, wrestling, swimming, equestrian, modern pentathlon, shooting, sailing and water polo.

Demonstration Sports
American football and lacrosse.

128 Events
(15 open to women)

Games officially opened by
Charles Curtis, Vice-President of the United States of America.

Olympic flame lit by
None

Olympic oath read by
George C. Calman (fencing)

IOC President
Henri de Baillet-Latour (BEL)

DID YOU KNOW?

In order to finance their visit, the Brazilians travelled with a cargo of coffee.

The three-tiered podium made an appearance.

American Pete Mehringer won the gold medal in freestyle wrestling in the light heavyweight division, after having taken a correspondence course to perfect his technique.

Jim Thorpe, who had been stripped of his medals in 1931, only took part in the Games with the collusion of journalists who had invited him to a press tribune.

Franz and Toni Schmid won an Olympic prize for mountaineering after they were the first to scale the north face of the Matterhorn.

Charlie Chaplin, Douglas Fairbanks, Marlene Dietrich, Mary Pickford and many other Hollywood stars were at the Games to entertain the athletes.

The Olympic Village, which consisted of 700 small houses, was exclusively reserved for the men, with women being put up in a hotel.

It was thanks to Hollywood that the first mascot, a dog named Smoky, made an appearance.

1936

Berlin

THE HEADLINES SCREAMED 'CORRUPTED Games' and 'A showcase for Hitler's power.' Reports observed that: 'Hitler's Germany has set out to prove to the world that it has once again become Greater Germany', and reflected: 'We have become figurines in a huge medieval clock at Nuremburg, moved by a mechanism assembled over the past four years.'

Those four years had revealed the true nature of the ruling regime of the country hosting the Games. Hitler had been appointed Chancellor in 1933, and proclaimed Führer of the Third Reich in 1934. In September 1935, he passed laws establishing two categories of Germans to ensure 'the protection of German blood and honour': racially pure 'citizens' and 'subjects'. Hitler intended to use these Games to prove his political and ideological theories, although Théodore Lewald, whose father was of Jewish descent, remained head of the German Olympic Committee, and Jewish fencer Helena Meyer, an Olympic champion in 1928, was selected.

Germany rose to the occasion like never before, with 4.5 million entrance tickets sold and a thousand special trains conveying spectators to events. The super-prepared German athletes won 33 gold medals, compared with only three in Los Angeles. However this demonstration of Aryan racial superiority hit an unexpected stumbling block in the huge successes enjoyed by African-American athletes. Despite Hitler's best efforts, the stars of the Games were Woodruff, Johnson, Metcalfe and, of course, the great Jesse Owens.

In Berlin's Olympic Stadium, 100,000 spectators raise their arms in salute and subvert the Games from a festival of sport into a celebration of the Reich.

1936
ATMOSPHERE

THE DISFIGURED GAMES.

For the 11th time, the world has seen its physical elite face each other. Nations have measured the evolution of the human body by success in such enormous tournaments.

For those who would judge the select group of athletes who take part in the Olympics not as complete human beings but as star performers, they proved a total success in demonstrating pure strength and showmanship.

In terms of both public and muscular triumph, the Berlin Games appear to have served sport's cause marvellously.

But unfortunately, the spirit of sport has never been so deeply corrupted. We leave Berlin and her rain of flags with deep misgivings that the spirit of sport has not been served.

The only Olympic ideal that remains is that of competition.

The Los Angeles Games served as a publicity campaign for a region whose sole beauty is a marvellously temperate climate. All that seemed to matter there were telegrams and telephones ringing with phrases like, 'Los Angeles, unbroken blue skies', 'California, a delight to the lungs, for the best human performance'.

By contrast, the Berlin Games are a grotesque demonstration of a national political regime. It begs the question: 'What of the Tokyo Games in four years? A diatribe for the Asian race?'

The Games no longer purely exist for sport; they have become a vehicle for other forces. IOC members are no longer free-spirited gentlemen of sport, but government representatives. The host country of the 1940 Olympic Games was decided in the offices of ministries of foreign affairs.

This must be stopped at once. Sport should be supported by the leaders of our countries, it should not be forced to succumb to them.

The very idea of sport is in danger from an extremism rooted in national ambition.

1 The big moment draws near as the penultimate carrier of the Olympic flame from Olympia hands over the flame to the German 1500m champion, Schilgen, at the stadium's eastern entrance.

2 Seated on the bleachers of the swimming stadium, the Philippine Welterweight boxer Simplicio de Castro appears amused as companions vie for his attention.

3 The 34-year-old Leni Riefenstahl filmed the Games for her documentary 'The Gods of the Stadium', an invaluable historical record of the 1936 Olympics.

4 In the team combined exercises, the Czechs compete second and are placed fourth in the official competition.

5 The photographers await Katherine Rawls' dive which would win her silver.

6 Spiridon Louis (GRE), winner of the 1896 marathon in Athens, meets the Führer, stealing the limelight from the aviator Lindbergh and the boxer Schmeling.

7 Who would guess that these eight elegant ladies were the Olympic champion gymnastics team, representing Germany? Second and third were Czechoslovakia and Hungary

8 2,000 flags, posters and banners decorated the Olympic Stadium. The streets of Berlin were even worse. These Games no longer belonged to Berlin: they had become the spoils of the Reich.

9 Under the watchful eye of Leni Riefensthal perched atop a watchtower-type structure, judges and time judges are arranged so as to appear infallible.

10 Despite the attention of her coach Erik Alderz, the tiny Swedish diver Nierling only comes 10th in the platform dive.

11 The Dietrich-Eckart Theatre provides a classical backdrop to the gymnastics tournament.

Four golds for Jesse Owens

The great Afro-American sprinter takes gold in the 100m, 200m, long jump and 4x100m events and sets almost as many world records – under the steely glare of the Führer Adolf Hitler.

In the 200m, Jesse Owens lives up to his undisputed title of the best sprinter in the world. He dominated his adversaries in 20.7 with apparent ease and setting a new Olympic record.

The first two finishers of the 12 100m sprint heats reduced the 68 entrants to 24 quarter finalists. Among heat winners were Berger, Van Beveren and Osendarp of Holland; Owens, Metcalfe and Wykoff of USA; Borchmeyer (GER), Hänni (SWI), Theunissen (SAF), MacPhee (CAN), Gyenes (HUN) and Strandberg (SWE). The outstanding performance of the heats was Owens' easy equalling of the world record of 10.3 seconds.

The quarter finals rooted out those who could not cover the distance in 10.7 seconds and the three Americans two from the Netherlands and a Briton reached the semi-finals. Powering into the lead in the first semi-final, Owens' time of 10.2 would have set a new world record but for the light tail wind but he still clocked 10.4 seconds.

The second semi was slightly less impressive but was won by Metcalfe, who stormed to 10.5 with his trademark final surge. In the final, Owens took gold in 10.3 with Metcalfe and Osendarp only 10ths of a second behind.

Owens achieves his best jump on his final attempt – an amazing 8.06m.

Wykoff was placed fourth, while Borchmeyer avoided last place in front of a fervent home crowd thanks only to an injury to Strandberg. Winning the Olympic 100m has never been harder. The superiority of the black American athlete is irrefutable.

Owens brought the day of the long jump to a glorious close. Despite the favourable wind, it was impossible not to be impressed by not only Owens' phenomenal 8.06m jump but by the number of athletes who can now break the 7.50m barrier at every jump. 7.15m was required just to get through qualifying and 16 achieved this.

The showdown between Owens (USA) and Long (GER) took place in front of Adolf Hitler, who spent the entire afternoon in the stadium.

With his blond locks and strong physique, Long seemed every inch the Aryan ideal in combat with the African-American. The tension was almost unbearable.

Their styles were quite different. Long appeared to throw his very being into each jump; Owens competed with nonchalance.

The American jumped 7.74m, then

7.84m: Long matched him jump for jump. Everything stopped in the stadium. For an hour, races were interrupted and for once, a single event held everyone's attention.

Long, driven by sheer will on his second last attempt, reached 7.87m, tying with Owens. When Owens heard the result, he approached his German rival and shook his hand, warmly offering his congratulations.

Then he headed to the jumping pit and began his run-up. Unusually, he kept low, sprinting like never before – not even in the 100m finals. He seemed to hang in the air and stay there until he had covered 7.94m!

Each had one attempt left. Long missed his, before Owens, taking off like a diver from a springboard, achieved 8.06m! Long was the first to shake his hand.

In the first 200m semi-final, Mack Robinson (USA) ran an exhilarating race, appearing to be a worthy adversary to Owens.

Yet only in direct competition can we truly compare athletes and in the final, Robinson, in the lane next to Owens, was a shadow of his former self, and seemed out of form from start to finish, as did Osendarp.

Jesse Owens put his powerful start to good use, thrilling the crowds who saw him explode out of his crouched position and attain full speed from the first stride.

This man must be possessed of the force of a compressed spring deep inside him – a power he is able to harness and release at a spilt second's notice.

Nature itself must be proud of what

After a fierce and unforgettable showdown in the long jump, Germany's Carl 'Lutz' Long (left), in the spirit of true sportsmanship, leans companionably towards America's Jesse Owens (right).

Owens gets through the 100m qualifying rounds at a stroll.

it has achieved in Jesse Owens.

In winning his third gold medal, Owens, true to current form, set a new Olympic record, after lowering it to 21.1 in the heats and repeating that time in the semi-finals.

He also achieved a world best for the distance run over the full curve of the track. Owens' time of 20.7 was only a 10th of a second outside Tolan's world 200m record of 20.7, achieved in a straight line.

The most striking impression is that in all his races, Owens starts in the lead and finishes in the lead.

He calmly raises his rhythm in between and appears to exert little effort, winning so decisively that there is no possible doubt as to his success.

The American 4x100m sprint relay team was to be split by controversy. Before the event it was made known

that the president of the US Olympic Committee Avery Brundage had decided to run it with an all-white team.

The Dutch team posed a serious threat, however, and the US Committee reassembled to discuss whether recourse to its black sprinters would be necessary to guarantee success.

Uproar followed when it emerged that Jesse Owens and Ralph Metcalfe would take the 4x100m relay places that trainer Lawson Robertson had promised to Marty Gluckman and Stam Stoller weeks before.

Fellow black medal winners Archie Williams and James LuValle could well have protested that they deserved the same consideration as Metcalfe and Owens for this event, but they were ignored.

Black Americans triumphed as they saved the day in the 4x100m. The stars and stripes was raised on the flagpole of honour and a new world record.

In the 4x400m relay, the US team was beaten by the UK amid protests from all sides and it is a miracle that the situation did not degenerate completely.

This new affair did nothing to ease existing tensions within the US camp. Gluckman and Stoller, the sole Jews on the American athletic team, were the only members of the squad to return to the States without having competed in a single event.

RESULTS

JESSE OWENS

100m
1 James 'Jesse' Owens (USA), 10.3
2 Ralph Metcalfe (USA), 10.4
3 Martinus Osendarp (HOL), 10.5
4 Frank Wykoff (USA), 10.6
5 Erich Borchmeyer (GER), 10.7
6 Lennart Strandberg (SWE), 10.9

200m
1 James 'Jesse' Owens (USA), 20.7
2 Matthew 'Mack' Robinson (USA), 21.1
3 Martinus Osendarp (HOL), 21.3
4 Paul Hänni (SWE), 21.6
5 Lee Orr (CAN), 21.6
6 Wijnand Van Beveren (HOL), 21.9

Long Jump
1 James 'Jesse' Owens (USA), 8.06m
2 Carl Ludwig 'Luz' Long (GER), 7.87m
3 Naoto Tajima (JAP), 7.74m
4 Arturo Maffei (ITA), 7.73m
4 Wilhem Leichum (GER), 7.73m
6 Robert Clark (USA), 7.67m
7 John Brooks (USA), 7.41m
8 Robert Paul (FRA), 7.34m

4 x 100m
1 USA (James 'Jesse' Owens, Ralph Metcalfe, Foy Draper, Frank Wykoff), 39.8
2 ITA 41.1
3 GER 41.2
4 ARG 42.2
5 CAN 42.7

Netherlands disqualified.

The triumph of youth

The Korean Son Kitei, 24, proves that the marathon is not just for aging athletes.

There is a myth in the world of sport that long-distance running is for the old. It is understandable that the young are more attracted to tests of speed and strength and may prefer to save trials of endurance until other faculties begin to dull with age.

Proof lies in the victory of diminutive Korean student Son Kitei, representing Japan in the marathon. Young and dignified, he is not the classic marathon runner.

Son emerged through the tunnel into the stadium as fresh and full of vigour as a 5,000m runner. He crossed the finishing line in style and, despite expectations, neither fainted nor faltered. He sat for a moment and savoured the relief of removing his running shoes.

We have seen so many outstanding performances this week that it comes as no surprise to see Japan's Son had set a new Olympic record for the marathon, having completed the 42,195 km in 2:29:19.

Nothing has been heard from His Excellency Juan Carlos Zabala, race favourite and the Argentine Ministry of Agriculture's official representative in Germany.

No doubt he will return to his country with a surprising amount of information on cabbage growing in Germany but many believe that the excessive place given to sport in his life got the better of him.

The view is that he had too much time to train and was worn out before the big event

The pointers are that he was over trained, he thought himself the strongest because he was the most shrewd.

With the defeat of the agricultural representative, never again will the Olympic oath be so smugly ridiculed.

From the very first minute, he appeared to take command of this race but after 25km, he seemed to fall asleep.

The Argentine government's man only held out until the 28km marker before he was overtaken by Japan's Son on his path to victory.

Son's triumph was a victory for quiet dignity as well as youth.

Son Kitei (JAP) was, in reality, Sohn Kee-chung of Korea, forced to compete under a Japanese name after his country's annexation.

The 1500m Race of the Century

New Zealand's Lovelock stormed to an amazing victory in a race that saw four runners beat the 3:50.0 mark, with two of them even smashing the world record.

Ny (SWE, left) and Cunningham (USA, no.746) control the race at the halfway point, ahead of the eventual winner. the New Zealander Lovelock (black jersey), and Italy's Beccali (behind Lovelock).

In the fierce battle for 1500m supremacy New Zealander John Lovelock gave a sensational performance.

Not only did he beat the world record to win by a respectable margin but he also appeared to accelerate out of the bends with a fresh pair of legs every time.

The UK has traditionally proved strong in this event but Lovelock's win broke that country's winning streak through pure ability.

As well as being the best on the track he ran the most intelligent race, an outstanding, faultless performance. No trickery and no fuss, he simply relied on his talent to eliminate all traces of fault from his technique.

Nevertheless, this 1500m race was never going to be a walkover because the starting line-up was of the highest calibre.

They were all legends, sharing a collective history of triumph and glory. Despite this, the assembled champions somehow managed to misjudge the race.

By running in tightly-knit groups, they were lulled into thinking that the pace was not particularly fast. France's Goix had begun to fall back by the halfway mark, but Cunningham, Ny, Lovelock, Beccali, Schaumburg, Boettscher, Cornes, San Romani and Edwards were jockeying for positions in the leading pack.

The stage was set for the battle that would end with five runners beating the Olympic record and two, the world record.

The timekeeper put things into perspective by pointing out that we were witness to one of the most amazing athletic feats of modern times. Lovelock had truly made his mark.

The new 1500m record holder John Lovelock is scarcely out of breath as he reflects on his new world record.

For the first 600m Lovelock wisely allowed himself to be carried along in the middle of a pack before effortlessly moving into third place behind Ny. At 1,200m he uncorked a sprint, upping the speed to such a pace as to break William Bronthron's world record by one second in 3:47.8.

RESULTS

1500m
1 John Lovelock (NZL), 3:47.8
2 Glenn Cunningham (USA), 3:48.4
3 Luigi Beccali (ITA), 3:49.2
4 Archie San Romani (USA), 3:50.0
5 Philip Edwards (CAN), 3:50.4
6 John Comes (GBR), 3:51.4
7 Miklos Szabo (HUN), 3:53.0
8 Robert Goix (FRA), 3:53.8

A CLOSE RUN RACE

In the semi-final of the women's 80m, Italy's Trebisonda Valla had run 11.6 seconds. Wind assistance meant the time could be accredited as an Olympic record, but not as a world record. Valla started the final as the favourite, but the result was so close, with four runners timed at 11.7, that it took the judges 30 minutes to select the winner from the photo-finish. After a nerve-shattering wait, Valla celebrates with her supporters, watched by a German official who manages a smile, despite the fact that the decision in Valla's favour left his compatriot Anni Steuer in second place.

ROWING

The Mighty Jack Beresford

Paired with Southwood in the double sculls, the British rower outclassed the German favourites to win his third Olympic title.

Beresford and Southwood are presented with a large wreath, marking their victory and Germany's frustrated ambitions.

Jack Beresford is unequivocal after the double sculls final: 'My best race ever!' That is really saying something as great performances have been a hallmark of his long career.

A single-sculls silver medallist at the 1920 Games, Beresford has won Olympic honours in every rowing combination. They have included gold in the quadruple sculls in 1924, silver in the eights in 1928 and gold again in the coxless fours in 1932. He is also the only rower to hold both skiff and sculls titles.

Beresford's father, Julius Beresford Wiszniewski, a coxed fours silver medalist in 1912, could never have imagined such a record for his son when he emigrated from Poland.

Yet of all Beresford's successes, this one will surely stand out. Beresford

and his partner, Leslie Southwood, ended a series of five consecutive German victories in front of 25,000 spectators, including Adolf Hitler, in ecstasy. The Britons overcame formidable obstacles to do so.

Six weeks before the Games their coach, Eric Phelps, told them their trip to Berlin was a waste of time as the

Beresford (left) wins his fifth medal in as many Olympic Games.

German design of boats were far superior.

To demonstrate his point, he challenged them in his single scull and was three lengths ahead within a minute. 'You need to slice through the water, not just float on the surface', Phelps told them.

For £50 and in just 17 days a dream boat was constructed on the lines of the German design.

En route to Berlin their craft disappeared. The Germans sportingly lent them another but they had to share with other crews. As a result Beresford and Southwood's training suffered.

In the nick of time, two days before the Games, their boat was found in a railway siding and, reunited with their pride and joy, Beresford and

Southwood saw off the European champions and race favourites, Kaidel and Pirsch (GER).

RESULTS

Double Sculls

1 Jack Beresford - Leslie Southwood (GBR), 7:20.8
2 Willy Kaidel - Joachim Pirsch (GER), 7:26.2
3 Roger Verey - Jersy Ustupski (POL), 7:36.2
4 André Giriat - Robert Jacquet (FRA), 7:42.3
5 John Houser - William Dugan (USA), 7:44.8
6 William Dixon - Herbert Turner (AUS), 7:45.1

Mastenbroek: the glory of hard work

Years of training pay off for the 17-year-old Dutch swimmer, who wins four medals, three of them gold.

Hendrika Mastenbroek has proved with four medals, including three gold, that persistence can pay off. From the age of 11, Mastenbroek has trained harder and longer than her rivals.

She arrived in Berlin, accompanied by her notorious coach Ma Braun, a week before the rest of the Dutch squad to gain the advantage of acclimatisation.

Braun's methods are controversial. Her swimmers sacrifice their adolescence to swimming but there is no doubt over the effectiveness of her methods. Hendrika swam every day of the Olympic competition and won all her events, with the exception of the 100m backstroke.

Observers say this shy Dutch girl, has yet to realise her full potential. Despite winning three golds and a silver at the 1934 European Championships Mastenbroek is still young.

She began the Games by winning the 100m freestyle in a new Olympic record of 1:05.9. Mastenbroek's only hiccup came in the 100m backstroke. Despite holding the world record for this event, she finished second to her compatriot Dina Senff. Tired after that morning's 400m heats, Mastenbroek swam the final in 1:19.2, 3.4 seconds outside her record.

The second gold came the following day with the Dutch 4x100m relay team, in a new Olympic record of 4:36.0.

Mastenbroek's final Herculean task was the 400m, in which she faced the formidable Dane Ragnhild Hveger.

Mastenbroek was motivated after Hveger, sharing out a large box of chocolates, snubbed Mastenbroek. The Dutch girl who took revenge where it mattered most – with victory in the pool.

Mastenbroek set another Olympic record at 5:26.4 and she said afterwards of her gold medal: 'This is better than a piece of chocolate.'

If Jesse Owens is the star of the stadium at these Games, Hendrika Mastenbroek is the queen of the pool.

The forbidding Ma Braun (right) is not renowned for her sense of fun but her methods take Henrika Mastenbroek to three gold medals.

1936

OLYMPIC ROUND-UP

JOHNSON'S TAKE-OFF.

During a recent trip to the United States, journalists predicted that, above all else, black Americans would be the stars of the US team this year.

This was confirmed on the very first day of the Games when Cornelius Johnson, second only to Jesse Owens in the athletic world, leaped to stardom. Clearing the high jump bar at 2.03m, he smashed the previous Olympic record of 1.98m set by Harold Osborn in 1924, earning a gold medal.

Johnson, who currently shares the world record of 2.07m with compatriot David Albritton, then attempted to clear 2.08m – a height never before jumped by man.

On his first attempt, Johnson cleared the bar but dislodged it on the way down. On his second, the bar wobbled then eventually fell. His final attempt also failed – with good reason this time.

Just as Johnson was about to start his run up, in the centre of the field Germany's Hans Woelke achieved 16.20m in the shot put, setting a new Olympic record and assuring him of a gold.

The shot landed just beyond the little flag with its interlacing rings, indicating the previous record of 16m set by Sexton in Los Angeles.

The passionate home crowd rose and roared their approval, stamping their feet and singing, oblivious to Johnson's own world-record attempt.

Johnson tried to start his take-off again but the uproar continued, a distraction for even the most focused of athletes.

Discouraged, Johnson took off but only jumped high enough to knock the bar with his chest.

Even without Johnson's fireworks, the high jump was an extremely high-calibre competition. Nine competitors jumped over 1.94m, two of whom jumped the two-metre mark, a ground-breaking standard never before attained in competition.

1. The Americans dominated the decathlon podium, with Glenn Morris (on the ground) emerging victorious ahead of Robert Clark and Jack Parker. Morris, a 24-year-old car salesman from Colorado, improved on his own world record with 7,900 points, based on the new set of tables introduced in 1934.
2. Ferenc Csik, a 22-year-old Hungarian medical student, is congratulated for his 100m freestyle gold medal by Holland's Willemijntje den Ouden, Olympic 4x100m champion. Csik died in an air raid in 1945, giving first aid to the injured.
3. Left to right, the three graces of platform diving – Germany's Käte Köhler (third place) and the Americans Velma Dunn (second) and Dorothy Poyton Hill (first, as in 1932).
4. Fifty participants test their endurance in the three-day event, but only 27 make it to the end. Three horses die in the process. Germany's Ludwig Stubbendorff (above) emerged victorious from the massacre on a horse named 'Nurmi.'
5. The all-around gymnastics event provided the Germans with yet another opportunity to inflame national pride.
6. On the podium, Italy's Trebisonda Valla celebrates her 80m hurdle gold. Judges take 30 minutes to separate her from Germany's Anni Steuer in the finish-line photo.
7. Söllner, Gaber, Volle and Maier show their pride after winning gold for Germany in the four-oared shell with cox.
8. 400m world record holder Archie Williams (46.1) confirms the superiority of the black American sprinters.
9. The sabre title did not escape the Hungarians, and Endre Kabos achieves a tournament record of 24-1 to take the individual gold. He lost his life on the eve of his 38th birthday during World War II when Budapest's Margaret Bridge was blown up.
10. After finishing third in Amsterdam and Los Angeles, Giulio Gaudini (ITA) defeats Édouard Gardère (FRA) to finally take gold in the foil in Berlin. He also wins his second team title; the first was in 1928.
11. The high jump is simple for Cornelius Johnson (USA), who does not even remove his sweat suit until the bar reaches 2m. Johnson goes even higher, achieving 2.03m.
12. After victory in the 100m and 4x100m, America's Helen Stephens tastes triumph for a third time when she turns down Hitler's offer of a weekend at his residence in Berchtesgaden.

BASKETBALL

Sleight of hand across several sports

Professor Naismith, the inventor of basketball, sees America take gold in Berlin.

The first Olympic basketball tournament was held outdoors. The final was affected by poor conditions.

The first Olympic basketball tournament ended in victory for the United States, ahead of Canada, Mexico, Poland, the Philippines and Uruguay. The result almost perfectly reflects the state of international basketball today.

The final the United States and Canada was plagued by heavy rain and the quality of play suffered as the players skated on a slippery surface, scarcely able to stop the muddy ball from sliding between their fingers.

The final score of 19-8 was mainly a result of the adverse conditions. This grand final showcased the tactics of the US team: take a 10-point lead, then close down the game.

The Canadians did not prove such easy pickings as their Estonian or Philippine counterparts.

The Americans were forced to sharpen up their attack and had to work hard to contain their Canadian opponents, only very occasionally allowing their extremely tight defence to slip.

To probe their adversaries' weaknesses, the Americans kept possession and force their opponents to chase the ball.

Swift attacks sliced open the opposition, before the rhyhm reverted to its former pace. By the end of the first half, the Americans had 15 points, while the Canadians had scored only one basket and two free points: four points in 20 minutes.

The Americans maintained their 11-point buffer for the remainder of the game, hypnotising their opponents with their ball control.

However, the Canadians managed to upset the US with rapier attacks and began to close in on their rivals with two baskets.

At 15-8, the Americans replaced two players and re-established their 11-point lead. Then they closed down the game.

The game was not spoiled by the US's tactic of playing for the whistle; indeed, quite the opposite. They showed intelligence and cunning,

proving that basketball is one of the most tactical sports around.

Dr. James Naismith, a PE teacher from Massachusetts, invented the game in 1891. A cent was added to the price of matches in the US tickets for a day, allowing Naismith to attend the

Played on a football pitch with two teams of 11, the version of handball performed in 1936 seems unfamiliar. Handball next appeared in its modern form in the 1972 Games.

Olympic debut of his creation.

He said: 'We played American football in the fall and baseball in the spring, but nothing in winter. My boss asked me to come up with something to keep our students amused during the bad weather.

'I remember racking my brains during the long winter nights at the end of December 1891. This went on for two weeks. Then, in one night, I wrote the original 13 rules of basketball.'

He said the students had a great time throwing the ball into the 'basket' but they cheated, throwing the ball against the balcony to make it slip into the basket.

To counteract that the professor said: 'The net to protect the basketball was invented two days later, and that is the story of basketball.

'This Olympic tournament is magnificent! But I'm going to let you in on a little secret: the game played by the Latin teams comes closest to the game I envisaged.'

1936

BERLIN XI OLYMPIAD

The Olympic flame was introduced for the first time. But in truth, there was another fire burning at the Olympics: until now, the Games had never before been used to such an extent to promote a cause. And this was the worst of all causes: Nazism.

THE GAMES IN BRIEF

Opening Date
1 August 1936

Closing Date
16 August 1936

Host Nation
Germany (GER)

Candidate Towns
Barcelona (ESP)

49 Nations Represented

4,066 Athletes
(328 women, 3,738 men)

21 Sports
(7 open to women)
Track and field, rowing, basketball, boxing, canoeing, cycling, equestrian, fencing, football, gymnastics, weightlifting, handball, field hockey, wrestling, swimming, modern pentathlon, diving, polo, shooting, sailing and water polo.

Demonstration Sports
None

129 Events
(24 open to women)

Games officially opened by
The German Chancellor, Adolf Hitler.

Olympic flame lit by
Fritz Schilgen (athletics)

Olympic oath read by
Rudolf Ismayr (weightlifting)

IOC President
Henri de Baillet-Latour (BEL)

DID YOU KNOW?

The Olympic flame took on an important symbolism with the first torch relay. The route, which was 3,000km long, took the torch from Olympia to the Games' host site, via seven countries (Greece, Bulgaria, Yugoslavia, Hungary, Czechoslovakia, Austria and Germany).

Another first was the fact that the 1936 Olympic Games were filmed and transmitted on 25 big screens throughout Berlin.

Basketball, canoeing and handball all appeared in the programme for the first time, while polo made its last appearance.

Two young girls were early record-beaters: 13-year-old Marjorie Gestring of the USA won a gold medal in diving, making her the youngest-ever gold medal winner. Dane Inge Sorensen, aged 12, won the bronze medal in swimming's 200m breaststroke to become the youngest-ever medalist in an individual event.

Hungarian water polo player Olivier Halassy won his third gold medal, despite having had a leg amputated beneath the knee following a tram accident.

1948

London

WORLD WAR TWO WAS BARELY OVER WHEN, in August 1945 London, selected in 1938 to hold the 1944 Games, was awarded the poisoned chalice of organising the Olympic revival of 1948. The world was healing its wounds and it was a time of austerity in a city that had shown courageous resistance and whose major priority was reconstruction. The Olympic Games would have to adopt the same tone.

The competitors were lodged in military barracks at Uxbridge and Richmond Park, or converted classrooms, in conditions that many athletes today would snub. There were problems in maintaining supply chains, and at times glaring inadequacies in conditions. These only got worse as the Games went on. Yet, given the circumstances, they were tolerated.

The Games were the first global sporting event after the war, despite the absence of the Germans (who were not invited), the Japanese (who declined the invitation), and the Soviets (who were in sporting isolation). The Games had to go on, and the London Games put them back on track.

It is true that there were limited resources, but there were symbols of the Games all around. And at the start of the television era, the event was brought into viewers' homes for the first time. Even if television sets were rare, the presence of cameras at Wembley Stadium and the Empire Swimming Pool were a promise of things to come.

Major Pierre Musy on Französin, representing Switzerland in the three-day event, completes the hastily-prepared endurance course. The winner was a Frenchman, Bernard Chevalier, on Aiglonne.

Blankers-Koen, housewife and champion

At 30, the Flying Dutchwoman is more than a proud mother: she wins the 100m, 200m, 80m hurdles and 4x100m relay.

A warm welcome for the queen of the London Olympics on her arrival in Amsterdam. Husband, children, local notables and supporters greet a champion who has just gone down in history.

Neither the birth of her children, nor the Second World War, could break Fanny Blankers-Koen stride. The 30-year-old mother of two has been the star of the London Games, a female Jesse Owens in puffed-out shorts, taking four gold medals. Never has a female athlete earned such adulation!

Born into a farming family, Francina (her real name) Koen escaped life on the land when her father became a lorry driver. In town, she left the local school, learnt home economics and spent her free time cycling, sewing and gardening. Her future seemed to lie in a life of domesticity.

Instead at 14 she took up competitive sport and two years later, her physical education teacher, hearing of her dream of Olympic glory, shaped her career by telling her, 'We already have plenty of good swimmers. Choose athletics' Under the

supervision of former triple jump champion Jan Blankers, the 18-year-old Blankers-Koen qualified for the Berlin Games, finishing sixth in the high jump and fifth in the 4x100m. Her greatest achievement in Berlin was obtaining Jesse Owens' autograph.

Slender and fast, she excelled at 800m, an event outlawed after several women collapsed in the 1928 final.

In the intervening years, she ran 100 yards in 11.0 seconds, the first of 11 world records, won bronze medals at 100m and 200m in the 1938 European championships and married her coach. During the war, she set world records for the high jump and the long jump. At the 1946 European Championships in Oslo, she took gold in the 80m hurdles and the 4x100m,

In the 100m on a water-logged track, Fanny Blankers-Koen, led after 20m and won with ease ahead of Dorothy Manley (GBR).

and finished fourth in the high jump.

At the London Games, on a water-logged cinder track, she entered eight races and won them all. In the 100m she left Dorothy Manley (GBR) trailing; in the 200m she humiliated

In the 4x100m relay Blankers-Koen (rear of shot, fourth from the left) takes the baton with a five-metre disadvantage and wins the race.

In the final of the 200m, Fanny Blankers-Koen gives a master class, finishing six metres in front of Williamson (723, GBR), Patterson (on the left, USA) and Strickland (on the right, AUS).

The 80m hurdles final was decided by the first hurdle. The medal winners are Blankers-Koen (on the inside lane), England's Gardner to her right, and Australia's Strickland, in the foreground (white vest).

Audrey Williamson (GBR), who had openly declared that Blankers-Koen was too old to represent a threat.

In the 80m hurdles final, Blankers-Koen set the only athletics Olympic record of the Games with 11.2 seconds. Finally, in the 4x100m, she started her leg in fourth place and crossed the finishing line first.

'All I've done is run fast. I don't see what people are making such a fuss about it', she protested.

I'm not sure we should believe her.

RESULTS

BLANKERS-KOEN'S FOUR WINS

100m
1 Francina 'Fanny' Blankers-Koen (HOL), 11.9
2 Dorothy Manley (GBR), 12.2
3 Shirley Strickland (AUS), 12.2

200m
1 Francina 'Fanny' Blankers-Koen (HOL), 24.4
2 Audrey Williamson (GBR), 25.1
3 Audrey 'Mickey' Patterson (USA), 25.2

80m hurdles
1 Francina 'Fanny' Blankers-Koen (HOL), 11.2
2 Maureen Gardner (GBR), 11.2
3 Shirley Strickland (AUS), 12.4

4x100m:
1 Holland (Xenia Stad-De Jong, Jeanette Witziers-Timmer, Gerda van der Kade-Koudjis, Francina 'Fanny' Blankers-Koen), 47.5
2 Australia, 47.6
3 Canada, 47.8

80m hurdles: Maureen Gardner (GBR, 135) loses after a desperate lunge for the line by Blankers-Koen (HOL, 692).

1948

OLYMPIC ROUND-UP

CABRERA MAKES CORPORAL.

You hear about athletes who wear the uniforms of the army and the police but an athletic fireman is a rarer find. The fire departments of the world have had one Olympic champion to date: Sergeant Henry Eriksson, the 1948 1500m champion. However, Sweden no longer has the monopoly on celebrity firemen. Buenos Aires, Argentina, is in the running with fireman and Olympic marathon champion Delfo Cabrera.

Cabrera, a stocky, 29-year-old fireman with jet black hair and a thick moustache, has been running since he was 10. His times were honourable, but little more: 15:25 for 5,000m, 32:00 for 10,000m.

Married and with a two-year-old child, Cabrera would certainly have come to the Games to represent his country, even if he had not met the coach of the San Lorenzo club, Francisco Moura, a few months before.

Moura had told him: 'I'm looking for a marathon runner. Will you hear me out?'

Cabrera asked, 'What's a marathon?'

Moura explained: 'You run 26 miles. It's easy, and not much more tiring than the 10,000m.

'You will have two team-mates to train you: Guiñez and Sensini. But keep quiet about the training. It's my secret. You will arrange to meet the spectators on 8 August in London.'

The three men had never run on the road before and completed the first marathon of their careers in London, finishing first, fifth and ninth.

Cabrera was amazed to have won: 'I am happy because it will encourage young people in Argentina to go running'.

Taking a personal telegram from President Peròn out of his trouser pocket, he added: 'Buenos Aires Head of Police and the Head of the Fire Service congratulated me after hearing the radio reports. They tell me I can expect to make corporal.'

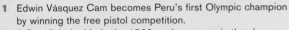

1. Edwin Vásquez Cam becomes Peru's first Olympic champion by winning the free pistol competition.
2. A Swedish double in the 1500m where, even in the absence of their compatriots Günder Hägg and Arne Andersson, both barred for professionalism. Henry Eriksson defeats the world record-holder Lennart Strand
3. and 4. The Hungarians excel in track and field: Imre Nemeth wins the hammer with 56.07m and Olga Gyarmati is the first ever woman's long jump champion, with 5.70m.
5. Leroy Cochran, the ninth of 10 children from a Mississippi family, easily wins the 400m hurdles and doubles his haul of gold in the 4x400m.
6. Delfo Cabrera, unknown before the Games, becomes the Olympic marathon champion 16 years after his fellow Argentine Juan Carlos Zabala.
7. Two US Olympic champions, Victoria Draves and Samuel Lee, platform diving winners, exchange views. Their compatriot Miller Anderson (centre), second in springboard diving, listens in.
8. Jesse Renick, captain of the US basketball team, is carried triumphantly by his team-mates after an easy victory over France in the final (65-21).
9. The decathlon was held in hellish conditions. Mondschein (USA, 616), Kistenmacher (ARG, 432) and Adamsczyk (POL, 445) seem to be running the 1500m on a vast lake.
10. Argentina's Pascual Pérez scores a bull's-eye in the final against Italy's Spartaco Bandinelli. Pérez almost did not compete as the officials initially confused him with his compatriot Pares and disqualified him for being over the weight limit.
11. The new 10.000m champion, 48 seconds faster than second-placed Alain Mimoun (FRA), Czechoslovakia's Emil Zátopek is supported by his team-mates and Yugoslavian friends.
12. The USA's pocket-sized Joseph Di Pietro, 4 feet 8 inches, lifts 105kg in the clean-and-jerk and wins with a total of 307.5kg.
13. First in the All-Around and Team competitions, second in the parallel bars and third in the fixed bar, Veikko Huhtanen shares first place in the pommel horse with his Finnish team-mates Paavo Aaltonen and Heikki Savolainen.

RIDING INTO VIEW

Mahmud, ridden by Alfred Blaser (SUI), puts in a swashbuckling
performance in the Three-Day Event team competition, to the
excitement of a large, and predominantly military, crowd. Blaser and
Mahmud were more photogenic than effective: their total of 59.25
faults was the best performance of the Swiss team, which could
only finish fourth behind the trios from the USA (gold), Sweden
(silver) and Mexico (bronze).

Micheline Ostermeyer gives a recital

After victory in the discus, the pianist Ostermeyer elicits another performance of the French National anthem by winning the shot-put.

Micheline Ostermeyer carries the weight of France on her shoulders. But they are solid enough to allow her to take a double Olympic victory in the most muscular of women's field events.

The Games had hardly begun. We were all still trying to find a little space for ourselves in this vast stadium when suddenly the Marseillaise was ringing out.

The crowd was on its feet, obscuring the Olympic flame, and the French contingent in the stadium looking to the tricolour and thinking of home, just across the water – all thanks to Micheline Ostermeyer.

Just three months ago, Ostermeyer graduated with honours from the Paris Conservatory of Music. It is ironic that on the first day of the Games, those delicate fingers could hurl a discus 41.92m to win the gold medal by 75cms.

I was sitting too far away to see the discus competition clearly, but I had an excellent view of the high jump, in which she placed third.

Then, on the sixth day of the Games, I had an excellent vantage point for Ostermeyer's performance in the shot put competition.

It was fine enough, despite the rain, to admire the elegance and grace of

Not a highly technical athlete but gifted with immense physical abilities and energy, Micheline Ostermeyer (1.79m and 73kg) wins the discus throwing competition, which was disappointing overall, on her last attempt.

MICHELINE SMILES BUT IS DISAPPOINTED

'Oh! Here you are again!' Micheline Ostermeyer said to me. 'There's no doubt about it, each time I want to meet journalists I'll have to win a world title'. 'Do I have to tell you that I'm happy? Certainly not! I am disappointed. I would have liked to have exceeded 14m.'

But her disappointment did not show. The champion is happy and that's all. She is so happy that she chatters a lot to all the journalists. Her joy is expressed in allegro like a czardas, with short fugues for placing a sentence over the top of the already fast delivery. Micheline's plans?

'The next thing is to improve in the high jump. Then, immediately after that, to go back to my piano. Since music is the future and the discus and shot are already in the past.'

her technique. After each throw, she returned to the bench and sat smiling on the sidelines, wrapped in a blanket.

At her turn again she takes her place in the circle, deep in concentration, focussing on her

technique despite the admiration of the crowd.

Quietly, and with absolute economy of energy, she powers into the throw. Three times, these demonstrations of poise and balance sent the shot a

fraction short of 13.6m.

Finally, she propelled it over 13.75m and became the first women's Olympic shot put champion, albeit slightly disappointed that she did not achieve her personal target of 14m.

LONDON XIV OLYMPIAD

The London Games were very austere, as they were poorly prepared.
They were also, however, the Games where a record number of countries
took part, and the first Games held in peace-time after World War II.

THE GAMES IN BRIEF

Opening Date
29 July 1948

Closing Date
14 August 1948

Host Nation
Great Britain (GBR)

Candidate Towns
Baltimore (USA), Lausanne (SUI), Los
Angeles (USA), Minneapolis (USA) and
Philadelphia (USA).

59 Nations Represented

4,099 Athletes
(385 women, 3,714 men)

19 Sports
(8 open to women)
Track and field, rowing, basketball, boxing,
canoeing, cycling, equestrian, fencing,
football, gymnastics, weightlifting, field
hockey, wrestling, swimming, modern
pentathlon, diving, shooting, sailing and
water polo.

Demonstration Sports
Lacrosse and Swedish system
gymnastics (Team).

136 Events
(31 open to women)

Games officially opened by
King George VI of England

Olympic flame lit by
John Mark (athletics)

Olympic oath read by
Donald Finlay (athletics)

IOC President
Sigfrid Edstroem (SWE)

DID YOU KNOW?

The Communist States took part in the
Games, and with them the first political
defection occurred: Marie Provaznikova,
President of the Technical Commission of
Women's Gymnastics refused to return to
Czechoslovakia.

In athletics, the starting block was used for
the first time.

Two Olympic Champions from the last
Games in 1936 managed to retain their titles
12 years on. They were Ilona Elek of
Hungary in women's foil fencing and Jan
Brzák of Czechoslovakia in the canoeing
Canadian pairs 1000m.

Karoly Takács, who was part of the
Hungarian world champion pistol shooting
team in 1938 lost his right hand in the war
when a grenade exploded. He taught
himself to shoot with his left hand and won
the gold medal in the rapid-fire pistol event.

In star class yachting, two father-son teams
won gold and silver medals: Hilary and Paul
Smart of the USA and Carlos de Cardenas
and Carlos de Cardenas Jr. of Cuba.

1952

Helsinki

THE 1952 OLYMPIC GAMES WERE FACED WITH perplexing issues. The first was the question of Soviet participation for the first time, in a host nation that had suffered greatly at the hands of its troublesome neighbour. Then, there were Germany and Japan, both banned from the 1948 Games. West Germany was now firmly in the Western bloc. A separate East German team first competed in 1968: until then, the two countries sent what was, in theory, at least, a joint delegation. As for China, invitations went to both the People's Republic and Chiang Kai-Shek's Taipei: fifty athletes from the former arrived five days before the Games ended. The latter stayed away in protest.

The Finns managed, with astonishing efficiency, to keep politics – and business, for that matter – away from the stadium. They embodied the spirit of the Olympics so well, with such warmth, thoughtfulness, enthusiasm, fair play, and organisational competence that some supported the idea of making Helsinki the permanent venue for future Olympic Games.

The fortnight began by ridiculing the Olympic Committee: at the opening ceremony, the great Johan 'Hannes' Kohlemainen, now 62, received the Olympic torch from Paavo Nurmi, aged 55, – the same Nurmi banned from the Games twenty years earlier because of supposed professionalism. Finland had never forgiven the IOC, and on that day alone, the long ovation had all the piquancy of revenge – a discreet expression of nationalist sentiment, and the only such display during an otherwise model Games.

She is Dana Zatopkova, the women's javelin champion. He is Emil Zátopek and he has achieved a remarkable hat-trick: the 5,000m, the 10,000m and the marathon. They both deserve a kiss!

Zátopek takes gold in his most spectacular victory ever

Four days after victory in the 10,000m, the Czech wins gold again after an epic 5,000m. And in three days, he competes in the marathon.

On the final curve of the 5,000m, Zátopek, looking tense, pulls away. Mimoun and Schade try to keep pace with him, while Chataway (left) has fallen after stepping on the curb.

The Helsinki 5,000m, the peak of athletic achievement, will go down in history as one of sport's most savage contests, fought to the bitter end, but also as a superior human challenge in which the physique, supercharged by a desire that is almost innate, was pushed to its very limits.

To comprehend what really happened on the final lap of the greatest 5,000m ever – perhaps the greatest track race ever – you'd have to see the entire event replayed many,

many times. It was a brutal war between four great athletes whose fortunes surged and ebbed from one moment to the next. Each saw his hopes shattered, restored, then shattered again as the race progressed. The crowd of 70,000 lost all sense of self or reason.

It is an astonishing feat for three men – and there would have been four, if Chataway had not fallen 80m from the finish – to complete 5,000m inside 14:10. Yet even the combined efforts of the foursome were eclipsed

by the intensity of the tragedy, to use the word in its ancient sense of grandeur and nobility.

One of sport's advantages over art is that neither master nor subject is static: athletes compose their works in constantly-evolving circumstances over which they do have only partial control. The unexpected, and the athlete's efforts to harness it, gives sport its richness. Split-second developments demand a complete surrender of self. The art of Émil Zátopek was to inflict pain with

carefully-calibrated cruelty. His brutality was expertly dosed to break his opponents' rhythm, crush their spirits and steer them into despair.

Only an athlete of Zátopek's abilities would dare mete out this sort of punishment. Who else could gain control of a race lap by lap, winning in record time a bloody, disjointed contest that was anything but favourable to record-making? Zátopek alone could ennoble his rivals by allowing them to demonstrate their remarkable talents even as he destroyed them.

His tactics allowed him to emerge successfully from a race he never looked in a position to win. He left the German prodigy Schade confused, troubled, unable to make sense of the race or his own abilities. Schade, though younger and more talented, lost because he had never before been subjected to such an onslaught.

The talent, or rather the many different talents, that make Zátopek virtually invincible, adorn his movements with such deep, vicious beauty that his surface appearance is almost transparent. His repertoire of

Zátopek is the clear winner of the marathon – the greatest display of the 1952 Games.

RESULTS

ZÁTOPEK'S TRIPLE

10,000m
1 Emil Zátopek (CZE) 29:17.0
2 Alain Mimoun (FRA) 29:32.8
3 Aleksandr Anufriev (SOV/RUS) 29:48.2

5,000m
1 Emil Zátopek (CZE) 14:06.6
2 Alain Mimoun (FRA) 14:07.4
3 Herbert Schade (GER) 14:08.6

Marathon
1 Emil Zátopek (CZE) 2:23:03.2
2 Reinaldo Gorno (ARG) 2:25:35.0
3. Gustav Jansson (SWE) 2:26:07.0

Mimoun, the only athlete to stay within range of Zátopek for the duration of the 10,000m, is dropped two kilometres from the finish, but maintains his second place.

fearful expressions and hysterical gestures defies description. They evoke Émile Anthoine's admirable maxim: 'Suffering is almost always the herald of joy.' And Zátopek admits that suffering sweetens the taste of victory.

Zátopek was just one of four heroes. Second was Schade, who thought it was all so easy, yet never came to terms with what was going on around him: the Czech's insane accelerations, the falls, Reiff's doomed attempts to revive the athlete he once was, Mimoun's serene presence.

The third hero was Chataway, who marched unflinchingly into battle, holding firm against his opponents.

And fourth was the French Algerian Mimoun, who appeared so relaxed, yet moved at such speed that his feet were a blur as he raced up the track.

At the bell, the four appeared moulded together. As they came out of the penultimate bend with 300m to go, Chataway surged into the lead. Only one man reacted, and with an astonishing turn of pace: Mimoun. Schade and Zátopek were momentarily dropped.

On the final curve, Zatopek ran wide and regained the lead. Chataway stumbled on the curb and fell. Mimoun, in spite of over excitement and exhaustion, drew alongside Zátopek, prepared to surpass even his

own expectations. This slight young Algerian with his tight curls, blue vest and shorts, was Zátopek's sole challenger in the greatest 5,000m event of modern times. The humble Mimoun, his head tilted towards his right shoulder, suddenly seemed a colossus himself. And he might indeed have won, if the incredible Zátopek had not conjured again that almost supernatural ability to deliver an extra spurt of acceleration, and jolted, like an engine firing, away from the Algerian and away to victory.

'I NEVER SUFFERED,' SAYS MIMOUN

Between Zátopek and Mimoun, there was no more than a few metres – five, at most.

The full meaning of this sprint against a man who, in previous contests, had left Mimoun behind after the second kilometre, if not before, became clear when he stepped off the podium and raised his arms to the corner of the stadium housing the seven hundred French supporters. The silver medal rewarded his sheer staying power. But had he found it difficult to match the pace set first by Schade and later by Zátopek, Reiff, Pirie and Chataway?

'No,' he responded, 'it was much easier than in the 10,000m, no doubt because the [attacks] were less sudden. I followed them easily, saving myself for the sprint.'

At what point did you plan to seize your chance?

'Only coming into the final straight – launching an attack with athletes of the calibre of Schade and Zátopek behind you would be suicidal, although you have to admire Chataway for taking that risk...'

And Zátopek took you by surprise?

'Exactly. I saw him draw level with me too late – the Czech had already picked up his pace. I reacted as quickly as I could, but Zátopek had already pulled well into the lead. You can't make up 5m on a runner of his class…'

Mimoun has no complaints about his silver medal. 'The form book said I should have finished behind Schade, but I wondered whether the German might be feeling the strain of setting the pace,' he said, before adding with a happy smile, 'Deep down, I was hoping for second, but I didn't want to admit it to myself.'

1952
OLYMPIC ROUND-UP

RECORD UPON RECORD FOR BRAZIL'S DA SILVA!

The splendid operatic strains of the Brazilian national anthem fade away and 60,000 spectators burst into applause.

Adhémar Ferreira da Silva, Olympic triple-jump champion, World and Olympic record holder, gazes at his gold medal with joy and disbelief… Without a single trace of vanity or ostentation, he makes a victory lap of the track to thank the public, brandishing his winner's bouquet just as, four days earlier, Paavo Nurmi had held the Olympic torch. The blonde, balding Nurmi was welcomed with respect and nostalgia, while the black, smiling Adhémar is greeted with the bubbling enthusiasm of the present moment.

Why? Because, during the triple-jump final, he had beaten his old world record of 16.01m no less than four times. Da Silva achieved 16.12m with his second jump, 16.09 with his fourth, 16.22 at his fifth attempt and 16.05 at the sixth. A magnificent string of achievements. And for the first time in fifteen Olympics, a Brazilian had become an Olympic champion – and some champion, too! We asked da Silva if the journey from South America to Finland had affected his performance adversely.

'At home, it's winter, and winter in São Paulo, where I live, is remarkably like summer in Finland. So I have to say, I've had no problems acclimatising.'

Adhémar is an outgoing character, but becomes strangely shy when asked his age. His features distort so much that his closed right eye almost touches the corner of his mouth. 'Twenty four,' he says, 'twenty-four-years-old.' Then, under his breath, he adds, '25, if you must know, but I don't like to admit it!' A skilled samba dancer, he loves singing more than anything else, and accompanies himself expertly on a pandero; a sort of concertina. He can also hold forth at length on any subject you care to suggest.

He has already pinpointed his next challenge: 'After the Games, I'm going to try to beat my own record. I think I can raise it to 16.50m!'

1 A historic 1500m final, in which the first eight beat Lovelock's old Olympic record – in spite of which, Luxembourg's Josy Barthel (406) takes gold with ease.
2 Bob Mathias, the American pastor, guarded by the angels of the decathlon, retains the title he won in London – and thanks the Almighty.
3 In the triple jump, Adhémar Ferreira da Silva beats his own World record with a jump of 16.22m. He retained his title at Melbourne in 1956.
4 The blonde Fanny Blankers-Koen (HOL, left), carrying a knee injury, pulls up in the final of the 80m hurdles.
5 In the 110m hurdles, the Americans make a clean sweep. Here, Harrison Dillard heads towards gold.
6 In the final of the football tournament, Beara, the Yugoslav goalkeeper, gathers up the ball ahead of the Hungarian strikers. But Puskas and Csibor, scoring twice, bring Hungary the title, confirming how far Hungarian football progressed between 1952 and 1954.
7 The eventual winner, André Noyelle (BEL), leads the decisive breakaway, before his compatriots Robert Grondelaers and Lucien Victor.
8 The American Bob Mathias, competing in the decathlon long jump event. He retains the Olympic title and sets a new World record of 7,887pts.
9 In the 100m, the first four are credited with the winning time of 10.4 seconds, but there is only one winner: the American Lindy Remigino (all white, in the centre, number 981).
10 In the two diving competitions, America's Patricia McCormick is sublime.
11 The finishing line judge, insisting that the winner of the 3,000m steeplechase should break the tape, misjudges Horace Ashenfelter's (USA) finishing sprint.
12 In the heavyweight division, the eventual winner Hayes Edward Sanders (USA) wins an early bout.

6

7

8

9

10

11 12

De La Hunty leaves behind Strickland

The Australian mathematician subtracts 0.1 seconds from the 80m hurdles and finds the formula for a new world record.

With her clean, efficient style, Shirley Strickland de La Hunty (third from right) streaks to victory in the 80m hurdles to take the Olympic title from former champion Fanny Blankers-Koen (to the left of Strickland de La Hunty).

Helsinki is a haven of peace. There may be psychological warfare going on between the contenders, but the only bombs being delivered in Helsinki are *bombes glacées*, and they have hundreds and thousands sprinkled on top. In such calm circumstances, it seems inappropriate to speak of ambushes, assassinations and wars in which mercenaries reap macabre rewards. Yet but for the Saint Bartholomew's Day Massacre and the repeal of the Edict of Nantes, which deprived French Protestants of their liberties, we might have heard a stirring rendition of the Marseillaise this afternoon, instead of a double helping of God Save the Queen followed by Advance Australia Fair - without so much as a topping of chocolate sauce.

For the winner of the 80m hurdles was Shirley Strickland, now known officially as Mrs Shirley Strickland de La Hunty. It turns out that to avoid beheading at the hands of Louis XIV's henchmen, the French protestant de La Huntes fled across the English Channel, and later emigrated to Australia. British pronunciation changed the name from Hunte to Hunty, and it was into this family that Shirley Strickland, born on 18 July 1925, in Guildford, Australia, married in 1950.

This fragrant young lady, her blond hair gleaming like the Australian sun, is the daughter of a professional runner named Violet. After graduating in physics and mathematics from Brisbane University, she went on to lecture in mathematics at the technical college in Perth, capital of Western Australia. It was here that she made her track debut in 1946, and met Mr Lawrence Edmund de La Hunty, whom she later married.

Under her maiden name of Strickland, she had already been turning heads. At the London Olympics, she competed against the imperious Fanny Blankers-Koen and came third in the 100m and 80m hurdles, second in the 4x100m relay, and finished fourth in the 200m in the same time as the bronze medalist.

Four years on, the new Mrs de La Hunty is in her prime. In the semi-final of the 80m hurdles, she slashed the World and Olympic record to 10.8. Her victory was wind-assisted, but in the final she set a legal record of 10.9. Blankers-Koen abandoned the final after hitting the first two hurdles. Strickland de La Hunty took bronze in the 100m sprint in 11.9.

At 5 feet 7, Shirley is tall, sweet and charming. After her victory, she was happy to sign autographs for her young fans. When the Australian ladies' team chaperone suggested that she stop signing any more autographs, Shirley responded: 'I'm a teacher. I love children and this makes them so happy. I don't mind giving up a quarter of an hour of my time to make them happy.'

Asked if she would continue to compete in track events, she replied: 'I don't think so. I like cooking lots of different dishes – I have French blood, you see – and as soon as I've learned all of my French Aunt Julie's recipes, I will give up the starting block for the stove! But I still don't know half of my dear aunt's recipes, so if the sixteenth Olympic Games takes place in Australia and I am still selected, I hope to win a gold medal in front of my fellow countrymen and my students.'

Let's hope we see you again in Melbourne in 1956, Shirley★! By then, the officials may have decided which national anthem to play when an Australian wins – unless, of course, France steps in with a counter-offer.

★At the 1956 Olympics, Shirley Strickland De La Hunty, now a mother, won the 80m hurdles in 10.7 – an improvement on her own Olympic record – and won the 4x100m in 44.5, a world record. She won a total of seven Olympic medals: three gold, one silver and three bronze. She was selected for the Rome Olympics in 1960, but her third pregnancy ruled her out of the competition.

RESULTS

80m hurdles
1 Shirley Strickland De La Hunty 10.9
2 Maria Golubnichaya (SOV/RUS) 11.1
3 Maria Sander (GER) 11.1
4 Anneliese Seonbuchner (GER) 11.2
5 Jean Desforges (GBR) 11.6
DNF: Francina 'Fanny' Blankers-Koen (HOL).

This level-headed young lady from Australia, married to a descendant of the Huguenots, is a great champion.

1952

HELSINKI XV OLYMPIAD

These Games took place in the middle of the Cold War, and the arrival of the Soviet Union for the first time led to various precautions being put in place. These proved unnecessary as the atmosphere that reigned in Helsinki really brought people together.

THE GAMES IN BRIEF

Opening Date
19 July 1952

Closing Date
3 August 1952

Host Nation
Finland (FIN)

Candidate Towns
Los Angeles (USA), Amsterdam (HOL), Minneapolis (USA), Detroit (USA), Chicago (USA) and Philadelphia (USA).

69 Nations Represented

4,925 Athletes
(518 women, 4,407 men)

19 Sports
(8 open to women)
Track and field, rowing, basketball, boxing, canoeing, cycling, equestrian, fencing, football, gymnastics, weightlifting, field hockey, wrestling, swimming, modern pentathlon, diving, shooting, sailing and water polo.

Demonstration Sports
Baseball and rugby.

43 Events
(35 open to women)

Games officially opened by
President Juho Paasikivi of Finland

Olympic flame lit by
Paavo Nurmi and Hannes Kolehmainen (athletics).

Olympic oath read by
Heikki Savolainen (gymnastics)

IOC President
Sigfrid Edström (SWE)

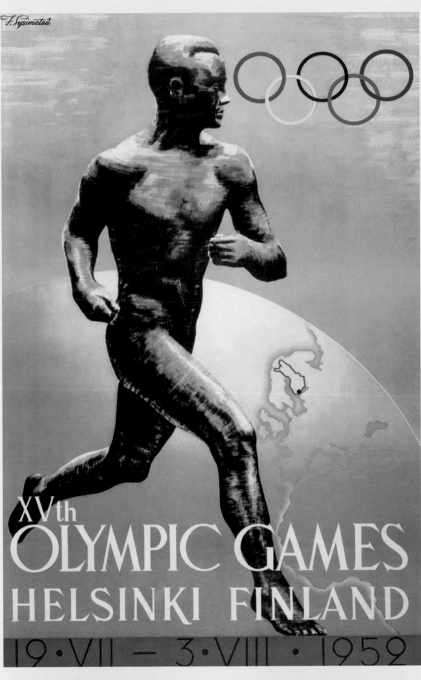

DID YOU KNOW?

Israel and the USSR took part for the first time. As the Games took place at the start of the Cold War, the Soviet athletes were housed in a separate village. However, nothing untoward happened between the athletes from East and West. Germany returned to the Games under the aegis of a new National Olympic Committee, the Committee of the Federal Republic of Germany (FRG). East Germany had also set up a new NOC, but had no athletes present.

Soviet Aleksandra Chudina achieved a unique triple as she won silver medals in the long jump and javelin and a bronze in the high jump. Dane Lis Hartel was one of the first women allowed to compete against men in the equestrian dressage, and won silver despite the fact that she was paralysed below the knees following a bout of polio. Madeleine Moreau, who came second in the 3m springboard diving contest, was the first non-American female medalist in this event since its introduction to the Games in 1920.

In 1924, Bill Havens had been chosen to represent the United States in the coxed eights rowing, but he declined, as he didn't want to leave his wife, who was pregnant. Twenty-eight years later, that very child, Frank Havens, won gold in the 10,000m Canadian singles canoeing event.

1956

Melbourne

FOR THE FIRST TIME, THE IOC SACRIFICED
the unity of the Games in time and place. Five years
after Melbourne's 1949 nomination to host the Games
in 1956, it emerged that the six-month quarantine that
Australian law imposed on foreign horses would cause
a major problem. Stockholm was therefore chosen to
host the equestrian events in May, while the rest of
the events would be held in Melbourne from the
end of November.

It was worth it: the Melbourne Games were a
resounding success. However, in the face of geopolitical reality, the world of sport had to admit its
insignificance, and act as a sounding board. Egypt,
Lebanon and Iraq boycotted the Games in protest at
the Franco-British expedition to the Suez Canal,
which followed the advance of Israeli troops into
the Sinai. Communist China did the same, to avoid
a meeting in Australia with Formosa (Taiwan).

Holland, Switzerland and Spain stayed away in
protest at Soviet intervention in Hungary, where the
uprising was crushed weeks before the opening of the
Games. At the Games, the Hungarian delegation was
warmly embraced; the Soviets received cold courtesy.
Their antagonism peaked when Hungary met the
USSR in the water polo tournament.

Two events which set the Games above the political
highs and lows went almost unnoticed; East and West
Germanys managed to agree to line up a single team,
while delegations from throughout the world mingled
during the closing ceremony – an innovative
celebration that became permanent.

In the sweltering sunshine, the eighty-eight road race participants discover the
Australian countryside. After 188 kilometres, the future world professional
champion, Italy's Ercole Baldini, took the title..

A bouquet for Murray Rose

After his 400m and 4x200m victories, the prodigious Australian confirms the host nation's superiority in the 1500m freestyle.

From left to right: George Breen (USA), Murray Rose (AUS) and Tsuyoshi Yamanaka (JAP) – third, first and second respectively in both the 400m and the 1500m.

M urray Rose's victory in the 1500m has confirmed Australia's invincibility in freestyle swimming. Its freestyle medal count – seven gold, three silver, two bronze – is proof indeed. Rose, 17, is the product of a system that turns out world-beating Australian swimmers (behind this triumph lies a twelve-week training camp led by expert coaches

RESULTS

1500m
1 Murray Rose (AUS), 17:58.9
2 Tsuyoshi Yamanaka (JAP), 18:00.3
3 George Breen (USA), 18:08.2
4 Murray Garretty (AUS), 18:26.5
5 William Slater (CAN), 18:38.1
6 Jean Boiteux (FRA), 18:38.3
7 Yukiyoshi Aoki (JAP), 18:38.3
8 Garry Winram (AUS), 19:06.2

and physiologists). British-born, he came to Australia with his parents before the war, aged one. He began to swim at a young age, and he has been preparing for these Games since he was twelve.

A wonderful technician with a 5 feet 11, 161 pound frame, Rose is as famous for his diet as he is for his records. He has never eaten meat, fish or poultry, nor tasted coffee or tea. His favourite dish is a concoction of fruit, soy beans and seaweed jam, prepared by his Irish mother. It clearly leaves him with a huge appetite for miles.

100m into the final, George Breen (USA), who had set a new world record in qualifying, swam the distance in 1:04.4 (compared to 1:02.4 on Wednesday) and still led at 400m – but Rose and Tsuyoshi Yamanaka (JAP), the 400m gold and silver medalists, were almost level.

At 800 metres, Yamanaka took over

the lead. Then Rose attacked. With remarkable ease, he established a convincing lead. At 900m, he was a second ahead of Breen, who was now closely followed by Yamanaka. Between 1000 and 1100 metres, Rose gained another second. At 1200m, Breen and Yamanaka were both four seconds behind. After 1300m, the Japanese dropped the American, and passed 1400 metres 4.5 seconds behind Rose. At this point, Yamanaka closed in on Rose, who already had the cushion he needed and finished with a comfortable 1.4 second lead. The podium was a repeat of the 400m result: Rose, Yamanaka, and yet another third place for Breen, who left Melbourne with a silver medal for the 4x200 and two bronze medals for the 400m and 1500m. No gold, but in consolation, he had set a world record.

After the race, Murray Rose admitted: 'After the 400m, my legs were

a bit tired, so I didn't overdo it in the 1500m heats. I was glad of the rest day before the final. This morning, I had a warm-up session in the pool. Then, the race plan was simple: to follow Breen up to 1300m, then sprint. I was in good form and the race went perfectly.' Three gold medals – a fine achievement for a boy who will only turn 18 in January. It is tempting now to say that in Rose, swimming has its Vladimir Kuts.

Dick Hanley points the finger: – for the Australians, swimming has become a professional.

The resounding domination of the Australians in freestyle swimming has not passed without comment in the Olympic village. In particular, Dick Hanley, the United States' entrant in the 100m, has accused the Australians of covert professionalism.

'The Australians [one of whom, Dawn Fraser, is pictured below] are now the best swimmers in the world because they train more than any of the American sprinters. It is not a question of natural superiority. The Australians train six hours a day; we train for one. If we could spend the same amount of time in the water as they do, we would be as successful, although I'm not sure the Americans would want to spend so much time swimming. For us, swimming remains a sport. For the Australians, it is fast becoming a full-time profession!'

Kuts – unbeatable!

The Soviet taught his opponents a lesson in the 5,000m, as he had already done in the 10,000m.

In a packed Olympic stadium, the fantastic atmosphere of the first day of the Games was re-created by the two main players of the dramatic 10,000m. Volodymyr Kuts and Gordon Pirie, pitted against each other again, this time in the 5,000m.

As in the 10,000m, the Soviet led from the 200m mark and maintained his lead throughout the race. He would have taken the lead at the gun had he not found himself boxed in at the start and taken half a lap to break out. Then the little Ukrainian began his infernal dance, unleashing burst after burst of speed, and little by little he wore down the pack of thirteen pursuers who were soon reduced to only three; the British trio of Gordon Pirie, Chris Chataway and Derek Ibbotson, as expected. The pace was fast – 2:40.0 at 1,000m, 5:26.0 at 2,000m – but only at this moment did the Soviet runner really begin to put his rivals under pressure, unleashing a violent attack on every lap as he entered the opposite straight. On this fairly poor track, it was more than sufficient to erode the resistance of the Britons, put to the sword by the brilliant Kuts.

Until this moment, Chataway had been the freshest of the British, daring to remain on Kuts' heels most of the time and even sometimes trying to run shoulder to shoulder with him; he now

RESULTS

A DOUBLE FOR KUTS

5,000m
1 Vladimir Kuts (USSR), 13'39"6
2 Gordon Pirie (GBR), 13'50"6
3 Derek Ibbotson (GBR), 13'54"4
4 Miklos Szabo (HON), 14'3"4
5 Albert Thomas (AUS), 14'4"6
6 Laszlo Tabori (HUN), 14'9"8
7 Maiyoro Nyandika (KEN), 14'19"
8 Thyge Thögersen (DEN), 14'21"

10,000m
1 Vladimir KUTS (URS), 28'45"6
2 Jozsef Kovacs (HUN), 28'52"4
3 Allan Lawrence (AUS), 28'53"6
4 Zdzislaw Kryszkowiak (POL), 29'5"
5 Kenneth Norris (GBR), 29'21"6
6 Ivan Chernyavsky (URS), 29'31"6
7 David Power (AUS), 29'49"2
8 Gordon Pirie (GBR), 29'49"6

Volodymyr Kuts sets an infernal pace for his rivals in the 5,000 m. Gordon Pirie (hidden, behind) cannot keep up, falling back a kilometre before the finishing line and settling for second place.

paid heavily for his efforts, and fell back and out of contention. This was at 3,500m; but Volodymyr Kuts was still not yet satisfied with his demolition work. He finished it off less than 500m later. Pirie and Ibbotson, having clung to the Soviet bravely, suffered the same fate as Chataway. Kuts attempted to shake them off several times before finally going clear: each time he put on a spurt, the Britons fought with a tenacity that in any other circumstance would have been enough to have kept them in with a chance.

KUTS: 'I HAD NO PLAN'

After Kuts had completed his lap of honour, savouring his delight like a child biting into a delicious fruit, the stiff, tall and phlegmatic Pirie went up to him, shook his hand and rested his head against the Russian. A chivalrous gesture, the knight's tribute to his lord. A little later, Gordon Pirie revealed the essence of his thoughts; 'Actually, I got off lightly. If the track had been decent, I would have lost my record too. What Kuts did on that track is admirable. Until these Games, my idol was Zátopek. Now it will be Kuts. He is terrific, and we still don't really know what he is capable of. Remember that he is almost a beginner: he has only really been running for five years.'

Then Volodymyr Kuts appeared, like a feudal nobleman. His features were unmarked; his carefully combed hair as smooth as if he had just come out of the bathroom in his Moscow flat. He still had his air of happiness, and his infectious and childlike joy. We talked tactics, and Kuts replied with humour: 'I only wanted to take the lead, continue to run in the lead, and finish in the lead. I had no plan concerning my lap time. Anyway, I didn't know exactly who was running behind me. What bothered me was simply feeling that someone was following me. I was determined to get rid of the threat. That was my only tactic. I was amazed when I realised I had been able to break up the race so quickly. I was ready to wind up the pace again if necessary. I could certainly have beaten the world record, because I am capable of running much faster than I have here. But I had no ambitions against the clock. All I wanted was to win.'

1956
OLYMPIC ROUND-UP

BOBBY MORROW, THE CALM SPRINTER.

For three years, Bobby Morrow has been indisputably the best sprinter in the world. His dominance reached its peak at the US Olympic qualifying tournament in in June. Bobby Morrow won all the heats, finishing a metre ahead of his closest rival in every round. America and the world felt that 'the Texas Flash', a physical education student at the Abilene Christian University, would be unbeatable at the Games. Then, in September, this confidence evaporated when, after a bout of food poisoning, Bobby was taken seriously ill with gastric flu. In the course of a month, Morrow lost seven kilos. He had not yet fully recovered when he ran in October's pre-Olympic meet in the United States. As he slowly returned to his form weight, he was understandably anxious.

A week before the qualifying heats and final of the Olympic 100m, Morrow was convinced victory was beyond him. He hadn't run 100m at maximum effort since his illness. He feared he would lack rhythm. 'I was reassured after my first heat,' Morrow told me. 'I began to feel I was no longer too far below my best. If I hadn't been ill, I am sure I'd have been in even better shape and I'd have won by an even wider margin.'

Morrow is twenty-one years old and married a classmate on 15 October. But his youth is tempered by a much greater maturity than you expect in a young man of his age. His mental maturity he owes to his struggles in life and in the stadium; his physical maturity he owes to a past as an American footballer, although he gave up football when he started university, on the instructions of his coach, who recognised the extent of his purely athletic potential.

Bobby Morrow speaks calmly, deliberately, avoiding any outburst of joy after this first success, anxious to save all his drive for the two following stages of his Olympic campaign – the 200m and the 4x100m – in both of which, for the record, he took gold.

1 The 21-year-old Soviet Larissa Latynina dominates the All-Around gymnastics tournament, and wins individual titles in the floor and the vault. Returning to the Rome and Tokyo Games, she would total eighteen medals during her career; nine gold, five silver and four bronze.

2 The Swede Lars Hall becomes the first modern pentathlon champion to retain his title.

3 Milton Campbell (USA) failed to qualify for the 110m hurdles during the US heats, so the 22-year-old sailor competed in the decathlon, and led the competition from start to finish!

4 Roger Bannister's pacemaker in his celebrated four-minute mile, Christopher Brasher, runs for himself in the 3,000m steeplechase, and takes gold.

5 In their boat 'Rush V', the Swedish crew takes the 5.5-metre title.

6 100m champion Bobby Morrow wins the 200m, ahead of fellow Americans Andrew Stanfield and W. Thane Baker.

7 The 50km walk has barely begun and New Zealander Norman Read (number 10) is already smiling. Does he already know he will walk away with the title?

8 Mustafa Dagistanli (TUR) has no mercy on Japan's Minoru Iizuka, who stands between him and the bantamweight title in the freestyle wrestling tournament.

9 Lev Yashin's legendary Soviets (seen here against the Germans) inherit the football honours from the Hungarians of Sándor Kocsis.

10 Already champion in 1948 and 1952, the Swede Gert Fredriksson retains his title in the 1000m kayak singles, adding the 10,000m title which he had already carried off in 1948 (he could only finish second in 1952). In Rome he would finish third in the 1000m.

11 Like Fredriksson in the K-1, Romania's Leon Rotman completes the double of the 1000m and 10,000m in the Canadian singles.

12 As they enter the final straight of the 800m, Thomas Courtney (USA, no. 153), Derek Johnson (GBR, no.137) and Audun Boysen (NOR, no.148) are at maximum speed. They finish in the same order.

6 10

7

8

9

11 12

Alain Mimoun, victory at last

The French athlete finally wins the Olympic gold he deserves – in his first marathon.

Dandenong Road was the strange-sounding street, whose charming houses hinted at suburban serenity behind Venetian blinds, along which Alain Mimoun pounded to victory in the marathon. Along the route, huge crowds had gathered. The men wore shirt sleeves, the women and girls light dresses, basking in the heat of a southern summer's day. As the athletes passed, a thrill ran along the road. Cricketers deserted their grounds to watch. Young women playing tennis lowered their rackets to applaud.

The most indifferent onlooker was the sun, no doubt anxious to make up for time lost since the opening of the Games. The heat was draining even for the spectators. It had become a decisive element in the race and weighed on the runners, sparing no-one.

The winner was not only the most talented athlete, but the bravest. In Alain Mimoun's features, after forty kilometres and more than two hours, sheer willpower illuminated his streaming face. Only his eyes retained the coolness of running water. Mimoun must have realised that luck was with him this time. Sport has been a waiting game for him. He had been thinking of this marathon for a long time. He had bought his running shoes in Finland, four years earlier.

He must have recalled that scorching day in London in 1948 when he had finished second in the 10,000m, and the Helsinki days where he ran magnificently in the 5,000m and 10,000m. On all three occasions, he had encountered the irresistible Emil Zátopek. Here, well before the tenth kilometre, Mimoun had looked around him and saw Zátopek was missing.

From that moment, he knew his day had come. The omens had been good. French marathon success came in cycles. A Frenchman had won in 1900. Another won in 1928. Now, twenty-eight more years had passed. He was wearing number 13. And the day before the race, he had learned by telegram that he had become a father.

Even after five kilometres, Mimoun was running with astonishing ease. At the fifteenth kilometre, Mimoun lay

Tired but happy, Alain Mimoun enters the Melbourne Cricket Ground with a comfortable lead on his pursuers to begin into a final, triumphant lap

second in a pack of thirteen men. The pace was easy and the decisive moment would not be long in coming. From the twentieth kilometre, there were only five men in the leading group, with Mihalic chasing a few metres behind. Thus, without accelerating, and maintaining the admirable pace he began with - and would retain as he made his final lap in the Olympic stadium - Mimoun saw

everything fall into place, in that long ascent towards the red flag marking the spot where the road turned back towards Melbourne. One after the other, his adversaries drifted away. In turn, Clark (GBR), Filin (SOV/RUS) and Ivanov (SOV/RUS) all disappeared. Only Mihalic (YUG) and Karvonen (FIN), perhaps thinking of the cool forests of his country, remained in sight of Mimoun.

And then, as he confided to us after the race, Mimoun wondered if he was alone too soon: 'I hadn't attacked. The others had fallen away. It would have been a mistake not to run at my own rhythm, although I wondered if I'd be in difficulty later on, because the pain in my legs was increasing. The thought of victory gave me wings.'

The Algerian-born Frenchman seemed extremely lucid to all that witnessed his run. He looked vaguely into the crowd. He was distracted by the cameramen who never left him during his solitary bid for victory. Around him there was only the crowd. He refused to drink cold water or splash it over him, fearing it could be deadly for his muscles.

Far behind, the Russians staggered and zigzagged, Zátopek ran with a broken stride, and Karvonen's eyes sunk into their sockets. Mihalic, pale, ran like an automation.

Mimoun continued at his unfailing rhythm into the thirtieth kilometre and the decisive phase of the race. His features took on a hard edge. After the race, he admitted; 'At that moment, I was in real difficulty. Remember, it was the first time I had run a competitive marathon and I was beginning to believe I wouldn't make it to the finish. I was going through hell. Luckily I was alone; otherwise, I might have doubted myself. But I couldn't hear anyone at my heels, so I reasoned that the others must be going through the same pain.'

Then, everything merged into an all-encompassing blur that enveloped the final landmarks of the route: the railway track, the bridge, the pink outer walls of the stadium, the tunnel, and, finally, the track, surrounded by 100,000 cheering voices.

Mimoun was amazingly fresh as he rounded the final lap of the track, before the blue French vest breasted the tape. At the finish line, he awaited the arrival of his opponents, running to embrace them as they finished, Mihalic, Karvonen and later, Zátopek. On this evening of the last day of the Games, Mimoun knew he was right; only they could understand the price he had had to pay to win the Olympic gold medal he had dreamed of for so long.

1956

MELBOURNE XVI OLYMPIAD

After Europe had hosted the Games ten times, and America
twice, it was the turn of a third continent: Oceania.

THE GAMES IN BRIEF

Opening Date
22 November 1956

Closing Date
8 December 1956

Host Nation
Australia (AUS)

Candidate Towns
Buenos Aires (ARG), Los Angeles (USA),
Detroit (USA), Mexico (MEX), Chicago
(USA), Minneapolis (USA), Philadelphia
(USA) and San Francisco (USA).

67 Nations Represented

3,184 Athletes
(371 women, 2,813 men).

19 Sports
(8 open to women)
Track and field, rowing, basketball,
boxing, canoeing, cycling, equestrian,
fencing, football, gymnastics,
weightlifting, field hockey, wrestling,
swimming, pentathlon, diving, shooting,
sailing and water polo.

Demonstration Sports
Australian football and baseball.

152 Events
(8 open to women)

Games officially opened by
The Duke of Edinbrugh

Olympic flame lit by
Ron Clarke (athletics)

Olympic oath read by
John Landy (athletics)

IOC President
Avery Brundage (USA)

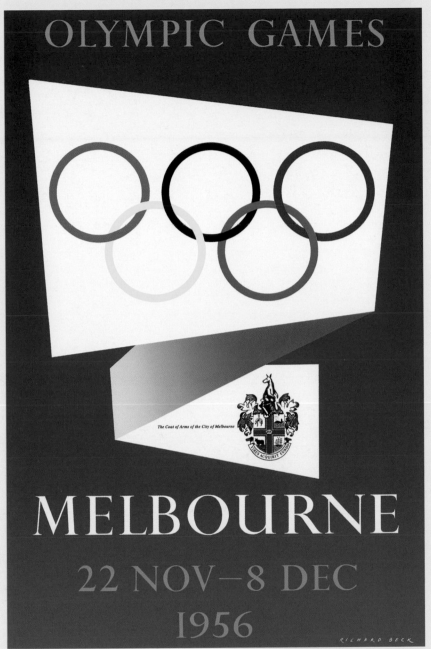

OLYMPIC GAMES

The Coat of Arms of the City of Melbourne

MELBOURNE

22 NOV–8 DEC

1956

RICHARD BECK

DID YOU KNOW?

Melbourne was chosen over Buenos Aires
to host the 1956 Olympic Games with a
majority of only one vote.

In athletics, Georgios Roubanis was the
first to use the fibreglass pole in the
individual pole vault. American Bob Mathias
had already done this in 1952, but in the
decathlon. Another first in these Games was
a false start in the marathon. American
hammer thrower Harold Connolly won the
gold medal and the heart of Czechoslovakian
champion discus thrower Olga Fikotová.
Their romance led to a marriage three
months after the Games.

The American basketball team, led by Bill
Russell and K.C. Jones, achieved the most
successful performance in Olympic history,
scoring twice as many points as their rivals
and winning every single match by at least a
thirty point margin.

In swimming, a fourth stroke made its
appearance: the butterfly was separated
from the breaststroke, and was contested
over 200m. But the 4x100m freestyle relay
was only introduced in 1960 and the 400m
individual medley in 1964.

American Pat McCormick won both diving
disciplines, just as she did in 1952. Even
though they were equal with a total
performance of 500kg, weightlifters Paul
Anderson of the USA and Humberto Selvetti
of Argentina were separated by weight –
bodyweight. The American winning gold
because he was lighter, weighing in at 137.9
kilograms as opposed to Selvetti's 143.5
kilograms. When American weightlifter
Charles Vinci presented himself to be
weighed, he was 200 grams too heavy to
fight in the bantamweight division. He was
given 15 minutes to get a severe haircut.
This proved a great help, and relieved him of
his excess weight, and he went on to win the
contest.

1960

Rome

GYMNASTS PERFORMING IN THE CARACALLA
Baths built in 2BC. Wrestlers grappling in the Basilica
of Maxentius, the site of bouts two thousand years
before. Marathon runners finishing beneath the
fourth-century Arch of Constantine. Sixty-four years
after the first Games in Athens – fifty-four years after
Italy had had to give away the 1908 Games after the
eruption of Mount Vesuvius – Rome provided a
stunning Olympic backdrop that had been handed
down from antiquity. Despite its classical roots,
however, the Olympic festival of sport was constantly
evolving. Qualifying standards had climbed so rapidly
in certain sports that some 1956 champions had been
unable to satisfy them to defend their titles.

A record eighty-three nations attended the Games,
their numbers boosted by representatives from many
African countries that had gained independence in the
four years since the Melbourne Games. Clement 'Ike'
Quartey, representing one of those new nations,
Ghana, created Olympic history by taking silver in the
light-welterweight boxing tournament, the first black
African Olympic medalist. Five days later, his
achievement would be eclipsed by Ethiopia's Abebe
Bikila, the bare-footed winner of the marathon.

As the Cold War cooled the international climate,
suffocating heat stifled Rome. This didn't prevent
modernity and tradition uniting for the fortnight of
the Games. The day before the Opening Ceremony,
Pope John XXIII blessed the Games in Saint Peter's
Square. Later, he enjoyed the canoeing semi-finals
from the window of his summer residence.

Not far from the Colosseum, the arches of the Basilica of Maxentius, the
former courts of justice, give the wrestling tournament a dream setting.

Wilma Rudolph – a picture of elegance

The young and beautiful American skips through the sprint events to three gold medals.

Wilma Rudolph's appearance at these Games could be described as a moment of illumination in a life of misfortune. She has lived her dream in the Roman summer, and with her velvety stride, exquisite bearing and seraphic calm, even at full tilt, nothing so beautiful has ever been seen on an athletics track. It is almost beyond belief that such beauty – shared for the first time by millions of television viewers, like in the first days of cinema – should mask such a cruel destiny.

Rudolph was one of twenty-two children living in the heart of a Tennessee ghetto, steeped more in the bitter sweat of the cotton pickers than in the energetic exhilaration of country music. Born premature, Rudolph, the twentieth of the brood, was a little girl of fragile health, weighing less than four pounds at birth. Polio, double pneumonia, scarlet fever: early childhood spared her little. She lost the use of her left leg at the age of four and spent two years bed-ridden. She learnt to walk normally aged seven.

Endless massages and the love of her family worked wonders. One fine day, her mother was amazed to see her playing basketball. Thanks to her size and her jump, Wilma was already outstanding beneath the nets when, during a summer course, she

In civilian clothing or on the track (crossing the 4x100m finish line ahead of German Jutta Heine), Wilma is a picture of elegance.

discovered her top speed. Her path was clearly mapped out - even more so in that running was a joy for this formerly handicapped 12-year-old. It led her straight to the 1956 Melbourne Games. On the third step of the Olympic podium for the 4x100m, the apprentice champion promised herself that next time she would take the place of the Australian Betty Cuthbert – right at the top.

During the four years that followed, 'Skeeter', as her friends continually called her – meaning mosquito, more because of her youth than her small

size – studied to become a teacher, and trained under one of America's best coaches, Ed Temple. When she arrived in Rome for the Games, she had just entered the history books as the first woman timed at under 23.00 seconds in the 200m. In a country with a sophisticated sense of aesthetics, the stage was set for a dazzling sight. More dazzling yet, for Wilma had wound herself like a vine around the black marble statue that was Ray Norton, and – carried away by this new love, her twenty years, the pure spirit of the Olympics and the

beauty of the setting – she shone.

The Games were a disaster for Norton. World record-holder in the 200m, winner of the American qualifying heats and favourite for the Olympic events, he finished last in the 100m and 200m finals. By contrast, nothing could touch the superb Wilma, victorious in the 100m, 200m and 4x100m, despite spraining an ankle the day before the 100m final. Wilma managed all this with her left foot in a bandage – but which did nothing to lessen the beauty of her stride.

Grace and Strength by Antoine Blondin

I n Greece, women were banned from the Olympic grounds on pain of death: the men fought naked and their women-folk might have been inclined to make unfavourable comparisons with their husbands. At Rome, on the whole, our wives emerge favourably from the aesthetic judgements we find ourselves forming from the heights of our terraces. All the genius of the Renaissance, which helped shape the image of woman as one of leisure and repose, is shattered under the whirling hams of wenches built like bas-relief woodcutters. Our 'sisters of the rib', as Adam said after his operation, seem animated by a demon that makes the rare splendours of athletic skill – so noble in men – ludicrous and futile. The worst of it is that this usurpation of tasks also tends to lead to the usurpation of physique. If the delightful male privilege of transforming oneself into a woman seems to belong exclusively to RAF NCOs, the opposite is the prerogative of these lady champions. In two weeks, a beard can grow long. After the Games, we suggest that those ladies who have won medals should undergo an examination. And, without going as

far as to add fine cuisine and darning to the programme of the Games, some proof of domestic skills should be provided.

For at the end of the day, watching the javelin throwers handle their lance like a broomstick, or the brilliant discus throwers grip their missiles as they might select a plate from the pile to let fly some crockery, we tremble at the thought of the fearsome weapon a rolling pin could become in the hands of little ladies such as Brown or Press; 100 kilos each, with the impetus to match. Yet there are exceptions. Here, it would be Iolanda Bala, the high-jumper from Bucharest, a slender daddy long legs with limbs like windmills. Or Wilma Rudolph, the black diamond, whom speed clothes like a silk robe, without a crease or crumpled edge. She alone seems to wear grace about her like a scarf as she crosses the line. And yet – alas! – for each Wilma Rudolph, how many brewers' mares!

In the 100m, Wilma Rudolph beats Hyman (centre) and Leone (right) in **11** seconds. This world record time is not ratified due to a tailwind of 2.47metres per second.

Dorothy Hyman (GBR), Wilma Rudolph (USA) and Jutta Heine (GER) – the 200m podium.

A triple exploit

S eptember 2, 100m: My stop-watch shows 11.0 seconds. Yet the world record was 11.3! The phenomenal black American Wilma Rudolph has won the 100m final in style, leaving the excellent Briton Dorothy Hyman, and the equally valiant Giuseppina Leone, trailing at least three metres behind.

The commentator confirms the result of the final: Wilma Rudolph, 11.0 dead. Unfortunately, her stunning performance will not be ratified, thanks to a tailwind of 2.47m/sec (the maximum permitted wind assistance is 2 metres per second).

September 5, 200m: Two women's finals take place in the Olympic stadium before a storm inundates the venue. Rudolph takes the lead 60m from the finish, and wins by four or five metres over Jutta Heine (GER). Into a strong head wind, Rudolph's 24.0 is worth a second less, at least.

September 8, 4x100m: Rudolph becomes the most titled athlete of the Rome Games. The US team do not repeat their semi-final performance of 44.4, the result of careful changeovers. Rudolph, not yet up to speed, is caught by the powerful Heine, before she accelerates away to a decisive victory.

Armin Hary breaks the ribbon

A photo finish was needed to decide between the German sprinter and David Sime (USA), both credited with 10.2.

The start (from left to right): Hary (GER), Radford (GBR), Figuerola (CUB), Norton (USA), Budd (USA) and Sime (USA).

The finishing line; Hary (foreground) dips ahead of Sime (far side).

be repeated: those preparatory rituals, those endless seconds of suspense as silence fell again. This time, Hary was slightly ahead of the starter's signal, by so little that whistles rang out everywhere. Our pleasure was deferred once again. On the starting line, Hary was paler still, and Sime more restless. Only Radford and Norton remained seemingly impassive. For the third time, silence fell, broken only by the noise of cameras. Then the real start took place, followed by the ten seconds of race – ten amazing seconds – which ended with the vision of Sime lying on the cinder track, pressing his face against it, slow to get up – as though he were afraid to learn that this final effort, torn from deep inside, had been in vain.

Thousand of Germans were chanting 'Hary,' and suddenly the German sprinter, from in the middle of the grass, raised his arms in victory. An official dressed in white had just informed him that he had won the finest 100m in the history of the Games. At that instant, Dave Sime, whose elegant musculature was still red – the colour of the cinders onto which he had fallen fallen full-length after a desperate dip for the tape – learnt he had been defeated.

He made his way slowly back to the starting line, wearily gathered up his tracksuit, and mechanically shook the hand held out to him by Armin Hary – the fastest man in the world. Then he headed sadly to the stadium exit, wiping off the sweat, the red sweat of a wounded man. At a distance, it is hard to imagine what those 10.2 seconds printed in a newspaper column really represent. It is hard to imagine the unbearable tension that precedes a 100m final, the silence that descends;

Sime gesturing his fists before him over and again in a convulsive gesture, challenging an invisible adversary; Norton's statuesque calmness; Hary's deathlike pallor.

Sixty thousand held their breath, taking in this jumble of images, the kind seen once in a lifetime. Sixty thousand pairs of eyes went from Hary to the starter. Sime could barely keep still and made the first false start, followed by the German. A falling leaf would set him off. Everything had to

Hary: 'My records weren't due to wind assistance'

The Americans had been unconquered in the 100m since 1932. Hary celebrates with Jesse Owen.

Nobody, apart from his own people, had believed in him. After the race, Armin Hary recalled this almost angrily: 'Perhaps they will now admit my records were not due to wind assistance.' This blond 23-year-old, born 22 March 1937 in Quierschied, had silenced his doubters. At 5 feet 11, 166 pounds, Hary is a neuro-muscular phenomenon. He arrived to contest the race of his life dressed like a tourist, in a straw hat and checked

shirt, carrying his starting block like a beach accessory. In the minutes leading up to the start, while the other runners moved in slow motion, Hary went to the starting line at a run. Nothing could disturb his serenity, not even the second false start, blamed on him. His race was then as clear as a bell. The secret to his start is simple: 'I have learned, through relaxation, how to achieve full stride very early in the race.'

RESULTS

100m
1 Armin Hary (GER): 10.2
2 David Sime (USA): 10.2
3 Peter Radford (GBR): 10.3
4 Enrique Figuerola (CUB): 10.3
5 Francis 'Frank' Budd (USA): 10.3
6 O. Ray Norton (USA): 10.4

A phenomenal decathlon

After a dramatic 1500m, American Rafer Johnson snatched the gold medal from the Formosan Yang Chuan-Kwang.

The day had begun badly for Rafer Johnson. Exhausted by his efforts the previous day, he had returned to the stadium with the slight advantage of 55 points over his rival Yang Chuan-Kwang, after an often dramatic struggle. He was still not properly awake, for a few hours of sleep had not been sufficient to erase the fatigue accumulated the previous day.

The 110m hurdles almost destroyed the world-record holder's hopes. It was expected that he and the Formosan would at least be equally matched. Thanks to a gusting headwind, Johnson only obtained a mediocre 15.3; in still conditions, Yang achieved 14.6. Suddenly, Yang led by 128 points, and the organisers held a large part of the responsibility: Yang and Johnson should have run in the same heat. When two athletes so clearly lead a competition, the done thing is that they have the same conditions.

In the discus, Johnson recovered, throwing 48.49m on his third attempt – far below his usual performance, but better than the Formosan's 39.83m. The result left Johnson ahead after seven trials, with 6,281 points against Yang's 6,137. Yang was known to be superior in the pole vault, but Johnson

Beaten in the 100m by his great friend and rival, Yang Chuan-Kwang (TAI), Rafer Johnson lost more ground in the long jump (7.35m against 7.46m).

Yang (right), exhausted and disappointed after the 1500m, supports his vanquisher.

67 points – a difference of 6.5 seconds in the 1500m. Yang chose his only option: to try to run away from Johnson. But the American stuck to Yang's heels like glue. Yang crossed the kilometre mark in 3.11; Johnson was still there. At 1250m, Yang attacked. Johnson responded with a slight delay. As they moved into the bend, Yang tried one last time, gaining five metres on the American. It was not enough. Johnson won the gold medal he had deserved at Melbourne by 58 points. On the finish line, the two men fell into each others arms. It was the most beautiful moment of the evening.

A BLACK ATHLETE CARRIES THE AMERICAN FLAG.

The first, and doubtlessly one of the most beautiful images of these Games was that of Rafer Johnson carrying the American flag during the opening ceremony. Thus, twenty four years after Berlin, a prestigious black athlete walked at the head of the delegation of the best athletes in the world. That alone was enough to justify and redeem the Olympic Games. Rafer Johnson, a student at the University of California in Los Angeles, was the first black to be elected head of an American student association. The previous day, Rafer had not been seen in any stadium, for he was practising carrying the flag. Johnson made his entry into the stadium shortly after another remarkable flag bearer, Christian d'Oriola – Olympic medal-winner in 1948, 1952 and 1956 – who carried the French tricolour.

Johnson finishes the 400m and the first day with a lead of fifty-five points.

limited the damage. Competing in two different vaulting areas, they made their final attempts almost simultaneously, Yang at 4.40m, Johnson at 4.20m. Both failed by tiny margins, but still notched up jumps of 4.30m (Yang) and 4.10m (Johnson).

Johnson had never before jumped 4m and retained a 24-point lead over Yang, his fellow student at the University of California in Los Angeles. Towards 8pm, they picked up their javelins. On the first attempt, Johnson threw 69.76m: Yang, with 65.90m, would have been 113 points adrift, if he had not thrown 68.22m on his second attempt. The gap was just

RESULTS

DECATHLON

1 Rafer Johnson (USA), 8 392 pts (10"9, 7,35 m, 15,82 m, 1,85 m, 48"3, 15"3, 48,49 m, 4,10 m, 69,76 m, 4'49"7)
2 Yang Chuan Kwang (TAI), 8 334 pts (10"7, 7,46 m, 13,33 m, 1,90 m, 48"1, 14"6, 39,83 m, 4,30 m, 68,22 m, 4'48"5)
3 Vassily Kuznetsov (URS), 7 809 pts (11"1, 6,96 m, 14,46 m, 1,75 m, 50"2 15", 50,52 m, 3,90 m, 71,20 m, 4'55"4)
4 Kutenko (URS) 7 567 pts
5 Evert Kamerbeek (HOL), 7 236 pts
6 Franco Sar (ITA), 7 195 pts
7 Markus Kahma (FIN), 7 112 pts
8 Klaus Grogorens (ALL), 7 032 pts

Abebe Bikila's amazing adventure

The marathon is won by the barefooted Abebe Bikila, a soldier and member of Ethiopia's Imperial Bodyguard.

Rubbing my eyes in surprise, I went in search of the Ethiopians' athletics coach, in the Olympic Village where they were staying. There, I came across a magnificent Viking, aged about forty: Onni Niskanen. Born in Helsinki of Swedish parents, Niskanen has been responsible for physical education in Ethiopia for fourteen years, after the government, wanting a trainer, asked Sweden for assistance. One of his tasks was to train Emperor Haile Selassie's Imperial Bodyguard. Four years ago, among the guards, he discovered a young man of astounding stamina.

His name was Abebe Bikila. He had been born in 1932 in a little village called Mout. Bikila joined the Imperial Guard as an adolescent. In four years, Niskanen turned him into a champion in the finest event of all for a soldier-athlete: the marathon. This is how the Ethiopian national anthem came to ring out under Constantine's Arch, a stone's throw from the Colosseum, close to the finishing line that this amazing barefoot marathon runner had crossed half an hour earlier. After a 42km race, the athlete arrived in a state of extraordinary freshness: his physical condition stupefied the doctors.

Abebe Bikila is a full-blooded Amhara, 5 feet 9 and 128 pounds, with regular features, dark brown skin, curly hair, a prominent and straight nose and pronounced lips. According to Niskanen, 'He only wears shoes when the ground could hurt him, but his stride is less relaxed. The skin on his soles is several millimetres thick and hardened like leather, and he feels no discomfort – quite the opposite.'

Bikila has run huge distances to achieve this success. 'He trains twice a day,' relates Niskanen, 'very early in the morning and at the end of the afternoon. He alternates between track session, mainly a series of 1500m runs after a very long warm-up, and long runs through the countryside. The countryside around Addis Ababa is well-suited to training; it is mountainous, and Bikila often climbs the hills at full speed. His powers of recovery are phenomenal; his resting pulse is less than 45 beats per minute.

At 6pm, as the sun goes down, Abebe Bikila (foreground on the right), is still just an unknown Ethiopian runner lost amid the pack.

He also does a lot of stretching and light weight-lifting.'

Disciplined by profession, Abebe Bikila trusts his coach implicitly: 'It hasn't sunk in that I've won – I can't believe it. Before the race, my trainer told me I had a chance. He told me to keep an eye on Rhadi and the Russians, and not to attack before the thirtieth kilometre. I ran at my own pace. Towards the end, I put on a spurt, and I still had reserves. I am happy for my country, for my Emperor and for my wife, who is waiting for me in Addis Ababa.'

Niskanen adds: 'I have believed in him since he ran two hours, twenty-one minutes and thirty-three seconds in the Olympic trials. The course was much more difficult there than in Rome – there was a 10km ascent – and the total difference in altitude was 250m, compared to just 90m in Rome. Addis Ababa is at an altitude of 8,000 feet, and the surrounding area goes up to 9,500 feet. The climate is good for training, but the altitude means times in long-distance events can be slow.'

And so, Abebe was thrown in at the international deep end. It was his third marathon. No doubt his ideal distance is 25km, but his range begins at 5,000m, where he has been credited with 14 minutes and 36 seconds.

'In the 10,000m, he has no great performances officially, but I am sure he is capable of running inside 29 minutes,' said Niskanen. 'He needs competition in order to toughen up and get to know his possibilities which I am sure are astonishing. I am also certain that at sea level, in good conditions, he is already capable of beating Zátopek's hour record – and he will attempt it as soon as he gets the chance. As he is a young runner, who only made his debut recently, I think that his career can go on for a long while yet, and he should be able to defend his title at the next Games in Tokyo. In the meantime he will run in the African Games in two years. Then we will see what progress Ethiopian athletes have made, as we have a lot of young ones.' Niskanen informs us that Ethiopia plans to call in another Scandinavian coach, as he can no longer do the job alone. He adds: 'Most of the young athletes that we are training were still too inexperienced for the current Olympiad, but you will see them in Tokyo. There is definitely no lack of talent.'

After seeing the excellent 800m runner Saïd here in Rome, and the marathon led by Abebe, we don't doubt Niskanen's optimism. In the sentimental context of the Games, this was obviously very pleasant to see. The Ethiopian athletes are not only a delight to behold, they are also an example to us all.

Bikila has just dropped the Moroccan Rhadi, and passes alone beneath the Arch of Constantine, achieving victory in bare feet.

1960
OLYMPIC ROUND-UP

GEREVICH GOES DOWN IN HISTORY.

There are moments that mark you for life, and the hours I spent watching the fencing tournament in that vast marble palace will stay in my memory for years to come. After Melbourne, the immense talent of the elegant and slim Rudolph Karpati was confirmed here in Rome. A touch helped him retain his Olympic title 4-4 in a final bout against the Pole Pawlowski. The Hungarians also have young Zoltán Horváth to be proud of; competing for the first time, he arrived just at the right moment to take back the torch of tradition. The victorious youth of Pawlowski and Horváth provided a striking contrast. Despite his fantastic footwork, Aladár Gerevich could not hold out against them; his reflexes betrayed him.

The semi-finals saw the elimination of 'old' Gerevich. Since his first appearance at the Olympic Games in 1932, he has brought glory to his country. Passionately dedicated to his art, he has devoted his life to sabre fighting. Now, in his fifties, he still wanted to prove that he was one of the world elite. He lost by only two touches, after a three-way barrage for two places. Despite the Hungarian's disappointment, his dignity was impressive, but his distress could be seen in his shining eyes. However, at the end of the team final two days later, Gerevich was all smiles again, as he added to his own Olympic total. Born 13 March 1910, Gerevich did not win his first individual medal until 1936 – a bronze in the sabre. He won his first title in London in 1948, in the same discipline, before extending his collection with the silver in 1952. In Helsinki he added the bronze medal in the team foil.

But it is precisely in the team foil that his longevity has most often been rewarded; with the Hungarian sabre team, he has taken the supreme title in 1932, 1936, 1948, 1952, 1956 and 1960 – six consecutive successes won over 28 years! A very young Olympic champion at Los Angeles at the age of 22, he was honoured once again in Rome at more than 50 years old!

1 Sime (USA) finishes the 4x100m relays ahead of Lauer (GER). But the Americans are disqualified and lose the title they had held since 1920.

2 The German eight (foreground) give a superb performance in the rowing, inflicting defeat on the Americans, also unbeaten since 1920.

3 Livio Berruti (ITA) becomes the first non-American in Olympic history to win the 200m, ahead of (left to right): Carney (USA, second), Johnson (USA, fifth), Seye (FRA, third) and Foik (POL, fourth).

4 Ingrid Krämer (GDR) achieves a diving double in springboard and platform.

5 In the long jump, American Ralph Boston reaches 8.12m to beat his countryman Roberson by a centimetre!

6 Borys Shakhlin (SOV/UKR) is the gymnastics king of the Rome Games with six medals, two of which are gold (all-around and parallel bars).

7 The Americans achieve a clean sweep in the discus. Al Oerter (59.18m) retains his title.

8 The Soviet Kapitonov dashed the hopes of Livo Trapé (ITA, left) and won the road race in the sprint.

9 The sabre is a Hungarian speciality, and the veteran Gerevich takes the seat of honour at the front.

10 A hundred metres from the finish of the 800m, Snell (NZL), in the black vest, is boxed in by Wägli (SWI), Moens (BEL), Schmidt (GER) and Kerr (JAM), on the left. A few metres further on he breaks away for victory.

11 Australia's Dawn Fraser retains the 100m title she won in Melbourne – a first in the history of women's swimming.

12 The podium for the 1000m kayak (from left to right): Szöllösi (HUN, second), Hansen (DAN, first) and Fredriksson (SWE, third). The Swede completed his extraordinary collection of medals – six gold, one silver and one bronze (from 1948 to 1960).

13 Rose (AUS, second), Konrads (AUS, first) and Breen (USA, third) share the 1500m freestyle podium.

A star is born

An 18-year-old American is the revelation of the boxing tournament. Cassius Clay, an eccentric out of the ring, is brilliantly effective in it.

The young Olympic middleweight champion is not yet Muhammad Ali, but it is already clear that he has a future. His talent and charisma are obvious.

Three Americans won gold medals in the boxing finals on the evening of 5 September 1960, but unfortunately for light-middleweight Wilbert McClure and middleweight Eddie Crook, the light-heavyweight Cassius Marcellus Clay was to steal the limelight when they returned to the United States. This eighteen-year-old from Louisville, Kentucky was the centre of attention from the moment he arrived in the Olympic Village.

'He's like a politician campaigning for an election,' laughed one of his team-mates. 'He's always introducing himself to the competitors of the other sports and giving them badges.' Clay surprised other boxers in the changing rooms with his pre-bout dancing. The surprise continued in the ring. After eliminating Becaus (BEL, stopped by

the referee in the second round), Shatkov (SOV/RUS, the 1956 middleweight champion) and Madigan (AUS) by unanimous decisions, he faced Zbigniew Pietrzykowski (POL), three times champion of Europe and bronze medalist in 1956, in the final.

For a moment in round one, Clay seemed to be in trouble. Disconcerted by his southpaw opponent, he took a flurry of punches and showed inexperience by closing his eyes against a combination. But in the second round, Clay kept out of reach with agile footwork and was able to lower his guard. Gaining in confidence, he went on the offensive and threw four hard rights to the Pole's face. He admitted: 'Even after round two, I knew I needed to win the final round.'

In the final three minutes, Clay

reached the peak of his art. Moving in and out, he unleashed a series of combinations. Abandoning his straight left, he drove a right cross through Pietrzykowski's guard. The Pole's face was covered in blood and he came close to a defeat by knock-out. When the bell came to his rescue, he was on the ropes, defenceless.

Six times winner of the Golden Gloves in Kentucky, twice the National Golden Gloves and twice US Champion, Clay easily qualified for the Games. But as he flew to the Olympic trials in California, his plane went through violent turbulence. Fearing the long journey to Europe, he told his coach Joe Martin that he was withdrawing. Martin reasoned with him for two hours in a Louisville park. In fact, without Joe Martin, Cassius Clay may never have entered the ring.

In October 1954, Clay, then aged 12, went with a friend to the Columbia Auditorium, where a black traders' market was being held. As the two friends went to go home, Clay discovered that his brand new bicycle had been stolen. He burst into tears and shouted for the police. A passer-by told him that an officer worked in the boxing hall beneath the auditorium. Distraught, Clay approached Martin, also a police officer, and told him he was going to knock the thief's block off. Martin advised him to learn to box first.

After six weeks of training, the 90-pound adolescent fought his first bout, winning on points. 'When I started boxing,' recalled Clay after his Olympic victory, 'all I wanted was to buy a house for my mother and father one day and a big car for myself.'

ROME XVII OLYMPIAD

The Roman Empire seized control of the Olympics from its rival, Athens,
until in 394BC the Games were abolished by Emperor Theodosius I.
Sixteen centuries later, the Games returned to Rome stronger
than ever, and the city provided a sumptuous setting.

THE GAMES IN BRIEF

Opening Date
25 August 1960

Closing Date
11 September 1960

Host Nation
Italy (ITA)

Candidate Towns
Lausanne (SUI), Detroit (USA), Budapest
(HUN), Brussels (BEL), Mexico (MEX) and
Tokyo (JAP).

84 Nations Represented

5,348 Athletes
(610 women, 4,738 men).

17 Sports
(6 open to women)
Track and field, rowing, basketball, boxing,
canoeing, cycling, equestrian, fencing,
football, gymnastics,weightlifting, field
hockey, wrestling, swimming, modern
pentathlon, shooting and sailing.

Demonstation Sports
None

150 Events
(29 open to women)

Games officially opened by
Giovanni Gronchi, President of Italy

Olympic flame lit by
Giancarlo Peris (athletics)

Olympic oath read by
Adolfo Consolini (athletics)

IOC Preseident
Avery Brundage (USA)

DID YOU KNOW?

An Olympic hymn, composed by Spyros
Samaras and Kostis Palamas, was played for
the first time at the 1896 Athens Olympics.
In the years that followed, various musical
works accompanied the opening ceremonies
until at Rome Samaras' and Palamas'
composition became the official Olympic
hymn.

Because of apartheid, Rome would be the
last Games in which South Africa would
participate until 1992.

Over 100 television channels broadcast
both live and recorded footage of the Games
to 18 countries across Europe as well as the
United States, Japan and Canada.

GAMES OF THE XVII OLYMPIAD

ROMA · 25.VIII-11.IX

ROMA MCMLX

HEAVY-WEIGHT B

JERK 217.5 kg

WORLD RECORD 215.5   OLYMPIC RECORD 20

164 L. Zhabotinsky

1964

Tokyo

HE PUTS THE TORCH TO THE OLYMPIC FLAME: Yoshinori Sakai, barely nineteen years of age, an athlete born not far from Hiroshima on 6 August 1945, the day the Enola Gay released the first atomic bomb, and three days before another B29 dropped the second over Nagasaki. The death toll was in the hundreds of thousands. Sixty per cent of Tokyo was destroyed. Nineteen years have passed since Japan surrendered. Emperor Hirohito, who declared the Games open, knows this better than anyone: he has been on the throne since 1926. He was there when Tokyo was selected to host the 1940 Games, and when Tokyo had to give them up due to the World War II.

Now, it's 1964 and Japan has put its past behind it. The country is no longer bellicose. It has been rebuilt, and is back on its feet. Spending on the Games is lavish: the budget is two billion dollars, a colossal sum. The organisation is flawless in every respect, and the first worldwide television broadcasts via satellite assured a global public.

The Games are a convincing display of Japanese efficiency, but lack emotion: the public is calm, polite, respectful and disciplined, but to Western eyes seeing Asia for the first time, seems cold. It may be easier to forget the catastrophes of recent history than to change the intimate habits of centuries of tradition. Nonetheless, tensions persist between China and the USSR, the United States and Cuba, and in Vietnam. During the Games, China, a conspicuous absentee, conducts its first nuclear tests.

Yuri Vlasov puts his glasses on; yes, he has read the scoreboard correctly. The hitherto invincible super-heavyweight has been defeated by his fellow Soviet and Ukrainian compatriot, Leonid Zhabotynsky, who has set a new world record of 217.5kg for the clean-and-jerk.

Geesink puts Japan in shock

By immobilising Akio Kaminaga in the open division, Antonius Geesink reduces a nation to tears.

Antonius Geesink, a judo instructor from Utrecht, had taught Asian Judokas a lesson in 1961, when he became the first non-Japanese world champion. But that was in Paris, not on Japanese soil.

Kaminaga didn't immediately notice his team-mates were sobbing. He laboriously got back on his feet, and for a moment he seemed to be weeping too. He was pale, but that was perhaps because of Geesink's kesa-gataine, or sash hold, seconds earlier. The room had held its breath for thirty seconds as the Japanese champion tried, furiously but in vain, to free himself from the Dutchman's unrelenting grip.

He had the look of a trout, exhausted by its own efforts. Geesink, his 253 pounds comfortably installed on Kaminaga's broad chest, his butcher's arms firmly around his rival's neck, having passed one of them under the shoulder of the Japanese, looked his rival ferociously in the eyes. He could have spent the whole evening in this position. It was over before the bell announced the end, and for Japan, watching on television, it was a moment of terrible anguish. Students wept in the restaurant, their hopes shattered with one blow.

Japan's total judo supremacy had been surrendered to a Westerner. The cameras, aimed at the Tatami – the rectangular matting – didn't allow viewers to decipher Geesink's

outstretched arm during the bout. He was pointing at the Japanese coach Matsumoto, who had been crouching at the edge of the Tatami yelling advice at Kaminaga. The gesture astonished the referee, who hadn't even noticed. He sent the Japanese eighth dan to his chair in a state of confusion. Geesink didn't miss a trick, and when a champion retains such clear-headedness in the heat of combat, it is

hard to imagine how he can be beaten.

And Geesink's supporters never doubted him. It was an excellent fight, better than the Paris bout in 1961 for the world title, also won by the Dutchman. Kaminaga, solidly poised on powerful legs, unleashed several sudden attacks which would have left any opponent but the giant Dutchman in shock. Kaminaga, who weighs in at over 100kg, managed to escape from

one hold, but only after a superhuman effort. In another move, he was thrown onto a third of a leg, which should have been worth a point to the Dutchman. Yet to general bemusement, the referee didn't react. It was the deciding kesa-gataine which made the Westerners in the room jump for joy, and reduced Inokuma, the Olympic heavyweight champion, and the rest of Japan, to tears.

Despite the efforts of Akio Kaminaga, the giant Geesink was never really put into difficulty, and it was a Dutchman who celebrated the introduction of judo to the Olympic programme.

Athletic perfection

The moment is approaching when the experts try to classify the giants of the Tokyo Games according to innate physical gifts and emotional impact.

It is entirely subjective to choose between Bob Hayes, the first human to run at thirty-six kilometres an hour, Abebe Bikila, unique in his ability to run at speed from dawn to dusk, Don Schollander, miracle record holder of Olympic titles for the crawl, the inexhaustible Dawn Fraser, and Peter Snell, who has unfortunately attained his greatest achievements against distinctly inferior opponents.

The Dutch giant Antonius Geesink also belongs to this exclusive club of athletes who have left their mark in the annals of sport. The judoka from the West has come as far as the land of the Samurai to prove that a white man with blond hair, formed in the European school, could surpass the most revered Japanese champions in their own ancestral pursuit.

The Japanese have been happy to dispatch their best judo teachers as missionaries across the world and conquer hundreds of thousands of new followers. Yet they have done so with the certainty that they would keep forever the seat of this growing religion. But this giant, not a monster but two perfect

athletes rolled into one, began the final combat against Kaminaga by raising his arms and flexing his jaws, inspired by the certainty of his fabulous superiority.

What role does brute strength play beside technique? The gospel of the judoka has as its central precept that it is always the most skilful who wins, even if he is physically weaker. This basic assertion gave way when weight divisions were created, but Geesink has as much technique as all the bearers of dans put together. He dominated the 220-pound mass of Kaminaga in every way. Geesink, a quiet man who spends his summers on the gulf of Saint-Tropez, held his opponent, absolutely drenched with sweat, staining the lapels of his slightly crumpled combat kimono,

in a victorious lock in which a bull could not have twitched as much as an ear!

The public in the Nippon Budokan Hall, a covered room modelled on the temple of Nara, from the period of the Yans (tenth century), with its octagonal form, its enormous, elegant pagoda roof, is still in shock.

Geesink quickly reverted to the courtesy and solemn rhythm required by ritual, and Japan, the best qualified judge, accepted both the verdict and the historic place he now held with surprising applause. As his masters sobbed, Kaminaga himself was the very picture of dignity. He had had the duration of that endless, Herculean lock to come to terms with the truth.

Dawn Fraser, wayward genius

Melbourne, Rome, Tokyo: the extraordinary Australian wins her third 100m title in consecutive Games.

Aged 27, Dawn Fraser is of advanced years for a swimmer. Yet she is young at heart, and full of mischief.

No author would have dared dream up such a heroine for a piece of fiction. Nothing seems to stop her. Neither convention nor criticism can deter her from fulfilling the destiny of her extravagant gifts in the water. It is almost as if she deliberately sought obstacles to overcome to enhance her unique achievements. Whatever the truth, she has attracted a continent of devoted admirers who greet her adolescent antics with affectionate lenience, perhaps recognising themselves in her childlike flaws. Her unruliness is matched only by her dedication.

Dawn Fraser is the youngest of eight children from Sydney docks. She suffered respiratory problems as a child, the result of playing in a disused coal mine. With the help of a irascible older brother, she learnt to swim at the age of five, began to compete at the age of eleven and was suspended for eighteen months at the age of fourteen after accepting some modest cash prizes. When she threw in her job at a sweet factory, her prospects didn't look good at all.

Back in the water, she was spotted by the celebrated coach Harry Gallagher, who had a quiet word in her ear. From the day she followed him to Adelaide, her life revolved around swimming. To 600km pool work a year, the Australian Swimming Union added eight weeks of gym work before the 1956 Olympic Games. Plus, for the first time in the history of Australian swimming, a winter training camp at the end of July. Only then did she make her international debut at the Games, duelling over 100m with her great rival and fellow Australian Lorraine Crapp and winning by a hand in 1:02.00, a

Left, Sharon Stouder, silver; right, Kathleen Ellis, bronze (both USA). Opponents come and go, but Dawn Fraser remains the 100m champion.

new world record.

Four years later, she arrived at the Rome Olympics after an extremely demanding journey, although the gastric problems she suffered there did nothing to prevent her from retaining her 100m title, as the legendary Duke Kahanamoku and Johnny Weissmuller had before her. Fraser's margin of victory over the great American Chris von Saltza was a gaping 1.6 seconds. The only Australian woman athlete to win gold, she celebrated her victory late into the Roman night away from the village. The following day, she refused to swim the butterfly leg of the 4x100m, which led to a falling out with her team mates and her directors. An escapade in Switzerland led the straight-laced ASU to ban her from international competition until 1962 for 'not performing to the best of her abilities in, and out of the pool.'

Her response was world-beating. On 23 October 1962, she swam 100m in 60.0 seconds. Four days later, she became the first woman to break the one-minute barrier with 59.9. On 29 February 1964, after lowering her world record to 58.9, Fraser was involved in a

road accident that killed her mother, knocked her sister unconscious, and left Fraser in a neck brace. Nevertheless, she won for the third time at the games in Tokyo, defeating the American Sharon Stouder, twelve years her junior. Fraser's time of 59.5 is even more remarkable in that she had taken a hand turn instead of the much faster tumble turn. Her triumph, less than seven weeks after the car crash, was one of the most moving moments of the Games.

This unprecedented third title should have put any other news about Dawn Fraser in the shade, to wit, her secret participation in the opening ceremony, her outlandish shirt, her bugle calls at the edge of the pool and even a bizarre episode in which she stole the Olympic flag flying over the Imperial Palace. Learning who she was, the police officers who had detained her respectfully offered her the coveted flag. The Australian Swimming Union, however, in a gesture of characteristic humourlessness, now intends to wreck the career of this most wayward, but also the most talented of swimmers by imposing a ten-year suspension.

A PHENOMENON!

As sporting progress becomes increasingly collective, remarkable individual talents are increasingly scarce. Before they can enjoy the spoils of success, those who have reached the summits of sport are prone to be elbowed aside by younger, more ambitious athletes. Not Dawn Fraser, who, even as she approaches her thirtieth birthday, is swimming faster than ever. Nothing can hold her back but her own personal limits – limits she tirelessly forces back, while maintaining a deceptively cheerful, easy going and informal manner. Fraser proves that physical strength is not the exclusive spoils of youth, provided the soul remains fresh and physical well-being, the foundation of athletic excellence, is maintained. In the qualifying heats for the women's 100m final, Fraser lowered the Olympic record she had set in Melbourne in 1956 by 2.1 seconds. Fraser's example proves that those who wish to win must constantly refine their technique.

Don Schollander, the first swimmer to win four

On his way to an unprecedented four gold medals, the young American outclasses his rivals in the 100m.

After ten metres, France's Alain Gottvalles led. At fifteen, Mike Austin (USA) replaced him. That was the world-record holder out of the reckoning. At the turn, Gary Ilman (USA) surfaced into a wave and lost his rhythm. That was the fastest qualifier out. After seventy metres, Austin began to fade, leaving the Scot Robert McGregor in the lead. Only then did Don Schollander, the world record holder for the 200m and 400m, increased his work rate. The closing stages were a bitter duel between McGregor and Schollander, the youngest man in the pool. At eighty metres, Schollander took the lead. McGregor reacted, regained the advantage five metres further on, then conceded. Schollander won in 53.4 seconds, with McGregor touching a tenth of a second later. The bronze medal was awarded to Germany's Klein after unofficial timings showed he had touched one thousandth of a second before Ilman.

Schollander rushed into his mother's arms, who used to double for Maureen O'Sullivan (Jane to Johnny Weissmuller's Tarzan) in water scenes. He had been hesitant before undertaking his packed Olympic programme. Fortunately, he stuck to his plans, which allowed him to become the first swimmer to win four gold medals in one Olympic Games.

RESULTS

FOUR TITLES FOR SCHOLLANDER

100m
1 Donald Schollander (USA), 53.4
2 Robert McGregor (GBR), 53'.5
3 Hans-Joachim Klein (GER), 54.'0

400m
1 Donald Schollander (USA), 4:12'.2
2 Frank Wiegand (GER), 4:14.'9
3 Allan Wood (AUS), 4:15.1

4x100m
1 USA 3:32.'2
2 GDR & GER 3:37.2
3 AUS 3:39.1

4x200m
1 USA 7:52''1
2 GDR & GER 7:59''3
3 JAP 8:03''8

The American Don Schollander, a 200m and 400m specialist, destroyed all comers in the 100m.

The fastest man in the world!

The American Bob Hayes flew through the final of the 100m in 10 seconds, after running a wind-assisted 9.9 seconds in the semis. Unbelievable!

No need for a photo-finish. Bob Hayes wins with a 0.2 second lead over Cuba's Figuerola and Canada's Harry Jerome.

The stadium is full, apart from a few vacant rows up in the stands. They are usually crowded with schoolchildren: today, they are either in the classroom or playing truant. It's a shame; they could have savoured one of those instructive history and geography lessons that sport sometimes provides.

An American from Florida and a Cuban from just across the Straits of Florida were disputing the exquisite prize of supremacy in pure speed, summing up, in its quintessence, the game every kid plays in every yard all throughout the world: 'Beat you there!' And millions across the world were absorbed in the game – the sort of child's play that reveals adult quarrels as nonsense.

On his way to the final, America's Bob Hayes had beaten the world record, admittedly with the help of the wind. Among those watching were Jesse Owens and, not far away, the German, Armin Hary, the current record holder. Hary licked his index finger to gauge the speed of the wind. He was right: the time was not official. Yet the memory lingers of a man

propelled solely by his humble human physique covering a hundred metres in less than ten seconds for the first time in the history of our species.

In the final, Hayes took on Cuba's Enrique Figuerola. A dense matrix of politics underlay the encounter, although no-one in the stadium cared for anything but the individuals on the blocks. It was only after the race that the search for some encrypted meaning began. It emerged in the warm, sincere handshake between the American and the Cuban, a rare event these days. It was a wonderful moment which left us believing, just for a while, that sport really can bring people together.

Bob Hayes, delighted over his gold medal. Four months before the Games, a serious leg injury led to fears that he would have to withdraw.

OWENS: HAYES IS FASTEST EVER

An aging Jesse Owens followed the final heats of the 100m with passion. In the past he had criticised Bob Hayes' poor start. Now, he revised his opinion. 'Bob is an exceptional athlete,' he said, 'although it is better to avoid comparisons between different eras. What is impressive in his case is his margin of victory. Sprinting has made enormous progress over recent years. The improvement in living standards in the majority of countries means better diet and hygiene. The use of starting-blocks, and advanced track construction, also helps, although improvements in preparation and also the greater time available for training are even more significant. Finally, because of the high level of competition, the best athletes must constantly excel themselves.

'I do not think that the future belongs inevitably to powerful sprinters. What makes modern runners strong is their resilience. With traditional timing, Bob would now be the sole world-record holder at 9.9 seconds. Sooner or later he'll achieve it. Bob Hayes is clearly the fastest man of all time.'

Peter Snell overcomes his fear of defeat

800m champion four years ago in Rome, the New Zealander retains the 800m and adds the 1500m.

Among the front runners of the 800m lead by Kiprugut, Snell bided his time before going into battle 100m from the finish (photos on the left). He applied the same tactic in the 1500m (to the right).

When they looked for him to award him his second gold medal, the Japanese officials began to panic. Peter Snell had taken refuge with his wife Sally behind a wall at the exit of the changing-room. I found them embracing tenderly, and looked away until the moment had passed. When he approached, taking slow, deliberate steps, he glowed with happiness. 'I'm tired,' he said, 'very tired.'

In the race, he had appeared supreme; less dominant, perhaps, than Herb Elliott in Rome, but a class above his opponents. Who would have guessed that Peter Snell was afraid of losing the race he valued the most?

'I was feeling very well after the semi-finals. I hadn't had to work too hard, in spite of the fast pace. It was the next day, on the eve of the final that I began to feel sluggish; my legs felt tender. In the race, I had only Burleson to fear, since Jazy and O'Hara were no longer there. But suddenly I was apprehensive: if Michel Bernard (FRA) set off like a whirlwind, as I feared he would, and Witold Baran (POL) took over from him, in all honestly, I doubted my chances. I didn't feel capable of running a fast race.' Little wonder: the final was Snell's sixth race in eight days. However, despite his fears, the race didn't turn out as expected. Bernard tried to light the fuse, but the powder wasn't dry and no-one in the group moved. Baran should have run his own race, but he tried to follow Snell, like the others.

'It wasn't as difficult as I feared,' says Snell, 'but I can tell you, I'm glad it's over.' He remains calm, steady,

level-headed, almost blasé, and with his customary reserve, he explains that he is satisfied. He doesn't wear his heart on his sleeve. He speaks of this dazzling triumph as if he's talking about someone else – as if it was a straightforward, everyday victory with

no historical significance. He did admit, however, that it was the 1500m that interested him, not the 800m.

'I may have given the impression that I wouldn't be competing in the 1500m. But at no time since I came to Tokyo did I consider withdrawing.

If it had been necessary to give up an event, it would have been the 800m.'

Snell had even stated that it was impossible, or at least very dangerous, to attempt the double in Tokyo. 'It was to confuse Jazy. I wanted to bluff him, to encourage him to concentrate on the 5,000m. I didn't want to have to take him on in the 1500m.'

I looked at Peter Snell with a sense of disbelief. He is so superior in everything he undertakes that his fears are hard to understand. He doesn't seem capable of self-doubt. Yet he had doubts. 'I don't say that to impress you,' he adds. 'I respect Jazy enormously. I think that he made a big mistake by choosing the 5,000m when he was probably stronger than ever in the 1500m. When we had run together in Meiji Park, a few days before the Games, he was highly impressive. I've never seen a better middle-distance runner, so graceful. I wanted to stop to watch him.'

'I hadn't competed seriously since April. The Games seemed like a long, dark tunnel.' He speaks softly, with a slightly stifled voice. Aged twenty-five, he has said his farewells to the Games. 'I won't be competing at the Mexico Olympics,' he says. 'This time next year, I may well have retired.' Like Herb Elliott, he is going to retire before reaching his maturity as a middle-distance runner. His only wish before retiring is to visit Europe and run a 1500m there. The distance isn't run in New Zealand: Snell ran the first 1500m of his life at the Olympic heats.

Third in the 1500m, John Davies raises the arm of his fellow New Zealander, Peter Snell.

1964
OLYMPIC ROUND-UP

BIKILA RISES THROUGH THE RANKS.

Once again, the slender figure of Abebe Bikila (photo 12) delighted us by the purity of his style and the remarkable radiance which this thoroughbred emanates, which brings to mind the radiance of the shepherds in the Bible. He is four years older now than in Rome, approaching thirty-two. He is still a member of the Emperor's guard, although he is a sergeant now, (he was a corporal four years ago), he is the same weight, fifty-six kilos, but runs even faster. He won in 2:15:16.2 in 1960. This time he achieved 2:12:11.2 to become the first marathon runner to keep his title.

'I did not lose my head at the Australian Ron Clarke's express train lead at the beginning. I knew my pace and I ran at top speed. I knew that I would make a comeback. When you asked me if I was better here than in Rome, I would reply yes, because I had more experience and greater self-assurance. I was sure to win this marathon in Tokyo, one hundred per cent. There was only one opponent I was dreading, and that was the Moroccan, Rhadi, who had made life difficult for me in Rome. But when I realised that he wasn't in the race, I was relaxed.'

He feared for a moment that he would not be able to run this marathon. 'I was operated on for appendicitis on 16 September,' he told us. 'Fortunately, I was allowed to resume training only eleven days later. It went better than I was expecting.'

The Ethiopian Abebe Bikila has decided not to bring his career to an end, thanks to his success here at Tokyo: 'I hope you will see me again in Mexico,' he said. 'The altitude suits me perfectly. I am used to it. And I think that Ethiopian sport will distinguish itself at the Mexico Games.'

One final detail: Bikila no longer runs barefoot. Ask him where he had his shoes made for the marathon, and he replies simply: 'I bought them at the Olympic Village. They are ordinary training shoes.'

1 The closing stages of the 10,000m: Australia's Ron Clarke is about to be passed by the American Bill Mills (722) and the Tunisian Mohamed Gammoudi, still third.

2 Wyomia Tyus (USA) wins the 100m in 11.4. beating her team-mate Edith McGuire and Ewa Klobukowska (POL), still a junior, by 0.2.

3 In the road race, Mario Zamin (ITA) wins the final sprint ahead of Rodian (DEN) and Godefroot (BEL).

4 In the 4x100m freestyle, 4x200 freestyle and 4x100m backstroke, the Americans, with Clark, Ilman and Schollander, are untouchable.

5 Borys Shakhlin (SOV/UKR), already triumphant in Melbourne and Rome, wins his final Olympic gold medal on the horizontal bar.

6 In the rain, the Welsh long jumper Lynn Davies achieves a leap of 8.07m and takes victory over the favourites Boston (USA) and Ter-Ovanesyan (SOV/RUS).

7 In female gymnastics, Vera Caslavska (CZE) puts an end to the supremacy of the Soviets.

8 In the light-heavyweight division, Italy's Cosimo Pinto (left) on his way to victory over Aleksei Kiselyov (SOV/RUS).

9 In the free rifle, Gary Lee Anderson, an American theology student, wins in a world record score.

10 In Greco-Roman wrestling, the Japanese bantamweight Ichiguchi (right) transforms Trostyansky (SOV/UKR) into a spinning top.

11 India regains the hockey title it had lost to Pakistan in 1960.

12 Recovering from appendicitis, the Ethiopian Abebe Bikila retains his title in the marathon wearing shoes this time.

13 In the deciding match of the water polo tournament, Hungary and Yugoslavia (pictured) cannot be separated (4-4). The results gives the Hungarians their fifth gold medal.

14 With a record throw of 69.74m, the hammer thrower Romuald Klim (SOV/BUL) inherits the title taken by Rudenkov (SOV/BUL) in Rome.

15 The Olympic sabre title, dominated by Hungarians since 1908. goes to another: Tibor Pezsa.

Deserved triumph for Valery Brumel

Despite difficulties adjusting to Japan, the world-record holder has not let his chance slip by.

Beaten on failed jumps in Rome (2.16m), Brumel takes his revenge, winning in the same way over John Thomas (2.18m).

Valery Brumel (SOV/UKR) got it all right, although John Thomas, the favourite four years ago, nearly defeated Brumel, the favourite here.

In Rome, Thomas, a twenty-year-old prodigy whose rivals surrendered in advance as they watched him train, had been disadvantaged by lack of experience at international level. The first man to clear 2.20m, Thomas was unused to being challenged. Yet he was beaten, and well beaten, by a trio of extraordinary Soviets, the products of sports schools spread out across the immense territory of the USSR. These classic high-jumpers, who peaked perfectly for the 1960 Olympics, identified their key competitor, and triumphed over him. Robert Shavlakadze took gold, jumping 2.16m and beating Valery Brumel, who had more failed attempts. Thomas

finished third.

This time, Brumel, the world-record holder with 2.28m, went one better. But he nearly suffered John Thomas's Olympic fate. The Games

The roll seems to have been invented for Brumel, who executes it to perfection.

are terrifying rigid in that they demand the optimal expression of an athlete's abilities at one moment, on one day, every four years. This explains how an athlete can achieve

the greatest performance of all time during his career, without ever climbing onto the central platform of an Olympic podium. Brumel admitted: 'I'm not in top form. I peaked too early. I didn't feel comfortable in the village. It took me a long time to adjust. I even found qualifying hard.'

Although a magnificent technician, Brumel failed his first two attempts at 2.03m, a height normally well within him. He cleared it at the last attempt.

'Then my form returned and I jumped better. I knew my strongest rival would be John Thomas. I'm not comfortable in long competitions. Clearing 2.14m was draining. Afterwards, my concentration came back, and got me over 2.18m. There was nothing in it*, but in the Games, all that matters is victory.'

*Brumel and Thomas both cleared 2.18m and were separated only on the number of failed jumps.

TOKYO XVIII OLYMPIAD

The Games were held in Asia for the first time ever. Asia was the fourth
continent to host the Olympics, following Europe, America and Oceania,
and Tokyo pulled out all the stops to make them a success.

THE GAMES IN BRIEF

Opening Date
10 October 1964

Closing Date
24 October 1964

Host Nation
Japan (JAP)

Candidate Towns
Detroit (USA), Vienna (AUT) and Brussels
(BEL).

94 Nations Represented

5,140 Athletes
(683 women, 4,457 men)

19 Sports
(7 open to women)
Track and field, rowing, basketball,
boxing, canoeing, cycling, fencing,
equestrian, football, gymnastics,
weightlifting, field hockey, judo, wrestling,
swimming, modern pentathlon, volleyball,
shooting and sailing.

Demonstration Sports
None

163 Events
(33 open to women)

Games officially opened by
Emperor Hirohito

Olympic flame lit by
Yoshinori Sakai (born in Hiroshima
6 August 1945).

Olympic oath read by
Takashi Ono (gymnastics).

IOC President
Avery Brundage (USA)

DID YOU KNOW?

The Tokyo Games were the first to be held
in Asia. The most touching symbol of the
Games was the final torchbearer, Yoshinori
Sakai; born in Hiroshima on the day the
atomic bomb exploded over the city, he
was chosen in honour of the victims.
Two new sports, judo and volleyball (both
men's and women's), were introduced
in Tokyo.
    In another first, competitors in the pole
vault used fibreglass poles.
    Tokyo was the last Games in which
athletics events were run on a cinder
track.
    The first 'fair play' prize was awarded by
the IOC. It was given to the Kall brothers
of Sweden who, during a regatta, gave up
their chance of victory to help two fellow
competitors who had capsized.

1968

Mexico

THE WORLD IS IN REBELLION. IN CHINA, THE Cultural Revolution is at its height. In the United States, activists are demanding an end to the intervention in Vietnam, and the Black community campaigns for civil rights. Student demonstrations paralyse France, Germany and Brazil. Czechoslovakia sees the Prague Spring crushed by the Soviet Union. Then, in Mexico, just ten days before the opening of the Games, government troops open fire on students, leaving more than 250 lying dead in Mexico City's celebrated Plaza of the Three Cultures.

The prospect of holding the Games at an altitude of 7,000 feet struck fear into the hearts of doctors, trainers and athletes alike. Other environmental factors characterised the Games: the track – synthetic – and the wind, which remained strangely constant at 2m/sec during the major finals. Other innovations combined to incite another revolution: in athletics, every record is broken up to 400m, including the relays. Africans monopolised the distance events from 1500m to the marathon. Dick Fosbury re-invented the high jump and Bob Beamon achieved the feat of the century with his giant long jump of 8.90m. Never have the Games been so affected by their setting. These exploits, and the emotion they aroused, made Mexico a global stage, on which Black Americans made peaceful protests, just six months after the assassination of Martin Luther King. Tommie Smith and John Carlos handed out badges marked 'Olympic projects for human rights' and raised black-gloved fists on the podium.

US team members Freeman (left), James (middle), and Evans (right, looking at the camera) explain their behaviour on the podium after the 400m to journalists. Freeman and Evans express their solidarity with the 'Black Power' movement.

Tommie Smith and John Carlos: 'We do not represent the United States'

After the 200m, two Black American athletes, took advantage of the Olympic stage to express anger at the 'victimisation' of their community.

Tommie Smith is elated at taking Olympic gold and setting a world 200m record – both with consummate ease. But the celebrations soon turn to controversy.

Several days ago, we reported that the Black American athletes were fraternising closely with the Black Africans. That day, the sprinter Melvin Pender told us: 'Something is going to happen during these Games.' That something happened as the battle for the pole-vault was reaching its climax. Tommie Smith and John Carlos mounted the podium to receive their 200m medals. Both wore the famous button bearing the slogan 'Olympic

RESULTS

200m

1 Tommie Smith (USA), 19.83
2 Peter Norman (AUS), 20.06
3 John Carlos (USA), 20.10
4 Edwin Roberts (TRI), 20.34
5 Roger Bambuck (FRA), 20.51
6 Larry Questad (USA), 20.62
7 Michael Fray (USA), 20.63
8 Joachim Eigenherr (GER), 20.66

Tommie Smith, the placid winner of the 200m, decodes the elements of his protest before the world's press.

projects for human rights,' a black glove, a black silk scarf and leotard under open jackets, black socks and no shoes. In their gloveless hand, they carried a running shoe that they placed on the podium before receiving their medals. During the US national anthem they raised their gloved fists to the sky and looked down instead of up at the US flag. Later, they told us: 'We are protesting against the shameful conditions black people endure in the USA and elsewhere. The United States are not united, because not all citizens are treated in the same manner. We do not represent the United States, but the Black population of the United States. We want to be close to all the Blacks worldwide. If, between now and Munich, certain problems are not dealt with, there will be a boycott by Black athletes.'

These words were not spoken in the heat of the moment. The two men were calm and composed. We asked them the significance of the running shoe they held in their hand.

'That's a different issue,' says Carlos. 'We were protesting because some of the records set during the Olympic trials in Lake Tahoe, Nevada, were not ratified because of the type of spike.'

In the press conference, they added: 'We have won medals and applause, but the Whites think that we Blacks are unthinking animals. When we do what they want, the Whites treat us as good boys. They think of us as circus horses. We are tired of it. We want to say to all the Whites: 'Take an interest in the injustice in the world, take an interest in the problems; or ignore them, but don't come to watch us run.'

They are probably wrong to protest about issues of such different orders. The shoes protest looks like a commercial matter, and pales into insignificance beside the civil rights struggle. Smith and Carlos were asked why their team mates Hines and Greene hadn't made the same protest. They replied that everyone was free to act in his own way, and that there were many ways of fighting the Black cause.

Crisis in the American Camp following the expulsion of Smith and Carlos

The Americans are at each other's throats following the Mexican Olympic Committee's decision to expel Tommie Smith and John Carlos, first and third respectively in the 200m, from the Olympic Village.

As we know, the two athletes appeared on the podium in black socks and a black glove brandishing a running shoe (the brand with which they had broken the records made unofficial by the International Federation). They lowered their heads while the national anthems were played and the flags rose. Following this they declared that they didn't feel united with their country but only with other Black Americans.

A press release was prepared. The two athletes were reprimanded and excuses were made to the International Olympic Committee, the Mexican Olympic Committee and the Mexican people. Smith and Carlos received a warning but there was no question of suspending them.

This press release had already been circulated when the order was given for its withdrawal. The IOC were not happy with the punishment. The American Olympic Committee decided, therefore, to suspend Smith and Carlos until a final decision was reached and asked them to leave the Olympic Village with the least fuss possible.

A deep sense of unease hung over the Olympic Village. Evans, finalist in the 400m, was seen staggering towards us and Green tore the letters USA from his tracksuit. But even the other Black members of the team were divided. About a dozen athletes, approximately one third, were considered fierce supporters of the protest. The others were opposed to any untimely demonstration, or else totally indifferent (like Hines and Davenport). The retired Olympic champion, Jesse Owens, president of the Committee of Retired American Olympic Champions, seemed very worried and conferred with the athletes and the leaders. Smith and Carlos took responsibility for their actions and agreed that they had achieved their aim no matter what happened in the future.

The medal ceremony, and Tommie Smith and John Carlos wait for the first note of the American anthem to lift their gloved fists and stare at the ground – something never witnessed before. It was seen as the only means for them to protest against the conditions imposed on Black people in the United States. Their punishment was unmerciful and immediate: suspension and expulsion from the Olympic Village.

Beamon out of this world!

By pulling off 8.90m in the long jump, the American has achieved a jump from another time. And it is, without doubt, the achievement of the century.

Flying high – Beamon's huge jump lands him a rightful place in history.

At the end of a hard training session, the joint-world record holder in the long jump, Igor Ter-Ovanesyan (SOV/RUS), told me: 'Human limits don't exist. Technique is always evolving. If man was able to conquer space, I don't see why someone shouldn't soon jump beyond 8.50m or 8.60m.' Ter-Ovanesyan had no idea just how right he was.

As the sky rolled overhead with heavy, thunderous clouds and the horizon passed vibrantly from blue to burgundy to purple, his words too took on an ominous hue. We were about to witness a long jump of such proportions that it might just qualify as space travel.

As the storm held back its downpour for a few moments, Bob Beamon perfected his run-up and hit the take-off board with the precision of a laser-guided missile. His take-off, the result of the perfect coincidence of power and speed, propelled him high into the air, and he performed an astonishing scissor movement with his unfeasibly long legs. Leaning over his lower limbs, Beamon remained suspended between the sky and the earth, rocket-like, for longer than seemed possible. He delayed his landing like a ski-jumper, and finally came down well beyond the range of the optical measuring device. Several verifications were necessary before Beamon, who had bounced twice after his terrific jump, performed a wild jig and finished up in the arms of fellow American Boston.

A shriek went up in the stand as the most fantastic result of these Games, and perhaps in athletics history, was displayed in fiery letters: 8.90m! Was there some mistake? No: with a legal tailwind of 2m/sec, Beamon had broken the world record by 55cm. Two records have fallen in similar conditions here: the triple jump (17.39m) and the women's 200m (22.5 seconds).

RESULTS

Long jump

1 Robert 'Bob' Beamon (USA), 8.90m
2 Klaus Beer (GDR), 8.19
3 Ralph Boston (USA), 8.16m
4 Igor Ter-Ovanesyan (SOV/RUS), 8.12m
5 Tõnu Lepik (SOV/EST), 8.09m
6 Allen Crawley (AUS), 8.02m
7 Jacques Pani (FRA), 7.97m
8 Andrzej Stelmach (POL), 7.94m

BOB BEAMON

Born 29 August 1946 in Jamaica (New York State).1.89m, 72 kg.

Debuts in 1961. At fifteen he has already cleared 7.33m in the long jump. He was also a triple jumper and achieved 14.12m in 1962.

His jump progress: 1962, 7.33m; 1963, 7.31m; 1964, 7.33m; 1965, 7.69m; 1966, 7.82m; 1967, 8.13m; 1968, 8.33m then 8.90m.

Beamon had already cleared 8.41m with a favourable wind. He had also been credited with 9.5 seconds for 100 yards. He is also an excellent college basketball player with ambitions to play in the NBA. He is a student at the University of Texas in El Paso.

Beamon: Is it a dream?

At first uncomprehending, Bob Beamon is then paralysed by the realisation of what he's done.

It is perhaps the most extraordinary moment in world athletics for a decade. We are at the foot of the stand level with the jumping pit, no more than six feet from the competitors, beside the French national coach Robert Bobin and long jump coach André Daniel. Beamon, long, supple and sinewy, sets off for his next jump. Daniel comments on his technique: 'Excellent run-up. Nice rhythm. Very good! Very good! What a take-off... oh my God! I have never seen anything like that in all my life!' He is astounded. 'Who was it who said that this young man didn't know how to jump? He has nothing to learn.' The board showed 8.90. We have just seen a jump of 8.90m, two metres away from us! Bursting with joy, Beamon suddenly lies down, gets up,

RESULTS

The first three in the Long Jump:
Beamon: 8.90m/8.04m
 (he stops after two attempts)
Beer: 7.90m/.8.19m/0/7.61m/0/0.
Boston: 8.16m/8.05m/7.91m/0/0/7.97m.

Former world record holder, Boston (USA), and Klaus Beer (GDR), regarded as a fine jumper, are relegated to the ranks of mere mortals at the feet of the astonishing Beamon.

Rain beats down on the stadium. Bob Beamon tries to rouse his spirits, but to no effect.

lies down again, rises to his knees and places his head between his hands. And then he cries. He is gripped by nausea. He raises his arms to the sky. His team-mate Boston takes him in his arms and tries to calm him. I hear him say: 'Hey man! It is impossible.'

The other competitors are struck mute in astonishment. Davies is pale; Ter-Ovanesyan's face is stone. Pani looks stunned. Daniel murmurs. 'This is absolutely incredible! The others are crushed.'

Then the rain begins to fall.

Beamon sits down beside us.

'I think I'm going to throw up. Tell me I'm not dreaming! Did I really do that? Do you think it will be beaten today?'

We tell him it will not be beaten for years to come.

Lee Evans' double victory

The American's record-breaking victory in the 400m demonstrates his athletic ability.

'Larry James ran perfectly over 395m', explained Evans. 'But I ran my race over 401m, which made all the difference.' Or rather, a lead of eleven hundredths of a second at the finishing line.

Lee Evans' victory was remarkable securing him an Olympic gold medal and a place in history on the hardest day he had ever endured.

When he left the Olympic Village in the morning, his eyes were still swollen with tears. Tommie Smith and John Carlos, expelled from the Olympic Village after their 'Black Power' protest, were his best friends, team-mates and comrades in a struggle that extended beyond the boundaries of both the stadium and San José State University, birthplace of the movement to defend civil rights at the Olympics. Evans, for his part, kept his civil rights badge pinned to his chest at all times.

He had spent most of the morning regaining his composure, assisted no doubt by the relaxation techniques of which he is a great fan, and by his strength of character. He knew he needed to win to prove himself and let the gold medal stand for 'the black

people in the United States and all over the world' – though he later added that he was also thinking of his white friends, both at University and in Europe.

He commented: 'For me, sport represented a means to win a scholarship and study at university, since I was not particularly privileged

in other respects. This is a personal opinion, but I believe this is one of the reasons why Black American athletes excel at sport.'

'In the race itself', he said with a wide grin, 'everything went as I hoped. I wasn't aiming for a world record, but I was convinced that to win, I would

need to run the distance in under 44 seconds on the day of the final. I was stronger in Mexico than I had been at South Lake Tahoe. So my time in the final didn't come as any surprise to me. I ran under 44 seconds at the US qualifying heats, but the spikes I wore in South Lake Tahoe meant that my victory was not officially recognised*. This is a double victory for me.'

* Lee Evans had beaten the world record, but was judged to be wearing non-regulation footwear.

After the race they had considered boycotting, James, Evans and Freeman (left to right) show their support for Tommie Smith.

RESULTS

400m

1 Lee Evans (USA) 43.86
2 G. Lawrence 'Larry' James (USA) 43.97
3 Ronald Freeman (USA) 44.41
4 Amadou Gakou (SEN) 45.01
5 Martin Jellinghaus (GER) 45.33
6 Tegegne Bezabeh (ETH) 45.42
7 Andrzej Badenski (POL) 45.42
8 Amos Omolo (UGA) 47.61

Al Oerter victorious on four continents

The American achieves an unprecedented four consecutive Olympic victories in Melbourne, Rome, Tokyo and now Mexico.

At the age of thirty-two, the American is still capable of beating his personal record, as his winning discus performance in Mexico proves. Milde (GDR) and Danek (CZE) take silver and bronze.

Al Oerter took off the towel that had been draped around his neck like a cape, having long ago dispensed with his rain-drenched tracksuit. With his bulging chest and blond locks plastered to his forehead, the incomparable Oerter resembled a gladiator. By the second round, the spectators could scarcely believe their eyes as they saw Oerter and Silvester's efforts fall short of the throws made by the Germans Milde and Losch. It appeared that the two Americans would have to battle it out for the bronze medal.

The discus throwers battled against the elements for over half an hour. Oerter nursed his own discus in a white cloth like a new-born child. Finally, the twelve competitors gave up

Milde (left) and Danek are powerless to prevent Al Oerter collecting his fourth consecutive gold medal.

and headed for the shelter of the stands, as the storm grew increasingly violent.

When the contest resumed, Oerter stepped confidently into the circle. He paced up and down several times, visualising a throw that would reach beyond the little flag that marked his Olympic record, to within reach of Silvester's fantastic world record.

He began to spin around in the circle. The discus flew out of his hand and hovered for what seemed an age in the black skies of Mexico City. When Oerter's throw of 64.78m was displayed, Silvester glanced at the scoreboard – and did a double take.

Oerter didn't even smile. As far as he was concerned, the battle was not over yet. Silvester, demoralised, made three foul throws. Oerter, meanwhile, unleashed three further throws beyond the 64m mark.

The four-times Olympic champion explained: 'I got off to a bad start – it was cold and I was nervous when I saw that my throws were not travelling well. But I managed to stay focused, and I knew I was going to win. I enjoy competing in these conditions!'

ALFRED 'AL' OERTER

Born 19 September 1936, Astoria, USA. Height: 6 ft 3. Weight: 277 pounds. University of Kansas. Electronic engineer at NYC aeronautical company.

Performance: 1955, 52.77m; 1956, 56.36m; 1957, 56.48m; 1958, 57.35m; 1959, 58.12m; 1960, 59.18m; 1961, 58.05m; 1962, 62.44m; 1963, 62.62m; 1964, 62.18m; 1965, did not compete; 1966, 63.22m; 1967, 62.03m; 1968, 64.78m.

ATHLETICS

Fosbury revolutionises the high jump

Four years after Brumel's belly-roll, Dick Fosbury pioneers a new technique – to great success.

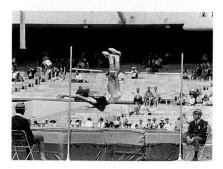

Fosbury stands, perfectly still, at a forty-five degree angle to the bar. He then carries out a bizarre series of movements to aid concentration, involving mysterious hand signals and a bending of his torso, almost to the point of losing balance.

He takes off, racing towards the bar at top speed in a wide arc. He reaches the bar and makes as if to perform a scissor jump. But as he launches himself into the air, he twists and flings his body backwards, passing over the bar in an almost horizontal position, before bringing his legs up towards his body as he lands on the other side.

This has been a remarkable international debut for Dick Fosbury. It was none the less strange to witness this new technique that departs so

abruptly from the Soviet 'belly-roll'.

Fosbury, unknown a year ago and with a personal outdoor best of 2.10m, cleared 2.18m, 2.20m, 2.22m, sailed over the American record of 2.24m, then attacked Brumel's world record of 2.28m. He missed, and Brumel's record remains intact, for now. But he has proved that it is sometimes worth challenging established practice.

Soviet coach Yuri Diatchkov's concern was written all over his face. The Soviet technique that he introduced had been adopted by the best trainers around the world. With his eye firmly riveted to his camera's viewfinder, Diatchkov has surely used more film than anyone else in the stadium. He has photographed all the athletes, both in training and competition, and especially Dick

Fosbury, with whom he is fascinated.

Last week, Diatchkov remarked: 'Fosbury's style is spectacular, but it is also very personal. I don't think that it will have much influence on the future of the high jump event.' Perhaps Fosbury's victory has made him change his mind.

When he returns to Moscow, Diatchkov will no doubt take a long, hard look at the Fosbury flop, which bears some resemblance to Lewden's scissor jump with an inwards turn, and the arched-back technique of Kotkas (FIN) and Weinkötz (GER) before the Second World War.

What will be the impact of this success, which has brought the US a title they last held in 1956? We can at least be sure of one thing: the Fosbury flop is bound to have its imitators.

Hines: King of the 100m

The Olympic 100m final pits eight black athletes against each other for the first time. The race lives up to expectations.

The stadium suddenly fell quiet. The eight finalists in the 100m had taken their positions and the reverent silence of the crowd heightened the magic of the moment. Eight athletes competing for one title. The semi-finals revealed no clear favourite, although they had been full of drama. The East German Heinz Erbstösser became the first sprinter in Olympic history to achieve a time of 10.2 and not qualify for the semi-finals. Then Charles Greene (USA), who had clocked 10.0 in his first two heats, collapsed on the grass after crossing the finishing line, clutching his thigh as if he had a muscular injury. In fact, he was having difficulty breathing – a bad sign for the bespectacled sprinter.

The two Cubans, Hermes Ramírez, who recorded 10.0 in the quarter-finals, and Enrique Figuerola, fourth in 1960 and second in 1964, were both eliminated. Melvin Pender, the fastest captain in the US Army, scraped into the final.

As the eight finalists lined up, all eyes were on Jim Hines (USA). The son of an Oakland construction worker, Hines had raised the world record to 9.9 in the semi-final of the US national championships Sacramento, California in June. It was the first accredited run under ten seconds, and followed a wind-assisted, and therefore illegal, run of 9.8 in qualifying. In the final at those championships, Hines was beaten by Greene, who consistently had the better of Hines until the Olympic trials, where Hines defeated Greene twice. In qualifying here at Mexico City, Hines too managed 10.0.

The Olympic final began with one false start. When, at last, the pistol cracked for the second time and the runners got away, it was the thirty-year-old Pender who took the early lead, before Hines and Greene drew level after 50m. At the 70m mark, Hines found another acceleration

and pulled away to win by a clear metre. Greene dropped off slightly, suffering cramp, and Lennox Miller (USA) beat him into second place.

Hines' time was officially given as 9.9 seconds. In fact, his real time was considerably faster than this. The electronic chronometer gave an

unofficial mark of 9.89 seconds. After taking into account the five hundredths of a second margin of error, this yields a more realistic time of 9.94 seconds. If Hines had been hand timed, his time would in all probability have been given as 9.8 seconds. This was hardly

surprising, given the altitude of seven thousand feet, and the new synthetic track. But this exploit, impressive though it may be, also brings to mind Bob Hayes. It seems this kind of champion only comes around every thirty years.

From the inside to the outside of the track: Greene (3rd), Montes (4th) and Hines (1st) – at the top of the picture with Greene – Miller (2nd), Pender (6th), Bambuck (5th), Jerome (7th) and Ravelomanantsoa (8th).

Wenden sinks the Americans

The young Australian coasts to victory in the 100m freestyle, his time of 52.2 seconds setting a new world record.

Five days after his success in the 100m, Mike Wenden (above, in lane four) again takes gold in the 200m, depriving Don Schollander (lane six) of a sixth Olympic title.

Enveloped in a cloud of spray, his arms a blur of movement, his boundless energy and enthusiasm catapulted him towards the finish. It seemed as though nothing could stop this human torpedo. The accumulated exhaustion of his last 4x100m relay race, swum in 51.7 seconds; the semi-final, which he finished in 52.9; the trio of American

Wenden swims 10 kilometres a day in training.

swimmers who set out to shatter him – none seemed to affect Mike Wenden.

As one glanced over at the scoreboard, where the swimmers' electronic times were immediately displayed, one understood why Wenden had made such an impression – he had swum 100m in an astonishing 52.2 seconds! His time smashed the former world record by

four tenths of a second.

It was a superb race between pure sprinters, such as the great, athletic Zorn, and resistance sprinters such as Wenden and Spitz, who gave off a more confident air. Zorn was doubtless foolish in attempting to leave the other swimmers for dead, covering the first 50m in 24 seconds, which put him on course to finish in 51 seconds. Wenden was happy to reach the halfway mark in 24.6 seconds.

Walsh, a pure sprinter like Zorn, had turned heads in the qualifying heats and the semi-finals. He wisely set off at a slower pace in the final. But he finished strongly, and from his lonely position over lane one, took second place. Wenden's strength lay in his ability to combine a base speed almost as fast as that of Zorn or Walsh with a stamina that comes from his former days as a 400m swimmer.

Wenden came to the Games as an outsider: he leaves them with two gold medals and a world record.

RESULTS

100 m

1 Michael 'Mike' Wenden (AUS) 52.2
2 Kenneth Walsh (USA) 52.8
3 Mark Spitz (USA) 53.0
4 Robert McGregor (GBR) 53.5
5 Leonid Ilyichov (SOV/RUS) 53.8
6 Georgi Kulikov (SOV/LAT) 53.8
7 Luis Nicolao (ARG) 53.9
8 Zachary Zorn (USA) 53.9.

Debbie Meyer a cut above the rest

The other ladies tried in vain to keep up with the young American as she streaked to gold in the 200m, 400m and 800m freestyle.

At the US Olympic trials, under the tutelage of coach Shermann Shavoor, Debbie Meyer, 16, had set world records in the 200m, 400m and 800m. At the Games, unsurprisingly, she was irresistible. Her performance in the 800m was typical: after 100m, she was a length ahead. After 200m, two lengths; after 300m, three lengths, etc. Every medal has a hinterland of pain and joy. If there was one thing this sixteen-year-old lacked, it was emotion. Meyer collected her three gold medals unopposed, as if it were as simple as buying a souvenir. She smiled and politely raised her hand to collect her third medal, then turned to shake hands with her defeated rivals. No other athlete has shown such dominance at the Mexico Games.

The American's explosive performance in the pool meant she became the first swimmer to win three individual gold medals in one Olympics.

RESULTS

MEYER'S TRIPLE VICTORY

200m
1 Debbie Meyer (USA) 2:10.5
2 Jan Henne (USA) 2:11.0
3 Jane Barkman (USA) 2:11.2.

400m
1 Debbie Meyer (USA), 4:31.8
2 Linda Gustavson (USA) 4:35.5
3 Karen Moras (AUS) 4:37.0.

800m
1 Debbie Meyer (USA) 9:24.0
2 Pamela Kruse (USA) 9:35.7
3 Maria Teresa Ramirez (MEX) 9:38.5.

Czech gymnast follows gold medal with gold ring

Defending champion Vera Caslavska has taken gold again in Mexico, just a few days before marrying a fellow Czech athlete in the Olympic Village.

The Czechoslovakian took six individual medals in Mexico: silver in the balance beam; and gold in the asymmetric bars, the floor, the vault and the all-around competition.

Standing on the podium, a pale young blonde girl with enormous eyes waved discreetly at Josef Odlozil. She was dressed in a black leotard, perhaps chosen as a symbolic reminder of certain recent events in her homeland.

Vera Caslavska retained the Olympic title she had won at Tokyo with a huge margin of 1.40 points over second-placed Soviet gymnast Zinaida Voronina. This meant she received her latest gold medal just a few days before her fiancé will place a gold ring on her finger. The marriage took place the next Saturday, in the Olympic Village. Odlozil would have preferred to keep the wedding a secret, so as to ensure a simple, intimate ceremony, but because of the Czechoslovakian delegation's popularity, he told us that the ceremony would be open to the press.

Caslavska will compete again this evening in the four finals of the apparatus events, hoping to take at least two further titles. 'After that', she said with a charming smile, 'I will be able to focus on a family life. I am finished with high-level competitions. Mexico will be my last Olympics.'

The Czechoslovaks, driven by national pride, fully justified their successes at the World Championships in Dortmund two years earlier. They missed out on team victory by 0.65 of a point.

But individually, Caslavska was invincible. Her performance on the balance beam, for example, sent a shiver through the crowd. When the judges awarded her only a 9.60, the audience was in uproar for five minutes until the appeal jury intervened to increase the mark to 9.80.

On the floor, Caslavska was exceptional – more athletic than the Soviets, and more acrobatic, too. She also had the wonderful idea of dancing (for her moves were dance-like) to the tune of 'The Mexican Hat Dance'. It is not hard to imagine the raucous reception that Caslavska received from the thrilled audience for this performance, and she earned a well-deserved 9.95.

From then on, she was unstoppable in her quest for victory. On the side horse vault, she took another 9.85. On the asymmetrical bars, she took risks and very nearly made a mistake that would have cost her everything, but ended up scoring a near-perfect 9.90. She had won.

The groom is an athlete, his bride a gymnast. They are now man and wife

ALL-AROUND COMPETITION

1 Vera Caslavska (CZE)
2 Zinaida Voronina (SOV/RUS)
3 Natalia Kuchinskaya (SOV/RUS)
4 Larissa Petrik (SOV/BLR)
5 Erika Zuchold (GDR)
6 Karin Janz (GDR)
7 Olga Karasyova (SOV/RUS)
8 Bohumila Rimnacova (CZE)

Zhabotynsky still the strongest man in the world

The Soviet's three-lift total of 572.5kg is more than enough to secure him victory.

In the absence of US heavyweight champion Robert Bednarski, Leonid Zhabotynsky comfortably won the super heavyweight contest. The challenge of Joseph Dube (USA), strikingly similar to Orson Welles, faded after the bench press.

Zhabotynsky was never really put to the test. After the snatch, the gold medal was within his grasp, even though he was some way behind his personal record of 572.5kg total lift.

After the press, Zhabotynsky and Dube were neck and neck, having both lifted 200kg. The Belgian Serge Reding, a bulging-chested librarian from Brussels, was close behind with a 195kg lift. Jean-Paul Fouletier had managed a respectable 167.5kg at the second attempt, but failed to lift 175kg. He injured his right wrist and needed a pain-relieving injection to continue with the remaining lifts. Unfortunately, this brought him no relief. Surprisingly, George Pickett (USA) failed to lift 190kg in his three attempts at the press.

In the snatch, Dube could only lift 145kg. Zhabotynsky, waiting in the wings of the Teatro Insurgents, where the event was being held, had gauged his opponent's limits. He lifted 170kg at the second attempt, and went into the jerk with a lead of 25kg.

A bitter duel was then fought out between Dube and Reding for the silver medal. Reding trailed by just 2.5kg after the snatch. Dube raised first 195kg, then 202.5kg, then 207.5kg. Reding, the last man up, needed to lift only 212.5kg. Reding kept his calm, lifted the 212.5kg and took the silver medal.

THREE-LIFT TOTALS

1 Leonid Zhabotynsky
   (SOV/UKR) 572.5kg
2 Serge Reding (BEL) 555.0kg
3 Joseph Dube (USA) 532.5kg
4 Manfred Rieger (GDR) 532.5kg
5 Rudolf Mang (GER) 525.0kg
6 Mauno Lindroos (FIN), 495.0kg
7 Kelevi Lahdenranta (FIN) 492.5kg
8 Donald Oliver (NZL) 490.0kg

Zhabotynsky impressed the crowd by holding the red flag in one hand throughout the Opening Ceremony. But the Ukrainian giant is even more impressive lifting the bar.

1968
OLYMPIC ROUND-UP

KEINO EXACTS A CRUEL REVENGE.

The 1500m brought together Jim Ryun, of the United States, hungry for victory in the only distance in which he had qualified, and the Kenyan Kipchoge Keino, looking for victory after two failed attempts in the 5,000m and 10,000m. One can imagine the mental states of these two men – Ryun, waiting for the Kenyan to attack after trying to intimidate him in the qualifying heats the night before; Keino, firmly resolved on humiliating the defending American champion who had beaten him a year earlier in Los Angeles. Once more, we were confronted with the troubling issue of Mexico's high altitude; and once more, we would see how wrong Keino had been not to put up a stronger fight in the 5,000m.

There are (we are led to understand) limits that athletes who train at sea level cannot surpass. Thus we could never have imagined Tunisian athlete Mohammed Gammoudi capable of running the 5,000m in thirteen minutes, fifty seconds in the rarefied air of Mexico City, nor much less of finishing as he did. And Keino could reasonably have assumed that Jim Ryun's high-altitude best would be 3:38.0, slower than his world record of 3:33.1. But he had already underestimated the devastating speed of the Tunisian Gammoudi, to his cost. The American's pace must now be neutralised at any price. This thinking led the Kenyan to change his tactics substantially from those he had used in the 5,000m.

Keino found in fellow Kenyan Ben Jipcho a loyal helper, who paces Keino. The first 1500m were run at an almost unprecedented pace: the first 400m in fifty-six seconds, the first 800m in 1:53.3. Jim Ryun was exactly four seconds behind – an enormous margin that could only have been reduced if Keino had tired. But the Kenyan had been wildly underestimated at this distance. He was generally believed capable of finishing in 3:38, or even 3:37. In fact, he crossed the line in 3:34.9, the second fastest time ever, after passing the 1200-metre mark in 2:53.4.

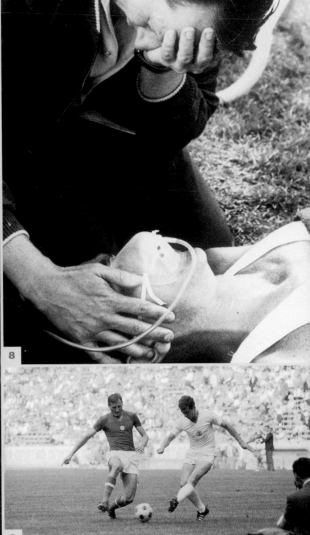

1. Sawao Kato, of Japan, sweeps to gold in both the individual all-around championship and the men's team competition.
2. Soviet 20,000m walker Volodymyr Holubnychy, a gold medalist in 1960 and bronze medalist in 1964, claims another gold medal in Mexico.
3. These four Norwegian canoeists (from left to right: Amundsen, Berger, Söby and Johansen) paddle to a shock Olympic victory in the kayak fours 1000m.
4. The pole vault has been won by a US athlete every year since the event was introduced in 1896. Bob Seagren continues the tradition with a vault of 5.40m.
5. Kipchoge Keino, of Kenya, who delivers a new Olympic record in the 1500m.
6. In the 5,000m, the gold medal is won by Tunisian athlete Mohammed Gammoudi, pictured here pulling away from Ron Clarke, of Australia.
7. In the individual horse-jumping championship, Bill Steinkraus (USA, pictured here) takes gold. Britons Marion Coakes and David Broome settle for silver and bronze.
8. The rarefied air in Mexico means several athletes need oxygen after a prolonged effort. Pictured here is Australian distance-runner Ron Clarke.
9. The Hungarians (pictured, on the left) defend their Olympic title in 1968, beating Bulgaria 4-1.
10. Wyomia Tyus, of the United States, retains her 100m title. Standing behind her to claim bronze is Polish sprinter Irena Szewinska Kirszenstein, winner of the 200m.
11. Despite the efforts of the Yugoslavs, no surprises in the basketball tournament, won by the USA (in white), victors every year since the event was introduced in Berlin in 1936.

George Foreman is American flag-bearer

Without fully understanding the attitude of his fellow black American athletes John Carlos and Tommie Smith, this young American boxer tries to demonstrate solidarity for the 'Black Power' movement – without forgetting to show that he is also competing as a US athlete.

His thoughts with the two expelled black American runners and a U.S. flag in his hand, Foreman shows no overwhelming joy at his boxing victory.

Though he did not know Tommie Smith and John Carlos personally, and confessed he did not understand their fisted salute during the 200m medal ceremony, George Foreman (USA), 19, regarded their exclusion from the Olympic Village an injustice and announced that he would withdraw from the final of the heavyweight boxing tournament in solidarity with them. Members of the American delegation convinced him to think again, including Barney Oldfield of Litton Industries, the sponsors of the programme for troubled adolescents that helped Foreman get back on track. He entered the ring on 27 October 1968, and after demolishing his rival, Ionas Chepulis (SOV/LIT), he held aloft a little American flag during the victory ceremony.

Foreman explained: 'He convinced me by taking me to see a Litton computer components factory just outside Mexico City. It was the first time the workers had ever met a "celebrity". Their enthusiasm made me understand how people see Olympic athletes. Their reaction also helped me understand that this was what I had been striving to achieve throughout my adolescence.'

Foreman had already vanquished the Italian left-hander Giorgio Bambini, and with no desire to disappoint his entourage – in particular his mother – or alienate the American Boxing Federation, he decided to contest the final. Before leaving the dressing room, the Texan heavyweight placed in the pocket of his gown a rosary given to him by a friend, and a small American flag offered by one of the US coaches.

In the ring, Foreman followed orders and used his left jab relentlessly to defend himself against the Soviet's attacks. 'I was so afraid of being hit', admitted the new Olympic champion, 'that each time he threw a punch, I closed my eyes. Luckily, my left jab proved sturdy and stopped him from getting too close – though it did prevent me from using my right jab.'

With the confidence his left jab had given him, Foreman went on the offensive. His jolting right crosses demolished Cepulis and the referee stopped the fight in the second round. When his trainer removed his gloves, Foreman took out his little American flag from his pocket and paraded around the ring, holding it aloft. 'To show good sportsmanship, a boxer should salute the judges and spectators from the four corners of the ring,' he explained. 'My waving the flag wasn't meant as a patriotic gesture or to take the opposite side from Tommie Smith and John Carlos. Since arriving at the Olympic Village, I have greeted the boxers I have come across in training, but instead of replying in English, they talk to me in a language I don't understand. I understood that it is your flag and your team colours that identify you.'

Born in Houston as one of seven children, he was brought up by his mother. His father, a railway worker, was often absent, either working or drinking away his salary.

As a teenager, Foreman was a petty thief, accosting passers-by to steal their wallets. But at the age of fifteen, he realised the error of his ways and gave up pickpocketing, although he continued to street-fight. He dropped out of junior high school and after a stint as a pot-washer in a restaurant, he was given a job in a furniture warehouse. After his idle attitude led to his dismissal, he joined the Job Corps, a programme for troubled adolescents. After six months spent in a conservation centre in Oregon, he requested a transfer to Pleasanton, California, an area renowned for its sports facilities, in particular its boxing ring. His friends had suggested that he should take his fights inside the ring. He began to focus on training, while continuing to study and learn different trades, including carpentry. After several fights, including a defeat in the Golden Gloves tournament, he dreamed of turning professional, but his coach convinced him to try out for the Olympic team first. The Army never called him up, and he was instead able to focus all his efforts on qualifying for Mexico.

RESULTS

Heavyweight final
George Foreman (USA) beat
Ionas Chepulis (SOV/LIT). Match
stopped by the referee in the
second round.

Classification:
1 George Foreman (USA)
2 Ionas Chepulis (SOV/LIT)
3 Giorgio Bambini (ITA)
   and Joaquin Rocha (MEX)

1968

MEXICO XIX OLYMPIAD

The world was in the grip of revolution and the Olympics were no exception, as the combination of the altitude and the new synthetic track produced 'historic' new records. Black American competitors caused a sensation both in the arena and out.

THE GAMES IN BRIEF

Opening Date
12 October 1968

Closing Date
27 October 1968

Host Nation
Mexico (MEX)

Candidate Towns
Detroit (USA), Lyon (FRA) and Buenos Aires (ARG)

113 Nations Represented

5,531 Athletes
(781 women, 4,750 men)

18 Sports
(7 open to women)
Track and field, football, modern pentathlon, sailing, gymnastics, swimming, fencing, rowing, basketball, shooting, wrestling, volleyball, cycling, weightlifting, field hockey, boxing, canoeing and equestrian.

Demonstration Sports
Pelote basque

172 Events
(39 open to women)

Games officially opened by
Diaz, President of Mexico

Olympic flame lit by
Enriqueta Basilio de Sotel (athletics)

Olympic oath read by
Pablo Garrido (athletics)

IOC President
Avery Brundage (USA)

DID YOU KNOW?

At 2,240m, the Olympic Games had never been held at such high altitude.

The German Democratic Republic's team competed under the name of East Germany.

Winners had to undergo drugs testing for the first time ever, and the Games had its first drugs disqualification when a Swedish entrant in the modern pentathlon, Hans-Gunnar Liljenwall, tested positive for excessive alcohol.

In athletics, cycling, rowing, canoeing, swimming and equestrian sports, official timings were taken both manually and electronically, although the electronic readings were considered to be the true times.

1972

Munich

THESE GAMES WERE TO BE THE GREATEST ever; Germany was determined to erase the shadow cast by the Berlin Games. Yet the nightmare that unfolded on the night of Tuesday 5 September made the Munich Olympics synonymous with fear. Masked Palestinian gunmen forced their way into the building in the Olympic Village housing the Israeli delegation, taking athletes and officials hostage and murdering two in cold blood.

For the first time in the history of the Olympics, the Olympic truce had been violated. The tragedy culminated in a shootout at the airport, where the Palestinians had planned to escape with their hostages. Nine more Israelis, five Palestinians and a police officer perished. By comparison, Mark Spitz's seven gold medals seemed meaningless and so too did the performances of two remarkable sixteen-year-olds, high jumper Ulrike Meyfarth and gymnast Olga Korbut. The 640kg lifted by the indomitable Soviet weightlifter Vassily Alekseyev, the cap worn by the exuberant David Wottle in the 800m, and the laughter of the magical Ugandan Akii Bua, 400m hurdle gold-medallist, could do nothing to relieve the sense of shock.

In the words of IOC President Avery Brundage, 'Peace must prevail over violence.' So the Games went on. East Germany and the USSR pushed the Americans to the limit and the Finns challenged the dominance of their African counterparts. Yet sport paled into insignificance in the face of tragedy, described as a 'tragedy in paradise' by 1956 Olympic discus champion Olga Connolly, an intimate witness to the terror. September 1972 was a black month indeed.

A face appears on the balcony of the Israeli residence in the Olympic Village. The face of horror.

TERRORISM

2.16am: 'It's gone badly wrong...'

On the morning of 5 September, gunmen belonging to the Palestinian faction Black September burst into the Israeli pavilion in the Olympic Village.

Never before had murder been committed in the Olympic Village. Palestinian terrorists stormed the Israeli apartment building at 31 Connoly Strasse, killing wrestling trainer Moshe Weinberger and weightlifter Yossef Romano. By the next morning, nine more had died.

7:41 am – News from Tel Aviv: the Israeli delegation has been attacked in their apartment by terrorists.

7:52 am – German police confirm Arab terrorists entered the Village between four and five in the morning.

8:20 am – An Israeli journalist gives the following account:

'The head of the delegation phoned me to tell me something had happened. At 6:30am I arrived at the Village and saw the body of Moshe Weinberger, gunned down on his bed. When another of the Israelis heard gunfire, he sounded the alarm but he was repeatedly shot. Three members of the team escaped in their night clothes. The rest were taken hostage.'

8:29 am – The terrorists threaten to fire again if police surrounding the compound do not withdraw.

9:14 am – The terrorists demand an aircraft to take them out of Germany.

9:19 am – The terrorists hand to an Olympic Games official a list of Palestinian detainees in Israel and threaten to kill the hostages if those named are not released before midday.

9:39 am – The Olympic Games resume with canoe-kayak heats.

On the top floor of the Olympic apartment where the Israeli delegation was based, an Israeli official held hostage is led onto the balcony by a fedayee.

10:39 am – Avery Brundage announces: 'The Games must go on.'

10:51am – The Palestinian organisation Black September claims responsibility for the attack.

11:39 am – Munich Chief of Police Shrelber announces that the Bavarian government is willing to pay unlimited sums for the release of Israeli hostages. They propose an exchange of Israeli for Bavarian hostages. The terrorists reject both proposals.

12:06 pm – The terrorists postpone their ultimatum from midday to 3pm.

12:58 pm – The sole Israeli yacht competing at the Games, Michaeli Yair and De Nir Ischah's Flying Dutchman, starts its final journey.

3:00 pm – German Chancellor Willy Brandt arrives in Munich.

3:02 pm – The second deadline is reached. There is silence in the Israeli compound.

3:35 pm – The terrorists extend their deadline to 5pm.

3:39 pm – The Egyptian basketball team refuse to play their match against the Philippines.

3:51pm – The Olympic Games are suspended until 10am the following day.

5:00 pm – German Minister for the Interior Genscher and Troeger, head of the Olympic Village, enter the Israeli building to resume negotiations.

5:45 pm – Genscher and Troeger leave, making no statement.

7:52 pm – The murder of Yossef Romano is made public. Injured in the morning's shootings, he was treated by the Israeli delegation's doctor, but could not be saved.

8:15 pm – Police officers take up position in a subway in the Village, apparently to open a possible escape route for a getaway car.

8:57 pm – The Palestinian with whom Genscher had been in negotiations emerges with Genscher and other German officials. Negotiations transfer to a section of the Village closed to journalists.

9:17 pm – Following negotiations at Police HQ, the leader of the Palestinian group returns to the Village and lines up the Israeli hostages on balcony.

9:21 pm – The terrorists prepare to leave for the airport with their hostages. Two helicopters land at 8:54pm and 9:15pm near besieged building.

9:27 pm – The IOC calls an emergency meeting for 10:00pm.

9:44 pm – A reliable source reveals that the German government may have been dealing directly with Egypt.

9:54 pm – A third helicopter lands outside the building.

10:10 pm – The terrorists leave Block 31 with hostages. A coach collects them.

10:15 pm – The coach drops them beside the three helicopters which fly them in the direction of the Fuerstenfeldbruck airport. Police enter Israeli quarters and discover the body of Yossef Romano as well as three Palestinians with serious knife wounds, proving Israelis defended themselves.

10:30 pm – An exchange of fire at the airport where the Boeing 727 was waiting for the terrorists and hostages. Contradictory rumours abound until a spokesperson for the German police explains: 'The hostages have managed to escape during the shoot out. Not all the terrorists fell into police hands, but the operation was still a success.' On hearing the news, the executive commission of the IOC decides that the Games should recommence at 10:30 on Wednesday morning, following the memorial service in honour of Mosche Weinberger and Yossef Romano. Sadly, as the minutes pass victory turns to sorrow as it emerges that the operation has, in fact, been disastrous.

2:16 am – Munich's Mayor Kronawitter confirms the news we have been dreading: 'All the hostages have been killed, four Palestinians have been shot dead and three others have escaped. A police officer has been killed and a helicopter pilot is seriously injured. What has happened is terrible; it has gone badly wrong.'

At the memorial ceremony, Israeli athletes are torn between feelings of sorrow and anger.

The situation evoked a strong sense of compassion but sadly the feeling was not unanimous.

Brundage: 'The Games must go on'

An emotional ceremony at the Olympic stadium.

Abebe Bikila and Jesse Owens are grief-stricken. The Olympic truce has been brutally violated.

Walter Troeger, head of the Olympic Village (left) and Elisshiv Ben Horin, the Israeli ambassador, place flowers at the scene of the tragedy.

Avery Brundage maintains that the Games are now more important than ever.

The delegations slowly entered the Olympic stadium, which should have rung with the sounds of athletic competition. Only sorrow filled it now.

The faces of the Israelis, in brown jackets and white capels, were tense; two young girls were on the verge of tears. The Munich Philharmonic performed the Funeral March from Beethoven's Heroica symphony. It was overwhelming.

The nationality of some athletes in plain clothes was difficult to identify. However, several Arab teams were noticeably absent. The Rhodesians, who had been expelled from the Games, were present.

Visibly exhausted, Willy Daume, the chairman of the organising committee, was the first to speak: 'Even in the world of crime, there are still taboos, a limit to dehumanisation that no-one dares cross. Those responsible for this atrocity have crossed this limit. They have brought murder to this great and beautiful gathering of people from around the world, a gathering dedicated to peace.'

The head of the Israeli delegation then addressed the crowd in Hebrew: 'Those who have died were true sportsmen, cut down in their prime.' He then listed the names of the victims. The crowd of 80,000 spectators all rose to their feet. 'In spite of this abominable crime, we have decided to continue competing in these Olympic Games, in a spirit of harmony and integrity.'

Gustave Heinemann then spoke: 'Over these last hours, mankind the world over has come to understand that hatred is a purely destructive force. It falls to each of us to fight the fanaticism that has rocked our world, in a quest to achieve harmony. The only barrier lies between those who strive for solidarity and peace and those willing to risk everything worth living for. Life requires conciliation.'

Finally, Avery Brundage, the IOC president, stepped forward: 'Any civilised human being is left paralysed by terror. The Games must go on. They will resume one day behind schedule.'

The Israeli delegation remained seated. Many athletes came to embrace them. The speaker gave details of the afternoon's events. No-one heard. Every heart was broken.

THE ISRAELI VICTIMS

As well as Moshe Weinberger and Yossef Romano, murdered in the Olympic Village, nine Israelis died in crossfire at Fuerstenfelbruck airport:
- Mark Slavin (18), Greco-Roman wrestler. had migrated to Israel from the Soviet Union just four months earlier.
- Eueser Halfin (24), also a USSR-born wrestler; migrated two years earlier.
- David Berger (28), lawyer and weight-lifter who migrated from the USA in 1969.
- Jeew Friedman (28), weightlifter. His father had been the sole family member to survive the concentration camps.
- Jaakow Springer (52), the only Israeli international weightlifting referee. Fourth Olympic appearance.
- Joseph Gutfreund (40), the only Israeli international wrestling referee. Fourth Olympic appearance.
- Kehat Shorr (53), one of the best coaches in Israel. Originally Romanian.
- André Spitzer (30), fencing coach. Brought up in Belgium. Married with a two-month old baby; his wife had traveled to Munich with him.
- Amizan Shapira (30), coach and teacher of physical education. Trained Esther Chachamarov, who reached the semi-finals of the 100m hurdles.

Mr Lalkin, head of the Israeli delegation, advocates the continuation of the Games, in spite of his grief.

Israeli journalists in the press gallery are in shock.

The Olympic Games, where the very purpose is to promote peace and brotherhood amongst athletes of all nations, cannot be permitted to become a forum where killers can be heard.

SWIMMING

Spitz, in all humility

Seven gold medals, seven world records. Yet these outstanding achievements on the part of the American seem almost derisory in light of the tragic events of the past few days – as Spitz himself is all too aware.

The press conference intended to showcase the enormity of Mark Spitz's achievements was inevitably affected by the recent events in the Olympic Village. Of the many things left unsaid at this rushed event, perhaps most notable were the concerns of the American officials to remove Spitz, a high-profile Jew whose fame extends well beyond the realm of sport, from the Village as quickly as possible. *Life* had already dedicated a cover to him after the US championships in Chicago. On the eve of the press conference, Spitz fronted *Time Magazine* and the *International Herald Tribune*, propelling him into the Who's Who of all-time celebrities.

After a 45-minute meeting with five hundred reporters, no-one can claim to know any more about Spitz than they already knew. Spitz pointed out that he could scarcely sum up twenty years in just five minutes, and had no more idea than anyone else where this

SEVEN TITLES AND SEVEN RECORDS...

August 28
200m butterfly
1 Mark Spitz (USA), 2:00.70

4x100m
1 USA (David Edger, John Murphy, Jerry Heidenreich, and Mark Spitz), 3:26.42

August 29
200m
Mark Spitz (USA) 1:52.78

August 31
100m butterfly
1 Mark Spitz (USA), 54.27

4x200m
USA (John Kinsella, Frederick Tyler, Steven Genter, Mark Spitz), 7:35.78

September 3
100 m
1 Mark Spitz (USA), 51.22

September 4
4x100m medley
1 USA (Michael Stamm, Thomas Bruce, Mark Spitz, Jerry Heidenreich), 3:48.16

On August 31, Mark Spitz, with his five gold medals, passes Schollander's medal tally [see p. 175]. In a statement, he announces his quest for Olympic gold is not over yet – two more to go!

tidal wave of fame was taking him.

Below are the questions and answers exchanged at the conference. Inevitably coloured by recent events, they almost always bear a humorous slant.

Q: So what's next?

A: Nothing in particular. Just to relax and try and watch the rest of the Games.

Q: Do you think the Games should be cancelled after the attack in the Village?

A: It's a tragedy. I have nothing to say on the matter.

Q: Have the athletes been kept informed?

A: No comment.

Q: Do your seven medals devalue your sport?

A: I've tried to do my best in each competition, but people will think what they want and I can't change that.

Q: Aren't the races in the programme too similar?

A: I swam against different competitors every time, so the races weren't as similar as all that.

Q: What was the difference between Mexico and Munich for you?

A: Four years and seven medals.

Q: The US didn't let you swim relays. Wasn't that a bit unfair?

A: (Peter Daland gets up and makes the most pertinent remark of the whole interview.) As men's coach of the US team, I see no problem with that. Surely it's better to make eight men swim once than four men swim twice.

Q: You were permanently in lane four; isn't it about time you started paying rent?

A: The facilities here are the best I've ever seen. I'd be glad to have an Olympic pool in my back yard.

Q: Why did you change coach after Mexico?

A: Personal reasons. It was better for me.

Q: Who, in particular, has helped you out here?

A: I have received three thousand letters. I haven't opened my mail yet this morning but if there was a letter from the US president, I would be happy.

Q: How have the four years between Mexico and Munich been?

A: Lots of hard work and uncertainty; there were no guarantees I'd do any better than in 1968.

Q: Who is the best swimmer of all time – apart from you of course?

A: I'm hardly in a position to answer that.'

With that, Spitz stood up and left. For the moment at least, there is no correlation between the swimmer's quite extraordinary track record and Spitz's alter ego as a University of Indiana dentistry student.

A sporting celebrity: Mark Spitz before five hundred journalists.

Why Spitz is a phenomenon

No man has ever come as close to embodying the majesty of dolphins as the American. Every atom of his being is efficient.

Spitz kicks off his incredible series of seven victories with the 200m butterfly.

Mark Spitz has dominated the butterfly since 1969, or more – his fifty yard record in the 9-10 age group still stands. His freestyle is also astonishing, and at the start of his international career, his coach Georges Haines steered him towards the middle-distance events. In 1967 he beat the world 400m record and he came close to clinching the 1500m title in 1966 when he recorded a time of less than seventeen minutes. He was a good deal lighter in those days.

Since 1968, he has favoured instead the 100m and 200m double in both freestyle and butterfly. It has turned out to be the best possible combination for picking up titles and medals by opening the doors to the relays. It certainly allowed him to swim in an enormous number of competitions for his country, his university or his club, Arden Hills.

Surprisingly, Spitz is not renowned for his rigorous training schedule. Although Sherm Chavoor claims Spitz has worked hard all year, especially on his arms, Andrew Strenk, his team mate at Arden Hills, says: 'Compared to the rest of the American team, Spitz's training is minimal. He's way behind Mike Burton in this respect. He's pretty erratic; sometimes he won't turn up, other days he's on top form and can swim 200m in 1:56 or 200m butterfly in 2:05 with his arms tied behind his back.'

Douglas Russell, who defeated Spitz in the 100m butterfly in the Games in Mexico, had also commented on his absence during the national team training camp in Colorado.

So where does Spitz's strength lie? Ever since he was a child, he has exhibited phenomenal flexibility, first noticed by his father and subsequently confirmed a hundred times over in underwater photographs and film footage. Every fibre in his body is efficient: the power in his arms, the rhythm and the fluidity of his stroke, the leanness of his muscles – giving him maximum strength at a minimum weight (160 pounds) – all this from an average sized American (six feet).

His spine curves gently and his legs arch back: exactly what the butterfly demands. A finer, more spectacular combination is impossible to imagine. Two moments in particular demonstrate his prowess: his performance in Leipzig, when he clinched victory for the USA against East Germany with a relay swim of fifty-four seconds, and the incredible acceleration between the 50 and 75m marks in the final in Chicago. His whole torso lifted clean out of the water. No man has better embodied the majesty of dolphins than Spitz.

His freestyle technique, though efficient, is not entirely smooth. His left stroke is slightly off-centre, undermining his stability. Yet he slices through the water with a steadiness unusual for a sprinter, swept along by an intensely powerful stroke. Admittedly, he is not especially fast over 25m but, as an ex-400m racer and 200m world record holder, his stamina makes him unbeatable in the second half of the 100m. He has worked hard to correct his slow starts and, in Munich, with all the muscular strength of his twenty-two years, he came close to achieving his ideal, covering the first 50m in a split time of just 24.56 – his fastest ever.

Outstanding in both butterfly and freestyle, excellent in backstroke, Spitz's only weakness is breaststroke. Above all, he possesses remarkable powers of recovery.

In 1968, former 400m world record holder Greg Charlton summed up Spitz's physical condition as follows: 'Mark is blessed with extraordinary powers of recuperation. He is the only American able to sustain peak form all year round. He is always full of drive, and has no weak points, unlike the rest of us. That's one hell of an advantage.'

Spitz has excelled in freestyle and butterfly in the 100m and 200m but he could equally have topped the field in the 400m, not to mention in backstroke, and therefore the medley. Indeed, Strenk reminds us that even at a very young age he was already the second best US backstroke swimmer in age-group events. No surprise then that at pre-Olympic training two weeks before the Games, Spitz beat backstroke specialists Ivey and Stamm in a 50m race. In spite of his shortcomings in breaststroke, he could have conceivably become a truly exceptional medley specialist. Put simply, he was born to swim.

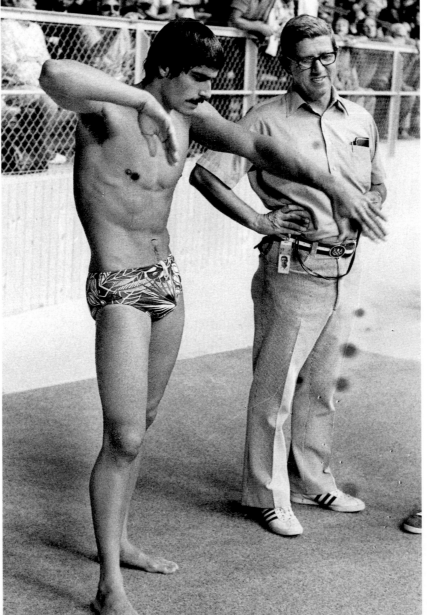

AN OLYMPIC ICON IN THE MAKING

At Mexico in 1968, Mark Spitz, an eighteen-year-old loner from California who had held world records in freestyle and butterfly since he was sixteen, had won gold in the 4x100m freestyle, silver in the 100m butterfly and bronze in the 100m freestyle – a medal haul others would have been proud of but which, for Spitz, was a disappointing under-performance. At Munich, now twenty-two, he dominated the pool, winning seven swimming finals, every one in world record time.

SWIMMING

Shane Gould – superstar at fifteen

The Australian finished the Games with three titles, five medals and three individual world records.

Shane Gould has everything under control. Herself, to start off with, but also the public, who cheer her on like a superstar, powering her along with burst of applause and whistles like something out of Carnegie Hall. Most important of all, she had the Americans, convinced they had her beaten after the 100m, in the palm of her hand.

After a breathtaking 200m in which not only Gould, with her winning time of 2:03.56, but also Shirley Babashoff (USA) with 2:04.33 and Keena Rothhammer (USA) with 2:04.92, smashed the previous world record, Rothhammer jumped for joy as she saw the electronic scoreboard. It wasn't victory she was after, it was a medal. Only Babashoff remained expressionless. But she must have recognised she was simply outclassed.

In the morning, during the qualifying heats, Gould appeared lighter in the water than in the 400m, apparently qualifying more easily. She seemed to be fully conscious that she was an ambassador visiting her opponents from another, future era.

THE PARENT'S ANGER

In a telephone statement to one of Sydney's daily papers, Shane Gould's father, Ron, announced that he and her mother would never again allow their daughter to be subjected to so ridiculous a schedule: 'Three races is a lot for an adult, but a fifteen-year-old girl* should never be made to compete in five individual races and a relay. And because she is Shane Gould, she is automatically expected to break a world record or win a gold medal in every race. My daughter is not a robot!'

Mr. Gould was even wondering if competitive swimming was the right choice for Shane. 'Judging by what I've seen in Munich, it's no life for a young girl. When Shane comes back to Australia, I'll force her to take a complete rest – no competitions until December. Then, with her mother, we'll decide on her future. It will be our decision, not the officials' or the coaches.'

*She will turn 16 on 23 November 1972.

With determination written all over her face, this fifteen-year-old is the best female swimmer in the world.

From the moment she began to compete at the Games, her times were without precedent: 50m in 29.2, sixty seconds dead for 100m... no, that is not a misprint, 100m in precisely one minute – and that's outside her world record of 58.5. To swim with such consistency, she couldn't adopt the mentality of a convalescent, which perhaps tarnished her performance in the 400m; instead, she had to take on the mindset of a great conqueror – the conqueror we expected her to be here in Munich. At 31.3 her final fifty metres were a fraction slower than Babashoff's (31 seconds) but in the end the American could do nothing but follow Gould home in her wake, such was the Australian's dominance.

So it was that the US swimmers were forced to play second fiddle to the Australian, in terms of both their motivation and their results – in spite, too, of their momentary conviction that they had escaped her iron rule. Two hundred metres in 2:33.5 is a tremendous feat and one which ought to provide food for thought for a number of male relay swimmers who could do no better in the men's 4x200m, not to mention swimming enthusiasts venturing near a pool anywhere in the world. The impact of this result is truly enormous. Shane Gould will go down in history. Given her continued technical shortcomings which cannot be solved overnight and which may prove a real obstacle in the 800m, where weight is the enemy, we can only admire her mental, as much as her physical strength.

Gould's third gold medal, in the 400m freestyle, was again a case of mind over matter and she accepted it with due gravitas. Defeat in the 100m the previous day forced her to recognise that she was no longer untouchable, as Debbie Myers had been in Mexico. Yet she remains a young girl, as she showed when she spontaneously abandoned the other two medalists mid-ceremony and darted over to her father. After getting up at 5am each morning to take her to the pool, he evidently deserved his victory kiss.

The fall of the American empire

Three seconds earlier and the USA would have won another title against the USSR.

Mediocre players, a strong Soviet defence line, and three extra seconds were all that was required to consign American invincibility to the past.

For the first time in the history of Olympic sport the American basketball team had been beaten. However, the eagerly anticipated final between the USA and the USSR ended in confusion, and in the closing seconds the Americans lost a game they thought they had won.

With three seconds remaining, Douglas Collins (USA) was awarded two free throws after a foul by Zurab Sakandelidze. Both went in and, for the first time in the match, the Americans had the upper hand and victory was in their grasp (50-49).

The Soviets inbounded the ball, but with one second on the clock, FIBA general secretary Mr. Jones was seen holding up three fingers in the direction of the scorers' table. Meanwhile, Vladimir Kondrashkin, the Soviet coach, rushed towards the referee, Mr. Righetto, to indicate that he had asked for a time-out, but no-one had heard him. At the insistence of Mr. Jones and, in spite of the

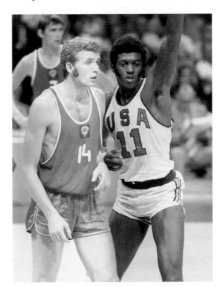

It was a heated final, interspersed with conflict and the ejection of Korkia and Jones.

protests of the American team, time-out was called and the Soviet players inbounded the ball once more. But as the two seconds already played were not put back on the clock, the horn sounded almost immediately, ending the game.

The crowd had already begun to surge onto the court and the American team were embracing each other. However, it was not over yet. Once again, Mr. Jones stepped in, ordering that three seconds be put back on the clock. To the apparent confusion of the Americans, Modestas Paulauskas lofted an inbound pass down court straight into the hands of Aleksandr Belov who scored unopposed.

A final score of 50-51 meant victory for the Russians who jumped for joy and lifted Paulauskas on to their shoulders in triumph. The Americans, outraged, protested against what they considered daylight robbery!

No-one will ever know if the final seconds were legitimate; the Americans lodged an appeal and the jury deliberated until 4:30 am without reaching a decision. However, the explanation given by Mr. Jones did nothing to convince anyone, least of all

Mark Iba, the American team's sixty-eight-year old coach. Iba declared the match a scandal and vowed that if the title was not handed back to his team, the USA would never compete again in an Olympic tournament!

The question was, had Mr. Kondrashkin really asked for a time-out between Collins' free throws? The debate raged on long after the end of the game and doubt will hang over the Soviet's victory, even though they clearly deserved to win the final, having dominated play for thirty-nine minutes and fifty-seven seconds. This was thanks, in no small part, to Sergei Belov, whose talent for mid-range shooting disrupted the flow of the American team, outpaced from the start. In spite of their dexterity and spring, the US players could only watch as Belov, Boloshev and Sharmukhamedov gave them a lesson in shooting hoops.

Kenya vs Finland

Scandinavia hands the middle-distance baton to Africa.

First of all, let us sing Finland's praises. The feats of two Finnish athletes yesterday were worthy of the golden era of Finnish athletics. Nearly half a century has passed since Finns won the 1500m, 5,000m and 10,000m in the 1924 Games. Then, in Paris, as now, in Munich, just two athletes were responsible for this hat-trick of wins: Paavo Nurmi won the 1500m and 5,000m, Ville Ritola the 10,000m. At Amsterdam four years later, victory was more widely distributed: Harry Larva took the 1500m, Ritola the 5,000m and Nurmi the 10,000m. Never again have athletes from one country bagged all three events at the same Games.

Not even Finland. In 1932, the 10,000m title escaped the Finns, and went to Poland. In 1936, the 1500m eluded them, and headed to New Zealand. Not since then has a Finnish name joined the list of champions in any of the three events – until now. The Munich Games have seen a resurrection in the fortunes of a nation of four and a half million inhabitants, among whom sport is not just a means of education but almost a religion.

Before Lasse Viren, only three athletes have achieved the double of the 5,000m and 10,000m, and they are among the legends of the Games: Hannes Kolehmainen in 1912, Emil Zátopek in 1952 (who also won the marathon) – and Volodomyr Kuts in 1956.

The Olympic programme dictated that Lasse Viren attained his magnificent double, and exited stage left, as Pekka Vasala entered stage right for the 1500m. True, there was something missing in Vasala's glory: a figure whose absence meant that Vasala's coronation as the finest 1500m runner of his generation could not be undisputed. The absentee was Jim Ryun, who missed the final after a silly accident. Ryun was eliminated in the fourth qualifying heat two days before the final. 550m from the finish, trailing the 1968 champion Kip Keino, Ryun was caught in a box. He tried to squeeze between the runners outside him, clipped the heel of the athlete in front, and fell onto the curb. The Ghanaian Billy Fordjour landed on top of him. Ryun's Olympic bid ended with a bruised hip, a scraped knee, a sprained left ankle, and a contusion of his Adam's apple. Ryan rose to his feet and began the chase, but he had lost seventy-five metres, and it was an impossible task. Afterwards, he commented: 'Everything was going well, I felt good - and the next thing I know, I was trying to figure out what had happened.' Sadly, from then on, he could only follow Kip Keino from the stands.

The irony is, Ryun should never have been in the same qualifying heat as Keino. His brilliant mile time of 3:52.8 was mistakenly entered as his best for 500m – when his best for 1500m was actually the world record of 3:33.1. Seeding should have given him a clear route to the final: instead, he was put in the same heat as the defending Olympic champion, which led to his heart-breaking fall.

It seems certain the Keino would have approached the final differently if Ryun had been taking part. He would have hit the front long before the 700m mark, where he chose to launch his first deft acceleration.

His goal was no doubt to diminish the Finn's hopes, despite the fact that Vasala, as Keino knew full well, had recently run 800m in 1:44.5. The closing stages were as scintillating as the final laps of the 5,000m had been. Keino was in his finest form, but he had waited too long to trouble Vasala. He merely induced him to cover the final two laps in 1:48.8, a time that seems incredible to those who have been able to study the race frame by frame.

Ryun, of course, haunts the final result. It is a shame that the shadow of doubt must hang over the achievements of the magnificent Pekka Vasala. However, it is beyond doubt that victory here would have had a quite different flavour if the world record holder had also been on the starting line.

The two great middle-distance superpowers of Olympic history, Finland and Kenya, are embodied in the inseparable figures of Pekka Vasala and Kip Keino.

1972

OLYMPIC ROUND-UP

SMILING KIP 'KENYA'.

Kip Keino cannot hide his childish smile, accompanied by peals of laughter that die away then reappear. Of all the winners coming voluntarily to the ordeal of the public interview, this one really does smile the most. 'Why are you surprised?' he says. 'Are other winners sad to be coming here? Winning the gold medal should make you forget how tired you are.' All the same, Keino seems as tired as he is smiley – and that's saying a lot.

'I had an easy race', he explains. 'Since I don't have much experience of the 3,000m steeplechase, I decided to stay at the back of the group until the last lap. It's easier to get over the hurdles, and there's no risk of being crowded. I decided to let things happen gradually. This is only the sixth 3,000m steeplechase I've run.'

Surely we've never seen such an inexperienced steeplechase runner, uncomfortable with the hurdles, take it on with such ease. 'I'm not very good at jumping the hurdles', says Keino, his beaming smile showing off all his teeth. 'I do what I can. I put my foot on top of the hurdle because I think that pushing on it means I can gain some ground on the other runners. Today, between hurdles, I was just taking it easy. The world record didn't interest me .'

And he still won't be interested tomorrow. You get the feeling that he only branched off into the steeplechase adventure to complete his medal collection. On the subject – which clearly does not fill him with passion – he says: 'I believe that the record can easily be broken; a fairly quick race should produce a substantial improvement in times.'

Keino laughs. Equally at ease here as on the track, he has a knack of getting out of every question. When you want to him to say that he has been ordered here by his country, he replies: 'I am Kip Keino, I run for Kip Keino, but yes, it's true that I am proud to represent my country, but only my country. I am Kip of Kenya, at least when I win.'

1. German super-welterweight Kottysch is sacred in the eyes of Poland's Rudkowski. He is victorious.
2. Russian Alexeïev's reign begins: he overcomes Germans Mang (GER) and Bonk (GDR).
3. American John Williams, at 18, becomes the first Olympic champion in modern archery. His secret is 42 hours of training every week!
4. Hennie Kuiper leads a group that includes Freddy Maertens (4th from the left) and Francesco Moser (following on behind). The Dutchman achieves his first great win.
5. Twenty-one of the thirty-three riders enrolled in the dressage competition are women. Germany's Liselott Linsenhoff is the first woman to become a true Olympic 'champion'.
6. Black Africa produces only middle-distance runners: Ugandan John Akii-Bua completes the 400m hurdles in 47.82, a world record.
7. Marathon winner Frank Shorter of the USA is congratulated by his team mate Kenneth Moore (4th).
8. One Dutchman follows another; but Willem Ruska (left) does better than Geesink: in addition to the all-category championship, he dominates the heavyweight tournament.
9. Gold in the 1500m and silver in the 5,000m in Mexico, Kip Keino does equally well in Munich: gold in the 3,000m steeplechase (shown here) and silver in the 1500m.
10. Yugoslav Lazarevic takes a free throw despite the opposition of Czech Karalic in the first handball final in September. His team will make their presence known.
11. With Kato, Kenmotsu, Kasamatsu, Nakayama, Okamura and Tsukahara (shown here), the Japanese dominate gymnastics competitions.
12. Since 1896, all pole-vaulting titles have been won by Americans. East Germany's Wolfgang Nordwig, at 29 years old, broke the run by chalking up 5.5m.
13. Silver in Tokyo, gold in Mexico, Italian Klaus Dibiasi retains his high-flying title, as he would do again, four years later, in Los Angeles!

Darling of the Games

Tiny Olga Korbut cracks at the crucial moment. Her team-mate earns herself a medal in her own inimitable style.

To the disappointment of the 11,000-strong crowd who turned out to cheer her on yesterday afternoon, the tiny Olga Korbut (SOV/BLR) has missed out on victory in the All-Around gymnastics competition. Two days ago, her freshness and enthusiasm during the first round of optional exercises had captivated the world, which fell in love with Korbut, who looks at least three years younger than her age, seventeen, and willed her to win. She emerged as a credible threat to her team-mate Lyudmilla Turischeva (SOV/RUS) and Karin Janz (GDR) in yesterday's All-Around competition.

She began the day by by stunning the room with a lively, energetic routine on the floor, peppered with technical moves which were indisputably worthy of an Olympic champion. She received a 9.8 and took the lead. A mark of 9.65 for the vault solidified her position.

With two disciplines to go, Olga Korbut, with 57.800 points, was ahead of Turischeva (on 57.725) and Janz (on 57.525).

In the team event, Korbut had

The public is enchanted: on the beam, tiny Olga Korbut takes the gold.

earned 9.7 on the asymmetrical bars. This time, she scuffed her feet on the mat as she mounted, fell during her routine, and missed her remount, due more to nerves than lack of skill.

When her score of 7.5 went up, she burst into tears. It was 5.15pm and the tiny Korbut had lost all hope of the gold medal – *any* medal. Astakhova, Olympic champion on the bars in 1960 and 1964, tried in vain to console her, as did Erika Zuchold (GDR). A spectator evaded the stewards and handed her a bouquet of dried flowers. The little Russian girl, tears streaming down her face, stood up, flowers in hand, and received a roaring ovation. Meanwhile, on the beam, Turischeva, despite a wobble, scored a cautious 9.4 under the watchful dry eye of Karin Janz, who took the lead (67.175 to Turischeva's 67.125). Only the final exercises remained: the asymmetrical bars for Janz, the floor for Turischeva.

First to go, Janz scored 9.7, a generous result considering she made a small error. Turischeva walked out onto the mat knowing she needed 9.8 to win the All-Around competition.

Her performance was impeccable: authoritative and well-rounded. For once, the flame within melted her icy exterior. She started with a double turn that demonstrated her confidence. It was the first move on the path towards the highest score of the Games: a near-perfect 9.9. Karen Janz applauded politely.

Olga Korbut dried her tears. Turischeva was the Olympic champion, ahead of Janz. Tamara Lazakovitch (SOV/BLR) took third, benefiting from the mistakes that left Korbut no higher than fifth. Thus ended two unforgettable hours of drama.

Lyudmilla Turischeva, born 7 October 1952 (5 feet 3) lacks the inspired sparkle of Korbut or Lazakovitch, but compensates with a robotic reliability and beauty, fronted by a serious face that is almost Asian in appearance. World champion in 1970, European co-champion (with Lazakovitch) in 1971 and Olympic champion today, she has compiled an outstanding record since her Olympic debut in Mexico City, where she finished twenty-fourth.

Turischeva has, so to speak, created her own gold medal, pursuing her own excellence without worrying about what is going on around her, doing what is necessary, when it is necessary, with discipline and precision. Maybe she is not an artist. She works to her own schedule, with near-military precision, under the eyes of her trainer. But how very majestic she is!

The young Belorussian gives everything to her sport, enchanting the public and the media with her charm and the vulnerability that would cost her overall victory.

Korbut is 17, Lyudmilla Turischeva almost 20: the difference in maturity accounts for the gap between them in the All-Around rankings.

MUNICH XX OLYMPIAD

Thirty-six years after the Berlin Games – remembered with such
horror – Germany became the setting for a hostage situation.
Once more, the Games showed that, despite themselves,
they were the perfect reflection of their time.

THE GAMES IN BRIEF

Opening Date
26 August 1972

Closing Date
10 September 1972

Host Town
West Germany (GDR)

Candidate Towns
Detroit (USA), Madrid (ESP) and Montréal
(CAN).

121 Nations Represented

7,123 Athletes
(1,058 women, 6,065 men)

21 Sports
(8 open to women)
Track and field, rowing, basketball, boxing,
canoeing, cycling, equestrian, fencing,
football, gymnastics, weightlifting, handball,
field hockey, judo, wrestling, swimming,
modern pentathlon, volley-ball, shooting,
archery and sailing.

172 Events
(43 open to women)

Games opened by
Gustav Heinemann, President of West
Germany

Olympic flame lit by
Gunther Zahn (athletics)

Olympic oath read by
Heidi Schueller (athletics)

IOC President
Avery Brundage (USA)

DID YOU KNOW?

Officials swore the Olympic oath for the first
time. In another first, the athletes' oath was
sworn by a woman.

Archery returned to the Olympic
programme after a 52-year absence.

Men's handball featured for only the
second time; it had been contested at the
last German Games in 1936, but as an
11-player event.

1976

Montreal

FIRST THERE WAS THE CANADIAN government's decision to gratify Communist China by revoking the visas of the Taiwanese, already resident in the Olympic Village. The IOC protested, then backed down, and the Taiwanese left. The Chinese stayed at home anyway, since the IOC had admitted Taiwan. Then there was New Zealand, whose rugby team had recently toured South Africa, banned from the Games because of apartheid. The shooting of several hundred black Africans by the South African police at a student protest in Soweto in June 1976 provoked the African nations to demand New Zealand's exclusion. When the IOC stood its ground, twenty-seven African nations withdrew, depriving the Games of John Akii-Bua of Uganda (400m hurdles), Mike Boit of Kenya (800m and 1500m), Mohamed Gammoudi of Tunisia (5,000m and 10,000m) and Filbert Bayi of Tanzania, the world 1500m record holder, whose duel with New Zealander John Walker, the world mile record holder, had been eagerly awaited.

The facilities at Montreal were big, beautiful and expensive (the projected budget had doubled from 1972 to 1976). Strikes during construction caused concern but the facilities were ready on schedule, although paint was still being applied in the hours before the Opening Ceremony.

Many new events were introduced into the programme including rowing, basketball and handball tournaments for women, although the Montreal Games are mostly remembered for the performances of Comaneci, Juantorena and Viren.

The Queen of the Games – or perhaps the Princess. Fifteen-year-old Nadia Comaneci approached perfection. With her unprecedented perfect tens, she is guaranteed a place in any Olympic top ten.

Nadia: the child of tranquility

Perfection exists: at Montreal, the tiny Romanian gains a perfect ten no less than seven times.

For all the little girls in the world who love gymnastics, a new inspiration: Nadia Comaneci, the diminutive, mousy-haired virtuoso whose performances before the staring eyes of the cameras outshone even Olga Korbut, the queen of the Munich Games.

As soon as her performance on the beam was over, Comaneci turned that minuscule face, pale and anxious, towards the luminous display boards. Then her score appeared, and it was her turn to light up with joy. Ten: the supreme achievement. It took her no more than an instant to take in, before she turned, walked calmly over to her team-mates and sat down, withdrawing into that deep internal stillness as the other gymnasts performed. At the post-event press conference, the new gymnastic Wunderkind charmed the media with a series of distant, elusive replies – even Olympic glory fails to unsettle her.

'Ten means you have attained perfection,' observes one questioner. 'What can you possibly achieve in the rest of your career?'

'I've achieved three tens in the gymnastic disciplines, but I've already had nineteen tens in my career. It's nothing especially new,' she replies, with poise. 'But I know I can still improve, and win more victories, other titles, other medals.'

The novelty was that Nadia made her perfect performance under the eyes of the Soviet team, a sumptuous array of gymnasts that includes Nelli Kim, Lyudmila Turischeva, Olga

On the beam, Nadia Comaneci draws admiration for her suppleness, her exquisite balance and the flow of her routine. It all seems so easy, and, for once, the public and the judges agree over the quality of her performance.

Nadia Comaneci's floor exercises are a joy to behold. Airy, light, full of impertinence, she also shows the technical mastery of a seasoned gymnast.

Korbut and the miniature Maria Filatova. The greatest team in the world, despite the growing threat of the Romanians.

Comaneci's rise has been prodigious, when you think that two short years ago no-one in the world of gymnastics even knew she existed. She first appeared in the World Championships at Varna in October 1974, in an out-of-competition performance given during the interval, as the panel judged the main competition. Nadia, born in November 1961, was not yet fourteen, and gymnastics has strict age rules. Only gymnasts aged fourteen on the day of competition can be admitted. The

French coach, Arthur Magakian, was stupefied and pronounced: 'This little Romanian will soon be the greatest gymnast on earth.'

A month later, she won the London tournament, and in May 1975, she celebrated her first great victory in the European Championships at Skien, when Lyudmila Turischeva, fourth, also emerged onto the world stage. By beating Nelli Kim (SOV/KAZ) and Annelore Zinke (GDA), Nadia

10/10: PERFECTION!

You think you've seen everything. You think that what's already been done could never be outdone. Then Nadia Comaneci arrives and perfection is redefined. Never before has the human body been more exquisitely manipulated both aesthetically and physically, to the limits of the possible. Beautiful is an under-statement. This stunning fifteen-year-old is inexorably bewitching. For the first time in the history of the Games the panel awarded the maximum score of ten for Nadia's display on the asymmetric bars. Korbut had just received a 9.90 in the same event but this was still no match for the genius who represented nothing other than perfection. This difference in score is indicative of the fantastic competitive performances by the Soviet and Romanian girls, alongside East Germany who, despite the great quality of their gymnasts and other factors in their favour, proved to be no match and were condemned to third place. The Romanians, despite their young age, have the steeliest of nerves. It really seems as though Comaneci is immune to external conditions. It takes just a couple of smiles for her to have the crowd in the palm of her hand. But the Soviets, with their consistency, should still win it.

The computer hadn't foreseen this! The first perfect ten in Olympic gymnastics cannot be displayed. 1.00 will have to do.

Comaneci started her reign in style.

But one can't help reflecting that four years ago, when Olga Korbut was wowing viewers throughout the world, Nadia was an eleven-year-old, spending four hours a day training at the state sporting academy of Gheorghia-Dej, the leading national centre for Gymnastics in Romania. At the age of six she was spotted by a national scout and placed in the care of Bella Karoly. She was subjected to physiological and medical testing, on the basis of which she was accepted by the school in Gheorghia-Dej – 'A remarkable complex', in Magakian's words. 'Like other centres, it provides comprehensive teaching of acrobatic training, apparatus work, training in choreography and physical expression. There is even a pianist to accompany floor exercises. To my knowledge there are ten centres in Romania, five for men and five for women.'

The Romanian team, who had won the bronze medal in Melbourne in 1956 and in Rome in 1960, went through a long period of decline before the government decided on a total restructuring of the system, particularly the development of the national centre at Gheorghia-Dej, 400km from Bucharest. 'With great care and precision, they then set about organising the scouting of very young

The delicate, doe-eyed child of 15 is the star of the Montreal Olympics.

Despite her young age, Nadia is the ambassador for her team.

talents through the schools' tests. And now people talk of a great gymnastic tradition in Romania. The team is young and very strong. They're going to surprise us again,' adds Magakian.

Nadia, the delicate Romanian doll measuring 5 feet 1 and weighing 90 pounds, follows a very strict diet. 'Fruit, milk, cheese and proteins,' said the Romanian Secretary General Emil Ghibu, 'but no sugar and definitely no bread.' This discipline has helped erase the memory of Olga Korbut, who had seduced the world at Munich. 'Her

impishness seduced them,' says Magakian, 'she had presence, a rapport with her audience. They loved her. It also has to be said that her programme offered a new gymnastic element that she brought to life at each section of apparatus. In Munich she was already seventeen, though so tiny. She is now twenty-one.' But Nadia Comaneci's superiority is clear. She is more slender, more supple, more elastic, and more precise in each movement. Everything she does is absolutely perfect.

'With Olga Korbut there are flashes of genius,' remarks Magakian, 'with Nadia Comaneci it's genius from beginning to end. There are no lulls in the sequences. On the beam, for example, her balance defies gravity. You wouldn't believe that the beam she is moving along is just ten centimetres wide. It requires not only exceptional strength in the legs but also a physical and mental preparation far greater than most could imagine. I know she is capable of performing her display on the beam fifteen times in a row without cracking.'

Nadia Comaneci's arrival on the scene is leading us into a new mesmerising era in this sport. Women's artistic gymnastics is tending more and more towards gymnastic dance, a tendency parallel to that of figure skating, influenced by the demands of television coverage.

COMANECI'S FIVE MEDALS

Individual All-Round
1 Nadia Comaneci (ROM), 79.275 pts
2 Nelli Kim (SOV/KAZ), 78.675 pts
3 Lyudmila Turischeva (SOV/RUS) 78.625 pts.

Asymmetric Bars
1 Nadia Comaneci (ROM), 20 pts
2 Teodora Ungureanu (ROM), 19.80 pts
3 Marta Egervari (HUN), 19.775 pts

Balance Beam
1 Nadia Comaneci (ROM), 19.95 pts
2 Olga Korbut (SOV/BLR), 19.725 pts
3 Teodora Ungureanu (ROM), 19.70 pts

Floor Exercises
1 Nelli Kim (SOV/KAZ), 19.85 pts
2 Lyudmila Turischeva (SOV/RUS) 19.825 pts
3 Nadia Comaneci (ROM), 19.75 pts

Team Competition
1 USSR (Kim, Turischeva, Korbut Saadi, Filatova, Grozdova) 466.00 pts
2 Romania (Comaneci, Ungureanu Constantin, Grigoras, Trusca Gabor), 462.35 pts
3 GDR (Escher, Kische, Gerschau Hellmann, Kräker, Dombeck) 459.30 pts

The end of the journey

Undisputed star of the tournament, American Sugar Ray Leonard, announces he'll never box again. We'll see about that ...

On the brink of a professional career and with an Olympic title under his belt, Leonard announces he's going to university. But when was a twenty-year-old ever certain about anything?

'The first time I saw him box I was staggered. It was like a reincarnation: the same moves, the same attitude, the same size, the same weight, the same skill, even the same first name. Thirty years later I had found Robinson at the same age.' So says Roland Schwartz, 63, President of the Amateur Athletic Union and attending the Games with the American boxers.

But Sugar Ray Leonard is not going to follow his predecessor along the often slippery paths of professional boxing. His career will be as remarkable for its brevity as his predecessor's was for its longevity. Yesterday Sugar Ray Leonard took his 137th and final victory in 142 bouts. At twenty years old, he's giving it all up, a decision he has declared 'irreversible.' He arrived in Montreal preceded by his reputation and left it crowned in glory.

The fight that marked the end of a journey, as he so accurately described it a little later, will go down in history of boxing.

Standing in the ring, looking great as brilliantly talented twenty-year-olds do, his face, childlike and unmarked even after five years in this violent sport, broke into a smile. He saluted the crowd with a bow.

The first bell sounded. In the fake guard of Leonard's opponent, Cuban Andres Aldama, who had not yet been taken the distance in the tournament, we were immediately reminded of the other Cuban, the speedy Angel Herrera. Leonard was cautious. 'I knew that the Cuban was particularly dangerous at a distance because of his big hook, so I got up close.'

With razor-sharp reflexes, spectacular side-stepping, lightning combinations to the body and face, Leonard made the fight his own. Then, from behind his guard, came a left hook that brought a flash of blood to Aldama's chin. The Cuban's knee touched the canvas: the big hitter had been hit, big time, and it was still only round two. Leonard's last round was balletic. Landing jabs, hooks and uppercuts, Leonard performed like a matador. The bell saved the Cuban from K-O.

Sugar Ray Leonard's final performance was over. There was delirium. He blew kisses to the crowd. Yet who had guessed that the hands inside those gloves were badly bruised? Schwarz spoke of this in interview: 'Without ice-packs to relieve the swelling, he wouldn't even have been able to clench his fist. But when you're chasing a childhood dream, you don't feel the pain.'

After the protocol ceremony, Leonard faced the press with rare maturity for a young man of his age. 'I'm ending my career today because I made that promise to my mother, my fiancée and myself. I set myself a goal and I achieved it. I want to be an example to young people. Being a champion is great but it's not everything. I want to be fulfilled, perfect my knowledge and be somebody.' In response to comments about the millions of dollars he could have made from boxing, he said, 'I've decided to go to the University of Burlington to study administration and public relations. Later on I'd like to get involved with training young people. My path is there, nowhere else.

'I want to use the intelligence I've been told I show in the ring in other areas. That will be my next fight.'

[Editor's note: Sugar Ray Leonard became WBC welterweight champion on 30 November 1979, and undisputed world champion in 1981].

The champion: his hands, cut to pieces after 142 fights, could also perhaps explain his great wisdom.

Alberto Juantorena – the cool Cuban

The new champion considers his unprecedented 400m and 800m double simply a stage of his life.

On the 400m podium, Juantorena shakes hands with Frazier (right) and Newhouse, the defeated Americans.

J uantorena is astonishing - prodigious. His incredible calmness takes everyone aback. Before the race, he was sitting calmly with his starting foot tucked under him then, on the starter's call, casually looked at his nails before kneeling down at his starting block. After the race had finished he was still absolutely serene. Lucidly analysing the two races that won him that many titles, Alberto Juantorena said: 'Of course I'm very happy to have won both competitions as that's never been done in the history of the Olympics. I won for my country. The hardest race was the 400m, though it's the one I prefer. As far as the race is concerned, it went exactly as I had hoped. My trainer and I have never sat down and planned how I was going to run a race.'

'I decided my tactics during the race. The conditions couldn't have been better for running. [Herman] Frazier [USA] and [Frederick] Newhouse [USA], whom I considered to be my two main opponents, were starting in front of me so I had them in my line of vision. I held back until the 300m mark then I went for it and got past them easily. In the final 50m I was certain I was going to win.'

Despite the double win Juantorena was disappointed at not beating the world record for the 400m as he had done so spectacularly in the 800m (1:43.50) four days earlier. To this the Cuban replied: 'You know, the world record for the 400m was set at altitude, which gives you a huge advantage. [Lee Evans, 43.86, at the Mexico Olympics in 1968]. Of course the record is on my mind, but later. I'm taking part in the relay here then I'm going to rest. What I'm doing here may seem effortless on the outside but believe me, these Olympic Games have used a lot of my energy. I'm certainly going to need strength next season when I'll be aiming to break records.'

Alberto Juantorena spoke about his sporting and professional future. 'I actually have a degree in economics but I have to pass the upper grade on the course at the University in Havana. I'm finding that it's important for a man to reconcile study and sport. Besides, it's a fundamental principle of Cuba's education system. My dream is to be an educated, well-rounded human being.'

Concerning his more distant future the Cuban remains evasive: 'It's difficult to predict that,' said Alberto, 'but I will probably defend my titles in Moscow 1980. I'll be twenty-nine years old and I may not be as strong as I am now even though I'll still be a new runner. Perhaps I'll have to choose between the 400m and the 800m.'

RESULTS

JUANTORENA'S DOUBLE

400m
1 Alberto Juantorena (CUB),44.26
2 Frederick Newhouse (USA), 44.40
3 Herman Frazier (USA), 44.95
4 Alfons Brijdenbach (BEL), 45.04
5 Maxie Parks (USA), 45.24
6 Richard Mitchell (AUS), 45.40
7 David Jenkins (GBR), 45.57
8 Jan Werner (POL), 45.63

800m
1 Alberto Juantorena (CUB),
   1:43.50 WR
2 Ivo Van Damme (BEL), 1:43.86
3 Richard Wohlhuter (USA), 1:44.12
4 Willi Wülbeck (FRG), 1:45.26
5 Steve Ovett (GBR), 1:45.44
6 Luciano Susanj (YUG), 1:45.75
7 Sriram Singh (IND), 1:45.77
8 Carlo Grippo (ITA), 1:48.39

Finishing the 800m after leading from the start, Alberto Juantorena beats Ibo Van Damme (BEL) and Richard Wohlhuter (USA), and sets a new world record.

Viren laps it up

After four anonymous years, the Finn reappears to perform the same 5,000m and 10,000m double as he did in Munich. He responds to the doping rumours by praising the benefits of reindeer milk.

As the final lap starts, seven athletes are still in contention. Then Viren accelerates, and Quax (NZL, 691) and Hildenbrandt (RFA, 420) concede victory.

he'll be hard to beat in the 5,000m.' The headline 'The return of the Messiah' is announced in the bible of Finnish distance running.

During the press conference after the 5,000m final, his fourth Olympic victory, Lasse Viren responded calmly to the sometimes aggressive interrogation. 'It's been said that artificial means have been used in Finland to improve athletic performance.'

'Absolutely not,' Viren replies. 'I just drank reindeer milk from Lapland. That's what works for me!'

Sinkkonnen backed him up; 'Viren has had no transfusions,' he asserted. But Viren, armed with ironic smiles, got himself out of the ambush of the press conference by acting the innocent: 'But what are all these stories of transfusion? I've never heard anything about it.' Suspicion can be a heavy burden, and is difficult to dispel. A blood transfusion can stimulate a tired body, and is undetectable. Besides, Viren can laugh at his detractors. He has four gold medals that will shine forever in the archives of Finnish middle-distance running. Today he succeeded in an exploit that put him up there with the Finnish god, Paavo Nurmi.

Lasse Viren's stunning double at the 1972 Games was still resounding around the world, yet his post-Munich performances met with derision. Could he explain his decline? I interviewed him several times during his fallow period, which he accepted with surprising equanimity: 'I'm not the sort of person who needs invincibility and world records,' he told me, with a disarming smile. 'I had a serious thigh injury and had to be operated on, but that's not important. I'm only interested in the Games.'

He claimed indifference to his reputation as a former Olympic hero, which was slowly deteriorating. And during those four years of purgatory, Kari Sinkkonnen, the head of Finnish athletics, took more or less the same view: 'We believe he'll have recovered totally in time for the Montreal

Games. He will be as hard to beat in the 5,000m as in the 10,000m.'

Last year we were in Helsinki for an evening meeting. The air was clear. The audience couldn't wait to see Viren run the 10,000m, as the policeman from Myrskyla, a small town 25km from Lahti, announced 'I'm here to win my Olympic selection.' After a three-week training camp in January in Puerto Rico and four weeks in Kenya in April at Thompson Falls, Viren was prepared for a dramatic return. He was covering a distance of fifty kilometres every day.

At the entrance to the stadium in Helsinki, we passed the legendary statue of Paavo Nurmi. Finland had lost Vasala, the 1500m champion in Munich, and Viren had been anonymous for four years: no-one believed a Finn would be the limelight in Montreal. But Viren's run that night

was an astonishing reverse of fortune. He exploded back onto the international stage with an astonishing 10,000m in 27:43. He ran the final kilometre in 2:36.1. Returning to its senses, the crowd joyfully accompanied him in this triumphant return. The legendary Finland had regained its hero. Viren explained his absence during the previous years: 'In 1973, the year after the Munich Games, I often celebrated my victory. I was invited everywhere. Then in 1974 and 1975 I had a serious thigh injury. I had to have an operation. Now it's 1976 and I'm back and I'm much better thank you!' He smiles.

On Canadian soil before the Games, we sought out the Finnish coaches to try to shed some light on this amazing comeback. 'There's no mystery,' says Kari Sinkkonnen. 'You're going to see him win the 10,000m and afterwards

'After the 10,000m my feet were in pain. I wasn't trying to publicise my brand of shoes.'

Lasse Viren: 'next, the marathon'

It was no longer just a good hand; it was becoming almost miraculous. In the 5,000m, fifteen metres from the line, Lasse Viren was smiling. Behind him, Hildenbrand (GER), Quax (NZL) and Dixon (also NZL), were grimacing with pain as they fought for second and third place.

Having already won the 10,000m, Lasse Viren added the fourth gold medal to his collection. Once he had crossed the line, Viren's lap of honour was more discreet than it had been after the 10,000m the other day. 'I was summoned by the IOC to explain why I took my shoes off after the race. I told the truth. It wasn't for publicity. I had blisters.'

He only learned three hours before the 5,000m that he would be allowed to take part.

Lasse Viren, four times Olympic champion, then spoke of his 5,000m victory: 'I was only worried twice during the event,' he said, 'The first time was when I realised that this race was going to be painful. I just did everything I could to get through it. The second time was 200m before the

finish line. I thought to myself: 'The milers will be on their way past – better watch out.' But I accelerated, and kept my lead to the end.'

Next to him, Dick Quax, the dignified New Zealander with the best time in the world this year, toys nervously with his moustache. Someone asks: 'Viren hasn't even been mentioned in four years, then comes back and surprises everyone in Montreal. What do you feel about it?'

'I'm disappointed,' he says, twice. It's clear that he doesn't want to say any more. His silence speaks for itself.

Then an American journalist aims a question for Viren: 'Do you dope your blood?'

Viren smiles. 'What do you mean by that?' he replies, 'I'm not aware of that kind of doping.'

'Do you raise your haemoglobin level using artificial means?'

'And how do you suppose that is done?' replies Viren, his face cupped in his hand maintaining his ironic smile. So we change the subject. Viren is certainly going to stay quiet about this problem. He would rather talk

about the marathon which is now going to feature in his training programme. The question is simple; does he feel capable of succeeding in a new challenge?

'To be honest with you,' he says, 'I have high hopes of winning the marathon too. Now I hope you'll excuse me from this press conference. I need to go and train.'

Portugal's Carlos Lopes offers the only resistance to Viren in the 10,000m, but he can't compete against the Finn's sprint finish.

Viren can't make it three in the marathon. He finishes fifth far behind Cierpinski (GDR in white, right), a true specialist.

A tale of two races

26 July, 10,000m – all eyes are on Viren who, except for his third place in the European Championships in Rome in 1974, he has not been involved in international competition for four years. He controls the race from start to finish, a curious, uneventful affair, not as close as the final four years ago. The best Africans are absent, and Dick Quax (NZL) has decided not to compete.

Carlos Lopes (POR), a magnificent athlete but lacking a sprint finish, ran a good race from the third kilometre, running between 2:44 and 2:42 per kilometre from the fifth to the ninth kilometre, at which point Marc Smet (BEL) who had fallen, and made it back to the bunch, was dropped. So too was Brendan Foster (GBR), uncomfortable from the seventh kilometre.

The race was now decided by the

finishing speed of Viren who, with his short, economic stride, followed Lopes until 450m from the end, before accelerating steadily and irresistibly past Lopes to retain his title more easily than he had acquired it in Munich. This despite an astonishing last 5,000m in 13:31 and a final 3,000m in 8:04. He ran the last lap in 60 seconds to join Zátopek, twice the 10,000m Olympic champion in 1948 and 1952, and out-performing Nurmi, winner in 1920 and 1928.

30 July, 5,000m – the 5,000m is a great tactical race. Nobody wants to take risks. Brendan Foster (GBR) suffers stomach pains over the previous days. Everyone is counting on their sprint finishes. But what a contest! Seven athletes are still together 400m from the end. All are capable of winning.

Progress has been slow; 2:41 at

1000m, 5:26.4 at 2,000 m, 8:16.3 at 3000m; it is like stepping fifteen years back in time. Suddenly the group comes to life under the impetus of Hildenbrand (GER), covering the fourth kilometre in 2:39.2, an astonishing acceleration compared to the preceding kilometre, covered in 2:50. At the bell Quax and Dixon, the best milers of the pack, seem most at ease. The pace increases spectacularly: 5:08.5 for the final 2,000m, 2:29.2 for the last 1000m, 1:57.5 for the last 800m. Then 400m from the finish, Viren flares out of the group and accelerates on the bend and along the next straight. Only Quax and Dixon go with him. At the start of the final straight Quax nearly levels with Viren, who retains his short lead. No runner, not even Nurmi, Ritola or Zátopek, had ever achieved a 'double double'.

Kornelia's coronation

Four titles, four world records and a unique double! Ender (GDR) takes all.

Reserved and discreet after her success, Kornelia Ender isn't cold or distant, just modest.

Kornelia Ender's success had met with little enthusiasm from the Canadian public – until now. With one of the great feats in Olympic history, this blond East German finally won over the crowd. And she knew it, bursting at last into spontaneous, radiant joy after so many victories, so many records, and a stunning milestone in women's swimming.

Later, it emerged that this was at the end of a three-year journey. At last, the doubt had gone from her mind.

Yes, she had beaten her rivals but, more than that, she had pushed back her own limits, winning the gamble she and her East German sporting leaders had taken, considered reckless beforehand, to try to win two consecutive finals. 'The decision was taken a month after I did a similar thing as part of my training,' she said.

It was 19.45 in Montreal when, to the rhythm of the Olympic march, the competitors in the 100m butterfly began their half-lap of the pool to get to their starting positions. Two minutes later came the presentation of the swimmers. Ender, in lane four, between Wendy Boglioli (USA) and Rosemarie Gabriel (GDR), received

only polite applause.
19.49 – The race starts. Ender wins in 1:10.13, equalling the world record.
20.02 – She tops the podium to the East German national anthem, her

Moments after winning the 100m butterfly, Ender appears for the 200m freestyle – unprecedented in the Olympic Games.

gold medal glinting in the spotlights.
20.05 – The medal ceremony ends.
20.11 – Ender returns for the 200m freestyle. 'In the little time I had I concentrated on relaxing as much as possible. I did flexibility exercises to stop my muscles tensing. I tried to focus. I knew Shirley Babashoff had the advantage of freshness, but I also knew I was capable of beating her.'
20.13 – She slowly removes her bathrobe and tracksuit and massages her calves and arms.
20.15 – As usual, she hits the water first. But at 50m Babashoff turns first, leads by 0.07 seconds. Although essentially slower, the American knows that she may have a chance if Ender hasn't fully recovered from her 100m butterfly. 'But,' admits the American, 'I actually couldn't go as fast as I had predicted. My arm stroke was a little shorter than it needed to be.'

On the last turn the two girls are in perfect synchrony, but then the East German's kick strengthens and the gap between them widens. Kornelia Ender swims the last 50m in 28.88. 'I learned a lesson in Cali (Colombia) last year, when Babashoff passed me in the last few metres after I started too quickly.

This season I have trained to follow Babashoff at the start then accelerate at the end.'

For the second time in her career Kornelia has swum 200m in less than two minutes – 1:59.26 to be precise.
20.29 – On the highest step of the podium, the crowd greets her with rapturous applause. Then, only then, Ender's face breaks into a smile.

Before the start, her warm-up movements accentuate her arm length.

ENDERS' TITLES

100m freestyle
1 Kornelia Ender (GDR), 55.65
2 Petra Priemer (GDR), 56.49
3 Enith Brigitha (NED), 56.65

200m freestyle
1 Kornelia Ender (GDR), 1:59.26
2 Shirley Babashoff (USA), 2:01.22
3 Enith Brigitha (NED), 2:01.40

100m butterfly
1 Kornelia Ender (GDR), 1:00.13
2 Andrea Pollack (GDR), 1:00.98
3 Wendy Boglioli (USA), 1:01.17

4x100m medley relay
1 GDR (Ulrike Richter, Hannelore Anke, Andrea Pollack, Kornelia Ender), 4:07.95
2 United States 4:14.55
3 Canada, 4:15.22

A record for all time

America's Jim Montgomery wins the 100m freestyle and breaks the fifty-second barrier (49.99).

The swimming events ended in apotheosis in the men's 100m freestyle, which saw Jim Montgomery, despite the great athleticism and eloquence of his compatriot John Naber, emerge as the greatest swimmer of the Games.

Between the semi-finals and the final, Montgomery, the Wisconsin Colossus – although he is one of coach James Counsilman's swimmers at Bloomington, Indiana – broke the world record twice, reducing it by no less than six tenths of a second and becoming the first man to accomplish the blue riband swimming event in less than fifty seconds – 49.99.

The fifty-second barrier had taken on mythical proportions. Montgomery's performance is even more impressive in that it has taken him less than twelve months to better his own time by 1.12 seconds – a distance of more than two metres at race speed.

Montgomery's greatness doesn't just stem from breaking this record, but also from having gone so far to do it. The 100m is the shortest competition in the Olympic programme (the 50m, last raced in 1904, was reintroduced in 1988), and

Two years ago Jim Montgomery set himself a goal: 'I calculated that, to be an Olympic champion in Montreal, I would have to swim in less than 50'. Since then I've been preparing myself physically and psychologically.' Above, he achieves that objective by the narrowest of margins.

Base speed and resistance: Montgomery becomes a new prototype for the 100m freestyle competitor.

consists of a single burst of energy. More of a time trial than a race, it leaves no room for error. The start and the turn is as important as the swimming. In 1964, Schollander beat McGregor, a faster swimmer, by virtue of a faster start. Four years later, Devitt won thanks to the first perfect turn of his life.

Despite an amazing semi-final in which Montgomery lowered the world record to 50.39, doubts remained. In the two previous big races in which Montgomery, after splendid qualifiers, had come up against great difficulties in the final, a mental weakness had emerged. Last year, in the US national championships, Montgomery broke a series of world records, then won the final by just one hundredth of a second with a much less impressive performance. During the Olympic trials last month, this scenario repeated itself.

Here, Montgomery tried to reassure everyone that he was going to bring it all together in a phenomenal first length. Only once has a human being started faster; Zacchary Zorn, in the 100m final of the Mexico Games,

reached the half-way point in twenty-four seconds. But that Zacchary was a false prophet: in the second length he paid the price of a week-long illness and finished last.

Montgomery was timed at 24.14 for the first fifty metres. But he still had to defend his lead from Jack Babashoff, with his frenzied arm rhythm, to his left, and the strong-legged Italian Guarducci to his right, who was shadowing him and taking maximum advantage of his wave.

No official timing could reinforce our confidence when, at about seventy-five metres, Jack Babashoff, whose arm rhythm was approaching dementure, closed the gap slightly. Montgomery merely accelerated. This was the man who, two days earlier, swam the second length of his leg in the 4x100m medley relay in 25.76 and seemed very satisfied with the result. Here he hardly swam his second length any slower – 25.85 – on the back of his remarkable first fifty metres. Beaten by 1.5m in a time of 50.81, Jack Babashoff became the second fastest swimmer of all time The size of the gap that separated him

from the man who beat him only added to Montgomery's achievement.

Jim Montgomery, however, was so superior to his rivals that there was little room for doubt. He could have made a mistake and still won. His margin of victory guarantees him a place in that elite group of swimmers who, in their time, were simply unbeatable including: Wenden (1968) and Spitz (1972). By finishing 0.82 seconds ahead of Jack Babashoff, Montgomery won more effortlessly than any of his predecessors. Not since Weissmuller in 1928 has an Olympic champion dominated the final so effortlessly.

RESULTS

100m
1 Jim Montgomery (USA), 49.99
2 Jack Babashoff (USA), 50.81
3 Peter Nocke (GER), 51.31
4 Klaus Steinbach (GER), 51.68
5 Marcello Guarducci (ITA), 51.70
6 Joe Bottom (USA), 51.79
7 Vladimir Bure (SOV/RUS) 52.03
8 Andrei Krylov (SOV/RUS), 52.15

1976

OLYMPIC ROUND-UP

KARPPINEN THE UNEXPECTED.

Eight medals out of eight mean East Germany has done what it came here to do. Eight medals (five gold, one silver, two bronze) was exactly the same result as last year at the World Rowing Championships in Nottingham. Curiously, the same three boats failed to win gold – the single, double and quadruple sculls all got off to a bad start. But it didn't prevent the implacable, impressive domination of East Germany. And if they had achieved eight gold medals, any uncertainty would have been removed from the sport of rowing, which would hardly be a good thing.

Yet you only need to look at the victories of the Finn Karppinen (photo 6) in the single-sculls and the Hansen brothers in the double-sculls to be convinced of a balance of power which may not be immediately visible but is a reality in the water.

The biggest surprise of the day was the victory of Pertti Karppinen in the single-sculls, as the race was dominated from start to finish – almost – by the brilliant Kolbe, who had the lead for three lengths. He descended the stream at thirty-two strokes per minute without seeming to over-exert himself, displaying power and agility at the same time. At the 500m mark he was still two lengths ahead of Karppinen, who had already begun a remarkable return.

The giant Finn, measuring 6 feet 7 and weighing 215 pounds, found himself at an advantage rowing into the wind, his oars punching the water with force. We kept expecting Kolbe, who was born to row and is gifted like no other, to suddenly display spectacular acceleration. But it was not to be. He lost it and was overtaken by a colossal effort from the imperturbable Karppinen, fifty metres from the finish. Karppinen was now Olympic champion and his efforts had paid off: his time of 7:29.03 into the wind is a fantastic achievement. Karppinen was the only one who had believed in his chances in this clash of the titans. Kolbe without doubt had shown too much complacency.

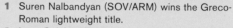

1 Suren Nalbandyan (SOV/ARM) wins the Greco-Roman lightweight title.
2 Leon Spinks wins the light-heavyweight tournament, in the fight following the middleweight final won by his brother Michael.
3 Favourites Poland lose the football final 3-1 to East Germany (in white).
4 A triple win for the Soviet triple jumper Viktor Saneyev who won in Mexico, Munich and Montreal.
5 The Hungarians (white caps, here against the Italian silver medalists) take the water-polo tournament by storm.
6 The Finn Karppinen is presented with the first of three gold medals in consecutive Games in the single-sculls.
7 Nadia Comaneci isn't the only one to merit a perfect ten – Nelli Kim (SOV/KAZ) also scores ten in the floor exercise and the vault.
8 Johanna Schaller, of East Germany, on course to win the 100m hurdles.
9 A title and world record for the American Bruce Jenner in the decathlon – he deserves a hug.
10 Is there no stopping Uljana Semyonova, over seven feet tall? The Japanese (fifth overall) couldn't, and nor could the Americans (silver medalists).
11 David Wilkie of Great Britain wins the 200m breast-stroke and becomes the only non-American male swimming champion at the Montreal Olympics.
12 At 34 years old, the Soviet weightlifter Vassily Alekseyev defends all his titles.
13 The unstoppable Tatyana Kazankina winning the 800m.
14 The German Alwin Schockemöhle becomes Olympic show jumping champion, with no faults.
15 Poland's Irena Szewinska achieves the last title of her Olympic career in the 400m. From 1964 to 1976, she won three gold medals, two silver and two bronze in the 100m, 200m, 400m and the 4x100m relay.

SWIMMING

Naber's finest hour

In sixty minutes the American John Naber wins gold in the backstroke and silver in the freestyle – incredible.

It takes physical strength, mental calmness, great powers of concentration and recovery, topped, above all, by unshakeable faith. Only exceptional athletes combine these qualities. John Naber is one. Before a crowd already won over by his innate charm, Naber, 20, a psychology student at the University of Southern California, lived his hour of glory.

It was 20.00 when, to music that evoked the coming of the gladiators, he arrived on his starting platform wearing his woollen cap, sandwiched between his team-mate Peter Rocca and Roland Matthes (GDR), who had beaten Naber's last world record (56.30). It wasn't complacency that lay behind Naber's smile. It was an implacable confidence in his capabilities. 'I was convinced I could beat the record of 56.19,' he later said.

He was unaffected by Matthes' two false starts in the 100m backstroke. This detachment was the product of an iron temperament, illustrated by Naber's flawless start. Surfacing almost a metre ahead of Rocca and

Untouchable in the 100 and 200m backstroke, John Naber takes his sport to a level never attained before.

RESULTS

NABER'S FIVE PODIUMS

100 m backstroke
1 John Naber (USA), 55.49
2 Peter Rocca (USA), 56.34
3 Roland Matthes (GDR), 57.22

200 m backstroke
1 John Naber (USA), 1:59.19
2 Peter Rocca (USA), 2:00.55
3 Dan Harrigan (USA), 2:01.35

200m
1 Bruce Furniss (USA), 1:50.29
2 John Naber (USA), 1:50.50
3 Jim Montgomery (USA), 1:50.58

4x200 m
1 USA (Michael Bruner, Bruce Furniss, John Naber, Jim Montgomery), 7:23.22
2 SOV, 7:27.97
3 GBR, 7:32.11

4x100m medley
1 USA (John Naber, John Hencken, Matt Vogel, Jim Montgomery), 3:42.22
2 CAN, 3:45.94
3 GER, 3:47.29

Matthes, he had half-won the race before it had really started, but it takes more than victory to satisfy a young man who said two days ago: 'Olympic victory is of no interest to me unless I give the best of myself.'

Naber turned in 26.36 seconds; Matthes, in 26.91. Naber held his lead and lowered the record to 55.59.

20.06 – Naber stays in the water and stretches with an innate theatricality. He waves to the crowd, to rapturous applause, and flashes his white teeth like a White House candidate before an election.

20.20 – On the highest step of the podium, Naber is still smiling.

20.50 – He returns to the pool for the 200m butterfly. He was the eighth qualifier in the morning, in the same time as Spitz in Munich. Between the formal ceremony and the call for the 200m, he has managed to rest for exactly thirty minutes.

Ever smiling, ever exuberant, the impressive John Naber came to swimming late, and became a phenomenon.

'I dozed, and relaxed in the training pool. My pulse wasn't any faster than normal before competition. I felt strangely calm. I had prepared for this situation in training and I had no fear of losing.'

After a length, Montgomery, with a faster base speed, turns. Naber is third. Half-way point, he turns slightly

ahead of Bruce Furniss. At 150m Naber still has a 0.04 second lead.

In the final length, the crowd screams. Furniss, breathing to the right, can see Naber. Naber can see nothing. 'In the final twenty-five metres I went through the pain threshold. I had a blocked ear and my head felt like it was going to explode.'

He finishes second in 1:50.50 – an achievement. 'I swim to go further into the search for myself,' he says. Naber must know himself a bit better than he did few days ago.

HE BEAT THE BUTTERFLY RECORD

John Naber overcame the fatigue of a gruelling week of competitions to win his second individual gold medal in the 200m backstroke. A historic race not only because the distance was covered in less than two minutes, but also because his time was faster than the 200m butterfly record, the butterfly having been considered a faster stroke until now!

MONTREAL XXI OLYMPIAD

The dramatic events of the Munich Games had left their mark, and
16,000 men were drafted in to look after security at the Games.
The real political threat, however, was the African boycott.

THE GAMES IN BRIEF

Opening Date
17 July 1976

Closing Date
1 August 1976

Host Nation
Canada (CAN)

Candidate Towns
Los Angeles (USA) and Moscow (SOV).

92 Nations Represented

6,028 athletes
(1,247 women, 4,781 men).

21 Sports
(11 open to women)
Track and field, rowing, basketball, boxing,
canoeing, cycling, equestrian, fencing,
football, gymnastics, weightlifting,
handball, field hockey, judo, wrestling,
swimming, pentathlon, volley-ball,
shooting, archery and sailing.

198 Events
(49 open to women)

Games opened by
HRH Queen Elizabeth II

Olympic flame lit by
Sandra Henderson (athletics) and
Stéphane Préfontaine (athletics).

Olympic oath read by
Pierre Saint-Jean (weightlifting)

IOC President
Lord Mickael Killanin (IRL)

Montréal 1976

DID YOU KNOW?

The Olympic flame arrived by air. It was
sent – in the form of an electronic signal –
to a transmitter pointed at an Intelsat
satellite, and then to a receiver where the
stored energy set off a laser beam that
restored it to a physical flame.
  Thanks to Clarence Hill, who won a
bronze medal for boxing, Bermuda became
the least populous nation (53,500) ever to
win an Olympic medal.
  Women's events were included for the
first time in basketball, team handball and
rowing.

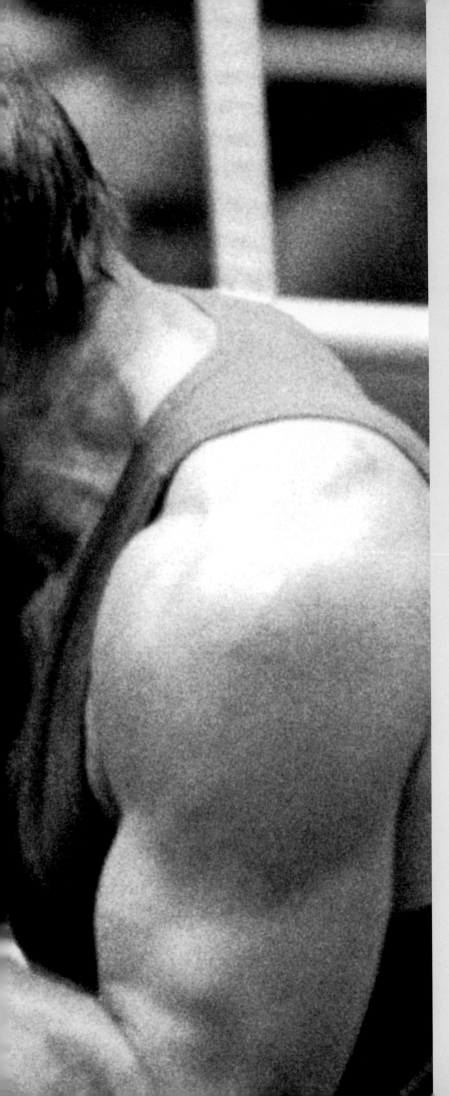

1980

Moscow

'THE SOVIET INVASION OF AFGHANISTAN
will seriously affect present and future relations
between us and the Soviet Union,' declared US
President Jimmy Carter in early 1980, and the boycott
of the Moscow Olympics became official on 20
January. Until 19 July, the date of the Opening
Ceremony of the Games, there was a fierce battle
between those who wanted to support the American
decision (Japan, South Korea, Canada, West Germany
and even China), those who wanted to participate
unconditionally (all the socialist bloc countries) and
those who wished to go to Moscow under individual
titles without emblems or national anthems (France,
Spain, Australia, Great Britain, etc.). A campaign was
even launched for an Olympic Games with neither
national anthems nor flags.

The pressure on the IOC and its Irish president,
Lord Killanin, was enormous. The Games had to be
saved. Though public opinion was divided, there was a
majority among the athletes in favour of participation.
On 19 July, eighty-one NOCs were represented.

These flawed Games earned unanimous praise for
the quality of the organisation, but they were tarnished
by excessive nationalism on the part of the Moscow
public. Despite this, and despite the numerous
absences, thirty-four world records and sixty-two
Olympic records were set.

On 3 August during the Closing Ceremony, Misha
the bear mascot shed a tear when the words 'See you
at the twenty-third Olympics' appeared.

Cuban Teófilo Stevenson had won all his bouts within the distance in 1972
and 1976. His third Olympic title was harder fought: Stevenson defeated Pyotr
Zayev (SOV/RUS) on points.

A great start for Dityatin…

The team competition saw the Soviets prevail, inspired by Aleksandr Dityatin's dazzling display.

After a twenty-four year wait, the USSR finally won the men's team event title. Since 1956 the Soviets had always conceded the Olympic crown to Japan. And this year it's theirs, to be celebrated by the people of Russia and, foremost among them, the six gymnasts; Aleksandr Dityatin, Nikolai Andrianov, Aleksandr Tkachyov, Eduard Azaryan, Vladimir Markelov and Bohdan Makuts.

It's a shame for the absentees. A Russian proverb says that the absent are always in the wrong, and that's certainly the attitude of the Soviets after this historic demonstration. Not for a moment were there any fears that this team had weak links (the last to be selected, Markelov, finished no lower than ninth). East Germany, coming second as predicted, finished 8.45 points adrift!

The outstanding gymnast was, unsurprisingly, Aleksandr Dityatin. The world champion at Fort Worth by a tenth of a point from the Olympic champion of Montreal, Nikolai Andrianov, increased his lead.

Here, he won by 0.25 points. It was a performance of great precision, carried out with metronomic regularity. Dityatin's great talent is for the rings, where he was awarded a well-deserved 9.95. The man known as the playboy of international gymnastics breezed through the events watched by an enthusiastic crowd that supported its men with gusto, although their support made little difference to the outcome: the Soviets were far superior to the rest.

We also learnt the qualifiers for the individual events. They followed the form book. Dityatin returned for six competitions, although he was the first to perform only once, for the rings. Andrianov bettered him in the floor exercises; Tkachyov, on the parallel bars; Magyar (HUN), on the pommel horse; and Deltchev (BUL), on the horizontal bar.

The real Lord of the Rings, as far as the Olympic world is concerned, has done it again.

RESULTS

Team Competition
1 SOV (Aleksandr Dityatin, Nicolay; Andrianov, Eduard Azaryan; Aleksandr Tkatchov, Bohdan Makuts; Vladimir Markelov), 598.60 pts
2 GDR, 581.5 pts
3 HUN, 575 pts

Individual All-Around
1 Aleksandr Dityatin (SOV/RUS), 118.65 pts
2 Nikolaï Andrianov (SOV/RUS), 118.225 pts
3 Stoyan Deltchev (BUL), 118 pts

Rings
1 Aleksandr Dityatin (SOV/RUS), 19.875 pts
2 Aleksandr Tkachyov (SOV/RUS), 19.725 pts
3 Jiri Tabak (CZE), 19,60 pts

Horizontal Bar
1 Stoyan Deltchev (BUL), 19.825 pts
2 Aleksandr Dityatin (SOV/RUS), 19.75 pts
3 Nikolaï Andrianov (SOV/RUS), 19.675 pts

Parallel Bars
1 Aleksandr Tkatchyov (SOV/RUS), 19.775 pts
2 Aleksandr Dityatin (SOV/RUS), 19.75 pts
3 Roland Brückner (GDR), 19.65 pts

Vault
1 Nikolaï Andrianov (SOV/RUS), 19.825 pts
2 Aleksandr Dityatin (SOV/US), 19.80 pts
3 Roland Brückner (GDR), 19.775 pts

Pommel Horse
1 Zoltan Magyar (HUN), 19.925 pts
2 Aleksandr Dityatin (SOV/RUS), 19.80 pts
3 Michael Nikolay (GDR), 19.775 pts

Floor
1 Roland Brückner (GDR), 19.75 pts
2 Nikolaï Andrianov (SOV/RUS), 19.725 pts
3 Aleksandr Dityatin (SOV/RUS), 19.70 pts

...and a beautiful finish!

Winning six medals in the apparatus finals, Dityatin brings his total to eight.

The gymnastics tournament culminated in the individual apparatus finals, with six male and six female qualifiers. More medals were awarded, eighteen to the men and twelve to the women, which always seems excessive compared to the single individual All-Around title. But those are the rules. In any case, the finals were spectacular.

The star of the show was Aleksandr Dityatin (SOV/RUS), who took part in all six finals and won six more medals – extraordinary, even if he only took gold in the rings. He collected four silver medals in the horizontal bar, parallel bars, the vault and the pommel horse, and won bronze in the floor exercises.

The tall, blond Aleksandr was even more brilliant and polished than at the World Championships in Fort Worth in December, in which America's Kurt Thomas had performed equally well, at least in certain events, notably the horizontal bar and the parallel bars.

Stoyan Deltchev (BUL) won the gold on the horizontal bar, raising the technical standard to an entirely new level. The elegant Aleksandr Tkatchyov (SOV/RUS) took consolation by winning the parallel bars – he had been hoping to do better than fourth in the All-Around competition.

On the pommel horse Zoltán Magyar of Hungary retained his crown. He has yet to find an opponent

With Deltchev outperforming him in the horizontal bar, Dityatin settled for silver.

to match him in this event, in which suppleness is paramount.

Nikolai Andrianov (SOV/RUS), All-Around champion in 1976, won the vault event, adding a gold to his silver in the All-Around competition. Victory allowed him to surpass the previous record number of medals won in men's gymnastics. His total went up to fifteen: seven gold, seven silver and three bronze between 1972 and 1980. His predecessor Boris Shakhlin (SOV/UKR) had won thirteen, seven of which were gold, between 1956 and 1964. It was a fitting end to Andrianov's glittering career. He will now devote himself to coaching.

Leningrad playboy Aleksandr Dityatin takes to the air, destined for a perfect ten – a mark he is the first male gymnast to attain. The bird man's only weakness was in the floor exercises, where he still managed a bronze medal – a podium in every discipline.

THE HISTORY OF THE PERFECT TEN

On the occasion of his vault event the Soviet Aleksandr Dityatin had the remarkable honour of becoming the first male gymnast to be given a score of ten in an Olympic competition, four years after Nadia Comaneci and Nelly Kim did the same in Montreal. Four more perfect scores were given for various events: Stoyan Deltchev (BUL) on the rings, Aleksandr Tkatchyov (SOV/RUS) on the horizontal bar and Zoltan Magyar (HUN) and Michael Nikolay (GDR) on the pommel horse.

Stevenson's treasure island

Cuba steals the show, and among its six Olympic champions, Teófilo Stevenson wins his third Olympic title.

Without forcing his talent, Teófilo Stevenson (left), the standard bearer of the brilliant Cuban team, gives Soviet Zayev a lesson in sober efficiency.

The boxing finals at the Olympiski complex were disappointing. The Americans, were sorely missed. No Howard Davis, no Spinks brothers, no Sugar Ray Leonard. Standards have been far below those set in 1976. Even the finest performers – Aldama, Gomez, Oliva – seemed dull and careless. The finals were even inferior to the early rounds in the same tournament, as boxers reached the finals exhausted from the preliminary rounds and paralysed by the stakes.

The highlight was the heavyweight final between Teófilo Stevenson (CUB) and Pyotr Zayev (SOV), in

The deputy dons his gloves.

which the Cuban won his third boxing gold medal in consecutive Games, going down in history with Laszlo Papp of Hungary, the Olympic champion who won the middle-weight title in 1948, then the light-middleweight in 1952 and 1956. Stevenson, the parliamentary deputy for Las Cunas, boxed mean and raw. Jabs with the left, light-footed side-steps, and big rights: three in the first round, three in the second and so on.

The robust Zayev, six inches shorter (5 feet 11 against 6 feet 5) wasn't humiliated in defeat, and forced the sculptured Cuban to work harder

than usual. Zayev hit Stevenson several times with his right. Even so, the Cuban's victory was indisputable, and Stevenson won't have been too exhausted by his latest Olympic adventure.

Zayev's predictable but honourable defeat was doubtless one of the least resented by the Soviets who, however, can't have imagined getting such a close result when the finals began. Yet Zayev's effort was a mere diversion in the face of a flood of Cubans. Of the eight finals, six produced Cuban champions, and it is to their island that we owe all that was good about this pugilistic marathon.

Salnikov the Czar

No victory was ever more widely predicted than that of the Russian in the 1500m freestyle.

There were celebrations at the Olympic pool in Moscow after East Germany's Rica Reinisch, in the women's 100m backstroke heats, beat the world record her team-mate Ulrike Richter had held for four years and that Reinisch herself had equalled there two days previously at the start of the 4 x 100m medley relay – 1:01.51. However, these celebrations were a mere appetiser before the *pièce de résistance* – the men's 1500m freestyle. The longest race of the programme was expected to crown the Soviet Vladimir Salnikov. Any other matters were mere distractions. The only questions were how Salnikov would decide to win, and who would come second.

Salnikov decided on the panache of a solo victory. He attacked from the gun. We're told, Salnikov listens to music during the marathon training sessions that have made him the most resilient swimmer in the world. It must be a particularly rhythmic soundtrack. Brian Goodell's world record (15:02.40) was already four years old, looked increasingly vulnerable as Salnikov extended his lead. He completed his lengths with almost mechanical regularity: the first 500 metres in 5:0.23, the first 1000 in 10:0.85. He reached 1,100m in 11:01.15. The last 400 metres he swam in 3:57.12, the last 200 in 1:57.46 and his last two lengths of the pool in 58.05. As he touched the pad, the

At the 1,100 metre mark, Vladimir accelerates, finally breaking the world record and the fifteen-minute barrier.

world record was his.

By completing 1500m in 14:58.27, Salnikov has become the first man to break the fifteen-minute barrier. This immortal feat will secure him a place in sporting history, fifty-eight years after Johnny Weissmuller, the legendary Tarzan – now in Acapulco suffering a serious illness – who conquered the one-minute barrier in the 100m. You can imagine how the crowd received the success of its champion. The silver medal, too, went to a Soviet swimmer, Aleksandr Chayev, who beat Australia's Max Metzker to the line. The crowd greeted their champions with cries of '*Molodiet*' – 'courageous.' Salnikov has

earned the title of the Czar of middle-distance swimmers, for this most challenging discipline cannot be won without unshakeable determination. Salnikov, a formidable warrior, will be the least controversial of Moscow Olympic champions. Unbeaten in the 400m, for three full years, he wouldn't have been surpassed, even if the Americans had been competing. Remember that the sixteen-minute barrier for the 1,500m was beaten exactly ten years ago by John Kinsella (USA, 15:57.1) and the seventeen-minute barrier, by another swimmer from across the Atlantic, Roy Saari (16:58.7) in 1964. It's amazing how things change over time!

[Editor's note: two days later, Vladimir Salnikov won the 400m in a new Olympic record time of 3:51.31.]

Invincible, a smiling Salnikov earns a place in history with a solo effort, as only the greats can.

RESULTS

1500m
1 Vladimir Salnikov (SOV/RUS), 14:58.27
2 Aleksandr Chayev (SOV/RUS), 15:14.30
3 Max Metzker (AUS), 15:14.39
4 Rainer Strohbach (GDR), 15:15.29
5 Borut Petric (YUG), 15:21.78
6 Rafael Escalas (SPA), 15:21.88
7 Zoltan Wladar (HUN), 15:26.70
8 Eduard Petrov (SOV/UKR), 15:28.24

Part one goes to Ovett

The favourite for the 1500m wins the first part of his all-British duel with Sebastian Coe – in the 800m.

Steve Ovett (279) wins the 800m ahead of Sebastian Coe (254), tricked by a slow pace. Nikolai Kirov (RUS, right) was third and Agberto Guimarães (BRA) fourth.

Last year, while Sebastian Coe was setting records, Steve Ovett was out of the spotlight. Coe was not fooled, and told journalists in Turin before the European Cup: 'I'm in good shape and I'm taking advantage of it, but there's no doubt that Steve will be strong in Moscow.'

Ovett is from a different mould: 'I'm not interested in world records like he is and never will be. I'm only interested in the one-on-one competition.' And in round one of their one-on-one went to Ovett.

'I had doubts about the 800m,' he confided to those close to him, 'but recent speed trials put my mind at rest. I had a psychological advantage over Sebastian in that I had nothing to lose in this race.'

Coe, meanwhile, made no excuses: 'I ran to try and beat my opponent and I did everything in my power. I didn't want to lead him out: it was windy, and you don't let a rival like that run in your slipstream. I thought I

Steve Ovett, normally introverted and modest, lets his hair down after the 800m.

would be able to come from behind, but I was too far back as we entered the finishing straight. That was my mistake. When the Russian started his

sprint on the opposite side, I saw him but I didn't react. You have bad days, and I wasn't at my best. Would it have turned out differently if I hadn't been running against my greatest rival? I don't know. There were some tussles, I don't like running in a group, my stride pattern is constricted. I'm not as relaxed as I should be. But in the end, it's simple: there was a runner who was better than me, and he deserves to be congratulated.'

Coe never pronounces the name of the man who is, alongside him, the best middle-distance runner in Britain. On the podium, he shook his hand without looking at him.

Steve Ovett was unavailable for comments after the race. He told French journalists 'I'd be happy to talk to you, but since I'm annoyed with the British press, it would be impolite to confide in anyone else.'

Fortunately, his joy spoke for him. His lap of honour and kisses to the crowd show that the rebel has a tender

side. His timidity is just one element of his personality: he keeps everything inside, including his stores of strength.

We can now look forward to the 1500m, and this time, it will be Coe who has nothing to lose.

Coe (second) stares into space. Ovett (first) smiles with joy. A satisfied Kirov (third) completes a surprise podium in the 800m.

Part two: Coe's Revenge

Beaten over 800m, his favourite event, Coe fights back over 1500m and wins.

Sebastian Coe's joy overwhelmed his phlegmatic instincts. He knelt on the track, kissed the ground and thanked the gods, looking to the sky as if projecting his joy into eternity.

We were wrong to think him more a stylist than a fighter. Since the 800m final – 'The most disappointing day of my athletic career' – Coe has proven he can fight. His intelligence resolved the conundrum of how to beat Steve Ovett.

'The 800m was the race I wanted to win. Even now, if I could choose, I'd prefer the 800m gold medal. But after a bad night after the final, I sat down with my father and analysed the race. This helped me to understand that I'd experienced the ultimate off-day, because this type of thing doesn't happen twice. I watched it several times on video and saw that the problem wasn't speed but tactics. I could tell from the video that if I went into the final 100m level with Ovett I could beat him, providing I was relaxed and didn't tense up. So that's how I ran: I didn't worry about anyone else; I was well-placed at the start of the last straight. The last 10m were tough and pushed me to the limit. But I'd rather have dropped dead on the track than lose.'

RESULTS

COE Vs OVETT

800m
1 Steve Ovett (GBR), 1:45.40
2 Sebastian Coe (GBR), 1:45.85
3 Nikolai Kirov (SOV/BLR), 1:45.94
4 Agberto Guimaraes (BRA), 1:46.20
5 Andreas Busse (GER), 1:46.81
6 Detlef Wagenknecht (GER), 1:46.91
7 José Marajo (FRA), 1:47.26
8 David Warren (GBR), 1:49.25

1500m
1 Sebastian Coe (GBR), 3:38.40
2 Jürgen Straub (GER), 3:38.80
3 Stephen Ovett (GBR), 3:38.99
4 Andreas Busse (GER), 3:40.17
5 Vittorio Fontanella (ITA), 3:40.37
6 Josef Plachy (CZE), 3:40.66
7 José Marajo (FRA), 3:41.48
8 Steve Cram (GBR), 3:41.98

Release for Sebastian Coe. He wins the 1500m, part two of his duel with Ovett. Straub of East Germany (right) finishes second.

Miruts Yifter puts Africa back on the map

The Ethiopian winner of the 5,000m and 10,000m is a pure product of his continent.

The 10,000m final, 27 July. Yifter, in front of his team mates Kedir and Tura, wins easily despite the effort of the Finns Maaninka (second) and Viren (fifth).

The 5,000m final, 1 August. With four races behind him, Yifter, ahead of his team mate Kedir, isn't as dominant, but wins all the same.

Miruts Yifter's 5,000m and 10,000m double was a triumph for a superb athlete who, in each race, gave us a stunning example of how to win with a final-lap sprint. It will endure as the classic image of the Games. Yifter's will be remembered as the greatest track performance of the Games, just as Lasse Viren's at Munich and Montreal. There are similarities between the two men. Neither is obsessed with records: both are more concerned with winning races – although neither man has an aggressive bone in his body.

Miruts always talks kindly of other athletes. He expresses great respect for Viren ('A courageous runner whose presence here, despite his poor form, is a homage to those who ran with him') and a fraternal affection for the Kenyans, particularly Henry Rono: 'He's my brother. It's a shame he can't be here. Africa owes him a lot and I have always been proud of his achievements.' What we have seen here makes us regret never having the chance to see the great distance runner of their generation at Montreal, because of the boycott. Would Lasse Viren have been able to repeat his Munich triumph if Miruts Yifter had been taking part? We'll never know. When Miruts was asked this question he was too much of a gentleman to hazard even the slightest opinion. 'Viren is a great runner,' he said. 'Of

A soldier and a patriot, Yifter is also a natural winner, radiant and at peace.

course I would have tried to win if I had been taking part in the 1976 Games, but I wasn't there.'

The Moscow Games – and this is some consolation for the disruption caused by the boycott – have rediscovered Africa, thanks to Yifter's proud leadership. After eight years we have witnessed again what Africa brings to the Olympic spirit, and the counterweight it brings to the artificial practices that threaten sport. Outside the stadium, in the Olympic Village for example, they are fine ambassadors. Inside it, they bring panache, treating each race as an adventure, given everything from the gun, giving the true tone to the Olympic anthem. Those who think that Olympic Games are moving towards extinction forget the emergence of the new Africa.

Miruts Yifter's defining quality is his spontaneity, which emerges as much in this training and racing as in his family life. He is the loving father of five sons and a daughter of whom the eldest is nine. Outside his running and his military career in which he is rising up through the ranks, he enjoys gardening and the pleasures of bringing up a family.

'And I've always enjoyed running,' he said. 'It's in my nature. I love to run for three or four hours a day in the woods near my house or in the hills, concentrating on my sprint finishes.'

Koch, of course!

In spite of her disrupted preparation, the East German's superiority is enough.

Marita Koch (GDR), the undisputed queen of the 400m, can bask in the glow of an Olympic gold medal at last. The injury that ruled her out at the semi-final stage in Montreal is now forgotten. Despite the fact that her preparation began late due to another injury, Marita Koch took the 1980 Olympic title by winning the fastest 400m in history, in which the first three finished in under 50.0. Christina Lathan, second at Montreal (as Christina Brehmer) in 50.51, finished third here, despite a time of 49.66.

So Koch is the new champion, and how could it have been otherwise? From the moment she took up 400m running, she has never been beaten. This year, less sylph-like than a year ago, Koch, a medical student from Rostock, was in complete control. 'I was wary of my opponents because this season, having been injured, I haven't run under 49 seconds – my

The world's fastest medical student: Marita, the 400m Olympic champion.

A smiling Marita: her unbeaten record intact.

RESULTS

1 Marita Koch (GDR), 48.88
2 Jarmila Kratochvilová (CZE), 49.46
3 Christina Lathan (GDR), 49.66
4 Irina Nazarova (SOV/RUS), 50.07
5 Nina Zyuskova (SOV/UKR), 50.17
6 Gabriela Löwe (GDR), 51.33
7 Pirjo Häggman (FIN), 51.35
8 Linsey MacDonald (GBR), 52.40.

best was 49.15.' She certainly hasn't come close to her world record of 48.60 seconds, although her winning time of 48.88 seconds is a new Olympic record. She would have liked to have tried for the 200m and 400m double. 'Unfortunately, it would have been impossible, given the schedule. With twenty minutes between the quarter final of the 200m and the final

of the 400m, it was out of the question. I would have risked too much and I could have lost the 400m. I knew my margin for error wasn't as great as some might have thought.' *

Since becoming European champion, Koch – who, let's not forget, was only twenty-three at the time – has been coached by Wolfgang Meier. That European title came six

years after her first East German title as a junior, and four years after becoming European junior champion in 1975. Last year, she became the first woman in history to beat 22 seconds in the 200m and the first woman to beat 49 seconds in the 400m.

* Bärbel Wöckel (GDR) won the Olympic 200m final in 22.03. Koch's world record stood at 21.71.

1980

OLYMPIC ROUND-UP

WESSIG, THE ALBATROSS FROM THE EAST.

Gerd Wessig has pushed back humanity's physical limits by jumping 2.36m. That is makes 40 centimetres more than his height. a look at your kitchen ceiling. Wessig flew over it unassisted, using nothing but a pair of agile feet and an arched back.

The cheers of the East German fans quickly turned into a song. The only word I could make out was 'Klasse'. This wonderful athlete has loads of it – Kolossal Klasse! It was a privilege to witness this twenty-year-old knock the cobwebs out of world high-jumping. Last year he jumped 2.21m. In the run-up to the Games, he achieved 2.30m. Here, he has beaten his personal best by six centimetres and set a new world record.

His joy was equal to his performance – altitudinous intoxication in an albatross from the East. Even when the bar went up to 2.38m, it didn't seem too high for him. His gracefulness defied weight and gravity. Floating before, during and after the competition, Wessig left the previous record of 2.30m, held by the great Dwight Stones, far behind and below him.

Wessig's habitually vacant expression is softened by a moustache. Victory had put a smile on his face – but it took only one question from the press to wipe it off again. The only question they had for him after his graceful victory was: 'What's your favourite food?' True, Wessig works as a cook near Schwerin. But he isn't fussy about his food. He likes everything, including food he doesn't prepare himself.

What else could they ask this young man, who had just stepped out of a hot air balloon? Oh yes! His emotions? 'I was relaxed. Not even the music annoyed me. No, I felt I could go very high. I wanted to take advantage of the moment and I succeeded.'

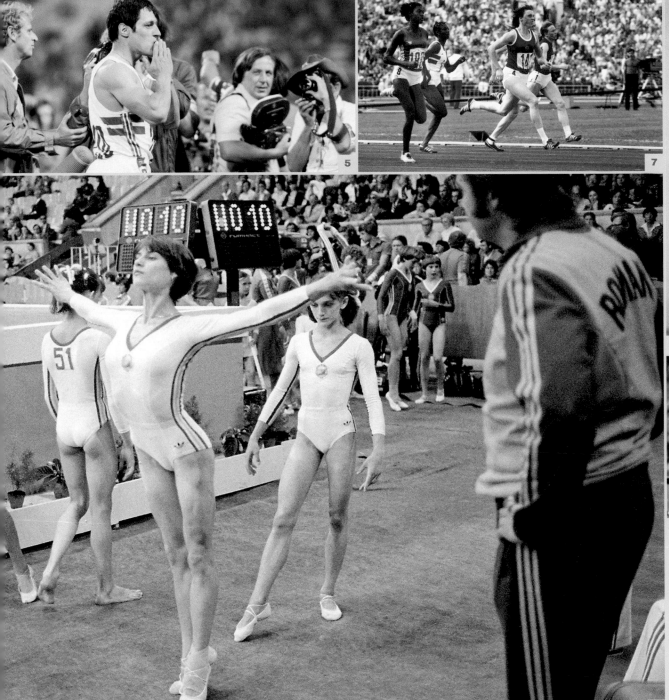

1 The Italians Generali (15), Villalta (12) and Meneghin (11) are powerless against Dalipagiç in a final that goes Yugoslavia's way 86-77.

2 The unknown Gerd Wessig jumps 2.36m to win the title and set a world record.

3 East German Birgit Fischer wins her first gold medal in the kayak singles. Between 1980 to 2000 she would win seven gold medals and two silver in the singles, the pairs and the fours.

4 East Germany, champions in Montreal, are brought back to earth by Czechoslovakia, who win the final 1-0.

5 For the first time a Finn wins the Finn class! Blond-haired Esko Rechardt brings honour back to his country.

6 In the absence of the Americans, Scotland's Allan Wells wins the 100m in the slowest time since electronic timing was introduced. He also came second in the 200m behind Italian Pietro Mennea.

7 In 1976 she was Bärbel Eckert. In 1980 she is Bärbel Wöckel but she's still a winner in the 200m. The East German beats Natalia Bochina (SOV/RUS, in red) and a young Merlene Ottey (JAM, in green).

8 In his first competition since an injury sustained in the World Championships in 1978, the hitherto unbeatable Alekseyev seizes up. After three failures at 180kg, he is eliminated.

9 As in Montreal, East German Waldemar Cierpinski wins the marathon, his second, equalling the achievement of the legendary Abebe Bikila.

10 The little girl has become a young woman and much of the magic has gone. Even so, Nadia Comaneci wins two gold medals (beam and floor) and two silver in Moscow.

11 The first part of a decathlon double 1980–1984 for Daley Thompson (GBR). His 8,495 points are enough to see off the two Soviet Russians Kutsenko and Zhelanov.

Koza's big moment

Despite a hostile stadium, Wladyslaw Kozakiewicz of Poland claims the pole vault title and the world record.

Wladyslaw Kozakiewicz clears every height at the first attempt up to 5.75m. Assured of the gold medal, he had the bar raised and set a new world record of 5.78m.

After four hours of attrition, Wladyslaw Kozakiewicz, 'Koza,' somersaulted with joy beside the jumping pit, as he does after every victory. He raised his face to the sky, almost inebriated with happiness, and brandishing his fist in a sign of victory. Koza, originally from Gdansk, was unfortunate in Montreal, where he was injured during his warm-up for the pole vault final. Here, victory and the world record of 5.78m were his.

No-one stood a chance against Kozakiewicz yesterday in a final that included two other Poles – Tadeusz Slusarski, the 1976 champion, and Mariusz Klimczyk – three Frenchman – Philippe Houvion, Thierry Vigneron and Jean Michel-Bellot – and Konstantin Volkov (SOV/RUS), the home crowd's blue-eyed boy.

But Kozakiewicz, 27, bemused his rivals, vaulting 5.35m, 5.50m, 5.60m, 5.65m, 5.70m and 5.75m, all at the first attempt.

It was unprecedented, despite the recent record-breaking exploits of Houvion and Vigneron. As night fell gently over the stadium and the sky turned to mauve, Kozakiewicz set about breaking Houvion's world record of 5.77m. Kozakiewicz beat it on his second attempt. The joyful chants from the stands, where Polish flags waved frantically, were deafening. The boos of the Soviet supporters were finally drowned out, as were the polite calls of the French, who had believed that

Jean-Michel Bellot and Philippe Houvion would stand on the podium. Their failure was part of the general disappointment for the French in the stadium events, where this great game of Russian roulette favoured only the few.

Vigneron failed at 5.55m (after vaulting 5.45m on the first attempt). Bellot seemed certain to win the silver medal, after clearing 5.35m, 5.50m and 5.60m on the first attempt. He had the bar raised to 5.65m. The choice seemed a little surprising but he was hoping, in vain, that his opponent was going to fail and he had taken the decision to go up five centimetres whatever the outcome. But at 5.65m everything turned against him. After vaulting 5.35m and 5.55m at his first attempt, Volkov cleared 5.65 on the third. So, astonishingly, did the thirty-year-old Slusarski, followed by Houvion. Bellot failed all three attempts. When the bar went up to 5.70m he was no longer in the competition.

It took Houvion two attempts to clear 5.25m and 5.45m, one at 5.55m and three at 5.65m. When he failed at 5.70m, he was level with Volkov and Sluzarski at 5.65m, but he had taken more attempts to get there, and therefore came fourth, with Bellot, fifth and Vigneron seventh.

The famous gesture of celebratory offence aimed at the partisan Russian crowd.

1980

MOSCOW XXII OLYMPIAD

Faced with an excessive number of absentees from the major events, a highly politicised atmosphere, a few dishonest judges and an overly chauvinistic public (especially in the Lenin Stadium), the Moscow Games were saved only by some outstanding sporting achievements.

THE GAMES IN BRIEF

Opening Date
19 July 1980

Closing Date
3 August 1980

Host Nation
Union of Soviet Socialist Republics (SOV)

Candidate Towns
Los Angeles (USA)

81 Nations Represented

5,217 Athletes
(1,125 women, 4,092 men)

21 Sports
(12 open to women)
Track and field, rowing, basketball, canoeing, cycling, equestrian, fencing, football, gymnastics, weightlifting, handball, field hockey, judo, wrestling, swimming, modern pentathlon, volleyball, shooting, archery and sailing.

203 Events
(50 open to women)

Games officially opened by
Leonid Brezhnev, President of USSR

Olympic flame lit by
Serge Belov (basketball)

Olympic oath read by
Nikolai Andrianov (gymnastics)

IOC President
Lord Michael Killanin (IRL)

OLYMPIAD 80
MOSCOU MOSCOW MOCKBA

DID YOU KNOW?

The first Games ever to be held in a Socialist country, Moscow was boycotted by most of the capitalist world. Only 81 countries took part, the lowest participation rate since 1956. Despite the boycott, three US citizens were present at the Moscow Games; they were Mike Perry, coach to the Swedish basketball team, Albert Mercado, representing Puerto Rico in the flyweight boxing event, and Bill Rea, competing for Austria in the long jump.

One unusual feature of the Moscow Games occurred in rowing, where in the coxless pairs the winners of both the gold (East Germans Bernd and Jorg Lanvoigt) and the silver (the Soviet Union's Youri and Nikolaï Pimenov) were actually identical twins.

Women's field hockey made an eventful debut at the Games when five of the six countries that qualified later withdrew because of the boycott, leaving only the USSR in the event. Czechoslovakia, India, Austria and Poland were all given a second chance to compete, and they did not hesitate to accept; nor did Zimbabwe, who were invited to enter just five weeks before the start of the Games. The players could not be selected until the weekend before the Opening Ceremony, but that did not stop Zimbabwe winning the event to everyone's great surprise.

1984

Los Angeles

IN THE WEST, RONALD REAGAN HAD defeated Jimmy Carter in the presidential elections of November 1980. In the East, Leonid Brezhnev had been succeeded by Yuri Andropov, who was then replaced after a fifteen-month presidency by Constantin Tchernenko. The names had been changed but the politics remained the same; on 5 May 1984, the USSR officially announced it was to decline the invitation from the Los Angeles Games Organising Committee, blaming anti-communist demonstrations in the USA. They claimed it was not a 'boycott' but rather a 'non-participation', because the safety of their athletes could not be guaranteed.

Seventeen countries, including Cuba, Poland, Bulgaria, Czechoslovakia, Ethiopia and East Germany, followed Moscow's lead. As in Moscow, medals in some events stood for very little; the boycotting countries had accounted for 58% of the gold medals at the Montreal Olympics.

Nonetheless, a record 140 nations took part. The US public expressed often exaggerated nationalism. The absentees were considered to be in the wrong, a view frequently and forcefully expressed by those who did attend. US TV channel CBS was criticised for showing only American competitors. Furthermore, the Games – the first to be staged without government financing – set an example of triumphant capitalism by making a $223 million profit. Even the star of the show – in a town where 'star' really means something – was 'Made in America'; Carl Lewis' achievements swelled the host nation's pride.

At the relay finish line, Carl Lewis is triumphantly hoisted onto his team-mates' shoulders after matching Jesse Owens' 1936 feat of victory in the 100m, 200m, long jump and 4x100m relay.

Lewis among the stars

Carl Lewis takes a big step towards a quadruple victory (100m, 200m, long jump and 4x100m relay) with a clear win in the 100m and an all-American celebration.

The 100m, the hardest of the four challenges facing the Fastest Man on Earth – won in 9.99 seconds.

The 200m, Lewis' second gold, was more straightforward than expected.

The sun sets behind the stands of the Los Angeles Coliseum, its last rays fading over the rococo façade, and Carl Lewis carries off the 100m gold in the Games' first moment of true emotion. It is only act one of the Lewis extravaganza.

In Row 2, Stand 27, an ecstatic Paul Tucker, 50, of New Orleans, unfurls an American flag and begins waving it. Next to him, his twelve-year-old son is standing on his seat. As Lewis rounds the bend, he spots the flag, takes it and starts his own brand of patriotic dance, inviting the crowd to join.

Pure Hollywood – Lewis is as talented at stage-managing the celebrations as at winning the race in under ten seconds of perfectly controlled sprinting. Exploiting local patriotism to the full, Lewis, wrapped in the flag, reinforces his iconic status. Michael Jackson, mark two.

'Winning his 100m final in near-perfect style, Lewis has won himself the well-deserved title of the Fastest Man on Earth. But what is that for a young man chasing immortality?' asked yesterday's Los Angeles Times. 'This is a man who wants to take everything life has to give.'

With his victory dance barely over, Carl Lewis was clearly searching for someone among the crowds. He came to a stop and threw himself into the arms of a tall, youthful-looking black man: John Carlos who, as bronze medalist in the 200m in Mexico, had taken to the podium with clenched raised fist to fight for black power. At home in Willingboro, New Jersey, Lewis, 7, was inspired to begin the career that brought him here.

Lewis left the Coliseum, avoiding the athletes' exit where at least a hundred journalists waited in vain. In the evening, he released a short written statement. It read:

'The 100m is the hardest test, because so much can go wrong. That is why I felt so emotional when I won. I got a good start, although not as good as the others. At 50m, I felt relaxed and confident. I have a reputation for being a good finisher and, because of that, I knew at the halfway point that I was going to win. When you have entered four events in a competition like the Olympic Games, it's like you're climbing a hill, and now I've won the 100m, I'm going down the other side. After the semi-final I was feeling all sorts of weird things in my legs. There was a strong headwind and I eased off because of that. I feel absolutely fine now. One down, three to go.'

It was a different story for Sam Graddy, who took silver in 10.19 seconds, compared with Lewis' 9.99. Graddy had said repeatedly that he felt he could beat Lewis, that nothing was impossible. Yet the 0.2 second gap between them was the biggest since Bob Hayes' win in Tokyo in 1964. Graddy grumbled: 'Well, maybe Carl was unbeatable today. I still think that if someone, some day is going to beat Lewis, it will be me. At the moment, Carl is perfect. He's using all his talents to the full. He's strong, but there are gaps in his technique, especially in the way he uses his arms. I'm 20, he's 23. I'll get better, and I'll beat him in the end. But for now, I think he can win the other golds he's chasing.'

A few days ago, Lewis said: 'Everything that is said about me, the stuff I read in the papers about all my opponents' ambitions and dreams of beating me, instead of worrying me, just makes me even more determined. They will all have the chance to show whether they can really beat me. As far as I'm concerned, I know that they can't, not here, not now.'

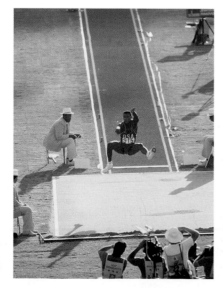

Over the long jump pit, scene of much suspense during the Games, a jump of 8.54m from the voracious and feline Lewis secures victory number three.

Lewis takes up the baton

Some 48 years after Jesse Owens' achievements, Carl Lewis makes history and reveals that he didn't do it on his own.

After the medal ceremony, he was hoisted onto his team-mates' shoulders, like a child who wants to see higher and further.

It was unclear whether Carl Lewis would show at the press conference. Then he arrived, flashing an uneasy smile at the clicking cameras and rustling papers. Lewis, preoccupied with prayer and salvation, suggested the American team had five members, not four. 'Without God, we can do nothing. It is thanks to Him that I was able to succeed in my Olympic adventure.'

He put his fourth gold medal on the table in front of him. Then came the comparisons with Jesse Owens. 'Owens is a legend, but he was also a man. I'm proud to have equalled him, but you shouldn't make comparisons. He is still Jesse Owens and I'm still Carl Lewis. We competed in different eras. I can honestly say I don't care what I've won, whether it's five dollars or five thousand dollars. That's not what's important. I've won four gold medals and you can't put a price on that.'

The 4x100m relay was the icing on Lewis' quadruple cake. In a time of 37.83 seconds, Lewis took over for the final leg from Calvin Smith with time to spare.

RESULTS

Four winning performances

100m
1 Carl Lewis (USA), 9.99
2 Sam Graddy (USA), 10.19
3 Ben Johnson (CAN), 10.22

200m
1 Carl Lewis (USA), 19.80
2 Kirk Baptiste (USA), 19.96
3 Thomas Jefferson (USA), 20.26

Long Jump
1 Carl Lewis (USA), 8.54m
2 Gary Honey (USA), 8.24m
3 Giovanni Evangelisti (ITA), 8.24m

4x100m Relay
1 USA (Ron Brown, Sam Graddy, Calvin Smith, Carl Lewis) 37.83
2 JAM 38.62
3 CAN 38.70

Just one point in it for Thompson

Ever full of surprises, Britain's Daley Thompson wins his second Olympic title, just one point short of the world record.

You have to expect the unexpected with Daley Thompson; he's an athlete capable of turning everything upside down. On the starting line of the 1500m – the grand finale of the decathlon competition – he gave a theatrical greeting to every one of the worthy competitors who would line up beside him on the blocks. Notting Hill's golden boy, with his famous moustache and permanent smile, appeared very relaxed – knowing that his six-year unbeaten run (since the 1978 European Championships in Prague) would remain unbroken after this race. Jürgen Hingsen, the 6 feet 7 giant from Leverkeusen, had failed to beat him in either the pole vault (where he managed only 4.5m against Thompson's 5m) or the javelin (60.44m against Thompson's 65.24). Thompson led by 209 points. All he had to do was finish the 1500m and a second Olympic title would be his. He also knew he had such a lead on Hingsen's world record – 104 points – that it was perhaps worth making that little extra effort in order to ice his gold medal cake with a new world record, and not just to please HRH Princess Anne, who had made a special trip to the Coliseum to cheer him on in his ten Herculean tasks.

Thompson, however, settled himself right in the middle of the pack, which had already stretched into single file; he was clearly not motivated by the idea of taking back the world record from Hingsen, who set a new record of 8,798 points in Mannheim last May.

Thompson stayed behind the Leverkusen giant, and finished in 4 minutes 35 seconds. He had missed setting a new world record by just two tenths of a second! He finished the event with exactly 8,797 points, one point off the record. He later explained that after the pole vault, he had realised that he could not break the 9,000-point barrier, and decided he did not want an incidental world record. On his lap of honour, he wore a Union flag and a t-shirt bearing two messages: on the front, 'Thanks America for a good Games and a great time' and on the back, 'What about some TV coverage?'

Daley Thompson, the gold medalist at the Moscow Olympics and the world champion at Helsinki, confirms his position as the world's greatest decathlete by defeating his arch rival Jürgen Hingsen of Germany once more, thanks to a fine 15.72m in the shot put which nearly equalled his own personal best.

The making of Moses

The god of the 400m hurdles is a legend in his own lifetime.

He enters the stadium like a king greeting his subjects, his intentions as clear as the sky above. This hard-won ground is his, and so too – probably – is the winners' podium; as he scans the stadium, the murmur of the crowd ran with him. Swept along by some ancient conquering instinct, Ed Moses is perfectly at ease in the role of hero, and gives off an air of casual disdain.

'He's been really nervous. He's had a difficult day,' says his wife Myrella, dressed in a long white robe. Below, her husband is stretched flat out on the track like a highway workman worn out by the sun. 'When you're on the track, the slightest sound can put you off. I think it was a camera that set me off so quickly,' he said later. He leads from start to finish, and soon after was bent double in an attempt to draw even a little breath from his lungs in a scene reminiscent of the American Olympic trials on the very same track.

'People have said that I was tired after the race, that this one would be my last. I'm telling you that that's not the case.' This is the sort of criticism faced by those who make winning their life's work. For Ed Moses, it's been like this for the seven years and 105 races.

The title was there for the taking, history was ready to be written; it was time for the execution, time to apply the blindfold. The only question was, what would it take to beat him?

Perhaps only his annihilation.

Edwin Moses, always the winner, has matured in the guise of a priest of athletics, a veneer of dignity forever gracing his pensive face, head held high to listen quietly and attentively to those around him. If you are alone in a class of your own, you can be forgiven for carrying yourself like a king.

There has never been any arrogance in his words, however. 'I am happy to have been through what I've been through over the last eight years. Why have I been so successful? I think I'm very lucky. I know that athletes like Harris have some very special qualities and are becoming a threat. I will have to be very careful. I'm not sure what I'm going to do; I have mentioned the 800m but for the time being I'm going to try to get my world record for the 400m hurdles under 47 seconds at the meets in Europe that I will take part in.'

Moses, Olympic champion in Montreal in 1976 but a victim of the American boycott of the 1980 Moscow Games, has enhanced his image. Millions will remember this radiant man held tightly in the arms of his mother and his wife.

That scene will now drive the huge PR exercise that surrounds Moses. The man who delivered the Olympic sermon, the man who wanted to be a doctor until just two years ago, no longer represents just himself. At the end of this season Moses is set to change sponsors, having signed a $1.2m contract that will earn him some $2.5m in 1989. Whatever currency you work in, a quick conversion will give you a good idea of exactly how much of a star that makes him, despite the fact that he still lives in a flat near an airport.

When pushed for a comment on the rules regarding professionalism, Moses skirted the issue: 'The regulations of the International Federation are carefully drafted.' He pointed out that Renaldo Nehemiah, his 110m hurdles counterpart, had predicted Moses' second Olympic victory. Nehemiah really has fallen foul of the rules by becoming a professional American football player.

The cruel Moscow boycott forgotten, Moses is king of the 400m hurdles again.

A pioneer in his discipline, Moses recorded 17 of the 19 best times in history. Unbeaten for seven years with 105 consecutive victories, Moses inspired unreserved admiration.

Joan Benoit: out on her own

Joan Benoit (USA) strolls into the record books as the first ever winner of the women's marathon.

Joan Benoit declared before the race: 'I will run my own race, and not worry about the others.' After three kilometres, she broke away, finishing 1m 34secs ahead of Grete Waitz (NOR).

It took eighty-eight years for the Olympics to have its first female marathon winner. Joan Benoit transformed the face of women's marathon running by turning the killer race into a walk in the park. This tiny twenty-seven-year-old, 5 feet 2 and 102 pounds, didn't bother with strategy; three kilometres into the race, she pulled away from the pack with no further thought for her rivals.

'I decided to run my own race, without worrying about anyone else. In this kind of event, you have to set your own pace, to find the rhythm that suits you after a few kilometres. If you run with the pack, unless you get right at the front and do all the work, your rhythm will change frequently and that's the worst mistake you can make in a marathon.'

At the US Olympic trials on 12 May, Benoit pulled off a huge achievement. At 2:31:04, her time was

not brilliant, but just seventeen days earlier she had been lying in a hospital bed following a cartilage operation.

'I carried the injury for weeks. Seventeen days before D-Day, it was

Cap in hand, Joan Benoit runs her lap of honour, having just become the first Olympic women's marathon gold medalist.

so bad I took my doctor's advice to have surgery – he assured me that I'd be on my feet within a week.'

The situation is reminiscent of Abebe Bikila, who had his appendix

removed weeks before taking his second gold in Tokyo.

A few years ago, Benoit took the job of coach to Boston University's women's athletics team. However, her ambition got the better of her and she resigned from the job to devote herself fully to her Olympic preparations.

'I was running 200km per week and it wasn't leaving me much time for other things. I train every day and always on my own, because I think that prepares you mentally and gets you ready for the suffering that is part of every marathon.' Three kilometres into the race, Benoit seemed to have tuned out everything except the clock ticking in her brain. 'I always hoped I'd get some help from athletes behind me, but that was the last I saw of them. It wasn't until we approached the stadium that I really believed I could win, because when I looked back I couldn't see any of my rivals.'

Behind one giant lurks another

Germany's Michael Gross threatens American domination as he follows his 200m freestyle title with gold in the 100m butterfly.

Michael Gross has had a hard day, but a good one – a world record and an Olympic title in an event in which he was expected to get a silver at best: the 100m butterfly, the only one of the three individual events for which he was not the favourite. Between him and victory lay the Cuban-born American Pablo Morales, a slim, handsome young man with a style so light, fluid and natural that he was being compared to Mark Spitz. Morales had won the US trials in 53.38 seconds and was rumoured to be capable of even better.

The West Germans, meanwhile, were boasting loudly of their new weapon, Michael Gross. A few days ago, Gerd Heydn, who works for the German news agency, SID, said, 'If Michael swims to the best of his abilities, he can do it in 53.0 or 53.1 seconds. But maybe Morales will do even better; it could all come down to just a fraction of a second.'

Although the heats this morning did not see a direct confrontation between them, they did at least allow their times to be compared. Morales emerged four tenths of a second faster – the same

Michael Gross beats favourite Pablo Morales of America in the 100m butterfly, setting a new world record of 53.08 seconds.

Andrew Jameson (GBR, fifth, right) witnesses the joy of Michael Gross after the 100m butterfly.

'No-one can catch me in the final 50 metres' – Michael Gross' message to the Americans before the 200m freestyle.

gap separating his world record from Gross' European record of 53.78 seconds. But man-to-man combat is a different game.

The final produced the battle everyone had been waiting for. Neither Morales' starting leap nor his long glide yielded anything to Gross, despite the advantage the German's huge arm span allowed him. With an elegant and majestic style that bore no relation to that of Gross, Morales seemed to be pulling clear, but he was to learn to his cost the blessing Gross had in his huge arms and hands. Despite leading at the

turn, Morales held only a hundredth of a second advantage. Morales raised his stroke rate and all of a sudden shook off his German opponent. This sharp acceleration proved formidable, for it upped the rhythm without shortening his stroke. Gross had lost: logic dictated it – but logic didn't know Michael Gross. Much had been made of Gross's talent and size, less about the severity of his training regime: his fifteen to eighteen kilometre runs each morning, the two-hour pool sessions each afternoon, the gymnastics and stretching. His fighting spirit was not

well documented.

The finish in a butterfly is riskier than in a freestyle race because the style involves a simultaneous arm movement rather than an alternating stroke. The swimmer whose hands are furthest forward will beat the swimmer whose arms are on the downward push. Gross had a tiny advantage at the finish and won by just fifteen hundredths of a second (53.08 to 53.23). For the second time in two days (the first being the 100m breaststroke), beating the world record was not enough to take Olympic gold.

Mary Decker writhes in agony as the other 3,000m runners pull away. The stadium goes silent, before the booing begins.

The women's 3,000m saw a long-awaited contest between the reigning 1500m and 3,000m world champion Mary Decker (USA), and a shy South African from a farm in Bloemfontein in Orange Free State, Zola Budd, who had beaten Decker's 5,000m world record in January 1984. Qualifying for British citizenship through her paternal grandfather, Budd had been brought to the UK by the Daily Mail newspaper, and was thrust out of South Africa's sporting isolation and into the media spotlight. Her encounter with Mary Decker, her athletic idol, was surrounded by hype. After 1600m, Budd, Decker, Wendy Sly (GBR) and mile world record holder Maricica Puica (ROM) began to pull away. Moving into the straight, Decker hit one of Budd's legs. Seconds later, they collided again. Budd, running, as always, in bare feet, was deeply spiked; Decker lost balance and careered off the track, pulling a muscle as she hit the ground.

Sly led Puica into the final lap, before the Romanian cruised into the lead on the back straight to win easily by more than fifteen metres.

Booed to the line by the partisan crowd, Zola Budd finished the race in tears, seventh. After the race, Decker rebuffed her repeated apologies, although Puica suggested Decker had been at fault for passing on the inside.

Karppinen joins Ivanov in record books

Finland's Karppinen beats Peter-Michael Kolbe to take his third single sculls gold at Lake Casitas, equalling a Russian record.

Montreal, 1976: Pertti Karppinen comes from behind to beat World champion and race favourite Peter Michael Kolbe (GER).

Finland's Pertti Karppinen has taken his place in history at Lake Casitas by winning his third Olympic single sculls gold. Only one athlete has achieved the feat before him: Russia's Vyacheslav Ivanov, between 1956 and 1964. As the hero of the hour explained: 'Winning the single sculls is something special. People remember your name, whereas in the other events they remember the country and that detracts from your win. Plus, the single scull is the boat everyone starts in; all the greatest rowers did it at some stage, before graduating to other events.' Karppinen came from behind to beat West Germany's Peter-Michael Kolbe in the last seconds of a historic battle reminiscent of the face-off between the two Jacks, Kelly (USA) and Beresford

men were neck-and-neck, but just twenty metres from the finish an exhausted Kolbe could do no more and Karppinen snatched victory, finishing 1.95 seconds ahead of his rival. The gap was tighter than in 1976, when Karppinen won Finland's first-ever rowing gold by 2.64 seconds. In those days he still wore his big horn-rimmed glasses, which have now been replaced with contact lenses.

Adding a third gold to his Montreal and Moscow titles marks a great comeback for Karppinen. Just after the Moscow Games, a new type of shell was introduced with a fixed seat, movable riggers and foot rudder; it suited some – Kolbe among them – but not others, including Karppinen. While Kolbe was winning world titles in 1981 and 1983, Karppinen rowed in the double sculls with his brother Reïma, with whom he took gold at the 1981 World Championships. Last year, however, the International Federation took the decision to ban the new-style shell, which was said to favour those rowers ill at ease in choppy waters. Vehmaa-born Karppinen decided to return to his favourite shell. The single scull undoubtedly suits his personality: when Finland emerges from its long winter, he heads not for the lakes but for the sea. 'There's more space to be alone,' he says.

Moscow, 1980: reigning world champion Karppinen confirms his supremacy.

RESULTS

KARPPINEN'S TRIPLE GOLD

Single Sculls
1976:
1 Pertti Karppinen (FIN), 7:29.03
2 Peter Michael Kolbe (GER) 7:31.67
3 Joachim Dreifke (GDR) 7:38.03

1980:
1 Pertti Karppinen (FIN), 7:09.61
2 Vassily Yakusha (SOV/AZR), 7:11.66
3 Peter Kersten (GDR), 7:14.88

1984:
1 Pertti Karppinen (FIN) 7:00.24
2 Peter Michael Kolbe (FRG) 7:02.19
3 Robert Mills (CAN), 7:10.38

Los Angeles, 1984: Eight years on, Kolbe once again counts the cost of Karppinen's strong finish.

(GBR), at the 1920 Games, or the equally legendary Ivanov-Mackenzie battle at the 1956 Melbourne Games.

Four-times world champion Kolbe led for most of the race, gaining a half-

length lead over the Finn from the start. However, the Finn refused to let the gap grow and slowly gained on his opponent, finally drawing level 120m from the finish line. For 100m the two

The Finn pulls off a single sculls hat trick to equal the feat of Ivanov (SOV/RUS) 1956–1964. The giant fireman from Parsio would be back to compete in the 1988 Games.

Mary Lou soars to gold

Dynamic Mary Lou Retton, 16, becomes the first-ever American gold medalist in women's gymnastics.

The delirious American crowd gave an overwhelming reception for Mary Lou Retton, the Barbie doll with incredible muscle tone and power and exceptional rhythm and take-off – not to mention nerves of steel. She is amazing to watch, even if her style is very different from the grace of Nadia Comaneci, although she has the same coach, Bela Karolyl, brought to America in 1981 by a fat pay-cheque.

At the start of the individual All-around event, Retton's lead over Ecaterina Szabó (ROM) was 0.15 of a point. It soon became obvious that Mary Lou was starting with her two weakest exercises, the asymmetric bars and the beam, where her power could not be used to its fullest. She knew, however, that by finishing with the floor and vault, she was maximising her chances – it was a sound strategy, since it meant that everything would rest on the final apparatus.

Szabó caught up with her rival with a 10 on the beam – the only gymnast to execute four somersaults on the dangerous apparatus – against Mary Lou's 9.85 on the asymmetric bars. Half an hour later, the Romanian took to the floor and scored 9.95. Mary Lou didn't score as well on the beam, achieving 9.80. Back to square one.

Szabó completed the vault and the asymmetric bars with two 9.90s; but it was not enough, for Mary Lou was on the home stretch. Leaping around the floor as if on a trampoline, the crowd were enthralled. US coach Don Peters held up two outstretched hands – as far as he was concerned, her performance merited the maximum marks. His opinion was swiftly shared by the panel, and Szabó's lead narrowed to 0.05.

Only the vault remained. Mary Lou won two well-deserved 10s. A perfect score, this time unanimous (even on the part of the Romanian judge). Szabó's lead of 0.05 of a point was reversed, and sixteen-year-old Mary Lou Retton became the first American woman to win Olympic gold for gymnastics.

Retton's Italian ancestory deposited in her a heightened sense of self-expression through movement. Her physique does the rest.

1984
OLYMPIC ROUND-UP

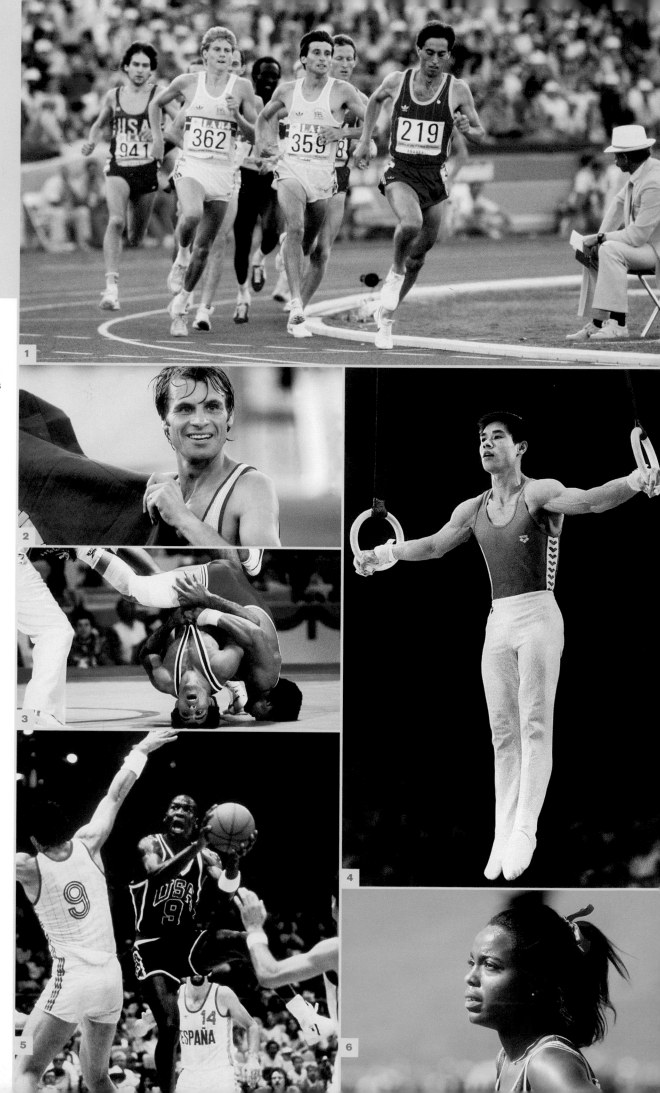

THEY HAVE DONE IT AGAIN!

The Americans have seized their ninth title as Olympic basketball champions (photo 5), and the manner in which they attained victory was almost insolent. There was no contest.

Despite a slightly disappointing performance against Germany and Canada in previous rounds (disappointing because of their huge potential – everything is relative), the USA were impressive against Spain, demonstrating categorically the breadth and depth of their talent. The Dream Team were back on form, playing basketball that was simply out of this world and spurred on by a cheering crowd throughout the game.

Their defence was better than ever, which was no mean feat as this aspect of the game had always been their strong point. Meanwhile Bobby Knight's team did just as brilliantly in attack, skilfully combining tactic with imagination.

Shattered by the Yankees' devastating victory, the distraught Spaniards had no choice but to put on a brave face. It was the only way to avoid further humiliation after such a crushing defeat. Against a tough American defence, the Spaniards grew clearly frustrated with their throws and became particularly clumsy (achieving less than 37 per cent). In a breathtakingly skilful and tremendous game from the Americans, Michael Jordan (number nine in photo 5) retorted with a dazzling performance that was truly worthy of his reputation.

With a final thirty-one point lead, it was an unquestionable victory for the Americans. But there was one man who saw success in the making. 'The result was obvious from the start of the game. It was meant to be; I'd decided it should be,' said coach Bobby Knight, directly after the final.

You see, basketball is easy if you are American. Sadly, it's a different story for the rest of the world.

1 Sebastian Coe (359) wins his second consecutive 1500m title in Los Angeles. A tactical masterpiece. Cram (GBR, 362) comes second, Abascal (ESP, 219), third.

2 Portugal's Carlos Lopes, aged 37, claims his first Olympic title in the marathon.

3 In blue, James Martinez (USA) topples Papadopoulos (GRE, in red) to take third place in Greco-Roman style wrestling (69kg).

4 Chinese Li Ning, one of the star gymnastic attractions in Los Angeles.

5 'Jordan glides through the air like a plane,' admired the Spanish trainer, Diaz Miguel.

6 American Evelyn Ashford was rejected in the 1976 trials and absent in 1980, but she finally achieves her dream in 1984 with a superb 100m victory.

7 American jockey Joe Fargis seizes the show jumping title with 'Touch of Class'.

8 Tracy Caulkins (USA) takes gold medals for the 200m and 400m medley relay.

9 North Africa celebrates its first representation in women's athletics with victory, as Morocco's Nawal el-Moutawakel wins the 400m hurdles.

10 Alexi Grewal (USA, left) beats Steve Bauer (CAN, right) in the men's road race. Dag Otto Lauritzen (NOR, in red) came third.

11 The astounding Australian team gains time on the USA in the final of the team pursuit.

12 Matt Biondi (USA) (left) congratulates his team-mate Ambrose 'Rowdy' Gaines (still in the water), who has just completed the triumphant last leg in the 4x100m freestyle relay.

13 American Valerie Brisco-Hooks (364) claims the first 200m-400m double in Olympic history. Here she is seen ahead of Kathryn Cook (left, GBR, third) on the 400m.

14 'Outlandish' Luis Doreste and Roberto Molina (ESP) take gold for Spain in the Men's 470.

15 Synchronised swimming makes its Olympic debut: Graceful Tracy Ruiz (USA) pockets two gold medals (solo and duet).

Elvström, a Viking warrior

Four-times Olympic sailing champion, from 1948 to 1960, the fifty-six-year-old Dane is participating in the Tornado Regattas with his daughter Trine.

The Vikings are men of legend. Pol Elvström keeps his legend as the world's most successful sailor and born navigator alive in the Tornado class, with his daughter Trine.

He is a true warrior, whose veins run with saltwater and Viking blood. Sailing genius Paul Elvström is a classic Scandinavian sea-god and four-time Olympic gold medalist – in the Firefly class at Torquay in 1948, and the Finn monotype class at Helsinki in 1952, Melbourne in 1956 and Naples in 1960. Elvström has not stood on the Olympic podium again since.

But today, 24 years after winning his last medal, he is representing his country again at the Long Beach Olympic Regatta, at the helm of a Tornado high-speed catamaran with his daughter Trine, who was not even born when he won his last medal.

With chiselled features and a silver beard, Elvström is the very image of Neptune. His countless victories have made him the favourite target of other crews. His opponents were previously obsessed, not with winning the regatta, but with defeating the mighty Elvström by stealing the wind from his sails. In those fierce naval battles, Elvström lost not just his sailor's luck, but the mysterious inspiration that enabled him to predict the winds and foresee tides and currents.

Sailing is a unique sport. Physical condition and training are only effective if an athlete possesses the ability to understand the elements and forecast the weather. It is a sport where age is no object and can actually prove to be an advantage. That would explain Elvström's exceptional endurance. He has also managed to keep his physique, sparkle and imagination thanks to his outdoor lifestyle in Denmark.

On top of his four Olympic gold medals, Elvström has claimed eight world titles in six different monotype sailing classes. He has succeeded as a skipper and as a crew member, especially with his pupil and fellow Dane, Hans Fogh. He also designed Bes, a large-scale racing sailboat, which he launched in the Three-Quarter Ton Cup. At the Los Angeles Olympic Games, Elvström is steering a double-hulled Tornado catamaran for the first time.

'I saw his Tornado debut in 1982,' says Patrick Seitert, former manager of the French Sailing Federation and a well-informed spectator. 'He competed in the Kiel Century regattas to please his daughter Trine, but he did not win anything and was really quite far behind the others.'

But in 1983, Elvström became European champion in the Tornado class and excelled in Antibes and at Kiel Week. This year he took the Ski Yachting Cup and gained third place in Hyeres Week, qualifying for the World Championship Team Cup.

Silver medal winner in the Flying Dutchman class at Kiel, Yves Pajot used to say: 'There are good days where you sense everything, even the slightest change in the wind, and others where you simply can't rely on instinct.' It seems like Elvström is always having a good day. It is almost as though his Viking ancestors made a pact with the elements.

But how long can this star of the sea continue to shine? 'Sailing with my daughter Trine has given me back my youth. I'm enjoying myself just as much as I did at her age,' he admitted.

[Ed: Elvström finished fourth in the Tornado class at the 1984 Games.]

1984

LOS ANGELES XXIII OLYMPIAD

After half a century, the Coliseum opened its gates once more to
Olympic athletes – the name may have been the same but the city was
very different. As, of course, was the sport, as the number of events
open to – and even exclusively reserved for – women continued to grow.

THE GAMES IN BRIEF

Opening Date
28 July 1984

Closing Date
12 August 1984

Host Nation
United States of America (USA)

Candidate Towns
None

140 Nations Represented

6,797 Athletes
(1,567 women, 5,230 men)

22 Sports
(14 open to women)
Track and field, rowing, basketball, boxing,
canoeing, cycling, equestrian, fencing,
football, gymnastics, weightlifting, handball,
field hockey, judo, wrestling, swimming,
modern pentathlon, volleyball, shooting,
archery and sailing.

221 Events
(62 open to women)

Games officially opened by
Ronald Reagan, President of the United
States of America

Olympic flame lit by
Rafer Johnson (athletics)

Olympic oath read by
Edwin Moses (athletics)

IOC President
Juan Antonio Samaranch (ESP)

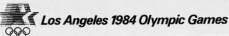
Los Angeles 1984 Olympic Games

DID YOU KNOW?

The Soviets organised revenge on the
Americans, with fourteen Socialist countries
refusing to participate in the LA Games. This
was a much smaller number than at Moscow,
but those fourteen nations had accounted
for 58 per cent of the gold medals at the
1976 Olympics.

Los Angeles was the only candidate to
host the Games, and it organised them
without government financing, using existing
facilities and with extensive support from the
private sector. After the Games made a
$223m profit, they became the model for
future Olympics.

The women's marathon featured in the
Olympic programme for the first time ever, as
did rhythmic gymnastics, synchronised
swimming and the women's cycling road race.

In another first, professional players were
allowed in the football tournament, as long
as they had never played in the World Cup.
France beat Brazil 2-0.

1988

Seoul

THE 1988 OLYMPICS TOOK PLACE IN A strangely symbolic location – Korea, a nation divided by the Bamboo Curtain along the thirty-eighth parallel since the 1953 armistice. The DMZ or de-militarised zone, fifty kilometres from Seoul, is a place of incomprehension, distrust and even contempt. The hut at Panmunjom – engaged in negotiations since 1952 – is the most explicit and distressing illustration of this sentiment.

When the International Olympic Committee chose Seoul to host the twenty-fourth Olympic Games on 30 September 1981, they were bombarded with criticism and disapproval. Boycott threats soon followed. The death of 269 passengers on a Korean Airlines Boeing, suspected of spying and struck down by a Soviet Sukhoi in 1983, didn't help.

The future began to look brighter when Mikhail Gorbachev was appointed General Secretary of the Communist Party of the Soviet Union in March 1985. Somewhere between glasnost and perestroika, the Olympics were saved. Apart from some countries that remained hopelessly devoted to North Korea, the entire world was flocking to the Land of Morning Calm. Sadly, this geopolitical rapprochement is not how the Seoul Olympics will be remembered. They will go down in history as a Games of scandal and doping. Ben Johnson and his steroids – and the disgraced sprinter's disqualification – was just one of a long string of weightlifters, judoka, pentathletes, Bulgarians, Hungarians, Spaniard, Australians, Britons…

Florence Griffith-Joyner outshines her opponents with 10.54 in the 100m and 21.34 in the 200m, a new world record. She seems to be running in a world of her own.

Ben Johnson, the time bomb

On Monday night, it emerged that the Olympic 100m champion was under investigation. Reliable sources suggest that he will be declared positive.

Ben Johnson (left) is elated as he finishes ahead of Linford Christie (third), Carl Lewis (second) and Robson Caetano da Silva (sixth). The victory was short lived.

Rumours had been circulating for twenty-four hours. The word was that the third champion of the Games was to be disqualified.

Members of the IOC Medical Commission, chaired by Prince Alexander de Mérode, were refusing to comment. However, it had been clear since the start of the Games that the recommendations he had made to the Executive Board had been taken on board by the IOC administration. Two Bulgarian gold-medalist weightlifters had already been disqualified, along with other weightlifters and a pentathlete.

A reliable source informed us that a 'B' test was already underway following the positive test result of a 'great personality at the Games'.

Late on Monday 26 July in Seoul, a Korean newspaper was already printing the headlines that would hit the news stands in the early hours: 'Olympic champion and world record holder Ben Johnson tests positive'.

Canadian Olympic Committee officials were still refusing to comment, although the CAC conceded that it had been informed of a positive doping case, confirmed by the 'B' test, relating to one of the Canadian team members. Johnson, however, was not officially named. Meanwhile, the athlete himself was nowhere to be found. Rumour had it that he had already left Seoul.

The Organising Committee for the Games, headed by Juan Antonio Samaranch, met as usual on Tuesday

morning in Seoul to examine the IOC reports, especially those of the IOC Medical Commission. At midnight in Paris the Executive Board met in secrecy to discuss the issues raised and to give a ruling on the recommendations made by the IOC Medical Commission.

The IOC Executive Board, masters in the art of disqualification, had irrefutable evidence against one of the biggest names in athletics. John Holt, General Secretary of the IAAF, answered press enquiries with a crisp 'No comment'. He did mention, however, given the seriousness of the rumours, that the IAAF had been notified of a case, which only the IOC had the competence to announce publicly, following meetings on

Tuesday morning. Visibly shaken, Holt said that previously when the IOC had informed international organisations, it was because allegations were very serious. 'It may just be a rumour, but we are prepared for the worst.'

It was said, in Holt's discreet British manner, as though the IAAF still hoped that the scandal would subside without harming the reputation of world athletics in general. But by then it was clear that the Medical Commission had no intention of keeping quiet. It had not hesitated to talk publicly when two Bulgarian gold medalists tested positive. At the time of writing, it seems unthinkable that Prince Alexander de Merode and his experts will play the hiding game, despite having agreed to be harsh and

Carl Lewis still looks shattered by his defeat, despite the respect shown by the ecstatic Canadian fans.

uncompromising if need be.

If the worst turns out to be true, the implications are clear: sport at its highest level is the subject of systematic manipulation. Johnson, who has been seeing an endocrinologist for several months, was supposedly being treated for the thigh injury that ruled him out of competition in February. It would be astonishing if his coaching team, which has highly sophisticated

methods at its disposal, including gene therapy, had been imprudent enough to prescribe the world record holder a product easily detectable by IOC laboratories, and specifically, the Seoul laboratory, which is known to be extremely diligent.

The explanation, however, could be simple, as Professor Arnold Beckett, a pharmacologist with a global reputation and a member of the IOC Medical Commission, told us last night. The doctors who treated Johnson undoubtedly carried out their own tests to satisfy themselves that Johnson would be able to compete at Seoul without running into trouble. However, they may not have had access to the latest test protocols available to the IOC and the international sports federations. Traces of anabolic steroids remain detectable six or seven months after their use. Since this type of doping product is subject to qualitative, not quantitative

analysis – unlike testosterone or caffeine – infinitesimal residues are enough to convict athletes treated with these products long before testing.

Professor Beckett leads us to believe that, following the expulsion of the Bulgarians, the IOC Medical Commission had not always been able to impose its standards on certain lax international federations. This is why, at Seoul, the IOC has refused to allow the international federations to become involved in testing.

On Tuesday morning in Seoul, as the day began, the world was still awaiting the IOC Executive Committee's announcement of the sanction against Ben Johnson, a sanction that will then have to be ratified by the IAAF. If the IOC announces his expulsion, Carl Lewis will become the Olympic 100m champion. As for the world record of 9.79, it can only be struck off by the IAAF. The record will revert to

Johnson's time of 9.83, set in Rome, when there was no suspicion of doping. The sanctions decided by the IOC cannot be back-dated – although if Johnson's guilt is confirmed, the IAAF has the power to ban him for life.

As the Canadian national anthem plays, Lewis looks disappointed and confused, while Johnson wears a mocking grin.

A strange angel

After his 100m setback, Carl Lewis stages a comeback in the long jump, yet remains as distant as ever.

As he walked leisurely along the corridor, he told the frantic press, penned in behind a velvet rope doubled up with a police cordon: 'Yes, I'm back, but there'll be no press conference.' With that, he disappeared into the white brick maze of the athletes' toilets. Carl Lewis is keeping his distance, and that includes in the long jump, where his supple gracefulness is either thrilling or chilling. He is detached and unconventional, with an air of self-importance. But it only takes a child to slip past the guard to make him forget his airs and graces.

Carl Lewis has retaliated against Ben Johnson's wild streak with his own eccentricity. Insinuations of homosexuality are being made of the 27-year-old Lewis. Lewis himself has probably taken a rebellious delight in promoting himself and his recent record with feathers, glitter and glamour, which temporarily destroyed

his pious image. But here in Seoul, the fundamentalists heaved a sigh of relief as he proved himself to be an athlete like any other. Or unlike any other. Carl Lewis shows a physical beauty perhaps never seen before on a running track.

In the time it took to run two races – this time without Johnson's competition – and take five jumps, Lewis scarcely ruffled his feathers. He showed slight irritation when asked to jump first, when he had already been given permission to jump last because of his participation in the qualifying heats of the 200m.

By jumping 8.72m, he added to an incomparable series of jumps that has made him, as a sprinter and as a long jumper, that amazing contradiction: an athlete who has often won, but has never set any records.

Carl Lewis didn't return to the long jump after his 200m heat. His American team-mates passed on the

With 8.72m, in his fourth jump, Carl Lewis wins the long jump competition.

information that his refusal to take part in the sixth attempt was not linked to an injury: another day and another final awaited, and a glimmer of gold reflected in his eyes, which now expressed an anxious charm. He left the track with his sister, who has the same haughty gait, at his side, looking as strange as ever in his tracksuit, like a white knight flaunting his fortune and individuality. He seems to be a stranger in the world of sport – a world he would abandon if he ever came back down to earth.

RESULTS

LEWIS'S TEN BEST JUMPS

8.79m Indianapolis, 1983
8.79m New York, 1984
8.76m Houston, 1982
8.76m Indianapolis, 1988
8.75m Indianapolis, 1987
8.72m Seoul, 1988
8.71m Los Angeles, 1983
8.71m Westwood, 1984
8.71m Los Angeles, 1984
8.76m Rome, 1987

Saturday 24 July, 1.30pm: Ben Johnson set a world record of 9.79 to win the 100m final, and signs the photo finish.

Tuesday 27 July, 10.30am: Ben Johnson has been disqualified! Carl Lewis is declared the winner and signs the new photo finish. But Johnson's shadow (right) hangs over the Games.

Bubka against himself

Not yet twenty-five, the world record holder in the pole vault has finally become an Olympic champion.

Bubka's first two 5.90m jumps carefully, you can see he made a real mess of things. But Bubka always manages to find a brilliant jump when he needs it. And he found it in his last attempt.' He went on to add: 'The hierarchy has been respected.'

It was shortly after 5pm that Bubka made his winning leap. After so many problems, he finally cleared the bar by a huge margin, in typical Bubka style.

According to the experts, never before had Bubka reacted with such joy when he had won, even when setting world records. Lying flat out in the landing pit, he let out an ecstatic cry, then bounded back to his seat in the shade, hardly able to contain his excitement. The world champion and record breaker was finally Olympic champion. After five years dominating the pole vault, he truly deserved his title.

Serhei Bubka claims the Olympic title with a 5.90m vault, far from his best. But it was very close!

Four hours into the pole vault competition, trouble was brewing. Grigory Yegorov (SOV/KAZ) was in spectacular form, judging by the way he sailed over 5.80m and into the lead, ahead of the favourites Serhei Bubka (SOV/UKR) and Rodion Gataullin (SOV/UZB). Four vaulters still had hopes of a medal: three Soviets – Yegorov, Gataullin and Bubka – and an American, Earl Bell, the oldest of the four, third in Los Angeles and sixth in the 1976 Montreal Olympics.

Bell was the last to be eliminated, failing at 5.75m three times. When Yegorov cleared 5.80m, Bell's final successful jump of 5.70m left him in the bronze medal position – ahead of Bubka, the double world champion and the world record holder at 6.06m. In any other competition, a jump of 5.70m would have been a sideshow. But

this was an Olympic final, and Bubka had never been in a competition like this before. He later confessed that he had never known such pressure: 'Everybody was waiting to see what I was capable of. It was unbearable.' He had every reason to feel under pressure. He had started to jump at 5.70m, but needed two attempts to clear the bar. When he did, finally, he grazed the bar on the way down. Add that to a tactical error: he passed on three heights (5.75m, 5.80m, 5.85m) and the only man to have ever reached six metres was on the point of elimination, at a height he would usually have found laughable.

Yegorov failed at 5.90m, leaving Gataullin leading at 5.85m. Bubka failed twice at 5.90m, and now faced his final attempt. Victory, or bust. The French vaulter, Philippe Collet, observed discreetly: 'If you watch

RESULTS

Pole Vault

1 Serhei Bubka (SOV/UKR) 5.90m
2 Rodion Gataulllin (SOV/UZB) 5.85m
3 Grigory Yegorov (SOV/KAZ) 5.80m
4 Earl Bell (USA) 5.70m
5 Philippe Collet (FRA) 5.70m
6 Thierry Vigneron (FRA) 5.70m
7 Istvan Bagyula (HUN) 5.60m
8 Philippe D'Encausse (FRA) 5.60m

The incredible Flo-Jo

The easy victor in the 100m performs even better in the 200m, smashing the previous world record.

When a champion acquires universal celebrity status and her hitherto private existence takes on a new public dimension, she will often strive to achieve further success. We are torn between admiration and astonishment after Florence Griffith-Joyner's 21.34-second 200m. She has taken the event further than several generations of athletes and ten seasons of athletics. A young woman of twenty-eight, who has been chasing glory for a decade, has taken a little over twenty seconds to become the very incarnation of speed.

Even more than in the 100m – her world record was wind-assisted – Griffith-Joyner has opened a new chapter in sprinting history and reclassified as mediocre performances those that until recently would have been considered electrifying.

It is strange to note that the incredible Flo-Jo belongs to a generation of athletes that has either retired or is ageing. She was a candidate for the 1980 US Olympic team, but the boycott meant she had to wait eight years, take second best several times and win a World Championship gold medal as a member of the 4 x 100m relay team before her metamorphosis.

The transformation took place in the off-season, which she had previously spent writing poetry and children's stories in which the fairy's magic wand turned pumpkins into princesses, and eating fattening snacks.

Florence Griffith-Joyner delights in her second 200m gold medal. An exceptional victory.

It is like something out of a slushy novel. While the majority of champions carried on as normal, Flo-Jo appeared at the end of last winter looking as though she had met a wizard with a miraculous elixir. It's a plot she could have used in one of her books for little girls. Her coach Bob Kersee's method has two inspirations: one is Ben Johnson's training programme; the other, Carl Lewis's performances on the track. The former means increased power and technical efficiency, the latter means relaxation and acceleration What we saw on the track at the Seoul Olympics proves that Griffith-Joyner has taken on these two identities. Her power oozed from every pore in her thighs, the hypertrophy of which contrasted with the relative slenderness of her torso. As for

her gait, it reproduced Lewis's perfect equilibrium and harmonious, linear movements.

The spectacle was captivating and intriguing, and turned the tables on athletes who had always beaten Flo-Jo. This time, they barely saw her heels. A 200m Olympic medal had never been won by such a wide margin since Fanny Blankers-Koen's 1948 victory. Flo-Jo eclipsed past winners, outshone Marita Koch, whose 21.71 world record had stood the test of time. As in the 100m, Griffith's opponents managed to save face for the first half of the race. If there is a secret to her success, it is the way she maintains her initial pace while the others begin to tire.

THE HIDDEN INGREDIENTS
After running the first 100m in 11.11, she ran the second half in 10.23, far

outstripping all her rivals, and beating Grace Jackson by 0.22 of a second. Heike Drechsler lost 0.35 seconds. Another monument in the history of athletics, this double 200m record proves that talent, given time and determination, and a disciplined willpower, can win through.

What lies hidden behind Griffith-Joyner's feat contains all the ingredients needed for a better understanding of her explosion into the annals of sport. But there are still missing links in the chain that check our unqualified enthusiasm.

145 KILO SQUATS!
The biography of this Californian athlete teaches us that she reads the Bible every day, prays before meals and phones her mother twice a day. She also mentions that she has been training hard all winter and squat-lifts 320 pounds, or 145 kilos. Like a good wine, she has become fuller bodied and has improved with age.

It is hard to believe that Flo-Jo came close to abandoning athletics in 1986 because of an unhappy love affair, when today she is reaping the benefits of her winter efforts and is set to earn millions of dollars in 1989.

Unreal and mysterious, the black panther has got its claws out and has escaped from its cage. But don't worry: it no longer snacks between meals.

THE VOICE

Florence Griffith-Joyner's voice and physique have changed completely since the Rome World Championships last year. Her new, deeper voice would easily allow her to be one of the basses in the Golden Gate Quartet. And with a body like a champion bodybuilder she could easily become a bodyguard. In the space of a year, Flo-Jo has changed dramatically. Far, far too much to be able to show her simple admiration, she began to smile half way through the 100m final as she left an excellent Evelyn Ashford trailing at more than three-tenths of a second. Last year Griffith was a 10.96 runner. The world record she set in Indianapolis is 10.49. Listen to the difference. It is in the voice.

The Kenyans' clean sweep of the distance events

The poor East African nation dominates the 800m, 1500m, 3,000m steeplechase and 5,000m.

'Remember what I predicted at Auckland, this winter, during the World Cross Country Championships,' says Mike Koskei. 'We'd use cross country as the base for dominating the track. Well, we've done it!' The coach of Kenya's light cavalry has kept his word.

Paul Ereng won the 800m; Peter Rono, the 1500m; John Ngugi, the 5,000m; Julius Kariuki, the 3,000m steeplechase. The marathon title evaded Douglas Wakihuri, second, by fifteen seconds; in the 10,000m, Kipkemboi Kimeli, third, was less than four seconds from victory.

'It was a simple question of planning and dedication. We have the human material to succeed; it's enough to know how to prepare it. Our results here are the logical outcome.'

The week prior to the athletics programme at the Games, we were struck by the ease, relaxation and discipline of the Kenyan team. It was a far cry from the disorganisation that used to characterise the Africans. Whether they're Kikuyu, Masai, Nandi or Turkana, the athletes selected for the Games feel Kenyan, above all else.

'For the first time, we've followed strict selection criteria,' Koskei continues. 'There were no exceptions, even for world champions. Look at Konchellah and Kipkoech: they won world titles at Rome last year, but this year, they've been ill, so they've been replaced. We've drawn up very strict rules, it's no longer a question of roving the globe earning money here and there. And we've excluded several athletes capable of competing at Olympic level because they lack the discipline. And, for the first time, we've organised middle-distance qualifying heats along the lines of the US trials. Every athlete present at Seoul is there at the top of his form.'

Just like the US sprint squad, it's sometimes easier to win an Olympic medal than to qualify for the Kenyan team. 'It's true,' says John Ngugi, world cross country champion and now Olympic 5,000m champion. 'It isn't

unheard of to see a boy who finished third in the Olympic trials have a higher place in the Olympic final. It's a matter of confidence. In my case, I've always followed the pace on the track, where I always set it in cross country. In cross country, I didn't get bogged down in tactics, but on the track, I ran in the group – until today!'

Last year, at Rome, I was out of form because of a cyst behind my knee. My time hadn't come yet. To beat the Europeans, you have to force them out of their usual routine – break up their traditional race pattern. Surprise them. They like steady-tempo running, so you have to give them what they don't like – accelerations. That's why I attacked after a thousand metres and ran a 58-second lap.'

As surprising as Ngugi's tactics is the rate at which Kenyan athletes emerge. One champion falls ill, and some unknown kid appears to take his place, and sometimes does even better. 'Above all, it's thanks to the contribution our US coaches have made to our training techniques,' says Peter Rono, the new Olympic 1500m champion. 'I've been at Mount Saint

Peter Rono (centre), 1500m champion in Seoul, celebrates with his compatriots Kipchoge Cheruyot (right, seventh) and Joseph Shesire (left, eleventh).

Mary College, Maryland, for two years now. That's where I've learnt how to train. I had natural ability; my coaches have turned me into a champion.'

The universities of Texas, Washington State, New Mexico and Maryland have all opened Kenyan offices, through which have passed Henry Rono, Samson Kimobwa and Julius Korir (Washington State University), Billy Konchellah (Wayland Baptist University), Paul Ereng (University of Virginia), Julius Kariuki (Riverside Community College) and a multitude of Koskeis and Sangs. There are two noteworthy exceptions, however: Ngugi, who's a soldier and rarely steps foot outside his homeland, and Wakiihuri, the marathon runner, who lives in Japan with Seko.

At the Rome Olympics in 1960, Nyandika Maiyoro finished sixth in the final of the 5,000m in an African record time of 13:52.8 minutes. Seraphino Antao and Bartonjo Rotich were semi-finalists in the 100m and 400m hurdles, respectively. The first Olympic medal won by a Kenyan was at Tokyo in 1964, when Wilson Kiprugut won the bronze in the 800m, a year after Kenya's independence. But Kenya exploded into Olympic history at the 1968 Games, when Kipchoge Keino defeated local favourite Jim Ryun in the 1500m, winning in an Olympic record time of 3:34.9. Keino also took second in the 5,000m – an event in which he had finished fifth four years earlier. His team-mate Naftali Temu won the 10,000m. Kenyan track athletes won eleven medals in six events ranging from the 4x400m relay to the 10,000m.

Boycotts in 1976 and 1980 interrupted the Kenyan emergence. Nonetheless, at Seoul, as the box below demonstrates, a global superpower in distance running has been confirmed, not from the wealthy industrialised nations, but from poor, mountainous East Africa.

RESULTS

1968: 1500m: Kipchoge Keino 3:34.9 **10,000m:** Naftali Temu 29:27.4 3,000m steeplechase: Amos Biwott 8:51.0 **1972: 3,000m:** steeplechaase: Kipchoge Keino 8:23.6 **4x400m:** Charles Asati, Hezakiah Nyamau, Robert Ouko, Julius Sang 2:29.83 **1976: 1980:** Boycotts **1984:** 3,000m steeplechase: Julius Korir 8:11.80 **1988:** 800m: Paul Ereng 1:43.45 1500m: Peter Rono 3:35.96 5,000m: John Ngugi 13:11.70 3,000m steeplechase: Julius Kariuki 8:05.51

John Ngugi completes his final lap in 62.2 seconds, to finish ahead of Dieter Baumann by four seconds.

SWIMMING

Kristin Otto leaves them KO

With six gold medals, four of them individual in three different strokes, the great East German is a true champion.

The butterfly-freestyle combination is standard among great swimmers, from Spitz to Ender. Kristin Otto adds the backstroke.

evening: 'The 50m isn't really my speciality.' We almost believed her. Then, sure enough, she delivered her usual daily performance, except that this time, what she achieved was truly breathtaking: four individual titles, unprecedented in women's swimming. Neither Debbie Mayer in Mexico, nor even Kornelia Ender in Montreal, achieved such a feat. Still more bewildering was the fact that Otto not only dominated in freestyle and butterfly, but also, unlike her two great predecessors, was equally untouchable in backstroke.

When a male or female swimmer performs in this way, minds are inevitably cast back to the yardstick of Mark Spitz's monumental record at the 1972 Games in Munich. As long ago as Friday, the matter was raised with Otto. Even if it were impossible for her to surpass the American, she was asked if she sometimes thought of him during these Games. She openly laughed out loud and retorted: 'No, the fact that I was here meant that I had a chance of winning. But I would have been content if I had only won one or two gold medals.'

She came to within a whisker of the great Spitz, and this considering that she had not been permitted to go further in her ambitious plan because there were only two relays for women compared to three for men. The truth

There was probably only one way out for Kristin Otto's rivals: to go on strike. Put yourself in their shoes for a moment: over the past four years they have risen in the early hours to swim thousands of kilometres, breakfasting on gallons of chlorine – in short, they've put themselves through the mill in pursuit of their sporting ambitions. And after all that effort, what have they got to show for it? Nothing, or next to it. A little silver on Otto's right, a smattering of bronze on Otto's left. It would be enough to put you off competing altogether.

Meanwhile, Kristin Otto has hit the jackpot and has accumulated a healthy collection of medals, six of them gold!

More than enough to put a few noses out of joint. Take yesterday, for example: during the 50m final, in the middle of prime time, Kristin, who hadn't produced the best time in the

qualifying heats, wasn't out of the centre of the television image for a second. Two days earlier, she had come close to admitting that she could not be counted on for Sunday

In lane four, Otto is next to Stellmach (GDR) and Plewinski (FRA) at the start of the 100m.

RESULTS

OTTO'S SIX TITLES

50m freestyle
First in 25.49

100m freestyle
First in 54.93

100m backstroke
First in 1:00.89

100m butterfly
First in 59.00

4 x 100m freestyle relay
First in 3:40.63 - GDR
(Otto, Meissner, Hunger and Stellmach)

4 x 100m medley relay
First in 4:03.74 - GDR
(Otto, Hörner, Weigang and Meissner)

In the 100m butterfly, Kristin Otto powers on towards her fourth title.

is that she has done just as well as the Californian.

It remains to be seen how this will now change her destiny, as this woman has experienced everything in six years with her first world title in Guayaquil in 1982. At twenty-two, her record remains for posterity. She has done it all: six Olympic titles, six world championship gold medals and eight first places at the European championships is truly exceptional.

So, the story ends there for the moment: there is no way of knowing where she will choose to go from here. She is a little lost in terms of direction and you can understand why. Really, people just want to know her plans for the coming year but she is living one day at a time this September. One thing is certain: eventually, she will be a sports correspondent, a profession she is training for at the University of Leipzig. Without doubt, this is why she does not shy away when the microphones are in close proximity. Although sometimes this reflex betrays her. She admits: 'I like to swim. And,

sometimes when I'm asked if I feel like I've missed out on my youth, I don't understand how anybody could ask such a question.' This is really only a minor detail. She is not today being asked to win the Pulitzer Prize. She does not give herself away when asked about her true feelings, beyond a few trivialities. To one journalist who asked her if she has any idea what awaits her when she returns home to Leipzig, she replied that it would be wrong to think in individual terms: 'There will be a celebration of the whole team. There is

no reason to separate us.' We only know that her achievements will not make her a millionaire. Unlike the Soviets, the East German authorities have promised nothing to the athletes who shine at Seoul. Meanwhile, taking Kristin Otto at her word, she will calmly go back to the journalism department at university in October, as if nothing exceptional has occurred in her life – although after what she has just experienced, it may be hard to find life, or anything else, very exciting from now on

SWIMMING

Biondi in Seventh Heaven

The best men's swimmer of these Games has equalled Mark Spitz's number of medals (seven).

Matt Biondi, seen here during the 100m freestyle, was unable to win all the individual events. However, as part of the American relay team, he managed to achieve a historic triple success.

The NBC commentator drove himself into a frenzy, repeating into his malfunctioning microphone: 'A historic result on this, the last day of the swimming events: with seven medals, including five gold, Matt Biondi has become the second greatest swimmer in history, after Mark Spitz. As for the East German Kristin Otto, she has become, quite simply, the greatest, winning six gold medals.'

There is nothing to add. The swimming events of the twenty-fourth Olympiad have been of an exceptional standard, with eleven world records. Despite a redistribution of medals as a result of the increasing strength of new nations, Matt Biondi and Kristin Otto, the stars of the Games, carried off an astounding collection of medals.

True, the strength of their teams protected them from unwelcome surprises in the relays. But the outcomes of the 50m were more uncertain.

With two world records on Saturday and another two on Sunday, the rhythm of the final weekend did not falter. It all started with an upset of gigantic proportions in the men's 100m backstroke, when Japan's Daichi Suzuki touched 0.13 seconds before David Berkoff (USA), and 0.15 before Igor Polyanski (SOV/RUS). Berkoff and Polyanski had been trading world records in the spring, and were the two outstanding favourites. Then Biondi finally set his first individual world record: 50m in 22.14. It was a good result for the international federation, too, who will no longer

have the embarrassment of the unratified, out-of-competition record of 22.18, held by Peter Williams, a South African, and therefore non grata at the Olympics.

There were still two records to go on the last day. Firstly, Tamas Darnyi (HUN), who doubled his medal tally with victory in the 200m medley. It

4x100m medley: Biondi (standing, left) swims butterfly. Jacobs finishes in style.

was Darnyi's second world record of the Games after the 400m individual medley – he missed the two-minute barrier by just 0.17 seconds.

The medley relay finished in another world record, set by the US team. It was a fitting finale, although it didn't stop East Germany claiming world supremacy. The medals tallies

speak for themselves: twenty-eight medals (eleven gold) for East Germany, eighteen medals (eight gold) for the USA. Biondi and Evans won five individual golds between them.

RESULTS

MATT BIONDI'S SEVEN MEDALS

50m	First (22.14)
100m	First (48.63)
200m	Third (1:47.99)
100m butterfly	Second (53.01)
4x100m relay	First (USA, 3:16.53)
4x200m relay	First (USA, 7:12.51)
4x100m medley	First (USA, 3:36.93)

Louganis takes a springboard to glory

Despite an accident in the preliminary rounds, the American retains his title.

Greg Louganis is a phenomenon! Of Samoan and North European ancestry, and given up for adoption by his fifteen-year-old parents, he overcame a childhood blighted by racism and dyslexia to become the geatest diver in the world, and the favourite to win two gold medals at the 1980 Olympics – which he then missed due to the boycott. At the 1982 World Championships he accomplished the feat, and repeated it at the 1984 Olympics.

At Seoul, he was back – and not even a shocking blow to the skull could distract him from his task. On his ninth dive of the preliminary round, a reverse two and a half somersault in the pike position, he hit his head on the board and fell limply

USSR in 1979,' he said, 'and it was much more serious than this. I was unconscious for twenty minutes and I had to withdraw from the competition.' Luckily, this was not the case at Seoul, where he paid a small penalty for a grave mistake. 'On take-off, I didn't push my hips far enough in front. I admit that I didn't even realise until my head hit the board, and then, of course, I received a shock, in every sense of the word,' he explained with a little smile.

However, the shock was not enough to make this first-class athlete give up. 'It obviously rattled my confidence, but after a very long warm-up session before the final, I regained my composure.' A fine performance followed, allowing for a momentary lapse on the fourth dive of the final.

The impact: Greg Louganis, double champion in Los Angeles (springboard and platform diving), attempts a single reverse somersault during the ninth of the eleven qualifying dives from the springboard. His head hits the springboard. He climbed out of the pool aided by officials, but was able to continue, finishing third in the qualifying rounds and reaching the final, which he then went on to win.

into the pool below – proving that even the best diver in the world can make an elementary mistake. Doubtless, the accident brought the champion public sympathy and may have affected the judges. But at the press conference after the medals ceremony, Louganis played down the incident, saying that it was more spectacular than serious, and more frightening than painful: 'No, honestly, I was in no pain today. I hit the platform during a competition in the

From then on, everything was back to normal. His victory was never contested, despite the skill of the Chinese divers.

It was the first of two possible gold medals on the road to becoming the first diver in history to retain two Olympic titles. Louganis was unbeatable even without the generosity of the judges. This was particularly obvious in his last dive when, despite a more than clumsy entrance into the water, he totalled eighty points. So was

Louganis overmarked? Probably, even if his heir, the faultless Tan Liangde, showed his sense of fair-play in replying at the press conference: 'No, I don't think the judges have been unfair.'

But diving is a gentleman's game: Louganis himself had already dismissed the excuse of injury as a reason for possible failure in the platform event.

The double Olympic champion in 1984, Greg Louganis retains both titles at Seoul: unprecedented!

1988
OLYMPICS ROUND-UP

HESSLICH THE GIANT

His are eyes closed, his jaw clenched, his face ridden with tics and his right hand on the zipper of the suit he closes sharply and nervously before the start. Before each race, Lutz Hesslich descends into intense concentration. It is almost frightening to watch. Then comes the explosion.

His two 1000m match sprints in the final against the Soviet Russian, Nikolai Kovsh, are awe-inspiring. During the first sprint, he attacks from 500m, after a stop. Kovsh, using lenticular wheels, allows himself to be surprised by Hesslich. To get his heavy bike moving, the giant East German with thighs of steel takes 60m, and when it comes to the home straight, it is a simple matter of maintaining his speed.

During the second sprint, the Muscovite takes the initiative but is then overtaken by Hesslich at breakneck speed.

Lutz Hesslich, his second Olympic title now assured, (photo thirteen) goes to cry, like a child, on his coach's shoulder. Monsters can sometimes prove touching. Even so, his new crowning seemed planned. In the absence of the only rivals of his calibre, his East German compatriots, King Hesslich reigned supreme.

Four times world champion (1979, 1983, 1985, 1987), Lutz Hesslich achieved a second 1000m match sprint gold medal at the Games, his first having been in Moscow eight years ago. He thereby joined the century's leading figures in track cycling.

In a press conference he was asked which of his two Olympic gold medals he had gone through the most torture for. 'This one,' he replied. 'Not so much here in Seoul, but before, to qualify in my country. For three years, the world's four best sprinters have been East Germans and it's very hard to stay the best over there. The only regret I have about my career has been inflicting all this stress on my wife, because I must be almost unbearable. But I find I have to behave like that. It's my way of preparing myself and collecting all my nervous energy.'

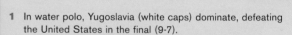

1 In water polo, Yugoslavia (white caps) dominate, defeating the United States in the final (9-7).
2 Volleyball: Timmons (smashing) and the United States retain their supremacy at the expense of the USSR (3-1).
3 Weighing in at more than 95kg, Hitoshi Saito (right) saves the honour of Japanese judo, achieving his country's only gold medal. On the left, Stöhr (GDR).
4 In double sculls the Dutch pair, Florijn-Rienks, win by a narrow margin.
5 A grave disappointment for Romario: Brazil are beaten in the final of the football tournament by the USSR (2-1).
6 Aleksandr Kareline (SOV/RUS), Greco-Roman wrestling champion in the super-heavyweight, division, recovers after his final against the Bulgarian Gerovski.
7 With a superb leap of 7.40m, the American Jackie Joyner-Kersee passes Heike Drechsler (GDR) in the long jump.
8 The surprise podium for the 400m hurdles, where 'king' Moses (left) is overtaken by his fellow American Philipps (centre) and the Senegalese Dia Ba (right).
9 In the 100m backstroke, the Japanese Suzuki causes an upset by defeating the American Berkoff.
10 The Canadians Carolyn Waldo and Michelle Cameron, the gold medal-winning duo in synchronised swimming.
11 In the semi-finals of the table tennis tournament, the pair from South Korea concede defeat to the eventual Chinese winners.
12 Men's basketball. After dismissing the United States in the semi-finals (82-76), the USSR (red) dominates the final, defeating the Yugoslavs 76-63. At the back stands the star, Arvidas Sabonis.
13 Track cycling. At speed, Lutz Hesslich (GDR) has an easy ride.
14 The Soviet handballers (white) apply themselves to deliver against a surprising team from South Korea (32-25).
15 Women's basketball. An easy win for the United States in the final against Yugoslavia (77-70), despite the energetic Mujanovic (12).

Lewis wins and Canada recovers her pride

A week after the Ben Johnson scandal, Canada recovered her pride thanks to Lennox Lewis, 23, from Kitchener, Ontario, who defeated Riddick Bowe (USA) when the referee stopped the fight in round two.

'In the ring, two Canadian officials took me for a doping test,' said Lewis. "They kept shouting at me: 'Don't shake hands with anyone! Don't drink anything!' They only began to relax when the sample had been provided and carefully stored away."

Another scandal worried Lewis: the dodgy decision that cost light middleweight Roy Jones (USA) gold against Park Si-hun of South Korea. "I was in the changing-rooms with my gloves on, when Jones went down," said Lewis. "I thought that there would be a wave of sympathy for the next US boxer, my opponent, Riddick Bowe. So, to be sure I would win, I was going to have to go for the KO.' Lewis visibly held Bowe's punching lower in contempt, and let him take the initiative at the start, allowing Bowe to deliver body punches. Lewis notably took three uppercuts, one making his nose bleed. "That was good," said Lewis. "It woke me up." In the second round, Bowe was then given a rude awakening and after 43 seconds of fighting, the match had to be stopped, quite rightly, by the referee. A professional future now awaits the Canadian.

Süleymanoglu, as strong as an ox

No dispute: Naim rules. He has taken the 60kg title, improving on six amazing world records.

Only two years ago, he was on the other side of the border. He was a national hero and recognised on every street corner. He was someone you gave up your place for in packed restaurants. He was fame itself and his name was Suleimanov, which later became Shalamanov, although he, like his parents, was of Turkish origin. At the first opportunity he left for the country of his ancestors. Then came more fame and a new hero's lifestyle for this child who had grown up so quickly. He was placed under the protection of the prime minister.

On arriving in Turkey, Shalamanov became Süleymanoglu, hero to 55 million Turks. In Seoul he passed his first great right of passage.

In the stands, nearly a hundred Turkish flags waved. Behind the scenes, the cheers were led by the president of the Turkish Olympic Committee, Jerfi Firatli, and by the IOC member Ali Sinan Erden.

His former Bulgarian coach, Abadjiev, had said: 'I'll only have to look him in the eye and Naim won't be Olympic champion.' But the master must have given the eye to the wrong man, as his new protege, the Bulgarian Stefan Topurov, was utterly beaten. The 145kg he had lifted at Cardiff during the European Championships melted in the summer sun down to 137.5kg.

He had long been eliminated when Süleymanoglu went on the platform to attempt 145kg. It was done both quickly and well. 'Now, let's get down to business!' he seemed to mutter, before lifting 150.5kg as if it were nothing. It was a new world record. He gave a small gesture of disdain which seemed to say, 'You see, easy.' Then 152.5kg also seemed easy, giving him an incredible second world record. Where was it all going to end? The Turkish crowd was hysterical: screaming and waving.

Topurov had taken a drubbing, lifting 15kg less than the king.

He was exhausted but picked himself up and made a second attempt to challenge Süleymanoglu in the clean-and-jerk. Topurov swayed beneath 165kg, but resisted and completed the lift. At 175kg, it was an even closer call,

but he emerged unscathed. While Süleymanoglu overcame the same weight, Topurov's collapse began. Drunk with exhaustion, the Bulgarian was eliminated at the next increase in weight.

The competition was over. Now it was time for Süleymanoglu to turn on

the style. The bar rose at 177.5kg, 185kg, 187.5kg, and stays at 188.5kg for a second attempt. In three swift movements, the bar rose, a smile appeared on Süleymanoglu's face, he directed a fixed stare at his fellow countrymen, and relaxed. 'Easy, too easy,' Süleymanoglu seemed to be

saying. 'Give me something more solid.' The crowd was going wild. Turkish flags were waving frantically. Bulgarian flags were at half mast.

The next weight was 190kg. It was incredible. Süleymanoglu resumed his zombie-like shuffle. With a dry movement and a quick squat, the cast iron lifted off, wobbled, swayed in the air, but Süleymanoglu stabilised it. It was his thirty-third world record and his sixth of the evening.

Concentrated and sure of himself, the neo-Turk Naim Süleymanoglu breaks every record in his category and wins in a class of his own.

RESULTS

WEIGHTLIFTING 60KG

1 Süleymanoglu (TUR), 342.5kg (world record)
2 Topurov (BUL), 312.5kg
3 Ye Huanming (CHN), 287.5kg
4 Min Joon-Ki (KOR), 280kg
5 Yosuke Muraki (JPN), 277.5kg
6 Giannis Sidriopoulos (GRE), 265kg
7 Kazushige Oguri (JPN), 260kg
8 Tolentio Murillo (COL), 260kg

Steffi Graf: real gold

Germany's Steffi Graf adds a gold medal to her Grand Slam. An unprecedented achievement in women's tennis.

Until Saturday 1 October, the expression 'Gold Grand Slam' did not exist. It was coined to define the feat of Steffi Graf, awarded a gold medal at the Seoul Olympic Games, just three weeks after winning a Grand Slam on the Flushing Meadows courts. No sooner had tennis returned to the Olympic Games than the young German seized her opportunity to pull off an incredible performance – a performance comparable to Bob Beamon's 8.90m long jump in Mexico, or Ben Johnson's 9.79 second 100m, if the time had been allowed.

Graf's achievement is unequalled in the annals of tennis, which had been

After winning the demonstration tournament in Los Angeles at the age of 15, Steffi Graf repeats her performance at Seoul. This time it's for a real Olympic title.

absent from the Olympic Games from 1924. And in those days, nobody even spoke of Grand Slams. Nevertheless, the record books show that no Grand Slam has ever been achieved before in an Olympic year. So even if tennis had remained an Olympic sport between 1924 and 1988, neither Donald Budge (1938) nor Maureen Connolly (1953), Rod Laver (1962 and 1969), nor Margaret Court (1970) would have found themselves in a position to carry off the same achievement as Steffi

Graf in Seoul! Does this unique achievement mean that the 19-year-old German is the greatest tennis champion of all time? Does she already rank above Suzanne Lenglen, Helen Wills, Maureen Connolly, Margaret Court, Billie Jean King, Chris Evert and Martina Navratilova? We'll have to wait a season or two to know. Meanwhile, one thing seems certain: Steffi Graf has devastating ability, which is all the more deadly as she is physically stronger than her

main rivals. Her mental strength seems unshakeable, while her taste for hard work and training surpasses that of her rivals.

Given the circumstances, Graf can be expected to dominate world women's tennis for five to six years, or at least while she has the will power to dedicate herself to competitive sport.

However, at the same time, could the success she has enjoyed this year not be considered exceptional, even for her? Chris Evert and Martina

Navratilova are playing far from their best tennis, while Gabriela Sabatini has not yet fulfilled her enormous potential. This year has definitely been a turning point for Steffi Graf, leaving her isolated at the top of the pyramid of women's tennis. It remains to be seen who will be able to resist her in years to come.

Gabriela Sabatini seems the obvious choice. She is the only player to have defeated Steffi Graf this year, and when the two meet at the most important tournaments, Roland-Garros, the US Open and the Olympic Games, the young Argentine always pushes her to really up her game before allowing her to win. Even if Steffi Graf is capable of winning almost all her matches during the year on top form, the pressure that Gabriela was capable of applying is likely to increase, much to the delight of women's tennis fans.

RESULTS

FIVE HISTORIC FINALS

Australian Open
Melbourne
6 to 24 January 1988
Steffi Graf (GER) bt. Chris Evert (USA), 6-1; 7-6; 7-3

French Open
Paris
23 May to 5 June
Steffi Graf (GER) bt. Natasha Zvereva (RUS) 6-0; 6-0

Wimbledon
20 June to 3 July
Steffi Graf (GER) bt. Martina Navratilova (USA), 5-7; 6-2; 6-1

US Open
New York
29 August to 11 September
Steffi Graf (GER) bt. Gabriela Sabatini (ARG), 6-3; 3-6; 6-1

Olympic Games
Seoul
19 September to 1 October
Steffi Graf (GER) bt. Gabriela Sabatini (ARG) 6-3; 6-3

SEOUL XXIV OLYMPIAD

The Seoul Games were marked by a long-awaited reunion of athletes from the West (who had not competed at Moscow) and the East (who were absent from Los Angeles). However, they were perhaps made more famous by the drugs scandals that marred the events.

THE GAMES IN BRIEF

Opening Date
17 September 1988

Closing Date
2 October 1988

Host Nation
South Korea (KOR)

Candidate Towns
Nagoya (JAP)

159 Nations Represented

8,465 Athletes
(2,186 women, 6,279 men)

23 Sports
(17 open to women)
Track and field, rowing, basketball, boxing, canoeing, cycling, equestrian, fencing, football, gymnastics, weightlifting, handball, field hockey, judo, wrestling, swimming, modern pentathlon, tennis, table tennis, shooting, archery, volleyball and sailing.

237 Events
(86 open to women)

Games officially opened by
Roh Tae-woo, President of South Korea

Olympic flame lit by
Chong Sun-man, Kim Won-tak and Sohn Mi-chung (athletics)

Olympic oath read by
Ms Hug-jae (basketball)

IOC President
Juan Antonio Samaranch (ESP)

DID YOU KNOW?

Despite Cuba, Ethiopia and Nicaragua boycotting the Games, participation rates were at their highest ever with 159 nations present.

For the first time ever, all three golds in the equestrian dressage were won by women.

Swedish fencer Kerstin Palm competed in her seventh Olympic Games, a new women's record.

Table tennis was introduced for the first time and tennis returned to the programme after a 64-year absence.

Germany's Christa Luding-Rothenberger, who had won two medals in the Calgary Winter Games, went on to take silver in the cycling match sprint in Seoul.

1992

Barcelona

EVERYONE WAS THERE, OR NEARLY: POST-apartheid South Africa, after a long absence from the Games; the Baltic states Estonia, Latvia and Lithuania, alongside another fifteen nations emerging from the disintegration of the Soviet Union, reassembled in the Commonwealth of Independent States, although their national anthems and flags were used as a matter of protocol. The Germans competed under one nation after the absorption of East Germany in 1990. North and South Yemen had merged. Croatia, Slovenia and Bosnia came separately, as war still raged in Yugoslavia. Their enemies from Serbia and Montenegro were also present.

Only the Palestinians was missing: they would not be represented at the Olympics for another four years.

Everyone was there, then, or nearly: amateurs, of course, but professionals, too – admitted for the first time. This meant that even more of the greatest athletes in the world could be seen in action: Luis Enrique or Guardiola in football, Chris Boardman in cycling, and above all the inspirational American basketball players of the NBA, together in an unbeatable Dream Team.

Everyone was there, then, or nearly, and Juan Antonio Samaranch, the Catalan president of the International Olympic Committee, was proud of these first Catalan Games and the enthusiasm they provoked. The organisation was impeccable. Not even the extraordinary security measures could chill the atmosphere.

A dream for some, a nightmare for others: the Angolans are denied the ball by Clyde Drexler, Charles Barkley and Chris Mullin.

Dream of dreams...

Deploying their inspirational skills, the United States take back what they considered their birthright: the Olympic basketball title.

Magic Johnson, Pat Ewing, Scottie Pippen, Karl Malone, Larry Bird, Charles Barkley, Michael Jordon. The US Dream Team was the principal attraction at the Barcelona Games and the public turned out in droves.

A dream has passed. We saw it disappear at the end of the corridor, ball in hand. Magic. With Jordan, Pippen, Ewing and Barkley, the man Chuck Daly declared was a joy to coach: 'But five weeks isn't enough!' Before the match, Daly divulged his feelings in USA Today, perhaps intended to be read to the sound of violins: 'I will remember it until the day I die. I can look at my gold medal' – bear in mind he hadn't won it yet – 'or put on a video of the Dream Team. Nobody will be able to take the shared experience away from me.'

All that remained was the small matter of the final. The evening before, even the most nocturnal Dream-Teamers were in bed early for the first time of their Spanish vacation; tucked in by midnight, as against the usual three or four in the morning routine they had become used to.

They played their last training match against members of the Spanish police to thank them for taking care of security. Now, they were ready.

So were the Croats, who did themselves proud. If the medal ceremony was full of genuine joy, it was because their Croatian rivals had shown that basketball was now universal enough to produce quality players all over the world.

'Sure, he could play in the NBA. He could play anywhere,' Mullin assured a journalist. 'Yeah, Toni Kukoc can play the game!' And with more skilful team-mates than Vrankovic or Arapovic, Kukoc might have done even better than with sixteen points, three out of five three-point shots – one of which was right in Pippen's face – five rebounds and nine assists.

And Drazen Petrovic, can play, too, allowing himself a spat with his

shadow, Michael Jordan. And Dino Radja was in fine form: twenty-five points, five out of six outside the three-point line, a fine shooting touch.

Not that we should pretend there

was any suspense, even if the half-time score of 56-42 meant the Americans still had to play carefully. At least it saved us one of those pitiful collapses that reduced Angola and others to their knees, after a sort of dereliction of duty. Croatia made a game of it, after a fashion: the result was never in doubt, but there was at least a game to watch, which was a sort of moral victory for the team coached by Petar Skansi. This was despite Michael Jordan's cruel comment, 'Our hardest matches were in our training sessions at Monaco.' The contest ended 117-85 (the Dream Team's closest result), and closed with an enigmatic smile on Kukoc's lips, as if he were looking into the future.

A cruel representation of the American dominance; Charles Barkley holds on to the ring and doesn't let go.

With a deficit of just 32 points, the Croats, in red, hold out better than any squad against the extraordinary Michael Jordan.

Michael Jordan stood on the podium with a flag draped over the Reebok logo on his official tracksuit. 'His own idea,' according to Barkley. Drexler, commenting on the endorsement situation, said: 'This way, everyone wins.' They'd certainly won: they felt immense, beautiful and proud. So did the Croations. 'For us,' Petrovic explained, 'silver is like gold. Finishing second is ample compensation for what we went through to get here. It's Croatia's first team 'gold' and we are very proud. We want to dedicate it to our people. The match may not have been spectacular, but I think we played at the level of the Dream Team for extended periods. We are happy men.'

MAGIC'S DREAM

Magic Johnson's happiness illuminated the Olympic tournament

He's always been 'Magic': full of joy and flair, Earvin 'Magic' Johnson, a natural leader, steered the Dream Team towards Olympic glory, while keeping his childlike spirit, the spirit of a child delighted to be living in a land of giants. 'If I'm on court, I'm always happy,' Magic repeated throughout the tournament. 'It's serious, but it's also fun. For me, the Olympic Games are the most important thing in my life. It's unforgettable, not just because of the basketball, but because of all the excitement. It's amazing to see the other athletes come to our training sessions, asking for our autographs and if they can take photos of us. I can't believe it.'

Magic, basketball demi-god touched by the demons of Aids, once more defied logic. He was no longer the man who declared himself HIV positive to all the world. He was quite simply a kid, tall (6 feet 8) and strong (218 pounds) for his age... You forget he's 32 and has his torments. All you noticed were his mischievous eyes, spontaneous laugh and his simple, shared happiness. 'I really enjoyed myself,' he said leaving the court. 'I experienced an extraordinary feeling and when the national anthem was played, I felt really emotional on the podium!' At the final whistle, the US team gathered round their emblematic star.

IN FLIGHT OVER BARCELONA

The sprawling city of Barcelona provided a mesmeric backdrop to the diving competition, which lived up to the magnificent setting with a series of stunning performances in a tournament dominated by Chinese athletes, who took either silver or gold in every diving category. Mingxia Fu (CHN), 13, already the youngest ever world diving champion, won the women's Platform Diving competition by 49.8 points (a record she would break four years later, retaining her title by 92.36 points). Her compatriot Min Gao won the women's Springboard tournament by 58.26 points. The Chinese also took both Synchronised Platform titles, and Shunwei Sun (photo), replaced Greg Louganis on the podium of the men's Platform Diving. It was a stunning triumph for a sports system that regiments its athletes from an early age, and one that marked the beginning of a period of dominance that continues to this day. How can the West compete?

CYCLING

A triumph of humility over technology

Chris Boardman's athleticism is overshadowed by his equipment.

The relation between sport and technology is double-edged: sometimes athletes and coaches drive technological progress. Sometimes, the technologists themselves revolutionise sport. Whichever way it happens, technology is invariably easier to understand than the vagaries of the human machine. The bike designed for Britain's Chris Boardman by Mike Burrows and built by Lotus, the Formula 1 car designers, bike, was a carbon composite monocoque with low-drag aerodynamic cross-sections, formed with unidirectional and stitched high-strength carbon fibre in an epoxy resin matrix, it was something the press could really get its teeth into.

In the preliminary rounds of the men's 4,000m individual pursuit, Boardman rode the new machine to world records of 4:27.357 and 4:24.496, demoralising the other contenders. In the final, he lapped world champion Jens Lehmann. It was unprecedented. For much of the media, it was a triumph for technology over muscle-power, despite Lehmann's insistence: 'I was beaten by the rider, not the bike.'

Six months after his Olympic victory, Boardman walked out of a meeting with the Lotus executives. 'The company secretary asked me, "Did you think you could do it without our bike?" I excused myself and left.'

In 1993, the post-Lotus Boardman pulverised the world hour record. In 1994 he thrashed Miguel Induráin and Tony Rominger in the Prologue of the Tour de France, winning by the enormous margin of fifteen seconds and wearing the coveted yellow jersey for the first three days of his Tour de France career. By the end of the season he had won the world pursuit title on the track and the world time time-trial title on the road. Yet the stigma of high technology would hang over him until the end of his career. Cycling's world governing body retrospectively downgraded his repeated world hour records by creating a new category of 'Records set using special bicycles.' Boardman responded in his final ride as a professional athlete by riding a traditional bike, circa 1972, to a new world hour record, despite a debilitating and untreated bone disease for which the only treatment, hormone therapy, was banned due to anti-doping legislation.

This wonderful career stemmed from his Olympic victory. Yet at the time, Chris Boardman went through mixed emotions. 'I did not have a sense of elation. I saw others dancing with joy and leaping up and down on the podium, but I had only a sense of shock. Everything I had worked for over two years, and in a matter of seconds it was all over. It took four an a half minutes to change my life.'

Chris Boardman didn't consider himself favourite: 'With or without the Lotus bike, I didn't believe I would win. I was just this guy from Hoylake – other people won the Olympics, not me.'

'If I had not won at Barcelona, I would have faded into the background'. Instead, Boardman's pursuit victory led him to a professional career and the yellow jersey of the Tour de France.

RESULTS

400m Individual Pursuit

1 Chris Boardman (GBR)
2 Jens Lehmann (GER) overtaken
3 Gary Anderson (NZL) 4:31.061
4 Mark Kingsland (AUS) 4:32.716
5 Philippe Ermenault (FRA) 4:28.838
6 Cedric Mathy (BEL) 4:33.942
7 Adolfo Alperi Plaza (SPA) 4:34.760
8 Ivan Beltrami (ITA) 4:36.541

LADY RAMBO

There are two halves to Jackie Joyner-Kersee. There's her brother Al Joyner, Olympic triple jump champion at Los Angeles and husband of Florence Griffith Joyner. Then there's Kersee, as in Bob, Jackie's husband and coach to this glittering world of athletes. Talking about Jackie, Bob has said, 'if there's a female version of Rambo, it must be her'. Coming second in the heptathlon at Los Angeles in 1984, Jackie Joyner-Kersee took her five-point defeat against Nunn of Australia very badly. Since then, she's not stopped proving she's the best. World long jump champion in 1987 and 1991 and winning gold medalist in Seoul have proved the point. With world titles for the heptathlon in 1987 and Olympic titles in 1988 and 1992, she's the only athlete to have significantly exceeded 7,000 points in this discipline. Born on 3 March 1962, her parents named her Jacqueline after President Kennedy's wife. Her grandmother once said, 'one day, this girl will be First Lady of something.' At 30, Jackie Joyner-Kersee has proved her right.

Outrunning his demons

Always placed, Linford Christie, the British athlete born in Jamaica, has become the oldest 100m champion in history.

Beside Linford Christie, number 695 (left to right): Adeniken (NGR, sixth), Ezinwa (NGR, eighth), Burrell (USA, fifth), Mitchell (USA, third), Fredericks (NAM, second) and Stewart (JAM, seventh).

Linford Christie has capped the best season of his life with the Olympic 100m title. Aged 32, he is the oldest 100m champion in Olympic history by four years. His second place in the semi-final behind former world record holder Leroy Burrell (USA) was his first defeat of the year. In the final, Burrell was blamed for a false start, and, with his nerves in tatters, never threatened. Bruny Surin (CAN) had the fastest opening phase, followed by Frankie Fredericks (NAM). By 60m, Christie had caught and dropped them both, and was still extending his lead when he crossed the line.

However, the man who may be the most fiercely competitive sprinter in athletics today has been has always been a slow starter. He was born on 2 April 1960 in St Andrews, Jamaica. His destiny lay on a distant horizon

and he took off in pursuit of it, but the road that led him to victory in Barcelona has been long and full of obstacles. He once punched a policeman who accused him of stealing an expensive car, and hurled insults at another who visited the family home to lecture an unruly brother. He ended up realising that throwing punches and unleashing torrents of abuse only brought temporary relief. It finally clicked that a little sweat and toil might bring him to even sweeter revenge.

In 1985, he didn't even make the British relay team for the European Cup. He came back the following year to win his first major title, the 200m in the 1986 European indoor Championships, aged almost twenty-six. 'People have always said that I'm too old. But it's never too late. If the mind is willing, the body will follow.'

Second in the 100m final four years ago after Ben Johnson's disqualification, Christie has maintained his competitive edge at an age when most sprinters have long ago given up. This burning desire is just one aspect of a complex man who combines magnetic charisma with a prickliness that has sometimes cost him friends. After a false start at the Tokyo World Championships, for instance, Christie claimed that the bronze medal won by Mitchell, was, by rights, his. And when he was promoted captain of the British team, he lambasted his teammates for their big-headedness after winning the 4x400-metre relay at the Tokyo World Championships when they should have been hanging their heads in shame after their individual performances. Yet these outbursts are perhaps no more than the corollary of the enormous demands he makes

of himself, and this prickly nature has now attained the prize Christie has coveted for so many years.

There has also been controversy: at Seoul, Christie's career almost drowned in a cup of ginseng, the only substance, it would appear, that assisted him. 'The newspapers have big imaginations,' Christie says sweepingly.

Linford Christie is now an Olympic champion. Any cutting remarks will be saved for another day. 'I've only ever thought of one thing,' he told the press: 'to get from A to B as quickly as possible.' As the only finalist to run sub-10 seconds, this prickly, but engaging personality has finally fulfilled the ambitions that have fuelled his long and outstanding career.

The exemplary Hassiba Boulmerka

The symbolic figure of the woman who gave Algeria its first Olympic title.

With her hands across her chest and pointing to her jersey, she screams, 'Algérie, Algérie, Algérie'. The spectators don't fully understand, but they still applaud Algeria's first-ever Olympic champion. Her country has been through a troubled year and Hassiba Boulmerka's nerves are clearly frayed. Her victory in the 1500m has confirmed the world title she achieved a year ago in Tokyo. With her country's national flag tied around her neck, she takes the traditional lap of honour.

Since the start of the year, this woman from Constantine has been on the move between Paris, Italy and a training camp in Zinnowitz, Germany. Even if she doesn't say so, life as a role-model for women can't be easy in a country of rampant religious fundamentalism.

A simple matter of marking the athletes of the Russian Federation before unleashing a burst of blistering pace to take the win.

Her first words to the press are surprising for a young woman proud of her independence and determined to live her own life. 'I don't get involved in politics,' she says, 'I'm just an ordinary woman defending my country. I have run for the martyrs of my country and I offer this Olympic title to the father of our country, President Mohamed Boudiat, a true democrat, assassinated at Annaba. I run for a peaceful, free and tolerant Algeria.' Strong words from someone who doesn't get involved in politics. Hassiba hardly mentions the race, a clean-cut event with little suspense, because Hassiba was clearly the best. 'I want to be a model for both men and women.'

'I have run for a peaceful, free and tolerant Algeria.' The clenched fist gets the message across!

RESULTS

1500m
1 Hassiba Boulmerka (ALG), 3:55.30
2 Lyudmila Rogacheva (CEI),3:56.91
3 Qu Yunxia (CHN), 3:57.08
4 Tatyana Dorovskikh (CEI), 3:57.92
5 Lui Li (CHN), 4:00.20
6 Maite Zuniga Dominguez (ESP), 4:00.59
7 Malgorzata Rydz (POL), 4:01.91
8 Yekaterina Podkopayeva (CEI), 4:2.03

Queen Krisztina

Hungary's triple champion, Krisztina Egerszegi, is the star of the Olympic pool.

If the Danube was ever as blue as Krisztina Egerszegi's blue eyes, then all the music written in its honour was well worth it. With her perfect figure, long legs, brown locks of hair and beaming smile, she has lit up every corner of the pool during the six-day Olympic swimming programme.

Since winning her first Olympic title at Seoul for the 200m backstroke when she was fourteen, this child prodigy has grown three inches and now weighs 121 pounds.

After last summer's European Championships, where she tried out her Olympic programme to brilliant effect, a Hungarian newspaper instantly doubled its sales by asking whom Krisztina was going to marry on its front page. Thousands of love-struck men must have had their dreams shattered. Krisztina just laughs if anyone broaches the subject. Just as she laughed yesterday evening after her victory in the 200m backstroke.

'Whenever I'm in the water, I'm smiling,' she says. 'But there are lots of things behind this smile – lots of sacrifices.' Since she first dipped her toes into the water at the age of four, she has covered so many kilometres that the one thing that can bend her smile into a frown is talk of training for six hours a day, including Sundays. But even her frown is enchanting, as she shows when she mentions the one sacrifice she would not make: 'I will never shave my head even if it is proved that it would make me go faster. It looks so ugly.'

In Hungary she is called the 'mouse' – the literal translation of

'My main goal at Barcelona was to retain my title in the 200m backstroke.' She did, adding the 100m backstroke and the 400m medley for good measure.

'Eger'. It's hardly an aquatic nickname, but Hungary has no sea and hardly any live fish in its not-so-blue Danube. Nonetheless, in a swimming pool, this mouse is capable of anything: Olympic champion and world record holder in the 100m and 200m backstroke and gold medal winner in the 400m individual medley, she would probably have taken the

200m individual medley as well, but dropped it from her schedule fearing it would be too much.

Yesterday was a day of celebration for the Hungarians. Tamás Darnyi won his second gold medal in the 200m individual medley, making him the unrivalled champion in both the 200m and 400m individual medley for over seven years. But it

wasn't until the last length that he took the lead. 'Everyone's getting older,' he says with a smile.

In the 400m medley, the final 100m of freestyle was enough…

… to defend the winning lead she opened in the backstroke.

BARBARA KENDALL FOLLOWS IN HER BROTHER'S WAKE

Sailboarding was first introduced to the Olympics at Los Angeles in 1984 and the first women's competition took place at Barcelona. The New Zealander, Barbara Kendall, whose brother Bruce took gold at Seoul, was the first woman to win this competition, but not without a few problems that included surfing between everything from dead rats to fridges and the floating mass of plastic bags that filled the Parc de Mar in Barcelona's harbour. Four boats were assigned to clear away all this rubbish on a daily basis, which wasn't decisive in that every competitor faced the same problem.

Kendall's achievement was all the greater in that she had overcome serious injury. Seven months before the Games, Barbara was hit by a training boat that left her with a fractured wrist and severed tendon. Despite her injuries, she sailed through the competition.

Scherbo has every right to be proud

Belorussian gymnast Vitaly Scherbo takes six gold medals. In Olympic history, only Mark Spitz has won more at a single Games.

Considered a favourite, an overconfident Vitaly Scherbo fails to qualify for the final of the horizontal bar. This and the floor exercise are his two disappointments.

Vitaly Scherbo has always been a player. A showman, even, to quote his national coach, Aleksandr Arkeyev, and one with a particular penchant for the Olympic Games. The Barcelona Games have provided the perfect stage for a young Belorussian who had hitherto been used to vaunting his bad boy reputation and collecting the booby prize. He came to Spain hoping to come away with the gold medal in the All-Around competition, but leaves with six gold medals, including team combined exercises, All-Around, long-horse vault, rings, parallel bars and side horse. The only titles he failed to take were for the horizontal bar and floor exercise.

Any other gymnast would be attempting to explain how he came to earn six gold medals. The question Scherbo has to answer is how he came to fail in two disciplines. Part of the answer is that he doesn't fit the traditional mould. He is a little boy lost in the world of gymnastics, where conservatism and long-established tradition prevail.

Vitaly Scherbo failed to qualify for the horizontal bar and the reason for this was the obsessive attention he paid to the All-Around competition. Concentrating on what he saw as his weaker points, he sidelined the horizontal bar, believing he was already one of the best, gymnasts in this discipline.

His self-confidence, pride and talent could and should have led him to the podium. For want of a little more effort, more confidence in his coaches and the fact that in a world of Lilliputians, technique is continuously taking giant leaps forward, any progress he had made in this discipline was limited.

In the floor exercise, Scherbo had the great misfortune of falling just behind the cheery character of Li Xiaoshuang of China, who tried his luck and succeeded at the daunting backward triple salto that only Valery Lyukin had successfully attempted at

the Moscow European Championships in 1987. Xiaoshuang scored 9,925 and took gold, leaving Scherbo in second place. The Chinese team was in raptures, the coach in tears and the spectators suddenly remembered that they should have only been cheering for the Spanish.

Scherbo's lack of concentration showed. When he is nervous, his skin turns the traditional colour of an Alfa Romeo and his eyes look like those of a sick child with a human form of myxomatosis. But Scherbo actually made his exit on the first diagonal – an artist's exit.

Even if he is still only known to gymnastics fans, he has entered the history books after taking the second largest haul of medals in one Olympic Games. The first, as everyone knows, is the American, Mark Spitz, who collected seven gold medals at Munich in 1972. Scherbo's position is shared with Kristin Otto who also earned six gold medals in swimming at Seoul. Coming second only to Mark Spitz is still a mighty achievement.

'I was very focussed on becoming an Olympic champion,' he says. 'I saw people smile at my chances. I was almost the only one to have any belief in myself. The judges have never held me in high esteem. According to my coach, it's because I'm too arrogant.'

On the rings, a perfect right-angle. With six medals and a place in Olympic history, Vitaly has every right to look proud.

SCHERBO'S SIX TITLES

All-Around
1 Vitaly Scherbo (BLR), 59,025 pts
2 Hryhoriy Misyutin (UKR), 58,925 pts;
3 Valery Belenki (AZR), 58,625 pts

Parallel Bar
1 Vitaly Scherbo (BLR), 9,90 pts
2 Li Jing (CHN), 9,812 pts
3 Guo Linyao (CHN), 9,80 pts

Long Horse Vault
1 Vitaly Scherbo (BLR), 9,856 pts
2 Hryhoriy Misyutin (UKR), 9,781 pts
3 Yoo Ok-ryul (KOR), 9,762 pts

Rings
1 Vitaly Scherbo (BLR), 9,937 pts
2 Li Jing (CHN), 9,875 pts
3 Li Xiaoshuang (CHN), 9,862 pts

Pommeled Horse
1 Vitaly Scherbo (BLR) and Pae Gil-su (PRK) 9,925 pts
2 Andreas Wecker (GER), 9,887pts

Team Combined Exercises
1 SOV (Vitaly Scherbo, Valery Belenki, Hryhoriy Misyutin, Igor Korobchinsky, Alekseï Voropayev, Rustam Shapirov), 585,450 pts
2 CHI, 580,375 pts
3 JAP, 578,250 pts

1992

OLYMPIC ROUND-UP

MORALES, AT LAST.

'I now know dreams can eventually come true,' he says with a quiver in his voice and a gleam in his eye. At 27, Pablo Morales (photo 3) has finally achieved his holy grail after retiring from swimming for three and a half years. He returned eleven months ago, and has finally achieved his goal of the last eight years: the Olympic gold medal in the 100m butterfly.

After breaking the world record in the US trials, he was defeated at the 1984 Games by Michael Gross. Morales was 19 at the time, had little international experience and decided to place his hopes on the next Olympics.

In 1988, still the world record holder, Morales finished third in the Olympic trials. Only the first two qualified. 'I couldn't watch the Games on TV. It was too painful.'

Morales abandoned swimming in favour of studying law and for the next three and a half years didn't set foot in a swimming pool. Not until the Barcelona Games were just around the corner, did the thought of swimming take hold again. 'I realised I wanted to return to swimming and set myself some goals. I wasn't interested in how far a 27-year-old swimmer could go, I just set myself a number of targets.'

After a mere seven months' training, Pablo won the US trials. 'My second goal was to win gold. For several weeks I'd pictured a number of possible outcomes that included winning, losing and not qualifying for the final.'

Touching the wall and finally achieving his dream, Pablo Morales was overcome with joy and emotion. He had put so much into the competition that he had trouble staying upright on getting out the pool. On the podium, he wiped away a tear and fixed his gaze on his father in the public stands. His mother had died the previous September and she was uppermost in his thoughts. 'I'd have so liked her to be here today. I know that she was with me in spirit. My turn has come at last.'

1 On his futuristic bike, Chris Boardman never had anything to worry about from Germany's Jens Lehmann in the final.

2 Steve Redgrave and Matthew Pinsent add to their collection of gold medals after their win in the coxless pairs. The future looks promising too!

3 Emotions run high for supporters of Pablo Morales who, at 27, finally wins gold in the 100m butterfly.

4 Ethiopian Derartu Tulu (left) celebrates her victory in the 10,000m with her queen-in-waiting, South Africa's Elana Meyer. Barcelona marked South Africa's return to the Olympic Games.

5 Olympic double champion in the 50m and 100m freestyle, Aleksandr Popov beats the Americans at their own game.

6 Juan Giha Yarur (PER, second) and Bruno Rossetti (ITA, third) still manage a smile after losing in the skeet competition to Zhang Shan, a female competitor from China.

7 Unbeaten since 1983, Thomas Lange (GER) keeps his 1988 title and proves he is very much the strongest contender in the single sculls.

8 Satisfaction all round. Kevin Young beats Edwin Moses' previous world best with a new record of 46.78 in the 400m hurdles.

9 Unable to clear the first bar at a height of 5.75m, Serhei Bubka falls to earth with a crash. No points for that.

10 Jubilation when Kiko scores twenty-six seconds before the end of the game, bringing an Olympic title to the Spanish football team.

11 Cheered on by the home crowd, Fermín Cacho takes the lead in the 1500m – according to his race plan.

12 Carl Lewis concludes the Barcelona Games with his eighth gold medal in the 4x100m.

13 Fabio Casartelli (ITA) wins the road race. Silver medallist, Hendrik Dekker (HOL), looks just as happy.

14 Unable to attend the 1984 and 1988 Games, Cuban high jumper Javier Sotomayor finally comes away with a title that reflects his long dominance of the event.

For Cecilia

The deeply religious Mexican-American boxer Oscar De La Hoya wins for his mother, who died of cancer.

On the balcony is his father, in tears, and his cousin, often mistaken for his sister – 'She's watching on television,' the kid explains as he lists his many supporters. His mother, Cecilia, who died of cancer in Autumn 1990, at the age of thirty-eight, watches from higher still.

In the ring, the nineteen-year-old, 5 feet 5, kneels and, with a light touch of his glove, blows a kiss to the one he has lost. Oscar De La Hoya is the Olympic lightweight champion for her.

World Amateur Champion Marco Rudolph defeated him last winter in Sydney in the quarter-finals of the world amateur championships (17-13). This time, the protection that the referee could offer (and it has been said he offered the German plenty) was not enough. With one minute of the fight to go, De La Hoya threw a left hook, and Rudolph folded.

After the contest, De La Hoya held the Stars and Stripes aloft in one hand, and a Mexican flag in the other. It's acts like these which make people love Oscar. His talent and history too: the Chicano pride in his bruised eyes and for his staccato, shy speech – not very macho at all.

Will he now take the financial rewards which professional boxing offers? Lou Duva, who was never very far from Barcelona and the American team's clan of Latino supporters, has been chasing him for a long time.

This close marking was justified. Bruce Silverglade, who runs the famous Gleason's Gym in New York, assured Ring magazine that with the right coach, the kid would quickly have the makings of a professional world champion.

Oscar De La Hoya would dearly love to be able to listen to the sweet advice of his mother, Cecilia, who would now be very proud to see her niño coming out of the sports pavilion, surrounded by swarms of admirers and attentive journalists. In the ring, seeing the flag raised, he just about manages to contain his emotions. When he gets back to the changing-rooms, and has his obligatory moment at the NBC mike, he cracks, lowers his eyes, and lets the tears run. You can't help but like Oscar.

Highly motivated Oscar De La Hoya takes revenge on the German world champion Marco Rudolph.

1992
BARCELONA XXV OLYMPIAD

President Samaranch spoke of 'the best Olympic Games', referring to the welcome received by the athletes and media and the conditions in which they worked. These Games were the first to be held under the new geopolitical order; Games organised by professionals, for professionals.

THE GAMES IN BRIEF

Opening Date
25 July 1992

Closing Date
9 August 1992

Host Nation
Spain (ESP)

Candidate Towns
Amsterdam (NED), Belgrade (YUG), Birmingham (GBR), Brisbane (AUS) and Paris (FRA).

169 Nations Represented

9,344 Athletes
(2,708 women, 6,636 men)

25 Sports
(17 open to women)
Track and field, rowing, badminton, basketball, baseball, boxing, canoeing, cycling, equestrian, fencing, football, gymnastics, weightlifting, handball, field hockey, judo, wrestling, swimming, modern pentathlon, tennis, table tennis, shooting, archery, volley ball and sailing.

257 Events
(101 open to women)

Games officially opened by
King Juan Carlos of Spain

Olympic flame lit by
Antonio Rebollo (archery paraolympian)

Olympic oath read by
Luis Doreste Blanco (sailing)

IOC President
Juan Antonio Samaranch (ESP)

DID YOU KNOW?

Aged just 11, Spain's coxswain in the eights, Carlos Front, was the youngest competitor in the Olympic Games since 1900.

Barcelona gold medal winner Andreas Keller of Germany was the third generation of his family to win a medal for field hockey. His grandfather Ewin won silver in 1936 and his father won gold in 1972.

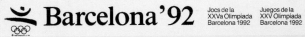

Barcelona'92

Jocs de la XXVa Olimpiada Barcelona 1992

Juegos de la XXV Olimpiada Barcelona 1992

Jeux de la XXVe Olympiade Barcelona 1992

Games of the XXV Olympiad Barcelona 1992

1996

Atlanta

THE SELECTION OF ATLANTA TO HOST THE 1996 Games was met with scepticism and disapproval: the United States again, and barely twelve years after Los Angeles. There was logic in the choice: the American chain CBS alone provided US$456 million of the US$898 million dollars in rights revenues. Atlanta is also the seat of Coca-Cola, faithful partner of the Games. However, the logic of the decision was seen by many to be deeply flawed.

But there were other symbols at play. Atlanta is the native city of Martin Luther King, the Baptist pastor with a dream who won the Nobel Peace Prize in 1964. And in this Southern city, it was a black man, Muhammad Ali, who lit the Olympic cauldron. He was crowned world champion in Rome, under the name of Cassius Clay, and then went on to win the world over with his talent and charisma.. And it was two black athletes, Michael Johnson and Marie-José Pérec, who pulled off the most magnificent feats of the fortnight.

Yet for all the jostling imagery, the Atlanta Games will be remembered for overcrowded and chaotic transport, a defective computer system, poorly-prepared and often incompetent on-site volunteers, a disturbingly biased crowd and an extremely mercenary attitude, especially around the Olympic Park. This was the site of a bomb explosion early on 27 July, which left one person dead and more than one hundred injured. It was as if Atlanta had to pay the price for its original sin: being chosen for the Centennial Games, ahead of Athens.

Marie-José Pérec, exhausted yet triumphant, wins her eighth race in seven days: to victory over 400m, she adds victory over 200m, beside a resigned Merlene Ottey (second) and an unsteady Mary Onyali (third).

Michael Johnson: 'I wanted to go down in history'

Thanks to his incredible 19.32, Michael Johnson win Olympic gold and breaks his own world record – all just three days after winning the 400m.

The fastest man in the world, Michael Johnson, crosses the finish line in triumph.

Q: Michael Johnson, you've achieved the double, and broken the 200m world record in the process. It must be a dream come true.

A: I can't even describe what I felt after beating the world record by such a margin. If the Games had taken place somewhere other than the United States, I would certainly have run 19.5 or 19.6, but the Atlanta crowd, who have been really extraordinary all this week, deserved

JOHNSON SEEN BY PÉREC: 'GRANDIOSE!'

Marie-José Pérec found the Texan's performance remarkable. 'In addition to what I did, he has the world record. What he's achieved is terrific. It was an extraordinary race. I think that Michael was grandiose. I know how hard it is to do what he did, and I know what he must have been through during each one of those races.'

this achievement.

Q: How did you achieve such a time?

A: As I positioned myself in the blocks, I said to myself, This is the medal you want; yes, this is the 200m medal that you couldn't have in Barcelona(*). Then it all pretty much fell into place as I envisaged. The track is fast, I was faced with great opponents like Frankie Fredericks, and, above all, my own motivation was enormous. I wanted to go down in history. A lot of athletes can claim to have a world record or a gold medal, but how many can say 'I've gone down in history!' I won the 200m and 400m at the Games, and beat the Olympic and world records.

Q: I suppose you must have thought about your idol, Jesse Owens?

A: His widow, Ruth, wrote me a letter after the American trials. For me, that was a great honour and a tremendous source of motivation. From the first round of the 400m to the final of the 200m, that letter never left me.

Q: What were your emotions in the run-up to the final?

A: Pressure. Enormous pressure. In all my life, I had never felt like that. For six months, whenever I opened a newspaper or turned on the TV, there was always something about the double. I also got lots of telephone calls from well-wishers saying to me: 'Just don't worry too much!' In fact, they did nothing but add to the pressure. (Smiles). But I've always said that to be at my best I need pressure. I like to be scared when I settle in the blocks. And that time, I was really very scared.

Q: It's like you're on another level…

A: People think things have always been easy for me. But I can tell you that since the beginning of my career, I've experienced pain, blows to my morale, injuries, and even food poisoning before the Barcelona Games. All these blows only made me even more determined. To find myself at this level today is a great relief, and

RESULTS

MICHAEL JOHNSON'S DOUBLE

200m

1 Michael Johnson (USA), 19.32
2 Frankie Fredericks (NAM), 19.68
3 Ato Boldon (TRI), 19.80
4 Obadele Thompson (BAR), 20.14
5 Jeff Williams (USA), 20.17
6 Iván García Sánchez (CUB), 20.21
7 Patrick Stevens (BEL), 20.27
8 Michael Marsh (USA), 20.48

400m

1 Michael Johnson (USA), 43.49
2 Roger Black (GBR), 44.41
3 Davis Kamoga (UGA) , 44.53
4 Alvin Harrison (USA), 44.62
5 Iwan Thomas (GBR), 44.70
6 Roxbert Martin (JAM), 44.83
7 Davian Clarke (JAM), 44.99
DNF: Ibrahim Ismail (QAT)

Michael Johnson's Games were ruined by food poisoning in 1992. His Atlanta double represented revenge and relief.

the true justification for everything I've been through.

Q: Do you feel that you are the best athlete on the planet?

A: That's for the public to decide. Personally, I find it hard to get interested in titles which aren't based on detailed facts and figures.

Q: Can you at least say that you feel you've achieved the perfect race?

A: Actually, I didn't have a very good start. I almost fell over when I came from the blocks. Then – alas! – like I always do, I rose too early. My coach also wanted me to box the air with my fists, on impulse, but I just settled for whirling my arms. All in all, I lost a few centimetres. That's what happens when you don't listen to your coach properly …(Smiles.)

Q: At what point in the race did you manage to set yourself right?

A: At the fourth stride. Then I managed to relax. I felt good, at the top of my game. I controlled the race perfectly from 80–90m and as I came out of the bend, I knew that I had never run so fast in my life.

Q: What did it feel like to run so fast?

A: When I was a kid, one day, my father gave me a go-cart. There was a big hill at the end of the street where I lived. And my favourite thing was to hurtle down this slope as quickly as possible and without stopping. So if you want to know how I felt, there's only one solution: go out, buy a go-cart, and find yourself a great hill!

Q: After having such an exceptional week, what other goals can you set yourself now?

A: In four years time, I'll be in Sydney. For what distance, I don't yet know. Ato Boldon is already saying that I am the fastest man in the world, but Jon Drummond maintains that only the winner of the 100m can claim that title. So, perhaps I'm going to have to convince Jon Drummond and run the 100m. (Smiles.)

Q: Generally speaking, do you think you have finally been acknowledged for your true ability?

A: Yes. I think that, for a long time, I haven't deserved all this glory. Before the Games, when I hadn't won a single gold medal, I was finding myself on the cover of all the magazines. Only after the 200m did I feel that I'd justified all that enthusiasm.

★ In Barcelona, Michael Johnson, with the world's best time, suffered food poisoning and was knocked out in the semi-finals.

Boldon (third), Sanchez (sixth), Fredericks (second), Marsh (eighth) and Williams (fifth) (left to right) are far behind. Nobody can keep up with Johnson, who cuts his world record from 19.66 to 19.32.

Pérec becomes a legend

Even before completing her fabulous 200m/400m double, Marie-José becomes the first athlete to retain her 400m title.

Pérec raises her arms in the 400m, watched by Nigeria's Falilat Ogunkoya (49.10, third) and Australia's Cathy Freeman (48.63, second).

It is the story of a life lived like a dream, from Basse-Terre to Paris, Tokyo, Barcelona and Atlanta. By winning the women's 400m final in Atlanta, Marie-José Pérec has become the first athlete, male or female, to retain an Olympic title at this distance. Four years after her victory in Barcelona, the athlete from Guadeloupe has done it again in Atlanta, a town that is also a symbol of the civil rights movement, and in the USA, her new home country, birthplace of the greatest athletics champions. A double significance, then, for the child from Basse-Terre, Guadeloupe, who was born to run, and to win – as she has, continually, for five years now, at the highest level.

It all started in 1991, a year which began for Marie-José with minor knee surgery. She had a hard time of it when she took up training again, but, to the amazement of her entourage, she soon had wings on her heels. Before leaving for the World Championships in Tokyo, she beat the

French national record twice, taking it to under 50 seconds. She arrived in Japan with a personal best of 49.32, which she had achieved on 29 June, in Frankfurt. The pressure was getting to her; she lost ten pounds before the final and was incapable of digesting the slightest scrap of food. She weighed just 119 pounds, and couldn't sleep. But, on the day of the final, everything unfolded like a dream. She was leading at 200m, maintained that lead at 300m, then, unsurprisingly, found herself all alone at the finishing line. The great German favourite Grit Breuer was beaten. 'I'm world champion,' exclaimed Marie-José after the finish. 'It's the start of a dream!' Aged twenty-three, Pérec became the first French female world champion in athletics. Her reign was only beginning.

The following year, the Olympic Games loomed. In Barcelona, she was the favourite, a role which she assumed perfectly. Pérec duly became Olympic champion ahead of the

Ukrainian Olha Bryzhina and began a new chapter in an already glorious career. The media seized upon her, and even went with her to see her grandmother Mam'tia in Basse-Terre, almost suffocating her with their requests. This budding glory seemed to cloud Pérec's focus, and she modelled for Paco Rabanne and posed for Claude Montana. Pérec had become a star. The girl who spent hours making-up her sisters and cousins for the February carnival in Guadeloupe became one of the models she dreamed of as a child.

Olympic and world champion over 400m, Pérec had won everything: on the eve of the 1993 season, she had to set herself new goals to satisfy her appetite for challenge. The 1993 World Championships in Stuttgart gave her the opportunity to do just this. She would run the 200m there. This new kind of challenge stimulated her desire, and gave her the courage to put her spikes back on after the all-too-numerous distractions stemming from

her Olympic title.

Everything went well until 21 July, the date of her victory at the Nikaïa Stadium in Nice over 100m. An hamstring injury left her doubting herself. In four weeks, she managed to recover and found enough within herself to reach the 200m final at the World championships. She only finished fourth there. Disappointed and frustrated, Pérec wanted a change of scene. No longer would she put up with the harsh paternalism of her old mentor Jacques Piasenta. At the start of 1994, they had one last clash at the Bercy Open, where Pérec withdrew at the last moment for no apparent reason, confirming their separation.

She dreamt of going back to live in the sunshine. The United States appealed to her – the American dream puts a twinkle in her eyes. She took off for Los Angeles and joined the stable of legendary sprint coach John Smith. With this champion-maker, she learnt self-management, discipline and relaxation. Normally so tense before each race, so anxious she made herself ill, Pérec learned to control her nerves.

With her gazelle-like stride, Marie-José Pérec seems to fly above the track. Only the grimace betrays any effort.

Landing in California as a champion, she became an athlete again, surrounded by other athletes who were not greatly concerned about her celebrity status.

With the help of John Smith's relaxation techniques, Pérec became a different woman. But that didn't change one thing: her desire to win, and in their first season together, Pérec and Smith added the only title missing from Pérec's CV: the European 400m in Helsinki. A second world title followed the next year in Gothenburg. All that remained was a taste of the American dream.

On the evening of 29 July, by retaining her Olympic title in a race she dominated, Marie-José Pérec became a legend. A legend of a little girl with long, thin legs, who jumped from rock to rock in the Herbes river. Of an adolescent who wanted to run the 400m, but who people thought was too thin. Of a young woman, who finally became the best athlete in the world in her discipline.

[Ed. Pérec won the 200m final, a metre ahead of Merlene Ottey (JAM), fifteen minutes before the men's 200m final, featuring Michael Johnson.]

RESULTS PÉREC'S DOUBLE

200m
1 Marie-José Pérec (FRA), 22.12
2 Merlene Ottey (JAM), 22.24
3 Mary Onyali (NGR), 22.38
4 Inger Miller (USA), 22.41
5 Galina Malchugina (RUS), 22.45
6 Chandra Sturrup (BAH), 22.54
7 Juliet Cuthbert (BAH), 22.60
8 Carlette Guidry (USA), 22.61

400m
1 Marie-José Pérec (FRA), 48.25
2 Cath Freeman (AUS), 48.63
3 Falilat Ogunkoya (NGR), 49.10
4 Pauline Davis (BAH), 49.28
5 Jearl Miles (USA), 49.55
6 Fatima Yusuf (NGR), 49.77
7 Sandie Richards (JAM), 50.45
8 Grit Breuer (GER), 50.71

In the 200m, as in the 400m some days earlier, Marie-José gives her opponents little chance.

Back to the Olympic ideal

Jefferson Pérez performs a public act of religious devotion.

Before the 1996 Games, Jefferson Pérez, a 22-year-old business management student at the University of Azuay, kneeled before an image of Christ at Quito's Franciscan cathedral and made a vow: if God allowed him to express his abilities in the 20km walk in Atlanta, he would make a gruelling pilgrimage. Before a global audience of billions, the greatest sporting event on earth hosted a private act of devotion which brought Pérez the gold medal and made him Ecuador's first-ever Olympic medalist, not to mention the youngest walking champion in Olympic history.

Pérez returned to the cathedral in Quito to give thanks for his success, and then returned to his hometown, Cuenca, 459 kilometres away – on foot. It took eleven days to cover the distance, walking, jogging and running at altitudes between 2,500 and 4,800m. 'I feel that I am an instrument of God's will,' he explained. 'I want this instrument to be in excellent condition, so that whenever God wants to use it, it will be ready.'

After finishing fourth in the Sydney Olympic 20km walk, Pérez retired, but found competition irresistible, and returned, stronger than ever. At the 2003 World Athletics Championships in France, Pérez took the world title, setting a new world record.

Preparing for the 2004 Olympic Games, he declared: 'The essence of the Olympic movement is to achieve the perfection of the individual.' Pérez's spiritual appeal to the Olympic ideal is the antithesis of the modern sporting ethos – useless to the pedlars of soft drinks, chocolate bars and credit cards who have turned sport into an advertisement. Whatever you believe, that is surely an excellent reason to cheer for Jefferson as he walks towards glory in Athens.

'When I took the lead, I felt so tired... I was half-asleep. It felt like a dream, but I thought, I must go for it, even if I die.' Jefferson Pérez's surprise victory brought Ecuador its first Olympic medal of any colour.

BAILEY CONSIGNS BEN JOHNSON
TO OBLIVION

This Jamaican-born Canadian won the
Olympic 100m in a new world record,
one year after winning the world title.
Any confusion between Donovan Bailey
and Ben Johnson ends there. Bailey
was not generated by a cynical
scientific production line. It was only in
1991, at the age of twenty-three, that
he decided to try his hand at the circuit,
'for fun'. By then, he had an economics
degree, co-owned a flourishing financial
consulting firm with his brother, drove a
Porsche and spent most of his evenings
partying. In the athletics circle, Bailey
was not regarded favourably. But he
has talent, as Frankie Fredericks
convinced him. The Namibian had
cause to regret his encouragement:
despite running 9.89 in the final, he had
to settle for yet another second place,
just like in Barcelona. Dennis Mitchell
(right), finished fourth – after running
9.99. But it was Donovan Bailey who
shouted for joy at the finishing line.
With a run of 9.84 seconds, he had
become the fastest man in the world.

The legend of King Lewis

Carl Lewis, at the age of thirty-five, takes home his fourth long jump gold medal, and his ninth in all, making him truly the athlete of the century.

If someone wrote a novel based on his life, it would have all the ingredients of a bestseller. A career inspiring hatred and respect. Blood, sweat and tears, often of happiness, sometimes of despair. Nothing would be missing. He has even left posterity a stunning photographic record.

On Monday evening, Frederick Carleton McKinley Lewis (born 1 July 1961, Birmingham, Alabama) gave us a new image, one of almost childlike emotion, on the podium where he was about to receive the ninth gold medal of his phenomenal career.

'I had the privilege of starting my Olympic career at home, in America. I want to finish it by winning a final gold medal, at home, in America.'

In the Olympic trials, Lewis finished eighth in the 100m (four consecutive races in two days was too much for an athlete in the sixteenth year of his career) and fifth in the 200m (quite a performance considering he was in lane one). This left the long jump, the discipline in which he was triple Olympic champion.

After jumping 8.50m to become quadruple Olympic champion, a feat which only discus thrower Al Oerter had achieved, he had these words for a group of his rivals, including James Beckford and Joe Greene: 'Boys, I promise you that this is the last time I'll bother you. After this, I'll leave you in peace. Promise.' The future will be theirs. The past and the present belongs to Carl Lewis.

After missing the last World Championships, Carl Lewis, at the age of 35, seemed to be a finished athlete. He alone still believed.

RESULTS

THE NINE TITLES OF CARL LEWIS

100m
First in 1984 (9.99) and in 1988 (9.92)
200m
First in 1984 (19.80)*
4 x 100m
First in 1984 (37.83) and in 1992 (37.40)
Long jump
First in 1984 (8.54m), 1988 (8.72m)
1992 (8.67m) and 1996 (8.50m)

Equal second in 1988 (19.79)

Me Sacha – not Tarzan

As he did in Barcelona, Aleksandr Popov completed the 50m/100m double, a feat achieved before him only by Johnny Weissmuller.

Popov is the first person since 1928 to retain his Olympic title over 100m. The jinx is broken.

'Johnny Weissmuller – I know him, of course, but I have never met him.' Aleksandr Popov, 'Sacha', flashes an impertinent smile at the American journalist who has just asked the inevitable question about Johnny Weissmuller, the only man until now to have won two Olympic 100m titles, in 1924 and in 1928.

Popov had been desperate to win at Atlanta. His supremacy over 100m, already went back almost five years. However, after his victory, he was almost perfectly polite, incessantly advocating harmony, and was extremely impertinent. He said things like: 'But I respect everybody, all my opponents, the crowd, Gary Hall too … It matters little to me to beat an American in Atlanta… Anyway, I'd like to thank Gary for having pushed me like this, for giving me a bit more determination.' What a great comedian. And the funniest thing is that the American media dived straight onto this moving happy ending…

If ever one day you want to convert someone to swimming, show them Popov in action. If that doesn't work, don't waste your time. Popov has all the qualities of the perfect swimmer, from the physique, the formidable strength in his arms and legs, the giant arm span, and perfect technique, described by Mark Spitz as 'the genius of movement'.

Popov has two further qualities without which even the most talented swimmer will never become a

champion: intelligence, and the dogged determination that allowed him to push an excellent Gary Hall, his American rival, out of the way, just as he had Matt Biondi four years ago. What's more, the expression 'Slavonic charm' might have been invented for him.

He has also made an almost miraculous return from injury. As a child, he fell from high in a tree and broke his left leg. The wound still affects him today, 'although, fortunately, not in the water'. He started training at eight years old and was quickly spotted and entered into the state training programme in the backstroke. There he stayed until the moment the USSR needed a champion who could one day defeat Biondi and his successors in the 100m freestyle.

This champion was to be Aleksandr Popov, brought up by Gennadi Touretski, coach guru at the Volgograd school, as his own son.

In 1991 Popov made a dazzling start in the European Championships, winning the 100m in 49.18. Since then he has won almost everything, thanks to 'talent, hard work, support and, inevitably, energy drawn from being near opponents'. He has put this energy towards winning 'the most difficult race of my career, but also the one that I perhaps enjoyed the most'.

Programmed to be a 'hero of the glorious USSR', Aleksandr Popov could have gone down with the Soviet Union. Instead, he became a perfect post-USSR champion. No longer truly Russian – 'A country where it is not easy to be a champion who succeeds' – and not yet really Australian, his winter retreat – 'A country with no culture'. Aleksandr Popov is from everywhere and nowhere: perhaps his true country is the water.

Beating the Americans on their home turf became an obsession: now the Russian can smile.

Over both the 50 and 100 metres, it was in the final metres where Popov got the better of Hall.

POPOV'S DOUBLE

50m
1 Aleksandr Popov (RUS), 22.13;
2 Gary Hall, Jr (USA), 22.26;
3 Fernando Scherer (BRA), 22.29;
4 Jiang Chengji (CHN), 22.33;
5 Brendon Dedekind (SAF), 22.59;
6 David Fox (USA), 22.68;
7 Francisco Sanchez (VEN), 22.72;
8 Ricardo Busquets (PUR), 22.73.

100m
1 Aleksandr Popov (RUS), 48.74;
2 Gary Hall, Jr (USA), 48.81;
3 Gustavo Borges (BRA), 49.02;
4 Pieter van den Hoogenband (HOL), 49.13;
5 Fernando Scherer (BRA), 49.57;
6 Pavlo Khnykin (UKR), 49.65;
7 Ricardo Busquets (PUR), 49.68;
8 Francisco Sanchez (VEN), 49.84;
9 Pavlo Khnykin (UKR), 49"65 ;
10 Ricardo Busquets (PRI), 49"68 ;
11 Francisco Sanchez (VEN), 49"84.

Michelle Smith makes waves

After dominating the 400m individual medley, the Irish girl wins the 400m freestyle. Her receives a cool reception.

Imagine for a moment how it must feel when, a few minutes after having become Olympic champion for the second time in forty-eight hours, you are received as Michelle Smith at the press conference.

'In Ireland,' began an American journalist, 'your story is being described as fantastic. Why, in your opinion, does the United States not seem as receptive to your fairy story?'

'What do you mean by fairy story?'

'To be frank, your dazzling progression is reminiscent of that of the Chinese swimmers, two years ago. Don't you think so?'

Michelle Smith, from Dublin, born in 1969, resident in the Netherlands since 1993, has emerged in an era where it is not better not to make waves. Improving your 400m time by eighteen seconds in fifteen months is not the best route to anonymity. Since

Poor in the breast-stroke, the Irish girl makes up time in the butterfly and crawl to win the two individual medley races.

Smith's smiling ended in 1999, when she was suspended for tampering with a drugs test.

SMITH'S FOUR MEDALS

400m
1 Michelle Smith (IRL), 4:07.25
2 Dagmar Hase (GER), 4:08.30
3 Kirsten Vlieghuis (HOL), 4:08.70

200m butterfly
1 Susan O'NEILL (AUS), 2:07.76
2 Petria Thomas (AUS), 2:09.82
3 Michelle Smith (IRL), 2:09.91

200m individual medley
1 Michelle Smith (IRL), 2:13.93
2 Marianne Limpert (CAN), 2:14.35
3 Lin Li (CHN), 2:14.74

400m individual medley
1 Michelle Smith (IRL), 4:39.18
2 Allison Wagner (USA), 4:42.03
3 Krisztina Egerszegi (HUN), 4:42.53

Over 400m, Michelle Smith has progressed eighteen seconds in fifteen months. Too good to be true, according to some observers.

the revelations of some years ago regarding the old East German system, and the more recent display by the Chinese at the 1994 World Championships and the Asiatic Games five weeks later, the world of swimming became wary of sudden improvements, especially when they occur in a 27-year-old.

Smith then married Dutch discus thrower Erik DeBruin, suspended for four years for steroid abuse. Her attempts to explain her progress failed to convince her audience.

Ordinarily, she would have been excluded from the 400m after her application arrived late. Ireland's IOC representative, Dermot Sherlock, twisted FINA's arm to allow her to compete. This would not have made too many waves if this episode had not ruled quadruple gold medalist Janet Evans out of the final. Evans then conceded that she had doubts about Smith's dazzling progression. Given that Evans' utterances are regarded as Gospel truth in swimming circles, even an Irish lass, however well she was usually regarded by the Good Lord, would find herself tarnished.

The end of a mighty reign

Miguel Induráin bows out with a gold against the clock.

CYCLING

Modern sport is fertile ground for icons and myth-making, and especially cycling – that gruelling, grinding, solitary effort that attracts the obsessed and the bloody-minded. In 1992, Britain's Chris Boardman rode his revolutionary Lotus carbon monocoque bike to victory in the 4,000m individual pursuit. Four years later, an even greater cycling icon was brought to the Atlanta Games, carefully packaged inside the ribcage of that Spanish colossus, Miguel Induráin. At rest, Induráin's massive heart was said to beat 28 times per minute. At peak performance, it multiplied its spasms by more than seven times to 210 beats per minute. This remarkable organ, fuelled by great, flotation-tank lungs with a capacity of eight litres, lay at the centre of one of the most extraordinary physiques in sporting history. As if this incredible engine wasn't enough, Induráin was impervious to stress. The voracious hunger that brought him five consecutive Tour de France wins between 1991 and 1995 was disguised beneath an exterior that was reminiscent of nothing so much as a huge, friendly whale.

Until 1996, the Olympic cycling events had been a mere stepping stone for riders wishing to turn professional. Induráin himself had taken part in the road race in Los Angeles in 1984, but had failed to finish. The 1996 Games allowed the finest professional cyclists to compete for the first time. By then, Miguel Induráin had become a living legend, as respected for his humility and generosity as for his athletic achievements. Yet in the summer of 1996 he had relinquished his Tour de France crown and finished eleventh, exhausted. Only a personal appeal from his Spanish compatriot Juan Antonio Samaranch, president of the International Olympic Committee, persuaded him to travel to Atlanta.

On 31 July, just ten days after the Tour had finished, Induráin finished just twenty-sixth in the road race, won by the Swiss rider Pascal Richard, who designed and wore a controversial Olympic champion's jersey for the following three years.

Three days after the road race, Induráin started the road time trial as the outstanding favourite. He had founded his unique succession of victories in the Tour de France on his ability in the time trials, which he frequently won by incredible margins. He was also the reigning world time trial champion, a title he had won in Colombia the previous year, beating fellow Spaniard Abraham Olano into second place. A terrible rainstorm blighted the Atlanta Olympic time trial. At one point, up to six inches of water cascaded along the streets, making progress almost impossible. However, the sun had returned by the time the final ten riders were due to race. Chris Boardman had the fastest split times when Olano and Induráin began to inch ahead. In the end, after 52.2 kilometres, just thirty-one seconds separated them. Boardman took a bronze medal to go with his gold of four years before. Olano, who would never quite live up to Spanish hopes that he would replace his legendary team-mate, took second place, while Olympic victory fell to the master, Miguel Induráin, capping a brilliant career and sealing his place in sporting legend.

His position is almost upright, compared with the aerodynamic tuck of Chris Boardman. But Miguel Induráin's flotation-tank lungs had to go somewhere. In any case, Induráin's power was such that it made little difference: an abnormally long thigh bone created an extremely efficient piston that drove him to victory in five Tours de France and the 1996 Olympic time trial title: the last victory of an extraordinary athlete, and a perfect gentleman.

1996

OLYMPIC ROUND-UP

KARCH KIRALY, AS GOOD OUTDOORS AS IN.

Winning the first Olympic gold medal for beach volleyball (pairs) in the rain, beside his team-mate Kent Steffes, Karch Kiraly (USA, photo 9) consolidated his reputation as the greatest volleyball player of all time, a reputation acquired during his indoor career, during which he won two Olympic gold medals (1984 and 1988).

It was after Seoul that this Californian father of two decided to venture onto the beach, quickly becoming the king of the beach, as his five Most Valuable Player awards from the Association of Volleyball Professionals prove (1990, 1992, 1993, 1994 and 1995).

It was a lucrative move: in 1995 Kiraly was the first volleyball player to pass the two million dollar mark in winnings! In 1993 his partner Kent Steffes became the youngest player to win a million dollars in prize money, at the age of twenty-five. Kiraly's distinctions don't end there: he remains the only beach volleyball player to have won tournaments with three different partners in one season. All this, despite long absence due to a shoulder injury sustained in 1995.

Faced with such quality, what could Michael Dodd and Michael Whitmarsh, ex-basketball players drafted by the Minnesota Timberwolves and the San Diego Clippers, hope for? Could they do as well as they did in the US trials where they earned their Olympic place by beating Kiraly and Steffes 15-8? Clearly not: their only success was to eliminate the Portuguese pair Brenha and Maia, who caused a sensation by stopping the Brazilians Zé Marco and Emmanuel, world champions from 1995 and favourites for the title. The way was free for Kiraly and Steffes.

The Americans took the men's title and the Brazilians took the women's, and what could be more logical than that: these two nations dominate beach volleyball, which was born a little more than half a century ago on a Californian beach. With Kiraly and Steffes, the sport has come full circle.

1   Miguel Indurain has a poor memory of the 1984 Games, during which he had to abandon the race halfway through. On his return twelve years later, he won the first individual road time trial since 1932. Here, he's on the podium with Abraham Olano (left) and Chris Boardman.

2   No weightlifter had ever succeeded in winning three consecutive titles, until Atlanta and Naim Süleymanoglu (TUR). A heavyweight competing as a featherweight.

3   A fantastic double for Russian Svetlana Masterkova: after the 800m (number 3700 here) on 27 July, she wins the 1500 metres on 3 August, after dictating the pace in both races.

4   Andre Agassi outdoes his father, who boxed for Iran in the 1948 and 1952 Games. Andre wins the tennis tournament, and goes on to become the only player to win each of the men's grand slam titles as well as the Olympics.

5   Ex-international basketball player Gadha Shouaa, 1.89m tall and with a huge arm span, reaffirmed her 1995 world title by winning the heptathlon. It was the first gold medal for her country, Syria.

6   Noureddine Morceli was expected to win in Barcelona but it was Fermin Cacho (left) who was victorious. The Moroccan Hicham el-Gerrouj was expected to win in Atlanta but this time Algerian Morceli triumphed over the Spaniard. The 1500m remains impossible to predict.

7   Celestine Babayaro nearly explodes with joy, as he scored Nigeria's first goal, against Argentina, in the final of the football tournament. Nigeria went on to win 3-2 and become the first African country to win the title.

8   Even playing within themselves, the Americans win the basketball competition with ease (95-69 in the final against the Yugoslavs), with a Dream Team including Shaquille O'Neal (airborne), Scottie Pippen, Karl Malone and Charles Barkley (left).

9   At the end of an all-American final, Karch Kiraly (aged thirty-five) partnered by Kent Steffes takes the first Olympic title in beach volleyball.

10 Cuba, already victorious in Barcelona, retains its women's Olympic volleyball title, beating China by three sets to one.

Atlanta 1996

7

8

9

10

Karelin saves Russia's pride

At the end of a titanic final, Aleksandr Karelin wins his third gold medal in Greco-Roman wrestling, Russia's only gold in this year's tournament.

Even in front of his home crowd, Siamek 'Matt' Ghaffari (USA, left) was powerless to stop Aleksandr Karelin (RUS), undefeated since 1989. 'You'd have to be King Kong to beat him,' he conceded.

Aleksandr Karelin, the giant from Novosibirsk, has lived up to his reputation, bringing back his third Olympic gold medal in a row. Nothing less was expected of him, although a lot more was expected of his Russian team-mates, far less dominant than envisaged.

Yesterday, the 8,000 spectators who crammed into the stands for this last day of Greco-Roman wrestling finally saw what they had been waiting for in the last bout of the afternoon. Matt Ghaffari, the American wrestler born in Teheran, Iran, faced the Russian ogre Aleksandr Karelin. Ghaffari entered the mat to the strains of the theme from 'Rocky'. Karelin walked in undaunted by the wildly pro-Ghaffari crowd.

Neither 130kg super-heavyweight held back, and colossal blow followed colossal blow.

After a rare pause, at the end of overtime, Karelin finally emerged victorious by one small point won with a common throw that looked no more dramatic than if the American had accidentally stumbled to his knees. 'To beat Karelin, you'd have to be King Kong', explained Ghaffari after his defeat, with humour and respect in equal measure.

The American has made victory over Karelin the goal of his whole life. He has photographs of Karelin in his locker, at home, and in his wallet. He never stops: when the referee sent the Russian to the ground for passiveness in overtime, we saw the worry emerge on Ghaffari's face. But the hunted animal didn't let himself get snared. And, once crowned, he commented with the superior air which nine years of invincibility lent him: 'I was seriously injured at the last European

Championships in March, followed by surgery. I have hardly fought since and Matt missed a good opportunity to beat me here.' For all that, what Karelin worries about is Russia's poor

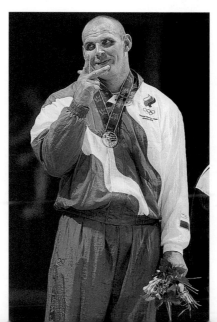

results: three medals, two of which are bronze, compared with three silver for the Americans and five medals, three of them gold, for the Polish. 'I think that it's a one-off,' analysed Karelin. 'The split of the Soviet Union has not damaged our work methods. But it's true that I am unhappy.'

As for his personal future, in spite of extravagant offers made by the wrestling organisers or by American football teams, he says he can't imagine himself anywhere other than in the homeland for which he has always competed. He doesn't think that his career as a wrestler is over: Ghaffari and co. can still tremble.

That makes three! Aleksandr Karelin, jubilant on the podium. Never before has a wrestler won three consecutive titles: Karelin achieves the feat in the showpiece super-heavyweight division.

ATLANTA XXVI OLYMPIAD

To celebrate the Centennial Games, something more than a show choreographed by Americans, for Americans – even a faultlessly organised show – was needed. However, this was anything but...

THE GAMES IN BRIEF

Opening Date
19 July 1996

Closing Date
4 August 1996

Host Nation
United States of America (USA)

Candidate Towns
Athens (GRE), Belgrade (YUG), Manchester (GBR), Melbourne (AUS) and Toronto (CAN).

197 Nations Represented

10,320 Athletes
(3,523 women, 6,797 men)

27 Sports
(21 open to women)
Track and field, rowing, basketball, badminton, baseball, boxing, canoeing, cycling (including mountain biking), equestrian, fencing, football, gymnastics, weightlifting, handball, field hockey, judo, wrestling, swimming, modern pentathlon, softball, tennis, table tennis, volleyball (including beach volleyball), shooting, archery and sailing.

271 Events
(108 open to women)

Games officially opened by
Bill Clinton, President of the United States of America

Olympic flame lit by
Muhammad Ali (boxing)

Olympic oath read by
Teresa Edwards (basketball)

IOC President
Juan Antonio Samaranch (ESP)

DID YOU KNOW?

A record 79 nations won medals, 53 of which won at least one gold.

Yachtsman Hubert Raudaschi of Austria became the first athlete to compete in nine Olympics, having first taken part in the 1964 Tokyo Games.

Beach volleyball, mountain biking, lightweight rowing, softball and women's football were all included for the first time.

Professionals made their debut in cycling, while in men's football each team was allowed to field three professional players, regardless of age.

2000

Sydney

TO END THE CENTURY AND THE MILLENNIUM, Sydney offered a Games full of records: there were close to two hundred nations present (eighty of which won medals), more than 300 events, 10,500 athletes, 16,000 media staff and almost 47,000 volunteers. The purpose-built Olympic stadium was the biggest yet, seating 110,000.

Despite this vast scale, the Games were perfectly organised, and restored the confidence of an Olympic movement shaken by the poor organisation and mercenary drift of Atlanta, growing concern over doping, and the corruption scandal surrounding the attribution of the 2002 Winter Games to Salt Lake City. Sydney was the breath of fresh air that sport desperately needed. It was as if the waters of its magnificent harbour had redeeming, purifying powers. Put more prosaically, Australia, whose population contains the largest proportion of people practising sports of any country on earth, a nation in which sport is a kind of religion, was a safe bet for a movement in desperate need of good news. Sydney provided it in abundance.

At the edge of the world, the uncertainties of the recent past paled beneath an eternally blue sky. In an extraordinary atmosphere of celebration and sporting achievement, Steve Redgrave, Marion Jones, Inge De Bruijn and Leontien Van Moorsel were among the heroes of the Games – not to mention the vulnerable, talismanic, inspirational Cathy Freeman, whose victory in her home nation had resonances beyond the confines of sport.

The unique design of the Sydney Opera House with its architecture, seen from the air: it became emblematic of the Games. The spectators are applauding the female triathletes, whose discipline is included in the Olympic programme for the first time.

Jones, like a whirlwind!

After winning gold medals in the 100m and 200m, and bronze in the long jump and 4x100m, Jones adds another gold in the 4x400m.

Of her incredible five medals, the most important for Marion Jones is the 100m. In a time of 10.75 seconds, she defeats Thanou (GRE, right) and Lawrence (JAM) by a wide margin.

Marion Jones falls to her knees in front of the clock. Her amazing lap as part of the American 4x400m team was an incredible piece of running and left the 110,000 spectators astonished. Tomorrow, a year from now or far into the future, her 100m will be certainly remembered, but so too will her third leg in the 4x400m relay.

She had already successfully competed in the 100m and the 200m, been through qualifying and the final of the long jump, winning the bronze, and had also run the 4x100m, but in this, her final race, the 24-year-old finished her lap in a time of 49.4 seconds (manual timing) and allowing the US team to win the race, adding a third gold medal to her collection. With a time like that, she could have challenged Cathy Freeman.

Just an hour earlier she had won her second Olympic bronze in the 4x100m. Disappointingly, there were several poor change-overs and the Americans even came close to disqualification after Nanceen Perry, replacing the injured Inger Miller on the third leg, had to grab Jones' wrist to hand her the baton. 'I was a bit disappointed after that race,' she admitted. 'We had a chance but we didn't take it. But when I joined the 4x400m team, I knew they were counting on me.' Jones wanted to finish off her amazing week in style.

The Americans were leading when Jones received the baton from Monica Hennagan, her university friend. 'I told myself that the last 100m would be a nightmare. But at the end of the race, I felt remarkably good,' Jones said. 'It's crazy,' said Pauline Davis (BAH). 'My legs hurt and I've run nowhere near as much as her.' Christine Arron was also amazed: 'She must recover really quickly.'

Jones' strength is mental as well as physical. She must have strong nerves

The 100m gold medal, a highpoint in the young but already long career of the American queen of the sprint.

The American women's relay team finish in first place in the 4x400m. It is the third gold medal for Jones and her fifth podium.

As focused and committed as Carl Lewis, Marion Jones heads for similar heights of excellence and achievement.

as well. She had to cope with the stress of competition and the shock when her husband, the shot putter C. J. Hunter, tested positive for drugs at the start of the athletics competitions. 'I will not allow anybody to ruin what I have made a lot of sacrifices to achieve,' she said.

She began her 400m leg cautiously, like somebody unaccustomed to the race. 'My last 4x400m was back when I was in school,' Jones said. She had only run one straight 400m this season, gaining her selection with at time of 49.54 seconds in April. This did not prevent her from assuring victory in Sydney by passing the baton to La Tasha Colander-Richardson with a considerable lead.

Her trainer, Trevor Graham, was not surprised by this performance and said: 'I know what she is capable of. I am convinced that if Marion trained for the 400m, she could break the world record.' That belongs to Marita Koch with a time of 47.60 seconds.

RESULTS

MARION JONES'S FIVE MEDALS

400m Freestyle
1 Marion Jones (USA), 10.75
2 Ekatarini Thanou (GRE), 11.12
3 Tanya Lawrence (JAM), 11.18

200m
1 Marion Jones (USA), 21.84
2 Pauline Davis-Thompson (BAH), 22.27
3 Susanthika Jayasinghe (SRI), 22.28

Long jump
1 Heike Drechsler (GER), 6.99m
2 Fiona May (ITA), 6.92m
3 Marion Jones (USA), 6.92m

4x100m
1 BAH (Savatheda Fynes, Chandra Sturrup, Pauline Davis-Thompson, Debbie Ferguson), 41.95
2 JAM (Tanya Lawrence, Juliet Campbell, Beverly McDonald, Merlene Ottey), 42.13
3 USA (Chryste Gaines, Torri Edwards, Nanceen Perry, Marion Jones), 42.20

4x400m
1 USA (Jearl Miles-Clark, Monique Hennagan, Marion Jones, La Tasha Colander-Richardson), 3:22.62
2 JAM (Sandie Richards, Cathrine Scott-Pomales, Deon Hemmings, Lorraine Fenton-Graham), 3:23.25
3 RUS (Yulia Sotnikova, Svetlava Gontcharenko, Olga Kotlyarova, Irina Privalova), 3:23.46

Representing for two nations

Cathy Freeman wins for Australia, and the Aboriginal community.

The pact between modern sport and nationalism has its ambiguities, and sport, including the Olympic movement, has sometimes struggled to contain the very nationalistic fervour it has fostered. Cathy Freeman carried the hopes of two nations into the 2000 Games: those of the host country, Australia, and those of the Aboriginal community into which she had been born. Already the first indigenous athlete to win a medal in an individual event by taking silver in the 400m at Atlanta, subjugation, disenfranchisement and white supremacy were not theoretical ideas to her. Freeman's grandmother, Alice Sibley, had been sent to a penal colony at the age of eight after being snatched by government agents. 'When we walked into new places, we were totally intimidated because we felt that, being black, we had no right to be there,' Freeman wrote in her autobiography. 'We felt bad about being black.' Even as Freeman lit the Olympic flame at the start of the 2000 Games, she was already totally focused on the race. Now, bearing a tattoo on her arm that read 'Cos' I'm Free,' she assumed the mantle of some illustrious precursors: Billy Mills, seven-sixteenths Sioux, who won the marathon at the 1964 Games for the USA; the Yaqui Juan Morales Rodríquez, seventh in the 1932 Olympic marathon for Mexico; and the extraordinary Jim Thorpe, part Sac and Fox, who had dominated the pentathlon and the heptathlon in the 1912 Games.

Sydney had been awarded the Games at a Monte Carlo ceremony in 1993. From that day on, Cathy Freeman's life centred on the women's 400m final at the 2000 Olympics. Her main rival should have been Marie-José Perec, the Guadeloupe-born French athlete who had become the first athlete of either sex to win Olympic 400m gold medals twice. However, Pérec seemed to have suffered an emotional breakdown, and fled Sydney without competing, alleging that she had been threatened by a stranger in her hotel room.

If anything, Pérec's absence increased the pressure on the home favourite.

Freeman, however, focused solely on self-control and enacted her race plan to perfection, starting fast, relaxing on the back straight and attacking out of the second bend. The crowd of 102,254 – the largest ever at an Olympics – roared deafeningly as she pulled clear to win by three metres ahead of Jamaica's Lorraine Graham and Britain's Katherine Merry.

Freeman sat alone on the track, enveloped in her green body suit, overwhelmed by the joyful crowd reaction, slowly allowing her achievement to sink in. Then she took her lap of honour, carrying not one but two flags: one for Australia, and one for the indigenous people of Australia.

Below, Freeman celebrates by trailing two flags behind her on her victory lap: one for Australia, the other for the aboriginal people of Australia: a double triumph for this inspirational athlete.

A race run and won according to plan: 'There was a voice in my head saying, 'Just do what you know.'

Savón: the king of the ring

Cuba's heavyweight star wins his third gold medal in as many Games, equalling the record of László Papp and his fellow Cuban Teófilo Stevenson.

In 1986, as the great Teófilo Stevenson, Cuba's three-times Olympic heavyweight champion from 1972 to 1980, worked towards his final world title, he sparred with an exciting eighteen-year-old named Félix Savón. It was the handover from one legend to the next. Stevenson had been the most impressive Olympic boxer since Cassius Clay, although the two men never met: Stevenson even turned down US$5 million to fight Ali, sticking to his revolutionary convictions.

His successor, Savón, was nicknamed Teófilo at school for his powerful physique, although he was no technical fighter: his discipline and sheer power made him the finest amateur of his generation. And just as attempts to arrange a bout between Stevenson and Ali had failed, so moves by boxing promoter Don King to get Savón in the ring with Mike Tyson came to nothing, despite King reportedly offering Savón $10 million to take the fight in the run-up to the 2000 Games

Savón first entered the Cuban sports system as a rower, although when he won a salsa contest on Cuban television, his father insisted he was born to be a dancer. That was before boxing coaches spotted him as a fourteen-year-old, and in 1986, four years after his first bout, Savón won his first world amateur championship. It was the first of a record-breaking six world amateur titles.

At the 1992 Games, Savón progressed to the final by defeating Dutch giant Arnold Vanderlijde 23-3 in the semi-final. It was the eighth time in eight bouts that Vanderlijde had lost to Savón: his consolation was to become the only boxer in Olympic history to win three bronze medals. In 1996 Savón's campaign was even more straightforward. In the final he defeated the former Nigerian light-middleweight David Defiagbon, now a Canadian heavyweight, by a farcical 20-2. In Sydney, Savón was in sombre mood, beating the Russian southpaw Sultanahmed Ibzagimov 21-14. It was one of four Cuban boxing gold medals at the 2000 Games, and consolidated revolutionary Cuba's position as the

With time running out, Ibzagimov (RUS) re-opened a cut under Savon's left eye, an injury originally suffered in the Cuban's 14-8 semi-final victory over Germany's Sebastian Kober.

For a moment, it appeared the gold medal bout might be stopped, but Australian referee Wayne Rose allowed it to continue. Savon won on points 21-13.

most successful Olympic boxing nation since 1972.

Savón retired from boxing with a career total of 592 victories against 17 defeats, after sixteen years at the summit of amateur boxing.

By winning his third Olympic boxing gold medal, Savón joins a tiny elite comprising only his compatriot Teófilo Stevenson and the Hungarian Lászlo Papp (champion at middle-weight in 1948 and at light middle-weight in 1952 and 1956).

RESULTS SAVON'S THREE WINS

1992 BARCELONA
1 Félix Savón fabré (CUB)
2 David Izonritei (NGR)
3 David Tua (NZL)
4 Arnold Vanderlijde (HOL)
1996 ATLANTA
1 Félix Savón fabré (CUB)
2 David Defiagbon (CAN)
3 Nate Jones (USA)
4 Luan Krasniqi (GER)
2000 SYDNEY
1 Félix Savón fabré (CUB)
2 Soultanakhmed Ibraguimov (RUS)
3 Vladimir Tchantouria (GEO)
4 Sebastian Kober (GER)

Savon missed the 1998 Games in Seoul due to a Cuban boycott. If he'd been there, he might have been celebrating his fourth gold medal here at Sydney.

Gebrselassie, small but mighty

Haile Gebrselassie retains his 10,000m title after a memorable duel with Paul Tergat.

Haile Gebrselassie stands on the starting line, his face stretched into that charming, ever-present smile. Gebrselassie carries joy with him: the joy of movement, the joy of competition, the joy of simply being alive. His, more than any other, is the peaceful face of sport, and before this, his last track event at the 2000 Olympics, the stadium is vibrant with energy, pulsing with anticipation before the start of the 10,000m. Gebrselassie was savouring every moment, delighting in every last second, beaming that infectious smile from the starting line. But, underneath it all, he was a deeply worried man.

'I had a cartilage problem. I shouldn't really have come to Sydney. But then, just a day or two before the opening ceremony, I changed my mind and made the decision to run.' Not since 1993, when he won the title of world champion at the age of 20, had he felt so nervous before a competition. This lack of confidence was, however, compounded by the memory of the 5,000m at Zurich in August, just before the Games. At the time he was already suffering from injury problems and, for the first time since the 1997 season and the challenge of Daniel Komen (KEN), he was troubled by a rival – another Kenyan, Paul Tergat. Tergat finished

eight tenths of a second behind the Ethiopian in the final of the 10,000m at Atlanta, four years ago. At Zurich, he was again at Gebrselassie's heels: the Ethiopian won the race with Tergat pushing him all the way to the finish-line. Gebrselassie's record is second to no-one, living or dead, but Tergat made sure he had no margin of error.

And in the Olympic 10,000m final, once again, Tergat was his main rival. Gebrselassie, the 10,000m world record holder, with a time of 26:22.75, knows every last centimetre of suffering involved in the race. The fact remains, he had not yet run a 10,000m all season, which added to his concern.

But the final was not about records.

It was the Olympic Games, and Gebrselassie had been dreaming of this race since he was a boy. When fellow Ethiopian Miruts Yifter had won the 10,000m in Moscow in 1980, somewhere in the Rift Valley, a young boy, one of ten children, had been listening to this victory on the radio, beneath his sacred tree, whose protective shadow now follows him throughout the world, even as far as Sydney. At least, that is what Gebrselassie believes. And he needed all the might of his 'waka' to be with him at this 10,000m, this immense, cruel battle, which is already notorious at the Olympics.

In the Olympic 10,000m final four

Beaten by Gebrselassie (ETH) by nine hundredths of a second, Paul Tergat (KEN, no 2393) has no regrets: 'He was the stronger runner.'

After a memorable duel with Paul Tergat (KEN, right), Haile Gebrselassie (ETH) retains his 10,000m title, following in the footsteps of Zatopek in 1952 and Viren in 1976.

years before, Gebrselassie had run the second half of the race quickly enough to have won eighteen out the previous nineteen Olympic 5,000m finals. He was a phenomenon, the greatest distance runner in history, and his achievements took place at a time when there were other excellent athletes who forced him to his extraordinary heights.

The 2000 final was a dazzling event, building up slowly over some twenty-seven minutes at an ever more remarkable pace. With nothing between them after twenty-four laps, the two men were destined for a battle over the last 400m. And that was how they found themselves, side by side on the final lap of the Olympic track, desperately searching for that final scrap of energy. Korir and another Ethiopian, Mezgebu, were there as well, but only to accompany them over the line. With 300m to go, Tergat, with his long legs, accelerated suddenly, taking Gebrselassie by surprise. 'I was saving my sprint for later,' Haile explained. 'Luckily, when I did start sprinting, Mezgebu moved out of the way so I could pass him. If he hadn't…'

Tergat rounded the final bend in the lead. Gebrselassie worked hard to close in on him. Then, there were just under 100m to go, and there was still a story to be written – a story of two men, completely different in stature and style, making one final effort, after which there would be nothing more to give. For a long time, for a very long time, Paul Tergat ate up the ground with his huge strides, which seemed to carry him inevitably towards victory. But all the time, Gebrselassie with his shorter, faster steps, like those of a sprinter, closed in inexorably on the Kenyan. The crowd rumbled and bellowed, and finally broke into a deafening roar as Gebrselassie threw himself at the line. Only a photograph could separate the two men. The electronic timing system separated them by just nine hundredths of a second after their 10km duel.

Both men greeted the outcome with dignity and generosity. 'It was extraordinary. I've never been in a race like that,' said Gebrselassie. 'I would almost like to give my medal to Paul, because he really was that good. I came so close to losing, and then I came through and won.'

'It was a highly competitive race,' said Tergat. 'I felt I ran well and attacked at the right time, but Haile was simply the stronger man.'

Once again, after the Atlanta Olympics and the World Championships at Athens and Seville, Gebrselassie has beaten Tergat. But that may not be the end of the story, for Tergat has announced his decision to leave the track in order to tackle the marathon. Gebrselassie is also considering the same move.

But is it too much to hope for another finish like this between these two extraordinary men at the end of the Olympics marathon in Athens? Can you rerun a perfect race?

Redgrave reigns supreme!

Winner in the coxless fours, the British oarsman has taken his fifth Olympic title in five Games.

Rowing is a noble sport: when the competition is over and the medals ceremony comes around, this proud discipline treats all its participants equally. There is no grand podium to place Caesar above Pompey. The medal-winners all stand on the same plane – the platform of honour. Normally. However, at the medal ceremony for the coxless fours, a chink appeared in this egalitarian protocol. The medals are traditionally awarded in the order in which the oarsmen sit in the boat. Not this time; and the flouter of protocol was none other than Princess Anne, daughter of Queen Elizabeth, a former Olympian herself and a member of the IOC, who gracefully sidestepped convention to honour the third oar in the victorious boat: a certain Steven Redgrave.

The Princess greeted this Officer of the Order of the British Empire with the respect he had earned the hard way, winning for the United Kingdom his fifth gold medal in five Olympic Games.

Redgrave has always been a champion of unparalleled ability, yet his rowing career began quite by chance. 'The person who has most influenced my life is a man called Francis Smith…', Redgrave explains. Without this fanatical rowing coach, Steven Redgrave would never have been tempted to join the local rowing club in his home town of Marlow. He was fifteen, already possessing the beginnings of the superb physique that later became his trademark, and took up rowing, at first with no notable successes. Never a brilliant junior, he worked his way through the ranks and quickly featured in the national team, although he narrowly missed out on selection for the Moscow Olympics in 1980. It was only four years later that he embarked on the journey that lead to glory. Until then, he had been considered primarily a solo oarsman, but the retaliatory Soviet boycott of the 1984 Games opened a window of opportunity for some ambitious younger athletes, Redgrave among them. He joined Richard Budgett, Martin Cross and Andrew Holmes in a coxed four crew. He was not yet 22, but the press was already speaking

of 'Steve Redgrave's crew.' It was a phrase that would echo down the years.

In 1986, his coach Mike Spracklen proposed that he join Andrew Holmes in a coxless pair. The World Championships programme had been modified, encouraging the two men to set themselves a lofty aim: to dethrone the imperious Abbagnale brothers from Italy in the coxed pairs, while at the same time becoming the world's best coxless pair. They never achieved the double, but they went down in history as the first to conquer the Italians.

Yet the Holmes-Redgrave pairing was not the dream team it appeared to be. The two men had little in common. Redgrave was prepared to sacrifice everything for victory; Holmes preferred to reserve time for his extra-curricular activities. In 1990 Redgrave joined Matthew Pinsent, the previous year's world junior champion, alongside Tim Foster. Initially, Pinsent did not warm to the idea; he was in a four that he enjoyed. But the two men quickly accumulated every possible, every imaginable, trophy. Moreover, their partnership worked both technically and personally: Redgrave named Pinsent the godfather of his youngest child. The two men dominated the coxless pairs with unprecedented tyranny. From 1991 to 1996 they won everything in their path, including two Olympic and four world titles. Then Redgrave decided the time had come to call it a day. The evening after his Atlanta win, he commented: 'If you ever see me in a boat again, you have my permission to shoot me.' Two months later, he announced his return to competition, embarking on another four-year odyssey that would take him to Sydney. Why? 'Because Australia is a beautiful country, and I was certain that the Games in 2000 would be a great event,' he said.

With Cracknell, Pinsent and Foster (left) in the coxless fours, Steven Redgrave (right) adds a fifth gold medal in five Games to his extraordinary record.

The Thorpedo

Two gold medals and two world records in the space of an hour: the Australian got everything right on his first day at the Olympics.

After an excellent preamble by Klim, Fydler and Callus, Thorpe starts the final leg of the 4 x 100m relay in the lead, ahead of the American specialist Hall. After an incredible effort, he secures victory for Australia.

'Walking into the pool in Homebush, I didn't know what to expect. I was only certain of one thing: I felt on top form! I felt relaxed and proud to be representing my country at the Olympics. The crowd was wild. It was like being at the Colosseum, and the swimmers were the gladiators.'

It was 16 September and Ian Thorpe was about to give the most convincing reply to all those who had thought the Olympic setting would unnerve him. He had broken record after record. After an ankle sprain in October last year, Thorpe continued swimming length after length, even with his leg in plaster, and came back with an arm action to match his criminally good leg action. The result was a short-course world record over 200m of 1:42.53 in mid-January.

The only thing left to test was his mental strength. Manfred Thiesmann,

Thorpe celebrates his triumph.

the German swimming coach, suggested Thorpe might be guilty of doping. Thorpe, who has been arguing in favour of blood tests since the age of fifteen, weathered the storm and, a couple of days later in Berlin, broke his own 200m world record.

At the Australian selection trials in May, he did not swim as well as normal.

At the Games, Don Talbot, the Australian coach, admitted that he had never seen Thorpe so nervous, despite

a margin of error of seven seconds.

However, on the first night of the finals, Ian Thorpe enjoyed an hour of complete bliss. At 7.15pm he won gold in the 400m. At 8.15pm he was part of the victorious Australian team in the 4x100m: 'Everything happened very quickly after the 400m. I had to say a couple of words to the press before going straight off to the recovery pool. Then they called me for the medal ceremony. I had got my swimming suit as far off as I could and then I realised that my three team mates were already almost under starter's orders. I had to run like a fool to join them. I got there just in time. As soon as I touched the wall, without looking at the board and without hearing anything, I knew that we had got the gold. I had just achieved my childhood dream. To dream of something and then to achieve it is the best thing that can happen to any of us! '

RESULTS

THORPE'S DOUBLE

400m

1. Ian Thorpe (AUS), 3:40.59
2. Massimiliano Rosolino (ITA), 3:43.40
3. Klete Keller (USA), 3:47.00
4. Emiliano Brembilla (ITA), 3:47.01
5. Dragos Cristian Coman (ROM), 3:47.38
6. Chad Carvin (USA), 3:47.58
7. Grant Hackett (AUS), 3:48.22
8. Ryk Neethling (RSA), 3:48.52

4x100m

1. Australia (Michael Klim, Christopher Fydler, Ashley Callus, Ian Thorpe), 3:13.67;
2. USA, 3:13.86;
3. BRA, 3:17.40;
4. GER, 3:17.77;
5. ITA, 3:17.85;
6. SWE, 3:19.60;
7. FRA, 3:21.00
Russia disqualified.

VDH is master of the waves

Unable to improve on the world record he set the night before, Pieter Van den Hoogenband still took gold in the 100m, deposing Aleksandr Popov.

'I was so nervous that in the final 15m, I kept saying to myself: 'I'm going to do it.'

RESULTS

VDH'S DOUBLE

100m
1 Pieter Van den Hoogenband (HOL), 48.30;
2 Aleksandr Popov (RUS), 48.69;
3 Gary Hall Jr (USA), 48.73;
4 Michael Klim (AUS), 48.74;
5 Neil Walker (USA), 49.09;
6 Lars Frolander (SWE), 49.22;
7 Denis Pimankov (RUS), 49.36;
8 Christopher Fydler (AUS), 49.44.

200m
1 Pieter Van den Hoogenband (HOL), 1:45.35;
2 Ian Thorpe (AUS), 1:45.83;
3 Massimiliano Rosolino (ITA), 1:46.65;
4 Josh Davis (USA), 1:46.73;
5 Paul Palmer (GBR), 1:47.95;
6 James Salter (GBR), 1:48.74;
7 Rick Say (CAN), 1:48.76;
8 Grant Hackett (AUS), 1:49.46.

VDH savours his victory over Alexander Popov.

International swimming has a new star. At 6 feet 3 and 167 pounds, Pieter Van den Hoogenband, 22, is the baby-faced giant who has stolen Aleksandr Popov's crown.

The Olympic 100m freestyle final has produced great champions: Weissmuller, Schollander, Wenden, Spitz, Montgomery, Gaines and Biondi. This time, Russia's Popov was attempting to make history by becoming the first man to win three consecutive Olympic titles in the event. Victory would have capped eight years of almost uninterrupted dominance in the sprint.

The tension was palpable. In Atlanta four years earlier, Popov met Hall before a wild, almost aggressive crowd. This time, no emotion showed on the faces of the favourites: Popov, the titleholder, Van den Hoogenband, the world record holder, and Klim, the former record holder.

Van den Hoogenband allowed Klim to lead for the first 50m, knowing that he could catch the slow-finishing Australian later. A first burst of acceleration after 25m gave him a one-stroke lead over Popov, and the advantage at the turn (23.32 against 23.44).

Overtaking Klim, Van den Hoogenband pulled away. Popov seemed to stall. Hall and Klim closed in on him, finishing only four and five hundredths of a second behind. VDH has become the first to hold Olympic titles and world records in the 100m and 200m since Mark Spitz in 1972.

'I CAN HARDLY BELIEVE IT'

'In both my events, I am up against giants,' said Van den Hoogenband on his arrival in Sydney, 'But I like that kind of challenge.' Van den Hoogenband defeated Thorpe in his home pool, in front of a home crowd, and stole his world record – a feat many believed impossible. Then, he brought Popov to his knees, breaking the Russian's long-standing world record in the semi-final, in a hitherto unheard of 47.84.

'I can hardly believe it', VDH repeated. 'I came here to try and win an Olympic medal in the individual and the relay. But I was in such good form that I did a lot more than that.' Meanwhile, Aleksandr Popov, nursing his wounds, could only say, 'See you in four years.'

Olympic giant

It was an immense challenge, but David Douillet has won his second Olympic title, beating Shinohara of Japan.

As the new century begins, the world of Judo rests on the shoulders of a giant – the finest, strongest fighter in the history of the discipline, one who has amassed four world titles and two Olympic gold medals, the second in the heavyweight division here at Sydney. His name is David Douillet, and his unparalleled record is just reward for a spectacular career.

Douillet had already spent two seasons without competing. Indeed, it is hard to say whether his greatest achievement was to win the Olympic tournament, or to appear at all. Doing so meant overcoming the torment that has wracked his thirty-year-old body. Until 21 September 2000, he shared his great international reputation with Yasuhiro Yamashita, the Japanese master from the 1980s. By defeating Yamashita's pupil, Shinichi Shinohara, in the final, he did more than merely throw his opponent into despair. At the instant of his winning move, Douillet decided that this would be the last time the world would see him fight. At thirty-one, he has retired from competition, leaving the Judo world in turmoil.

Three years ago in Paris, in the final of the World Championships, he won his fourth world title when his opponent, Shinohara, was disqualified. Shinohara thought that he had been denied the title in Paris, and last year in Birmingham he proclaimed himself the new holder of the two main titles (heavyweight and openweight), a double that Douillet had achieved once before, in Japan in 1995.

But great sportsmen always have what it takes. The scene was set in Sydney. It was the last day of the Olympics, and the French were having a last minute rush on the medals. Nobody could have dreamed of a better ending than this mighty clash. For the Judo world, this France-Japan confrontation was as important as France-Brazil World Cup Final held on 12 July 1998. It was a battle

The standard bearer for the French team (far right), David Douillet justified this honour by retaining his title, despite the best efforts of Shinohara (JAP, in blue).

David Douillet savours his achievement as he enters the pantheon of the greats. Right, the Estonian, Pertelson: his opponent in the semi-final.

between champions. Two days earlier, Douglas Cardoso, the Venezuelan fighter, failed to turn up at the morning weigh-in and was disqualified. He can at least boast that he wasn't beaten by Douillet.

Douillet's bout against the experienced Belgian Arnie Van de Barneveld was a model tactical battle. In the fourth round, Van de Barneveld received hansuko-make and disqualification. The Frenchman then

had three hours to prepare for his semi-final against the left-handed Estonian, Pon, runner-up in the World Championships. The two had never met. During Douillet's enforced absence from competition, spent strengthening his suspect back, Douillet had never forgotten his Judo. Although he had had to wait until mid-August and the tournament in Bonn to resume fighting, at Sydney Douillet was unstoppable. In the final,

Shinohara was exhausted from his semi-final against the young Tmenov, just twenty-three. After one minute and thirty-five seconds, Douillet attempted a right uchi-mata. The left-handed Japanese wrestler rolled onto the right hip of the Frenchman, and the two men fell to the mat. The referee from New Zealand awarded an attack yuko to the Olympic champion.

Long after the final, Yasuhiro Yamashita, embodying the disappointment of the Japanese, went to the judges' table to protest. It was rare move for the master, who believed – along with the rest of Japan – that the yuko should have been awarded to Shinohora. Shinohara, meanwhile, had left the arena, no doubt burdened by the day's events. He had hung on to the last, forcing Douillet to commit errors and concede penalties until, thirty-eight seconds from the end, the Frenchman performed another yuko. Douillet was champion.

On the podium, Shinichi Shinohara was unable to raise his head. Since the 1992 Barcelona semi-final and Ogawa's victory, no Japanese had beaten Douillet. Shinohara had thought that the path was finally clear for him, but Douillet had come back. On the podium, Douillet looked on top of the world.

DOUILLET: 'I WASN'T THINKING ABOUT THE PODIUM.'

'You shed tears on the podium. Were they because of your gold medal or because it was your last fight?'

'Tonight is full of both joy and sorrow. Joy, because of what I've got here in my hands [his gold medal]. Sorrow, because half of my life is coming to an end. Judo was my passion, my job, my pleasure, my sorrow and my life. My family, my children, my wife, my parents; they have all suffered for it. Everyone was there through the good times, and, above all, they were there through the bad times. Maybe that sounds like a cliché, but it really is true. I'm turning over a new leaf because I think I've done all I can within my sport. I've given all I have to give, honestly. That's why I have decided to bring it to a close today. So you see, there is a mixture of emotions. But at this particular moment, there is still more sorrow than joy. I need to try and put it out of my mind before the party!'

'What does it mean for you to have won the biggest collection of medals in the history of Judo, with six world and Olympic gold medals?'

'That is a small plus. Yamashita spoke to me about it. He told me to try and beat the record that we held together. But I didn't really believe that I could. That was not why I carried on. I carried on because I like to fight.'

2000
OLYMPIC ROUND-UP

MAURICE GREENE:
ANOTHER GOLDEN SPRINTER.

The two American sprinters who triumphed in Sydney 23 September on the Olympic track, surrounded by the flashes of a thousand cameras, did so as overwhelming favourites. Marion Jones, from Los Angeles, and Maurice Greene, from Kansas City, dominated their Olympic finals in the 100m, just as they have dominated their disciplines since Atlanta. Both are reigning double world champions, gold medalists both in Athens in 1997 and then in Seville last summer. After running 9.79s in Athens in June 1999, Greene is now the current world record holder. Neither missed their chance to claim a first Olympic title. For the twenty-four-year-old Jones and the twenty-six-year-old Greene, these Olympic titles are just reward for their unquestionable superiority.

On the podium, Maurice Greene let his emotions get the better of him in an uncharacteristic moment of sentiment during the raising of the Star Spangled Banner. Normally so expressive in his excitement, Greene looked once more like that young boy from Kansas City, who must so often have dreamed of one day standing there. Greene's success may have been less awesome than that of Marion Jones, but his twelve hundredths of a second winning margin over Boldon is still the largest winning margin since Carl Lewis beat Sam Grady by twenty hundredths of a second in Los Angeles. That is certainly some achievement, despite the fact that his time of 9.87 (slower than the 9.84 run by Bailey in Atlanta) is only the fifteenth fastest time ever. Maurice has already himself run five quicker races in his career.

Boldon started faster and challenged his training partner over the first 60m. Then Greene pulled away. They next met on the podium for the medal ceremony, joined by another gem from the Caribbean, Obadele Thompson. In truth, it was not Greene that made the difference, but Boldon who cracked, unable to maintain the rhythm with which he had begun. He only managed a time of 9.99.

1   Gold in the road race and road time trial, gold in the pursuit and silver in the points race: Leontien Van Moorsel-Zijlaard (HOL) is unbeatable on any surface.

2   Jan Ullrich (left) gets his own back on Lance Armstrong for the Tour de France by winning the road race. He also beat Armstrong in the time trial, getting silver behind the Russian Ekimov.

3   Heike Drechsler of Germany increases her collection of Olympic medals: two gold medals (1992 and 2000) and one silver (1988) in the long jump, and two bronze in the 100m and 200m in 1988.

4   Making her mark in the K2 and K4 (here), the German Birgit Fischer brings her medals total to seven gold (2 in K1, 2 in K2 and 3 in K4) and three silver, between 1980 and 2000.

5   Inge De Bruijn of the Netherlands is the queen of the pool. She won the 50m, 100m and 100m butterfly, all in world record times.

6   Maurice Greene (right) can enjoy himself. With Jonathan Drummond, Brian Lewis and Bernard Williams, he has won the 4x100m. This was his second title, along with the 100m.

7   The third javelin title for the 34-year-old Czech Jan Zelesny. He finished in second place in Seoul, but managed to dominate in Barcelona, Atlanta and Sydney.

8   Felix Savon (right) wins his third consecutive heavyweight title, equalling the record of the Hungarian Papp and his fellow Cuban Stevenson.

9   Andrea Raducan, gold medallist in the individual All-Around gymnastics competition, is not the winner for long. She is stripped of her title after a positive drugs test. The title goes to fellow Romanian, Simona Amanar.

100 Although they have won the title six times, the Hungarian water polo team had not been on the podium since 1980. Sydney marked the return to their traditional place.

11 Venus Williams, 20, wins gold in the tennis singles. She wanted her younger sister Serena to have a title, too. They won it in the doubles.

12 Trailing 2-0 against Spain, Cameroon equalise, and then win on penalties, to inherit the title from Nigeria.

Ullrich steps out of the shadows

Lance Armstrong's long-suffering understudy occupies centre stage in the Olympic road race, and beats the Texan in the time trial.

The history of sport is full of athletes who would have dominated their discipline if their careers had not coincided with some other, still greater figure. Gymnast Vladimir Artemov (SOV/RUS) was known as 'the eternal second' in USSR before he won the All-Around competition at the Seoul Olympics. Women's springboard diver Irina Lashko (RUS) never won Olympic gold, but took the silver medal at the 1996 Olympics after finishing second at the 1990 Goodwill Games, the 1991 World Championships, the 1992 Olympics and the World Cup in 1987, 1989 and 1993.

Jamaican sprinter Merlene Ottey became known as 'Ms Bronze' because of a string of 100m and 200m third places at the 1980 and 1984 Olympics, and the World Championships in 1987, 1991 and 1992. She did manage to finish second in the 1996 Olympic 100m and 200m.

Snooker player Jimmy White lost the final of the World championship six

The muscular Jan Ullrich was second favourite behind Lance Armstrong in Sydney.

Ullrich's style, based on power, contrasted starkly with Armstrong's lighter, quicker pedal stroke. Yet victory in the time trial was reserved for neither: the winner was Armstrong team-mate Vyatcheslav Yekimov (RUS).

Jan Ullrich celebrates, ahead of his two Team Telekom team-mates Aleksandr Vinokourov (KAZ, in the turqoise shirt of Kazakhstan) and Andreas Klöden (GER).

times (1984, 1990–94).

Cycling has its own role call of eternal seconds: Joop Zoetemelk, six times second in the Tour de France, just once the winner, had the misfortune to first come up against Eddy Merckx, then with Bernard Hinault. Raymond Poulidor, eight times a top three finisher in the Tour de France, never wore the yellow jersey. His career coincided with those of Jacques Anquetil and then Merckx.

When a twenty-two-year-old German from the Baltic coast named Jan Ullrich, the world amateur champion of three years before, finished second to his team-mate Bjarne Riis in the 1996 Tour de France, the cycling journalists of the world opened their German grammars and set to work, convinced that the next decade belonged to him. Crushing victory in the 1997 Tour de France confirmed their fears: here was the new Eddy Merckx, and he was still a kid.

Here again, things didn't quite turn out that way. As Ullrich shepherded Riis

to victory, the 1993 professional world champion Lance Armstrong abandoned the 1996 Tour de France somewhere in the Franche-Comte, beneath the pouring rain. A few months later, Armstrong learned he was riddled with cancer. In 1999, after multiple surgery

and debilitating courses of chemotherapy, Armstrong returned to the Tour and won. The American's inspirational miracle story was the German's tale of unfulfilled promise: Ullrich was a class above every other athlete in his sport – except Armstrong.

One team (Deutsche Telekom), two nations, (Germany, Kazakhstan), three close friends.

Both men went to Sydney knowing that success in the Olympic arena offered acclaim comparable to Tour de France victory. On Wednesday 27 September, Ullrich's Deutsche Telekom team-mates Aleksandr Vinokourov of Kazakhstan and Andreas Klöden, also German, finished nine and twelve seconds respectively behind their team leader Ullrich, amid allegations that by riding to trade-team rather than national tactics, they had breached Olympic ethics. Armstrong finished thirteenth, one minute 29 seconds behind Ullrich.

However, the Texan had staked all on the time trial, three days later. There, he was again beaten by Ullrich, who completed the 46.8km course 26 seconds faster. But it was not Ullrich but Armstrong's friend and team-mate Vyatcheslav Yekimov, who won, finishing eight seconds faster than Ullrich.

Returning home with a gold and a silver medal, Ullrich had stepped out of Armstrong's shadow for the first time since 1999.

Nemov, the quiet father

After his success in the All-Around competition, the Russian thought about his son, who he is yet to meet...

For once, he didn't flash that seductive smile. On the podium, Alexeï Nemov stood straight as a post. Only the constant bobbing of his Adam's apple betrayed his emotions. Far away, in Moscow, his wife Galina held their son, Alexeï Junior, born on 2 September 2000, when his father was already in Sydney. 'I can't wait till he is older and I can tell him about this evening,' Nemov said. Aged 24, strong and supple, Nemov always seems to land on his feet. So far in Sydney, he has won bronze in the team event and gold in the individual competition, with the apparatus finals still to come.

Even before the Games, he had a fine collection of world and Olympic medals. He also had a fine collection of fiancées, including the wonderful Svetlana Khorkina, 1996 Olympic champion on the asymmetric bars, and the 1997 Grand Prix champion, Elena Vitrichenko: Russian national trainer Leonid Arkaïev was strongly against the marriage of any of his pupils while they were still part of the national team.

'I've not changed my lifestyle completely. I sometimes like to go to bed at two in the morning, and sometimes I like to go out for a beer,' Nemov said yesterday after winning his title, and you can be sure he went out for one last night. But no more

Like a modern day Hercules, the new father has completed his twelve tasks.

than one: the competition isn't over, and the reigning world champion on the floor and pommeled horse still has work to do in the apparatus finals.

Yesterday was tense for him: after stumbling on his landing in the vault, he couldn't make any errors on the parallel bars. 'It was a difficult moment. As recently as a month ago, Nemov couldn't complete his parallel bar routine,' said Arkaïev. 'He has worked hard since then.' Afterwards, Arkaïev could breathe again.

Nemov's former team-mate, Dimitri Karbanenko, now representing France, commented: 'What he's achieved is fantastic. It's very difficult to go into the individual competition having finished first in the All-Around.'

Once upon a time, in their shared room in Lake Round, Karbanenko used to give advice to the young Nemov. Now, there is nothing more that he can teach Nemov about gymnastics, but maybe he can give him some advice about being a father.

Nemov is one with the angels, both in the vault and on the floor.

RESULTS

NEMOV'S TWELVE MEDALS

Gold
1996: Vault and team event;
2000: All-Around competition and
horizontal bar.

Silver
1996: All-Around competition;
2000: Floor.

Bronze
1996: Horizontal bar, floor and
pommel horse;
2000: Parallel bars, pommel horse
and the team event.

SYDNEY XXVII OLYMPIAD

Fifty-one nations won at least one Olympic title, and eighty NOCs went home
with at least one medal, setting a new record that offered proof – if proof
were needed – of the global nature of the final Games of the century.

THE GAMES IN BRIEF

Opening Date
15 September 2000

Closing Date
1 October 2000

Host Nation
Australia (AUS)

Candidate Towns
Berlin (GER), Istanbul (TUR), Manchester
(GBR) and Peking (CHIN).

199 Nations Represented

10,651 Athletes
(4,069 women, 6,582 men)

29 Sports
(25 open to women)
Track and field, rowing, basketball,
badminton, baseball, boxing, canoeing,
cycling, equestrian, fencing, football,
gymnastics, weightlifting, handball, field
hockey, judo, wrestling, swimming,
modern pentathlon, softball, tennis, table
tennis, volleyball (including beach
volleyball, taekwondo, shooting, archery,
triathlon and sailing.

300 Events
(132 open to women)

Games officially opened by
Sir William Deane, Governor of Australia

Olympic flame lit by
Cathy Freeman (athletics)

Olympic oath read by
Rechelle Hawkes (hockey)

IOC President
Juan Antonio Samaranch (ESP)

DID YOU KNOW?

North and South Korea walked out under the
same flag, while East Timor took part under
the Olympic IOA banner (Individual Olympic
Athletes).

New events included the triathlon and taekwondo, as well the women's modern
pentathlon and women's weightlifting.

Also included for the first time were blood
tests and EPO tests.

Athens, in the name of history

First to host the modern Olympic Games in 1896, Athens will in 2004 become the first to stage the Games in the third millennium.

Gianna Angelopoulos-Daskalaki, the charismatic leader of the Greek bid, can at last celebrate: Athens won the vote easily.

Eleven cities bid to host the 2004 Olympic Games: Athens, Buenos Aires, Cape Town, Istanbul, Lille, Rio de Janeiro, Rome, St Petersburg, San Juan, Seville and Stockholm. In March 1997, a short list of five was selected, which saw strong bids, especially from Istanbul and St Petersburg, rejected.

On 5 September 1997, the host city for the Games of the twenty-eighth Olympiad was selected from the five remaining candidates: Athens, Buenos Aires, Cape Town, Rome and Stockholm.

The first round of voting excluded Buenos Aires, making its fifth bid to host the Games. That South America has never hosted the Olympic Games should have worked in its favour, yet its presentation was considered poor, consisting of three slide-shows, with tango playing in the background.

The second round ruled out Stockholm, which perhaps suffered from a lack of domestic support until too late, compounded by isolated incidents of terrorism which prompted security concerns.

Cape Town was the third city to be excluded from the running. The presence of Nelson Mandela, whose beautiful, touching speech brought considerable weight to a very original presentation that was colourful and surprising, prompted IOC President Jacques Rogge to observe, 'It was a message of hope and confidence in Africa. We want to give you the opportunity to host the Olympic Games. Keep working on it.'

This left just two candidates. Rome and Athens. The fact that Rome already possessed most of the required amenities surely counted in its favour. Yet there remained a sense of guilt in the IOC that Athens had been deprived of the 1996 Games, for

which it had forcibly campaigned. However, in 2002, Ioannis Spanudakis, the managing director of the organising committee, commented publicly: 'Thank God we didn't get the Games in 1996. We would never have been up to it.' In 1990 the Greek bid had been hampered by political infighting, and the Athens team felt insulted when they failed to secure the centennial Games. However, they refused to give up, building on the undeniable emotional pull of Athens by continuing to construct stadiums and hosting more high-level competitions.

Most importantly, perhaps, they discovered the talents of Gianna Angelopoulos-Daskalaki, a unique personality who was capable of carrying the Athens bid. It is easy to imagine this multi-millionaire former Member of Parliament dressed as a vestal virgin and lighting the Olympic torch. In 1997, when Greece re-applied, she assumed leadership of the project, suppressed the squabbling inside the Greek camp and gave some structure to their preparations – even stretching the IOC's entertainment guidelines at her own expense.

At the final presentation, everything fell into place. Angelopoulos-

After the joy and celebrations caused by the decision of the Olympic Committee, the Greeks were quickly back down to work. They now have a commitment to meet.

The transport network has been redesigned for the arrival of the participants and the spectators.

In addition to the thirty-seven competition sites, work is also underway on the Olympic Village, which will house 1,600 athletes.

Daskalaki spoke for almost fifty minutes, in English and in French. She offered detailed explanations, occasionally using illustrations, keeping her audience in rapt attention. She could have won everyone over with her charm alone. Many IOC members admitted that they were as enchanted as if they had been borne away in a boat to Cythera. After this one-woman show, the feeling was widespread that Athens would go the distance. Their bid had flawless taste. The Greek team had carefully considered the men and women of the IOC and addressed their increasing preoccupations with economics and socio-cultural considerations. Without doubt, the sporting impact, Greek culture and Olympic history played a role, although the same can be said for

The Olympic movement, a product of the ninteenth century, became characteristic of the twentieth. In the twenty-first century, with new challenges, the task of building the Olympic future goes on.

Rome, which played exactly the same cards. The Italian presentation was also remarkable, with many veiled references and sporting and cultural memories. Rome had put together a formidable team for its bid, and Mayor Francesco Rutelli made an excellent impression. To cap it off, even Luciano Pavarotti made an appearance. Unfortunately, his 'O sole mio' was not enough. The vote went Athens' way by sixty-six to forty-one: the Olympics would return to the city where they had been reborn 108 years earlier.

Nobody could have predicted such a wide gap between the two Mediterranean cities. It was an enormous winning margin. Thomas Bach, president of the evaluation committee, was surprised, but he indicated that the choice represented the assessment of his committee, who read every word of every line, and sometimes the spaces between them.

Within months of the decision to give the Games to Athens, preparations were in crisis. The organising committee requested a delay in submitting their first official reports to the Executive Board. The general manager of the organising committee, Kostas Bakouris, was soon telling the press that all Olympic projects were 'beset with problems', and in 2000, alarmed after three years of inaction, the IOC threatened to take the Games elsewhere.

However, despite these teething problems, the legacy the Games will leave to the Greek people is likely to be huge, boosting the economy and strengthening the infrastructure. A new airport is under construction; public transport capacity will increase by fifty per cent, and 200 kilometres of ring roads, trunk roads and light railway are being added to the transport network – all inspired by the idea of hosting the Olympic Games. With a new ecological park, marina, aquarium and open-air theatre, Athens at the start of the third millennium is undergoing a complete transformation.

At the 112th session of the IOC at Moscow in July 2001, Beijing was preferred to Istanbul, Paris, Osaka and Toronto as the host to the 2008 Games. Juan Antonio Samaranch, the IOC President now nearing retirement, commented: 'The IOC did the world a favour. This will change China.' Olympic sponsors like Coca-Cola, Kodak, Schlumerger-Sema and Swatch quickly renewed their contracts.

2004

ATHENS XXVIII OLYMPIAD

The Greek bid to host the Centennial Games failed. But they built on the experience, and were successful: building on the undeniable emotional pull of Athens, the 2004 Games return to the city that saw their rebirth 108 years ago.

THE GAMES IN BRIEF

Opening Date
13 August 2004

Closing Date
29 August 2004

Host Nation
Greece (GRE)

Candidate Towns
Buenos Aires (ARG), Cape Town (RSA), Rome (ITA) and Stockholm (SWE)

201 Nations Represented

10,500 athletes

28 Sports
(26 open to women)
Track and field, rowing, badminton, baseball, basketball, boxing, canoeing, cycling, equestrian, fencing, football, gymnastics, weightlifting, handball, field hockey, judo, wrestling, swimming (including synchronised swimming, diving and water-polo), modern pentathlon, softball, taekwondo, tennis, table tennis, shooting, archery, triathlon, sailing and volleyball (including beach volleyball).

301 Events
(133 open to women)

IOC President
Jacques Rogge (BEL)

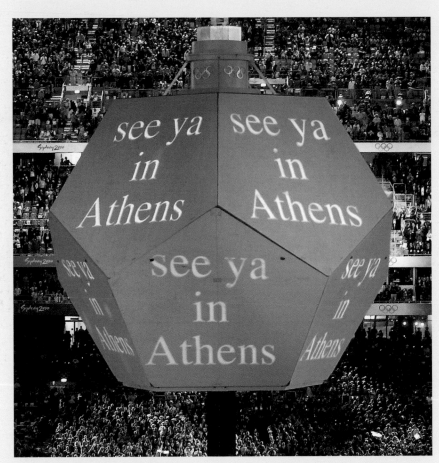

DID YOU KNOW?

The twenty-eight sports that make up the Olympic programme cover thirty-two Olympic disciplines.

The events will be contested on 37 different sites.

The number of accredited officials is likely to be around 5,500, while the number of journalists arriving to cover the Games will be about 21,500 – 16,000 for TV and radio and 5,500 for the written press.

The Olympic Village will house some 16,000 athletes and officials.

Some 45,000 people will be responsible for security at the Games: 25,000 police, 7,000 soldiers, 3,000 coastguards, 1,500 firemen, 3,500 private security agents and 5,000 specially trained volunteers.

The marathon course will follow the ancient route from the town of Marathon to the Panathenaic Stadium.

OLYMPIC CHAMPIONS
ATHENS TO ATHENS 1896–2004

ATHLETICS (MEN)

60m

| 1900 | Alvin KRAENZLEIN | USA | 7.0 |
| 1904 | Archibald HAHN | USA | 7.0 |

100m

1896	Thomas BURKE	USA	12.0
1900	Frank JARVIS	USA	11.0
1904	Archibald HAHN	USA	11.0
1908	Reginald WALKER	SAF	10.8
1912	Ralph CRAIG	USA	10.8
1920	Charles PADDOCK	USA	10.8
1924	Harold ABRAHAMS	GBR	10.6
1928	Percy WILLIAMS	CAN	10.8
1932	Thomas Edward TOLAN	USA	10.3
1936	James Jesse OWENS	USA	10.3
1948	Harrison DILLARD	USA	10.3
1952	Lindy REMIGINO	USA	10.4
1956	Robert 'Bobby' MORROW	USA	10.5
1960	Armin HARY	GER	10.2
1964	Robert HAYES	USA	10.0
1968	Jim HINES	USA	9.95
1972	Valery BORZOV	SOV	10.14
1976	Hasely CRAWFORD	TRI	10.06
1980	Allan WELLS	GBR	10.25
1984	Carl LEWIS	USA	9.99
1988	Carl LEWIS	USA	9.92
1992	Linford CHRISTIE	GBR	9.96
1996	Donovan BAILEY	CAN	9.84
2000	Maurice GREENE	USA	9.87

200m

1900	John Walter TEWKSBURY	USA	22.2
1904	Archibald HAHN	USA	21.6
1908	Robert KERR	CAN	22.6
1912	Ralph CRAIG	USA	21.7
1920	Allen WOODRING	USA	22.0
1924	Jackson SCHOLZ	USA	21.6
1928	Percy WILLIAMS	CAN	21.8
1932	Thomas Edward TOLAN	USA	21.2
1936	James 'Jesse' OWENS	USA	20.7
1948	Melvin PATTON	USA	21.1
1952	Andrew STANFIELD	USA	20.7
1956	Robert 'Bobby' MORROW	USA	20.6
1960	Livio BERRUTI	ITA	20.5
1964	Henry CARR	USA	20.3
1968	Tommie SMITH	USA	19.83
1972	Valery BORZOV	SOV	20.00
1976	Donald QUARRIE	JAM	20.22
1980	Pietro MENNEA	ITA	20.19
1984	Carl LEWIS	USA	19.80
1988	Joseph DE LOACH	USA	19.75
1992	Michael MARSH	USA	20.01
1996	Michael JOHNSON	USA	19.32
2000	Konstantinos KENTERIS	GRE	20.09

400m

1896	Thomas BURKE	USA	54.2
1900	Maxwell LONG	USA	49.4
1904	Harry HILLMAN	USA	49.2
1908	Wyndham HALSWELLE	GBR	50.0
1912	Charles REIDPATH	USA	48.2
1920	Bevil RUDD	SAF	49.6
1924	Eric LIDDELL	GBR	47.6
1928	Raymond BARBUTI	USA	47.8
1932	William CARR	USA	46.2
1936	Archie WILLIAMS	USA	46.5
1948	Arthur WINT	JAM	46.2
1952	George RHODEN	JAM	45.9
1956	Charles JENKINS	USA	46.7
1960	Otis DAVIS	USA	44.9
1964	Mike LARRABEE	USA	45.1

1968	Lee EVANS	USA	43.86
1972	Vincent MATTHEWS	USA	44.66
1976	Alberto JUANTORENA	CUB	44.26
1980	Viktor MARKIN	SOV	44.60
1984	Alonzo BABERS	USA	44.27
1988	Steve LEWIS	USA	43.87
1992	Quincy WATTS	USA	43.50
1996	Michael JOHNSON	USA	43.49
2000	Michael JOHNSON	USA	43.84

800m

1896	Edwin FLACK	AUS	2:11.0
1900	Alfred TYSOE	GBR	2:01.2
1904	James LIGHTBODY	USA	1:56.0
1908	Melvin SHEPPARD	USA	1:52.8
1912	James 'Ted ' MEREDITH	USA	1:51.9
1920	Albert HILL	GBR	1:53.4
1924	Douglas LOWE	GBR	1:52.4
1928	Douglas LOWE	GBR	1:51.8
1932	Thomas HAMPSON	GBR	1:49.7
1936	John WOODRUFF	USA	1:52.9
1948	Malvin WHITFIELD	USA	1:49.2
1952	Malvin WHITFIELD	USA	1:49.2
1956	Thomas COURTNEY	USA	1:47.7
1960	Peter SNELL	NZL	1:46.3
1964	Peter SNELL	NZL	1:45.1
1968	Ralph DOUBELL	AUS	1:44.3
1972	David WOTTLE	USA	1:45.9
1976	Alberto JUANTORENA	CUB	1:43.50
1980	Stephen 'Steve' OVETT	GBR	1:45.40
1984	Joaquim CRUZ	BRA	1:43.00
1988	Paul ERENG	KEN	1:43.45
1992	William TANUI	KEN	1:43.66
1996	Vebjorn RODAL	NOR	1:42.58
2000	Nils SCHUMANN	GER	1:45.08

1500m

1896	Edwin FLACK	AUS	4:33.2
1900	Charles BENNETT	GBR	4:06.2
1904	James LIGHTBODY	USA	4:05.4
1908	Melvin SHEPPARD	USA	4:03.4
1912	Arnold JACKSON	GBR	3:56.8
1920	Albert HILL	GBR	4:01.8
1924	Paavo NURMI	FIN	3:53.6
1928	Harri LARVA	FIN	3:53.2
1932	Luigi BECCALI	ITA	3:51.2
1936	John LOVELOCK	NZL	3:47.8
1948	Henry ERIKSSON	SWE	3:49.8
1952	Joseph BARTHEL	SWE	3:45.1
1956	Ron DELANY	IRL	3:41.2
1960	Herbert ELLIOTT	AUS	3:35.6
1964	Peter SNELL	NZL	3:38.1
1968	Kipchoge KEINO	KEN	3:34.9
1972	Pekka VASALA	FIN	3:36.3
1976	John WALKER	NZL	3:39.17
1980	Sebastian COE	GBR	3:38.40
1984	Sebastian COE	GBR	3:32.53
1988	Peter RONO	KEN	3:35.96
1992	Fermin CACHO RUIZ	SPA	3:40.12
1996	Noureddine MORCELI	ALG	3:35.78
2000	Noah NGENY	KEN	3:32.07

5,000m

1912	Johan 'Hannes' KOLEHMAINEN	FIN	14:36.6
1920	Joseph GUILLEMOT	FRA	14:55.6
1924	Paavo NURMI	FIN	14:31.2
1928	Vilho 'Ville' RITOLA	FIN	14:38.0
1932	Lauri LEHTINEN	FIN	14:30.0
1936	Gunnar HÖCKERT	FIN	14:22.2
1948	Gaston REIFF	BEL	14:17.6

1952	Emil ZÀTOPEK	CZE	14:06.6
1956	Volodymyr KUTS	SOV	13:39.6
1960	Murray HALBERG	NZL	13:43.4
1964	Robert SCHUL	USA	13:48.8
1968	Mohamed GAMMOUDI	TUN	14:05.0
1972	Lasse VIREN	FIN	13:26.4
1976	Lasse VIREN	FIN	13:24.76
1980	Miruts YIFTER	ETH	13:20.91
1984	Said AOUITA	MOR	13:05.59
1988	John NGUGI	KEN	13:11.70
1992	Dieter BAUMANN	GER	13:12.52
1996	Venuste NIYONGABO	BRD	13:07.96
2000	Million WOLDE	ETH	13:35.49

5 MILES

| 1908 | Emil VOIGT | GBR | 25:11':2 |

10,000m

1912	Johan 'Hannes' KOLEHMAINEN	FIN	31:20.8
1920	Paavo NURMI	FIN	31:45.8
1924	Vilho 'Ville' RITOLA	FIN	30:23.2
1928	Paavo NURMI	FIN	30:18.8
1932	Janusz KUSOCINSKI	POL	30:11.4
1936	Ilmari SALMINEN	FIN	30:15.4
1948	Emil ZATOPEK	CZE	29:59.6
1952	Emil ZATOPEK	CZE	29:17.0
1956	Volodymyr KUTS	SOV	28:45.6
1960	Pyotr BOLOTNIKOV	SOV	28:32.2
1964	William MILLS	USA	28:24.4
1968	Naftali TEMU	KEN	29:27.4
1972	Lasse VIREN	FIN	27:38.4
1976	Lasse VIREN	FIN	27:40.38
1980	Miruts YIFTER	ETH	27:42.69
1984	Alberto COVA	ITA	27:47.54
1988	Brahim BOUTAYEB	MOR	27:21.46
1992	Khalid SKAH	MOR	27:46.70
1996	Haile GEBRSELASSIE	ETH	27:07.34
2000	Haile GEBRSELASSIE	ETH	27:18.20

MARATHON

1896	Spiridon LOUIS	GRE	2:58:50"
1900	Michel THEATO	FRA	2:59:45"
1904	Thomas HICKS	USA	3:28:53"
1908	John HAYES	USA	2:55:18.4
1912	Kenneth McARTHUR	SAF	2:36:54.8
1920	Johan 'Hannes' KOLEHMAINEN	FIN	2:32:35.8
1924	Albin STENROOS	FIN	2:41:22.6
1928	Mohamed Boughera EL OUAFI	FRA	2:32:57"
1932	Juan Carlos ZABALA	ARG	2:31:36"
1936	SON Kitei (SOHN Kee-Chung)	JAP	2:29:19"
1948	Delfo CABRERA	ARG	2:34:51.6
1952	Emil ZATOPEK	CZE	2:23:03.2
1956	Alain MIMOUN	FRA	2:25:00"
1960	Abebe BIKILA	ETH	2:15:16.2
1964	Abebe BIKILA	ETH	2:12:11.2
1968	Mamo WOLDE	ETH	2:20:26.4
1972	Frank SHORTER	USA	2:12:19.8
1976	Waldemar CIERPINSKI	GDR	2h09:55.0
1980	Waldemar CIERPINSKI	GDR	2:11:03"
1984	Carlos LOPES	POR	2h09:21"
1988	Gelindo BORDIN	ITA	2:10:32"
1992	HWANG Young-cho	KOR	2:13:23"
1996	Josia THUGWANE	SAF	2:12:36"
2000	Gezhange ABERA	ETH	2:10:11"

110m HURDLES

1896	Thomas CURTIS	USA	17.6
1900	Alvin KRAENZLEIN	USA	15.4
1904	Frederick SCHULE	USA	16.0
1908	Forrest SMITHSON	USA	15.0
1912	Frederick KELLY	USA	15.1

1920	Earl THOMSON	CAN	14.8
1924	Daniel KINSEY	USA	15.0
1928	Sydney ATKINSON	SAF	14.8
1932	George SALING	USA	14.6
1936	Forrest TOWNS	USA	14.2
1948	William PORTER	USA	13.9
1952	Harrison DILLARD	USA	13.7
1956	Lee CALHOUN	USA	13.5
1960	Lee CALHOUN	USA	13.8
1964	Hayes JONES	USA	13.6
1968	Willie DAVENPORT	USA	13.33
1972	Rodney MILBURN	USA	13.24
1976	Guy DRUT	FRA	13.30
1980	Thomas MUNKELT	GDR	13.39
1984	Roger KINGDOM	USA	13.20
1988	Roger KINGDOM	USA	12.98
1992	Mark McKOY	CAN	13.12
1996	Allen JOHNSON	USA	12.95
2000	Anier GARCIA	CUB	13.00

200m HURDLES

1900	Alvin KRAENZLEIN	USA	25.4
1904	Harry HILLMAN	USA	24.6

400m HURDLES

1900	John Walter TEWKSBURY	USA	57.6
1904	Harry HILLMAN	USA	53.0
1908	Charles BACON	USA	55.0
1920	Frank LOOMIS	USA	54.0
1924	Morgan TAYLOR	USA	52.6
1928	David George BURGHLEY	GBR	53.4
1932	Robert TISDALL	IRL	51.7
1936	Glenn HARDIN	USA	52.4
1948	Leroy COCHRAN	USA	51.1
1952	Charles MOORE	USA	50.8
1956	Glenn DAVIS	USA	50.1
1960	Glenn DAVIS	USA	49.3
1964	Warren CAWLEY	USA	49.6
1968	Dave HEMERY	GBR	48.12
1972	John AKII-BUA	UGA	47.82
1976	Edwin MOSES	USA	47':63
1980	Volker BECK	GDR	48':70
1984	Edwin MOSES	USA	47':75
1988	Andre PHILLIPPS	USA	47':19
1992	Kevin YOUNG	USA	46':78
1996	Derrick ADKINS	USA	47':54
2000	Angelo TAYLOR	USA	47':50

3,000m STEEPLECHASE

1900	George ORTON (2590m)	CAN	7:34.4
1904	James LIGHTBODY (2590m)	USA	7:39.6
1908	Arthur RUSSELL (3200m)	GBR	10:47.8
1920	Percy HODGE	GBR	10:00.4
1924	Ville "Vilho" RITOLA	FIN	9:33.6
1928	Toivo LOUKOLA	FIN	9:21.8
1932	Volmari ISO-HOLLO (3460m)	FIN	10:33.4
1936	Volmari ISO-HOLLO	FIN	9:03.8
1948	Thore SJÖSTRAND	SWE	9:04.6
1952	Horace ASHENFELTER	USA	8:45.4
1956	Christopher BRASHER	GBR	8:41.2
1960	Zdzislaw KRZYSZKOWIAK	POL	8:34.2
1964	Gaston ROELANTS	BEL	8:30.8
1968	Amos BIWOTT	KEN	8:51.0
1972	Kipchoge KEINO	KEN	8:23.6
1976	Anders GÄRDERUD	SWE	8:08.2
1980	Bronislaw MALINOWSKI	POL	8:09.7
1984	Julius KORIR	KEN	8:11.80
1988	Julius KARIUKI	KEN	8:05.51
1992	Matthew BIRIR	KEN	8:08':84
1996	Joseph KETER	KEN	8:07.12
2000	Reuben KOSGEI	KEN	8:21.43

4,000m STEEPLECHASE

1900	John RIMMER	GBR	12:58.4

CROSS COUNTRY

1912	Johan 'Hannes' KOLEHMAINEN	FIN	45:11.6
1920	Paavo NURMI	FIN	27:15.0
1924	Paavo NURMI	FIN	32:54.8

CROSS COUNTRY (TEAM)

1912	SWE

1920	FIN
1924	FIN

3km (TEAM)

1912	USA
1920	USA
1924	FIN

5km (TEAM)

1900	GBR/AUS

3 MILES (TEAM)

1908	GBR

4 MILES (TEAM)

1904	USA

4x100m

1912	GBR	42.4
1920	USA	42.2
1924	USA	41.0
1928	USA	41.0
1932	USA	40.0
1936	USA	39.8
1948	USA	40.6
1952	USA	40.1
1956	USA	39.5
1960	GER	39.5
1964	USA	39.0
1968	USA	38.24
1972	USA	38.19
1976	USA	38.33
1980	SOV	38.26
1984	USA	37.83
1988	SOV	38.19
1992	USA	37.40
1996	CAN	37.69
2000	USA	37.61

4x400m (200+200+400+800m in 1908)

1908	USA	3:29.4
1912	USA	3:16.6
1920	GBR	3:22.2
1924	USA	3:16.0
1928	USA	3:14.2
1932	USA	3:08.2
1936	GBR	3:09.0
1948	USA	3:10.4
1952	JAM	3:03.9
1956	USA	3:04.8
1960	USA	3:02.2
1964	USA	3:00.7
1968	USA	2:56.16
1972	KEN	2:59.83
1976	USA	2:58.65
1980	SOV	3:01.08
1984	USA	2:57.91
1988	USA	2:56.16
1992	USA	2:55.74
1996	USA	2:55.99
2000	USA	2:56.35

HIGH JUMP

1896	Ellery CLARK	USA	1,81 m
1900	Irving BAXTER	USA	1,90m
1904	Samuel JONES	USA	1,80m
1908	Harry PORTER	USA	1,90m
1912	Alma RICHARDS	USA	1,93 m
1920	Richmond LANDON	USA	1,93 m
1924	Harold OSBORN	USA	1,98 m
1928	Robert KING	USA	1,94 m
1932	Duncan McNAUGHTON	CAN	1,97 m
1936	Cornelius JOHNSON	USA	2,03 m
1948	John WINTER	AUS	1,98 m
1952	Walter DAVIS	USA	2,04 m
1956	Charles DUMAS	USA	2,12 m
1960	Robert SHAVLAKADZE	SOV	2,16 m
1964	Valery BRUMEL	SOV	2,18 m
1968	Richard FOSBURY	USA	2,24 m
1972	Juri TARMAK	SOV	2,23 m
1976	Jacek WSZOLA	POL	2,25m
1980	Gerd WESSIG	GDR	2,36 m
1984	Dietmar MÖGENBURG	GER	2,35 m
1988	Gennadi AVDEÏENKO	SOV	2,38 m
1992	Javier SOTOMAYOR	CUB	2,34 m
1996	Charles AUSTIN	USA	2,39 m
2000	Serguei KLIUGIN	RUS	2,35 m

STANDING HIGH JUMP

1900	Raymond 'Ray' EWRY	USA	1,65 m
1904	Raymond 'Ray' EWRY	USA	1,50 m
1908	Raymond 'Ray' EWRY	USA	1,57 m
1912	Platt ADAMS	USA	1,63 m

LONG JUMP

1896	Ellery CLARK	USA	6,35 m
1900	Alvin KRAENZLEIN	USA	7,18 m
1904	Meyer PRINSTEIN	USA	7,34 m
1908	Francis IRONS	USA	7,48 m
1912	Albert GUTTERSON	USA	7,60m
1920	William PETERSSON	SWE	7,15 m
1924	William HUBBARD	USA	7,44 m
1928	Edward HAMM	USA	7,73 m
1932	Edward GORDON	USA	7,64 m
1936	James 'Jesse' OWENS	USA	8,06 m
1948	Willie STEELE	USA	7,82 m
1952	Jerome BIFFLE	USA	7,57 m
1956	Gregory BELL	USA	7,83 m
1960	Ralph BOSTON	USA	8,12 m
1964	Lynn DAVIES	GBR	8,07 m
1968	Bob BEAMON	USA	8,90 m
1972	Randy WILLIAMS	USA	8,24 m
1976	Clarence 'Arnie' ROBINSON	USA	8,35 m
1980	Lutz DOMBROWSKI	GDR	8,54 m
1984	Carl LEWIS	USA	8,54 m
1988	Carl LEWIS	USA	8,72 m
1992	Carl LEWIS	USA	8,67 m
1996	Carl LEWIS	USA	8,50 m
2000	Ivan PEDROSO	CUB	8,55 m

STANDING LONG JUMP

1900	Raymond 'Ray' EWRY	USA	3,30m
1904	Raymond 'Ray' EWRY	USA	3,47 m
1908	Raymond 'Ray' EWRY	USA	3,33 m
1912	Konstantinos TSIKLITIRAS	GRE	3,37 m

TRIPLE JUMP

1896	James CONNOLLY	USA	13,71 m
1900	Meyer PRINSTEIN	USA	14,47 m
1904	Meyer PRINSTEIN	USA	14,35 m
1908	Timothy AHEARNE	GBR	14,92 m
1912	Gustaf LINDBLOM	SWE	14,76 m
1920	Vilho TUULOS	FIN	14,50m
1924	Anthony WINTER	AUS	15,52 m
1928	Mikio ODA	JAP	15,21 m
1932	Chuhei NAMBU	JAP	15,72 m
1936	Naoto TAJIMA	JAP	16,00m
1948	Arne AHMAN	SWE	15,40m
1952	Adhemar FERREIRA DA SILVA	BRA	16,22 m
1956	Adhemar FERREIRA DA SILVA	BRA	16,35 m
1960	Józef SCHMIDT	POL	16,81 m
1964	Józef SCHMIDT	POL	16,85 m
1968	Viktor SANEEV	SOV	17,39 m
1972	Viktor SANEEV	SOV	17,35 m
1976	Viktor SANEEV	SOV	17,29 m
1980	Jaak UUDMÄE	SOV	17,35 m
1984	Al JOYNER	USA	17,26 m
1988	Kristo MARKOV	BUL	17,61 m
1992	Mike CONLEY	USA	18,17 m
1996	Kenny HARRISON	USA	18,09 m
2000	Jonathan EDWARDS	GBR	17,71 m

STANDING TRIPLE JUMP

1900	Raymond 'Ray' EWRY	USA	10,58 m
1904	Raymond "Ray" EWRY	USA	10,54 m

POLE VAULT

1896	William HOYT	USA	3,30m
1900	Irving BAXTER	USA	3,30m
1904	Charles DVORAK	USA	3,50m
1908	Alfred GILBERT	USA	3,71m
	Edward COOKE	USA	3,71 m
1912	Harry BABCOCK	USA	3,95m

1920	Frank FOSS	USA	4,09m
1924	Lee BARNES	USA	3,95m
1928	Sabin CARR	USA	4,20m
1932	William MILLER	USA	4,31m
1936	Earle MEADOWS	USA	4,35m
1948	Owen Guinn SMITH	USA	4,30m
1952	Robert RICHARDS	USA	4,55 m
1956	Robert RICHARDS	USA	4,56 m
1960	Donald BRAGG	USA	4,70m
1964	Frederick HANSEN	USA	5,10m
1968	Robert SEAGREN	USA	5,40m
1972	Wolfgang NORDWIG	GDR	5,50m
1976	Tadeusz SLUSARSKI	POL	5,50m
1980	Wladyslaw KOZAKIEWICZ	POL	5,78 m
1984	Pierre QUINON	FRA	5,75 m
1988	Serguei BUBKA	SOV	5,90m
1992	Maksim TARASOV	RUS	5,80m
1996	Jean GALFIONE	FRA	5,92 m
2000	Nick HYSONG	USA	5,90m

SHOT PUT

1896	Robert GARRETT	USA	11,22 m
1900	Richard SHELDON	USA	14,10m
1904	Ralph ROSE	USA	14,81 m
1908	Ralph ROSE	USA	14,21 m
1912	Patrick McDONALD	USA	15,34 m
1920	Frans Wilhelm PÖRHÖLA	FIN	14,81 m
1924	Clarence HOUSER	USA	14,99 m
1928	John KUCK	USA	15,87 m
1932	Leo SEXTON	USA	16,00m
1936	Hans WOELLKE	GER	16,20m
1948	Wilbur THOMPSON	USA	17,12 m
1952	Parry O'BRIEN	USA	17,41 m
1956	Parry O'BRIEN	USA	18,57 m
1960	William NIEDER	USA	19,68 m
1964	Dallas LONG	USA	20,33 m
1968	James Randel MATSON	USA	20,54 m
1972	Wladyslaw KOMAR	POL	21,18 m
1976	Udo BEYER	GDR	21,05 m
1980	Vladimir KISSELIOV	SOV	21,35 m
1984	Alessandro ANDREI	ITA	21,26 m
1988	Ulf TIMMERMANN	GDR	22,47 m
1992	Michael STULCE	USA	21,70 m
1996	Randy BARNES	USA	21,62 m
2000	Arsi HARJU	FIN	21,29 m

SHOT PUT 25,4kg

1904	Etienne DESHAMMER	CAN	10,46 m
1920	Patrick McDONALD	USA	11,26 m

SHOT PUT (BOTH HANDS)

1912	Ralph ROSE	USA	27,70 m

DISCUS

1896	Robert GARRETT	USA	29,15 m
1900	Rudolf BAUER	HUN	36,04 m
1904	Martin SHERIDAN	USA	39,28 m
1908	Martin SHERIDAN	USA	40,89 m
1912	Armas TAIPALE	FIN	45,21m
1920	Elmer NIKLANDER	FIN	44,68 m
1924	Clarence HOUSER	USA	46,15 m
1928	Clarence HOUSER	USA	47,32 m
1932	John ANDERSON	USA	49,49 m
1936	Kenneth CARPENTER	USA	50,48 m
1948	Adolfo CONSOLINI	ITA	52,78 m
1952	Sim INESS	USA	55,03 m
1956	Alfred 'Al' OERTER	USA	56,36 m
1960	Alfred 'Al' OERTER	USA	59,18 m
1964	Alfred 'Al' OERTER	USA	61,00 m
1968	Alfred 'Al' OERTER	USA	64,78 m
1972	Ludvik DANEK	CZE	64,40m
1976	Maurice 'Mac' WILKINS	USA	67,50 m
1980	Viktor RASCHUPKIN	SOV	66,64 m
1984	Rolf DANNEBERG	GER	66,60m
1988	Jürgen SCHULT	GDR	68,82m
1992	Romas UBARTAS	LIT	65,12m
1996	Lars RIEDEL	GER	69,40m
2000	Virgilijus ALEKNA	LIT	69,30m

DISCUS (GREEK STYLE)

1908	Martin SHERIDAN	USA	38,00m

DISCUS (BOTH MAINS)

1912	Armas TAIPALE	FIN	82,86 m

JAVELIN

1908	Eric LEMMING	SWE	54,83 m
1912	Eric LEMMING	SWE	60,64 m
1920	Jonni MYYRA	FIN	65,78 m
1924	Jonni MYYRA	FIN	62,96 m
1928	Erik LUNDQVIST	SWE	66,60m
1932	Matti JÄRVINEN	FIN	72,71 m
1936	Gerhard STÖCK	GER	71,84 m
1948	Kaj Tapio RAUTAVAARA	FIN	69,77 m
1952	Cyrus YOUNG	USA	73,78 m
1956	Egil DANIELSEN	NOR	85,71 m
1960	Viktor TSIBULENKO	SOV	84,64 m
1964	Pauli NEVALA	FIN	82,66 m
1968	Janis LUSIS	SOV	90,10m
1972	Klaus WOLFERMANN	GER	90,48 m
1976	Miklos NEMETH	HUN	94,58 m
1980	Dainis KULA	SOV	91,20m
1984	Arto HÄRKÖNEN	FIN	86,76 m
1988	Tapio KORJUS	FIN	84,28 m
1992	Jan ZELEZNY	CZE	89,66 m
1996	Jan ZELEZNY	CZE	88,16 m
2000	Jan ZELEZNY	CZE	90,17 m

JAVELIN (FREESTYLE)

1908	Eric LEMMING	SWE	54,45 m

JAVELIN (BOTH HANDS)

1912	Juho SAARISTO	FIN	109,42 m

HAMMER

1900	John FLANAGAN	USA	51,01 m
1904	John FLANAGAN	USA	51,23 m
1908	John FLANAGAN	USA	51,92 m
1912	Matthew McGRATH	USA	54,74 m
1920	Patrick RYAN	USA	52,87 m
1924	Frederick TOOTELL	USA	53,29 m
1928	Patrick O'CALLAGHAN	IRL	51,39 m
1932	Patrick O'CALLAGHAN	IRL	53,92 m
1936	Karl HEIN	GER	56,49 m
1948	Imre NEMETH	HUN	56,07 m
1952	Jozsef CSERMAK	HUN	60,34 m
1956	Harold CONNOLLY	USA	63,19 m
1960	Vassil RUDENKOV	SOV	67,10m
1964	Romuald KLIM	SOV	69,74 m
1968	Gyula ZSIVÓTZKY	HUN	73,36 m
1972	Anatoli BONDARCHUK	SOV	75,50m
1976	Juri SEDYKH	SOV	77,52 m
1980	Juri SEDYKH	SOV	81,80m
1984	Juha TIAINEN	FIN	78,08 m
1988	Serguei LITVINOV	SOV	84,80m
1992	Andrei ABDUVALIEV	TJK	82,54 m
1996	Balazs KISS	HUN	81,24 m
2000	Szymon ZIOLKOWSKI	POL	80,02 m

TRIATHLON

1904	Max EMMERICH	USA	35,7 pts

PENTATHLON

1912	James THORPE	USA	7 places
1920	Eero LEHTONEN	FIN	14 places
1924	Eero LEHTONEN	FIN	14 places

DECATHLON

1904	Thomas KIELY	GBR	6036 pts
1912	James THORPE	USA	8412 pts
1920	Helge LÖVLAND	NOR	6804 pts
1924	Harold OSBORN	USA	7711 pts
1928	Paavo YRJÖLÄ	FIN	8053 pts
1932	James BAUSCH	USA	8462 pts
1936	Glenn MORRIS	USA	7900 pts
1948	Robert MATHIAS	USA	7139 pts
1952	Robert MATHIAS	USA	7887 pts
1956	Milton CAMPBELL	USA	7937 pts
1960	Rafer JOHNSON	USA	8392 pts
1964	Willi HOLDORF	GER	7887 pts
1968	William TOOMEY	USA	8193 pts
1972	Nikolai AVILOV	SOV	8454 pts
1976	Bruce JENNER	USA	8618 pts

1980	Francis 'Daley' THOMPSON	GBR	8495 pts
1984	Francis 'Daley' THOMPSON	GBR	8798 pts
1988	Christian SCHENK	GDR	8488 pts
1992	Robert ZMELIK	CZE	8611 pts
1996	Dan O'BRIEN	USA	8824 pts
2000	Erki NOOL	EST	8641 pts

3km WALK

1920	Ugo FRIGERIO	ITA	13:14.2

3.5km WALK

1908	George LARNER	GBR	14:55.0

10km WALK

1912	George GOULDING	CAN	46:28.4
1920	Ugo FRIGERIO	ITA	48:06.2
1924	Ugo FRIGERIO	ITA	47:49.0
1948	John MIKAELSSON	SWE	45:13.2
1952	John MIKAELSSON	SWE	45:02.8

10 MILES WALK

1908	George LARNER	GBR	1:15:57.4

20km WALK

1956	Leonid SPIRIN	SOV	1:31:27.4
1960	Vladimir GOLUBNICHYI	SOV	1:34:07.2
1964	Kenneth MATTHEWS	GBR	1:29:34.0
1968	Vladimir GOLUBNICHYI	SOV	1:33:58.4
1972	Peter FRENKEL	GDR	1:26:42.4
1976	Daniel BAUTISTA	MEX	1:24:40.6
1980	Maurizio DAMILANO	ITA	1:23:35.5
1984	Ernesto CANTO	MEX	1:23:13
1988	Josef PRIBILINEC	CZE	1:19:57
1992	Daniel PLAZA	SPA	1:21:45
1996	Jefferson PEREZ	ECU	1:20:07
2000	Robert KORZENIOWSKI	POL	1:18:59

50km WALK

1932	Thomas GREEN	GBR	4:50:10
1936	Harold WHITLOCK	GBR	4:30:41.4
1948	John LJUNGGREN	SWE	4:41:52"
1952	Giuseppe DORDONI	ITA	4:28:07.8
1956	Norman READ	NZL	4:30:42.8
1960	Donald THOMPSON	GBR	4:25:30.0
1964	Abdon PAMICH	ITA	4:11:12.4
1968	Christoph HÖHNE	GDR	4:20:13.6
1972	Bernd KANNENBERG	GER	3:56:11.6
1980	Hartwig GAUDER	GDR	3:49:24
1984	Raul GONZALEZ	MEX	3:47:26
1988	Viatcheslav IVANIENKO	SOV	3:38:29
1992	Andrei PERLOV	RUS	3:50:13
1996	Robert KORZENIOWSKI	POL	3:43:30
2000	Robert KORZENIOWSKI	POL	3:42:22

ATHLETICS (WOMEN)

100m

1928	Elizabeth ROBINSON	USA	12.2
1932	Stanislawa WALASIEWICZ	POL	11.9
1936	Helen STEPHENS	USA	11.5
1948	Francina 'Fanny' BLANKERS-KOEN	NED	11.9
1952	Marjorie JACKSON	AUS	11.5
1956	Elizabeth CUTHBERT	AUS	11.5
1960	Wilma RUDOLPH	USA	11.0
1964	Wyomia TYUS	USA	11.4
1968	Wyomia TYUS	USA	11.08
1972	Renate STECHER	GDR	11.07
1976	Annegret RICHTER	GER	11.08
1980	Ludmila KONDRATIEVA	SOV	11.06
1984	Evelyn ASHFORD	USA	10.97
1988	Florence GRIFFITH-JOYNER	USA	10.54
1992	Gail DEVERS	USA	10.82
1996	Gail DEVERS	USA	10.94
2000	Marion JONES	USA	10.75

200m

1948	Francina 'Fanny' BLANKERS-KOEN	NED	24.4
1952	Marjorie JACKSON	AUS	23.7
1956	Elizabeth CUTHBERT	AUS	23.4

1960	Wilma RUDOLPH	USA	24.0
1964	Edith McGUIRE	USA	23.0
1968	Irena SZEWINSKA (KIRSZENSTEIN)	POL	22.58
1972	Renate STECHER	GDR	22.40
1976	Bärbel WÖCKEL (ECKERT)	GDR	22.37
1980	Bärbel WÖCKEL (ECKERT)	GDR	22.03
1984	Valérie BRISCO-HOOKS	USA	21.81
1988	Florence GRIFFITH-JOYNER	USA	21.34
1992	Gwen TORRENCE	USA	21.81
1996	Marie-José PEREC	FRA	22.12
2000	Marion JONES	USA	21.84

400m

1964	Elizabeth CUTHBERT	AUS	52.0
1968	Colette BESSON	FRA	52.03
1972	Monika ZEHRT	GDR	51.08
1976	Irena SZEWINSKA (KIRSZENSTEIN)	POL	49.28
1980	Marita KOCH	GDR	48.88
1984	Valérie BRISCO-HOOKS	USA	48.83
1988	Olga BRYZGINA	SOV	48.65
1992	Marie-José PEREC	FRA	48.83
1996	Marie-José PEREC	FRA	48.25
2000	Cathy FREEMAN	AUS	49.11

800m

1928	Karoline RADKE	GER	2:16.8
1960	Ludmila CHEVTSOVA	SOV	2:04.3
1964	Ann PACKER	GBR	2:01.1
1968	Madeline MANNING	USA	2:00.9
1972	Hildegard FALCK	GER	1:58.6
1976	Tatiana KAZANKINA	SOV	1:54.94
1980	Nadezda OLIZARENKO	SOV	1:53.43
1984	Doina MELINTE	ROM	1:57.60
1988	Sigrun WODARS	GDR	1:56.10
1992	Ellen VAN LANGEN	NED	1:55.54
1996	Svetlana MASTERKOVA	RUS	1:57.73
2000	Maria MUTOLA	MOZ	1:56.15

1500m

1972	Ludmila BRAGINA	SOV	4:01.4
1976	Tatiana KAZANKINA	SOV	4:05.48
1980	Tatiana KAZANKINA	SOV	3:56.6
1984	Gabriella DORIO	ITA	4:03.27
1988	Paula IVAN	ROM	3:53.96
1992	Hassiba BOULMERKA	ALG	3:55.30
1996	Svetlana MASTERKOVA	RUS	4:00.83
2000	Nouria MERAH-BENIDA	ALG	4:05.10

3,000m

1984	Maricica PUICA	ROM	8:35.96
1988	Tatiana SAMOLENKO	SOV	8:26.53
1992	Yelena ROMANOVA	RUS	8:46.04

5,000m

1996	WANG Junxia	CHN	14:59.88
2000	Gabriela SZABO	ROM	14:40.79

10,000m

1988	Olga BONDARENKO	SOV	31:05.21
1992	Derartu TULU	ETH	31:06.02
1996	Fernanda RIBEIRO	POR	31:01.63
2000	Derartu TULU	ETH	30:17.49

MARATHON

1984	Joan BENOIT	USA	2:24:52
1988	Rosa MOTA	POR	2:25:40
1992	Valentina EGOROVA	RUS	2:32:41
1996	Fatuma ROBA	ETH	2:26:05
2000	Naoko TAKAHASHI	JAP	2:23:14

80m HURDLES

1932	Midred 'Babe' DIDRIKSON	USA	11:7
1936	Trebisonda VALLA	ITA	11:7
1948	Francina 'Fanny' BLANKERS-KOEN	NED	11:2
1952	Shirley STRICKLAND DE LA HUNTY	AUS	10:9
1956	Shirley STRICKLAND DE LA HUNTY	AUS	10:7
1960	Irina PRESS	SOV	10:8
1964	Karin BALZER	GDR	10:5
1968	Maureen CAIRD	AUS	10:39

100m HURDLES

1972	Anneliese ERHARDT	GDR	12:59
1976	Johanna SCHALLER	GDR	12:77
1980	Vera KOMISOVA	SOV	12:56
1984	Benita FITZGERALD-BROWN	USA	12.84
1988	Yordanka DONKOVA	BUL	12.38
1992	Paraskevi PATOULIDOU	GRE	12.64
1996	Ludmila ENGQUIST	SWE	12.58
2000	Olga SHISHIGINA	KAZ	12.65

400m HURDLES

1984	Nawal EL MOUTAWAKEL	MOR	54.61
1988	Deborah FLINTOFF-KING	AUS	53.17
1992	Sally GUNNELL	GBR	53.23
1996	Deon HEMMINGS	JAM	52.82
2000	Irina PRIVALOVA	RUS	53.02

HIGH JUMP

1928	Ethel CATHERWOOD	CAN	1,59 m
1932	Jean SHILEY	USA	1,65 m
1936	Ibolya CSAK	HUN	1,60m
1948	Alice COACHMAN	USA	1,68 m
1952	Esther BRAND	SAF	1,67 m
1956	Mildred MCDANIEL	USA	1,76 m
1960	Iolanda BALAS	ROM	1,85 m
1964	Iolanda BALAS	ROM	1,90m
1968	Miloslava REZKOVA	CZE	1,82 m
1972	Ulrike MEYFARTH	GER	1,92 m
1976	Rosemarie ACKERMANN (WITSCHAS)	GDR	1,93 m
1980	Sara SIMEONI	ITA	1,97 m
1984	Ulrike MEYFARTH	GER	2,02 m
1988	Louise RITTER	USA	2,01 m
1992	Heike HENKEL	GER	2,02 m
1996	Stefka KOSTADINOVA	BUL	2,05 m
2000	Yelena ELESINA	RUS	2,01 m

LONG JUMP

1948	Olga GYARMATI	HUN	5,69 m
1952	Yvette WILLIAMS	NZL	6,24 m
1956	Elzbieta KRZESINSKA	POL	6,35 m
1960	Vera KREPKINA	SOV	6,37 m
1964	Mary RAND (BIGNAL)	GBR	6,76 m
1968	Viorica VISCOPOLEANU	ROM	6,82 m
1972	Heidemarie ROSENDHAL	GER	6,78 m
1976	Angela VOIGT	GDR	6,72 m
1980	Tatiana KOLPAKOVA	SOV	7,06 m
1984	Anisoara CUSMIR-STANCIU	ROM	6,96 m
1988	Jackie JOYNER-KERSEE	USA	7,40m
1992	Heike DRECHSLER (DAUTE)	GER	7,14 m
1996	Chioma AJUNWA	NGA	7,12 m
2000	Heike DRECHSLER (DAUTE)	GER	6,99 m

TRIPLE JUMP

1996	Inessa KRAVETS	UKR	15,33 m
2000	Teresa MARINOVA	BUL	15,20m

POLE VAULT

2000	Stacy DRAGILA	USA	4,60m

SHOT PUT

1948	Micheline OSTERMEYER	FRA	13,75 m
1952	Galina ZYBINA	SOV	15,28 m
1956	Tamara TYCHKEVITCH	SOV	16,59 m
1960	Tamara PRESS	SOV	17,32 m
1964	Tamara PRESS	SOV	18,14 m
1968	Margitta GUMMEL (HELMBOLDT)	GDR	19,61 m
1972	Nadezda TCHIZOVA	SOV	21,03 m
1976	Ivanka CHRISTOVA	BUL	21,16 m
1980	Ilona SLUPIANEK (SCHOKNECHT)	GDR	22,41 m
1984	Claudia LOSCH	GER	20,48 m
1988	Natalia LISSOVSKAÏA	SOV	22,24 m
1992	Svetlana KRIVELIOVA	RUS	21,06 m
1996	Astrid KUMBERNUSS	GER	20,56 m
2000	Yanina KOROLCHIK	BLR	20,56 m

DISCUS

1928	Halina KONOPACKA	POL	39,62 m
1932	Lillian COPELAND	USA	40,58 m
1936	Gisela MAUERMAYER	GER	47,63 m
1948	Micheline OSTERMEYER	FRA	41,92 m
1952	Nina ROMASHKOVA	SOV	51,42 m
1956	Olga FIKOTOVA	CZE	53,69 m
1960	Nina PONOMARIEVA (ROMASHKOVA)	SOV	55,10m
1964	Tamara PRESS	SOV	57,27 m
1968	Lia MANOLIU	ROM	58,28 m
1972	Faina MELNIK	SOV	66,62 m
1976	Evelin SCHLAAK	GDR	69,00m
1980	Evelin JAHL (SCHLAAK)	GDR	69,96 m
1984	Ria STALMAN	NED	72,30m
1988	Martina HELLMANN	GDR	72,30m
1992	Maritza MARTEN	CUB	70,06 m
1996	Ilke WYLUDDA	GER	69,66 m
2000	Ellina ZVEREVA	BLR	68,40m

JAVELIN

1932	Mildred 'Babe' DIDRIKSON	USA	43,68 m
1936	Tilly FLEISCHER	GER	45,18 m
1948	Hermine BAUMA	AUT	45,57 m
1952	Dana ZATOPKOVA (INGROVA)	CZE	50,47 m
1956	Inese JAUNZEME	SOV	53,86 m
1960	Elvira OZOLINA	SOV	55,98 m
1964	Mihaela PENES	ROM	60,54 m
1968	Angela NEMETH	HUN	60,36 m
1972	Ruth FUCHS	GDR	63,88 m
1976	Ruth FUCHS	GDR	65,94 m
1980	Maria RUENES	CUB	68,40 m
1984	Theresa 'Tessa' SANDERSON	GBR	69,56 m
1988	Petra FELKE	GDR	74,68 m
1992	Silke RENK	GER	68,34 m
1996	Heli RANTANEN	FIN	67,94 m
2000	Else 'Trine' HATTESTAD	NOR	68,91 m

HAMMER

2000	Kamila SKOLIMOWSKA	POL	71,16 m

PENTATHLON

1964	Irina PRESS	SOV	5246 pts
1968	Ingrid BECKER	GER	5098 pts
1972	Mary PETERS	GBR	4801 pts
1976	Siegrun SIEGL	GDR	4745 pts
1980	Nadezda TKATCHENKO	SOV	5083 pts

HEPTATHLON

1984	Glynis NUNN	AUS	6390 pts
1988	Jackie JOYNER-KERSEE	USA	7291 pts
1992	Jackie JOYNER-KERSEE	USA	7044 pts
1996	Ghada SHOUAA	SYR	6780 pts
2000	Denise LEWIS	GBR	6584 pts

4x100m

1928	CAN	48.4
1932	USA	46.9
1936	USA	46.9
1948	NED	47.5
1952	USA	45.9
1956	AUS	44.5
1960	USA	44.5
1964	POL	43.6
1968	USA	42.88
1972	GER	42.81
1976	GDR	42.55
1980	GDR	41.60
1984	USA	41.65
1988	USA	41.98
1992	USA	42.11
1996	USA	41.95
2000	BAH	41.95

4x400m

1972	GDR	3:22.95
1976	GDR	3:19.23
1980	SOV	3:20.20
1984	USA	3:18.29
1988	SOV	3:15.17
1992	SOV	3:20.20
1996	USA	3:20.91
2000	USA	3:22.62

10km WALK

1992	CHEN Yueling	CHN	44:32
1996	Yelena NIKOLAIEVA	RUS	41:49

20km WALK

2000	WANG Liping	CHN	1:29:05

ARCHERY (MEN)

INDIVIDUAL

1972	John WILLIAMS	USA
1976	Darell PACE	USA
1980	Tomi POIKOLAINEN	FIN
1984	Darell PACE	USA
1988	Jay BARRS	USA
1992	Sebastien FLUTE	FRA
1996	Justin HUISH	USA
2000	Simon FAIRWEATHER	AUS

TEAM (60 yards)

1904	USA

TEAM

1988	KOR
1992	ESP
1996	USA
2000	KOR

YORK ROUND (100, 80, 60 yards)

1908	William DOD	GBR

CONTINENTAL STYLE (50m)

1908	Eugène GRISOT	FRA

FIXED BIRD TARGET
(SMALL BIRDS)

1920	Edouard VAN MOER	BEL

FIXED BIRD TARGET
(LARGE BIRDS)

1920	Edmond CLOETENS	BEL

FIXED BIRD TARGET TEAM
(SMALL & LARGE BIRDS)

1920	BEL

POLE TARGETS (28m)

1920	Hubert VAN INNIS	BEL

POLE TARGETS TEAM
(28m)

1920	HOL

POLE TARGETS (33m)

1920	Hubert VAN INNIS	BEL

POLE TARGETS (33m)
TEAM

1920	BEL

POLE TARGETS (50m)

1920	Julien BRULÉ	FRA

POLE TARGETS (50m)
TEAM

1920	BEL

SUR LA PERCHE A LA HERSE
(156m)

1900	Emmanuel FOULON	BEL

SUR LA PERCHE A LA PYRAMIDE
(156m)

1900	Emile GRUMIAUX	FRA

AU CHAPELET (33m)

1900	Hubert VAN INNIS	BEL

AU CHAPELET (50m)

1900	Eugène MOUGIN	FRA

AU CORDON DORE (33m)

1900	Hubert VAN INNIS	BEL

AU CORDON DORE (50m)

1900	Henri HÉROUIN	FRA

DOUBLE AMERICAN ROUND
(60, 50, 40 yards)

1904	George Phillip BRYANT	USA

DOUBLE YORK ROUND
(100, 80, 60 yards)

1904	George Phillip BRYANT	USA

ARCHERY (WOMEN)

INDIVIDUAL

1972	Doreen WILBER	USA
1976	Luann RYON	USA
1980	Keto LOSABERIDZE	SOV
1984	SEO Hyang-soon	KOR
1988	KIM Soo-nyung	KOR
1992	CHO Youn-jeong	KOR
1996	KIM Kyung-wook	KOR
2000	YUN Mi-jin	KOR

TEAM

1988	KOR
1992	KOR
1996	KOR
2000	KOR

DOUBLE COLUMBIA ROUND
(50, 40, 30 yards)

1904	Matilda HOWELL	USA

NATIONAL ROUND
(60, 50 yards)

1908	Sybill NEWALL	GBR

DOUBLE NATIONAL ROUND
(60, 50 yards)

1904	Matilda HOWELL	USA

BADMINTON (MEN)

SINGLES

1992	Alan BUDI KUSUMA	INA
1996	Poul-Erik HOYER-LARSEN	DEN
2000	JI Xinpeng	CHN

DOUBLES

1992	BUL
1996	INA
2000	INA

BADMINTON (WOMEN)

SINGLES

1992	Susi SUSANTI	INA
1996	BANG Soo-Hyun	KUR
2000	GONG Zinchao	CHN

DOUBLES

1992	KOR

1996	CHN
2000	CHN

MIXED DOUBLES

1996	KOR
2000	CHN

BASEBALL (MEN)

1992	CUB
1996	CUB
2000	USA

BASKETBALL (MEN)

1936	USA
1948	USA
1952	USA
1956	USA
1960	USA
1964	USA
1968	USA
1972	SOV
1976	USA
1980	YUG
1984	USA
1988	SOV
1992	USA
1996	USA
2000	USA

BASKETBALL (WOMEN)

1976	SOV
1980	SOV
1984	USA
1988	USA
1992	SOV
1996	USA
2000	USA

BOXING

Light-Flyweight (48kg)

1968	Francisco RODRIGUEZ	VEN
1972	György GEDÓ	HUN
1976	Jorge HERNÁNDEZ	CUB
1980	Shamil SABIROV	SOV
1984	Paul GONZALES	USA
1988	Ivailo CHRISTOV (I. HUSEÏNOV)	BUL
1992	Rogelio MARCELÓ GARCIA	CUB
1996	Daniel PETROV	BUL
2000	Brahim ASLOUM	FRA

Flyweight (51kg)

1904	George FINNEGAN	USA
1920	Frank DI GENARO	USA
1924	Fidel LA BARBA	USA
1928	Antal KOCSIS	HUN
1932	István ÉNEKES	HUN
1936	Willi KAISER	GER
1948	Pascual PÉREZ	ARG
1952	Nathan BROOKS	USA
1956	Terence SPINKS	GBR
1960	Gyula TÖRÖK	HUN
1964	Fernando ATZORI	ITA
1968	Ricardo DELGADO	MEX
1972	Georgi KOSTADINOV	BUL
1976	Leonard RANDOLPH	USA
1980	Petar LESSOV	BUL
1984	Steven Mc CRORY	USA
1988	KIM Kwang-sun	KOR
1992	CHOI Chol-su	PRK
1996	Maikro ROMERO	CUB
2000	Wijan PONLID	TIIA

Bantamweight (54kg)

1904	Oliver KIRK	USA
1908	Henry THOMAS	GBR

1920	Clarence WALKER	RSA
1924	William SMITH	RSA
1928	Vittorio TAMAGNINI	ITA
1932	Horace GWYNNE	CAN
1936	Ulderico SERGO	ITA
1948	Tibor CSIK	HUN
1952	Pentti HÄMÄLÄINEN	FIN
1956	Wolfgang BEHRENDT	GER
1960	Oleg GRIGORIEV	SOV
1964	Takao SAKURAI	JAP
1968	Valery SOKOLOV	SOV
1972	Orlando MARTINEZ	CUB
1976	GU Yong-jo	PRK
1980	Juan HERNÁNDEZ	CUB
1984	Maurizio STECCA	ITA
1988	Kennedy Mc KINNEY	USA
1992	Joel CASAMAYOR JOHNSON	CUB
1996	Istvan KOVACS	HUN
2000	Guillermo RIGONDEAUX	CUB

Featherweight (57kg)

1904	Oliver KIRK	USA
1908	Richard GUNN	GBR
1920	Paul FRITSCH	FRA
1924	John FIELDS	USA
1928	Lambertus VAN KLAVEREN	HOL
1932	Carmelo ROBLEDO	ARG
1936	Oscar CASANOVAS	ARG
1948	Ernesto FORMENTI	ITA
1952	Jan ZACHARA	CZE
1956	Vladimir SAFRONOV	SOV
1960	Francesco MUSSO	ITA
1964	Stanislav STEPACHKIN	SOV
1968	Antonio ROLDÁN	MEX
1972	Boris KUZNETSOV	SOV
1976	Angel HERRERA	CUB
1980	Rudi FINK	GDR
1984	Meldrick TAYLOR	USA
1988	Giovanni PARISI	ITA
1992	Andreas TEWS	GER
1996	Kamsing SOMLUCK	THA
2000	Bekzat SATTARKHANOV	KAZ

Lightweight (60kg)

1904	Harry SPANGER	USA
1908	Frederick GRACE	GBR
1920	Samuel MOSBERG	USA
1924	Hans NIELSEN	DAN
1928	Carlo ORLANDI	ITA
1932	Lawrence STEVENS	RSA
1936	Imre HARANGI	HUN
1948	Gerald DREYER	RSA
1952	Aureliano BOLOGNESI	ITA
1956	Richard Mc TAGGART	GBR
1960	Kazimierz PAZDZIOR	POL
1964	Józef GRUDZIEN	POL
1968	Ronald Woodson HARRIS	USA
1972	Jan SZCZEPANSKI	POL
1976	Howard DAVIS	USA
1980	Angel HERRERA	CUB
1984	Pernell WHITAKER	USA
1988	Andreas ZÜLOW	GDR
1992	Oscar DE LA HOYA	USA
1996	Hocine SOLTANI	ALG
2000	Mario KINDELAN	CUB

Light Welterweight (63.5kg)

1952	Charles ADKINS	USA
1956	Vladimir YENGIBARIAN	SOV
1960	Bohumil NEMECEK	CZE
1964	Jerzy KULEJ	POL
1968	Jerzy KULEJ	POL
1972	Ray SEALES	USA
1976	Ray 'Sugar' LEONARD	USA
1980	Patrizio OLIVA	ITA
1984	Jeremy PAGE	USA
1988	Viatcheslav YANOVSKI	SOV
1992	Héctor VINENT	CUB
1996	Héctor VINENT	CUB
2000	Mahammat Kadyz ABDULLAEV	UZB

Welterweight (67kg)

| 1904 | Albert YOUNG | USA |
| 1920 | Albert SCHNEIDER | CAN |

1924	Jean DELARGE	BEL
1928	Edward MORGAN	NZL
1932	Edward FLYNN	USA
1936	Sten SUVIO	FIN
1948	Julius TORMA	CZE
1952	Zygmund CHYCHLA	POL
1956	Nicolae LINCA	ROM
1960	Giovanni 'Nino' BENVENUTI	ITA
1964	Marian KASPRZYK	POL
1968	Manfred WOLKE	GDR
1972	Emilio CORREA	CUB
1976	Jochen BACHFELD	GDR
1980	Andrés ALDAMA	CUB
1984	Mark BRELAND	USA
1988	Robert WANGILA	KEN
1992	Michael CARRUTH	IRL
1996	Oleg SAITOV	RUS
2000	Oleg SAITOV	RUS

Light Middleweight (71kg)

1952	László PAPP	HUN
1956	László PAPP	HUN
1960	Wilbert Mc CLURE	USA
1964	Boris LAGUTIN	SOV
1968	Boris LAGUTIN	SOV
1972	Dieter KOTTYSCH	GER
1976	Jerzy RYBICKI	POL
1980	Armando MARTINEZ	CUB
1984	Frank TATE	USA
1988	PARK Si-hun	KOR
1992	Juan Carlos LEMUS	CUB
1996	David REID	USA
2000	Yermakhan IBRAIMOV	KAZ

Middleweight (75kg)

1904	Charles MAYER	USA
1908	John DOUGLAS	GBR
1920	Henry MALLIN	GBR
1924	Henry MALLIN	GBR
1928	Piero TOSCANI	ITA
1932	Carmen BARTH	USA
1936	Jean DESPEAUX	FRA
1948	László PAPP	HUN
1952	Floyd PATTERSON	USA
1956	Gennadi CHATKOV	SOV
1960	Edward CROOK	USA
1964	Valery POPENCHENKO	SOV
1968	Christopher FINNEGAN	GBR
1972	Viatcheslav LEMECHEV	SOV
1976	Michael SPINKS	USA
1980	José GÓMEZ	CUB
1984	SHIN Joon-sup	KOR
1988	Henry MASKE	GDR
1992	Ariel HERNÁNDEZ	CUB
1996	Ariel HERNÁNDEZ	CUB
2000	Jorge GUTIERREZ	CUB

Light-Heavyweight (81kg)

1920	Edward EAGAN	USA
1924	Harry MITCHELL	GBR
1928	Victor AVENDAÑO	ARG
1932	David CARSTENS	RSA
1936	Roger MICHELOT	FRA
1948	George HUNTER	RSA
1952	Norvel LEE	USA
1956	James BOYD	USA
1960	Cassius CLAY (Muhammad ALI)	USA
1964	Cosimo PINTO	ITA
1968	Dan POZNIAK	SOV
1972	Mate PARLOV	YUG
1976	Leon SPINKS	USA
1980	Slobodan KACAR	YUG
1984	Anton JOSIPOVIC	YUG
1988	Andrew MAYNARD	USA
1992	Torsten MAY	GER
1996	Vasili ZIROV	KAZ
2000	Alexander LEBZIAK	RUS

Heavyweight (91kg)

1984	Henry TILLMAN	USA
1988	Raymond MERCER	USA
1992	Félix SAVON	CUB
1996	Félix SAVON	CUB

| 2000 | Felix SAVÓN | CUB |

Super Heavyweight (Over 91kg)

1904	Samuel BERGER	USA
1908	Albert OLDMAM	GBR
1920	Ronald RAWSON	GBR
1924	Otto VON PORAT	NOR
1928	Arturo RODRIGUEZ	ARG
1932	Santiago LOVELL	ARG
1936	Herbert RUNGE	GER
1948	Rafael IGLESIAS	ARG
1952	Edward SANDERS	USA
1956	Peter RADEMACHER	USA
1960	Francesco De PICCOLI	ITA
1964	Joe FRAZIER	USA
1968	George FOREMAN	USA
1972	Teofilo STEVENSON	CUB
1976	Teofilo STEVENSON	CUB
1980	Teofilo STEVENSON	CUB
1984	Tyrell BIGGS	USA
1988	Lennox LEWIS	CAN
1992	Roberto BALADO	CUB
1996	Vladimir KLITCHKO	UKR
2000	Audley HARRISON	GBR

CANOEING (MEN)

500m CANADIAN SINGLES

1976	Alexander ROGOV	SOV
1980	Serguei POSTREKHIN	SOV
1984	Larry CAIN	CAN
1988	Olaf HEUKRODT	GDR
1992	Nikolai BUKHALOV	BUL
1996	Martin DOKTOR	CZE
2000	Gyorgy KOLONICS	HUN

500m CANADIAN PAIRS

1976	SOV
1980	HUN
1984	YUG
1988	SOV
1992	SOV
1996	HUN
2000	HUN

1000m CANADIAN SINGLES

1936	Francis AMYOT	CAN
1948	Josef HOLECEK	CZE
1952	Josef HOLECEK	CZE
1956	Leon ROTMAN	ROM
1960	János PARTI	HUN
1964	Jürgen ESCHERT	GER
1968	Tibor TATAI	HUN
1972	Ivan PATZAICHIN	ROM
1976	Matija LJUBEK	YUG
1980	Ljubomir LJUBENOV	BUL
1984	Ulrich EICKE	GER
1988	Ivan KLEMENTJEVS	SOV
1992	Nikolai BUKHALOV	BUL
1996	Martin DOKTOR	CZE
2000	Andreas DITTMER	GER

1000m CANADIAN PAIRS

1936	CZE
1948	CZE
1952	DAN
1956	ROM
1960	SOV
1964	SOV
1968	ROM
1972	SOV
1976	SOV
1980	ROM
1984	ROM
1988	SOV
1992	GER
1996	GER
2000	ROM

500m KAYAK SINGLES

| 1976 | Vasile DIBA | ROM |

1980	Vladimir PARFENOVITCH	SOV
1984	Ian FERGUSON	NZL
1988	Zsolt GYULAY	HUN
1992	Mikko KOLEHMAINEN	FIN
1996	Antonio ROSSI	ITA
2000	Knut HOLMANN	NOR

500m KAYAK PAIRS

1976	GDR
1980	SOV
1984	NZL
1988	NZL
1992	GER
1996	GER
2000	HUN

1000m KAYAK SINGLES

1936	Gregor HRADETZKY	AUT
1948	Gert FREDRIKSSON	SWE
1952	Gert FREDRIKSSON	SWE
1956	Gert FREDRIKSSON	SWE
1960	Erik HANSEN	DAN
1964	Rolf PETERSON	SWE
1968	Mihály HESZ	HUN
1972	Aleksandr CHAPARENKO	SOV
1976	Rüdiger HELM	GDR
1980	Rüdiger HELM	GDR
1984	Alan THOMPSON	NZL
1988	Gregory BARTON	USA
1992	Clint ROBINSON	AUS
1996	Knut HOLMANN	NOR
2000	Knut HOLMANN	NOR

1000m KAYAK PAIRS

1936	AUT
1948	SWE
1952	FIN
1956	GER
1960	SWE
1964	SWE
1968	SOV
1972	SOV
1976	SOV
1980	SOV
1984	CAN
1988	USA
1992	GER
1996	ITA
2000	ITA

1000m KAYAK FOURS

1964	SOV
1968	NOR
1972	SOV
1976	SOV
1980	GDR
1984	NZL
1988	HUN
1992	GER
1996	GER
2000	HUN

10,000m CANADIAN SINGLES

1948	Frantisek CAPECK	CZE
1952	Frank HAVENS	USA
1956	Leon ROTMAN	ROM

10,000m CANADIAN PAIRS

1936	CZE
1948	USA
1952	FRA
1956	SOV

10,000m KAYAK SINGLES

1936	Ernst KREBS	GER
1948	Gert FREDRIKSSON	SWE
1952	Thorvald STRÖMBERG	FIN
1956	Gert FREDRIKSSON	SWE

10,000m KAYAK SINGLES (FOLDING)

| 1936 | Gregor HRADETZKY | AUT |

10,000m KAYAK PAIRS

1936	GER
1948	SWE
1952	FIN
1956	HUN

10,000m KAYAK PAIRS (FOLDING)

| 1936 | SWE |

CANADIAN SLALOM SINGLES

1972	Reinhard EIBEN	GDR
1992	Lukás POLLERT	CZE
1996	Michal MARTIKAN	SVK
2000	Tony ESTANGUET	FRA

CANADIAN SLALOM PAIRS

1972	GDR
1992	USA
1996	FRA
2000	SVK

KAYAK SLALOM SINGLES

1972	Siegbert HORN	GDR
1992	Pierpaolo FERRAZZI	ITA
1996	Oliver FIX	GER
2000	Thomas SCHMIDT	GER

KAYAK SINGLES 4x500m RELAY

| 1960 | GER |

CANOEING (WOMEN)

500m KAYAK SINGLES

1948	Karen HOFF	DAN
1952	Sylvi SAIMO	FIN
1956	Elizaveta DEMENTIEVA	SOV
1960	Antonina SEREDINA	SOV
1964	Liudmila KHVEBACKSTROKEIUK	SOV
1968	Liudmila PINAEVA (KHVEBACKSTROKEIUK)	SOV
1972	Julia RJABCHINSKAÏA	SOV
1976	Carola ZIRZOW	GDR
1980	Birgit FISCHER	GDR
1984	Agneta ANDERSSON	SWE
1988	Vania GECHEVA	BUL
1992	Birgit SCHMIDT (FISCHER)	GER
1996	Rita KOBAN	HUN
2000	Josefa IDEM-GUERRINI	ITA

500m KAYAK PAIRS

1960	SOV
1964	GER
1968	GER
1972	SOV
1976	SOV
1980	GDR
1984	SWE
1988	GDR
1992	GER
1996	SWE
2000	GER

500m KAYAK FOURS

1984	ROM
1988	GDR
1992	HUN
1996	GER
2000	GER

KAYAK SLALOM SINGLES

1972	Angelika BAHMANN	GDR
1992	Elisabeth MICHELER	GER
1996	Stepanka HILGERTOVA	CZE
2000	Stepanka HILGERTOVA	CZE

CRICKET

| 1900 | GBR |

CROQUET

SINGLES – 1 BALL

| 1900 | AUMOITTE | FRA |

SINGLES – 2 BALLS

| 1900 | WAYDELICH | FRA |

DOUBLES

| 1900 | FRA |

CYCLING (TRACK)

1000m MATCH SPRINT

1896	Paul MASSON	FRA
1900	Georges TAILLANDIER	FRA
1920	Maurice PEETERS	HOL
1924	Lucien MICHARD	FRA
1928	Roger BEAUFRAND	FRA
1932	Jacobus VAN EGMOND	HOL
1936	Toni MERKENS	GER
1948	Mario GHELLA	ITA
1952	Enzo SACCHI	ITA
1956	Michel ROUSSEAU	FRA
1960	Sante GAIARDONI	ITA
1964	Giovanni PETTENELLA	ITA
1968	Daniel MORELON	FRA
1972	Daniel MORELON	FRA
1976	Anton TKAC	CZE
1980	Lutz HESSLICH	GDR
1984	Mark GORSKI	USA
1988	Lutz HESSLICH	GDR
1992	Jens FIEDLER	GER
1996	Jens FIEDLER	GER
2000	Marty NOTHSTEIN	USA

OLYMPIC SPRINT

| 2000 | FRA |

4,000m INDIVIDUAL PURSUIT

1964	Jiri DALER	CZE
1968	Daniel REBILLARD	FRA
1972	Knut KNUDSEN	NOR
1976	Gregor BRAUN	GER
1980	Robert DILL-BUNDI	SUI
1984	Steve HEGG	USA
1988	Gintautas UMARAS	SOV
1992	Christopher BOARDMAN	GBR
1996	Andrea COLLINELLI	ITA
2000	Robert BARTKO	GER

4,000m TEAM PURSUIT

1908	GBR
1920	ITA
1924	ITA
1928	ITA
1932	ITA
1936	FRA
1948	FRA
1952	ITA
1956	ITA
1960	ITA
1964	GER
1968	DEN
1972	GER
1976	GER
1980	SOV
1984	AUS
1988	SOV
1992	GER
1996	FRA
2000	GER

ONE-LAP RACE

1896	Paul MASSON	FRA
1908	Victor JOHNSON	GBR

1/4 MILE

1904	Marcus HURLEY	USA

1/3 MILE

1904	Marcus HURLEY	USA

1/2 MILE

1904	Marcus HURLEY	USA

1000m TIME TRIAL

1928	Willy Falck HANSEN	DAN
1932	Edgar GRAY	AUS
1936	Arie VAN VLIET	HOL
1948	Jacques DUPONT	FRA
1952	Russell MOCKRIDGE	AUS
1956	Leandro FAGGIN	ITA
1960	Sante GAIARDONI	ITA
1964	Patrick SERCU	BEL
1968	Pierre TRENTIN	FRA
1972	Niels FREDBORG	DAN
1976	Klaus-Jürgen GRÜNKE	GDR
1980	Lothar THOMS	GDR
1984	Fredy SCHMIDTKE	GER
1988	Aleksandr KIRITCHENKO	SOV
1992	José Manuel MORENO	ESP
1996	Florian ROUSSEAU	FRA
2000	Jason QUEALLY	GBR

1 MILE

1904	Marcus HURLEY	USA

2 MILES

1904	Burton DOWNING	USA

5km TRACK RACE

1908	Benjamin JONES	GBR

5 MILES

1904	Charles SCHLEE	USA

10km TRACK RACE

1896	Paul MASSON	FRA

20km TRACK RACE

1908	Clarence KINGSBURY	GBR

25km TRACK RACE

1900	Louis BASTIEN	FRA

25 MILE TRACK RACE

1904	Burton DOWNING	USA

50km TRACK RACE

1920	Henry GEORGE	BEL
1924	Jacobus WILLEMS	HOL

100km TRACK RACE

1896	Léon FLAMENG	FRA
1908	Charles BARTLETT	GBR

12 HOURS TRACK RACE

1896	Adolf SCHMAL	AUT

5km POINTS RACE

1900	Ernesto BRUSONI	ITA

POINTS RACE

1984	Roger ILEGEMS	BEL

1988	Dan FROST	DAN
1992	Giovanni LOMBARDI	ITA
1996	Silvio MARTINELLI	ITA
2000	Juan LLANERAS	ESP

TANDEM

1908	FRA
1920	GBR
1924	FRA
1928	HOL
1932	FRA
1936	GER
1948	ITA
1952	AUS
1956	AUS
1960	ITA
1964	ITA
1968	FRA
1972	SOV

MADISON

2000	AUS

KEIRIN

2000	Florian ROUSSEAU	FRA

CYCLING (TRACK) (WOMEN)

500m TIME TRIAL

2000	Félicia BALLANGER	FRA

1000m MATCH SPRINT

1988	Erika SALUMÄE	SOV
1992	Erika SALUMÄE	EST
1996	Félicia BALLANGER	FRA
2000	Félicia BALLANGER	FRA

4,000m INDIVIDUAL PURSUIT

1992	Petra ROSSNER	GER
1996	Antonella BELLUTTI	ITA
2000	Leontien VAN MOORSEL-ZIJLAARD	HOL

POINTS RACE

1996	Nathalie EVEN-LANCIEN	FRA
2000	Antonella BELLUTTI	ITA

CYCLING (ROAD) (MEN)

INDIVIDUAL ROAD RACE

1896	Aristidis KONSTANTINIDIS	GRE
1924	Armand BLANCHONNET	FRA
1936	Robert CHARPENTIER	FRA
1948	José BEYAERT	FRA
1952	André NOYELLE	BEL
1956	Ercole BALDINI	ITA
1960	Viktor KAPITONOV	SOV
1964	Mario ZANIN	ITA
1968	Pierfranco VIANELLI	ITA
1972	Hennie KUIPER	HOL
1976	Bernt JOHANSSON	SWE
1980	Sergueï SOUKHOROUTCHENKOV	SOV
1984	Alexi GREWAL	USA
1988	Olaf LUDWIG	GDR
1992	Fabio CASARTELLI	ITA
1996	Pascal RICHARD	SUI
2000	Jan ULLRICH	GER

INDIVIDUAL TIME TRIAL

1912	Rudolph LEWIS	RSA
1920	Harry STENQVIST	SWE
1928	Henry HANSEN	DAN
1932	Attilio PAVESI	ITA
1996	Miguel INDURAIN	ESP
2000	Vjatceslav EKIMOV	RUS

ROAD-RACE TEAM WINNER

1912	SWE
1920	FRA

1924	FRA
1928	DEN
1932	ITA
1936	FRA
1948	BEL
1952	BEL
1956	FRA

100km TEAM TIME TRIAL

1960	ITA
1964	HOL
1968	HOL
1972	SOV
1976	SOV
1980	SOV
1984	ITA
1988	GDR
1992	GER

CYCLING (ROAD) (WOMEN)

INDIVIDUAL ROAD RACE

1984	Connie CARPENTER-PHINNEY	USA
1988	Monique KNOL	HOL
1992	Kathryn WATT	AUS
1996	Jeannie LONGO-CIPRELLI	FRA
2000	Leontien VAN MOORSEL-ZIJLAARD	HOL

INDIVIDUAL TIME TRIAL

1996	Zulfiya ZUBIROVA	RUS
2000	Leontien VAN MOORSEL-ZIJLAARD	HOL

DIVING (MEN)

SPRINGBOARD (3m)

1908	Albert ZÜRNER	GER
1912	Paul GÜNTHER	GER
1920	Louis KÜHN	USA
1924	Albert WHITE	USA
1928	Ulise DESJARDINS	USA
1932	Michael GALITZEN	USA
1936	Richard DEGENER	USA
1948	Bruce HARLAN	USA
1952	David BROWNING	USA
1956	Robert CLOTWORTHY	USA
1960	Gary TOBIAN	USA
1964	Kenneth SITZBERGER	USA
1968	Bernie WRIGHTSON	USA
1972	Vladimir VASIN	SOV
1976	Philip BOGGS	USA
1980	Aleksandr PORTNOV	SOV
1984	Gregory LOUGANIS	USA
1988	Gregory LOUGANIS	USA
1992	Mark LENZI	USA
1996	XIONG Ni	CHN
2000	XIONG Ni	CHN

PLATFORM (10m)

1904	George SHELDON	USA
1908	Hjalmar JOHANSSON	SWE
1912	Erik ADLERZ	SWE
1920	Clarence PINKSTON	USA
1924	Albert WHITE	USA
1928	Ulise DESJARDINS	USA
1932	Harold SMITH	USA
1936	Marshall WAYNE	USA
1948	Samuel LEE	USA
1952	Samuel LEE	USA
1956	Joaquin CAPILLA	MEX
1960	Robert WEBSTER	USA
1964	Robert WEBSTER	USA
1968	Klaus DIBIASI	ITA
1972	Klaus DIBIASI	ITA
1976	Klaus DIBIASI	ITA
1980	Falk HOFFMANN	GDR
1984	Gregory LOUGANIS	USA
1988	Gregory LOUGANIS	USA
1992	SUN Shuwei	CHN
1996	Dimitri SAUTIN	RUS
2000	TIAN Liang	CHN

SYNCHRONISED SPRINGBOARD (3m)

2000	CHN	

SYNCHRONISED PLATFORM (10m)

2000	RUS	

DISTANCE

1904	William DICKEY	USA

PLAIN HIGH DIVING (10m)

1912	Erik ADLERZ	SWE
1920	Arvid WALLMAN	SWE
1924	Richmond EVE	AUS

DIVING (WOMEN)

SPRINGBOARD (3m)

1920	Aileen RIGGIN	USA
1924	Betty BECKER	USA
1928	Helen MEANY	USA
1932	Georgia COLEMAN	USA
1936	Marjorie GESTRING	USA
1948	Victoria DRAVES	USA
1952	Patricia McCORMICK	USA
1956	Patricia McCORMICK	USA
1960	Ingrid KRÄMER	GER
1964	Ingrid KRÄMER	GER
1968	Sue GOSSICK	USA
1972	Micki KING	USA
1976	Jennifer CHANDLER	USA
1980	Irina KALININA	SOV
1984	Sylvie BERNIER	CAN
1988	GAO Min	CHN
1992	GAO Min	CHN
1996	FU Mingxia	CHN
2000	FU Mingxia	CHN

PLATFORM (10m)

1912	Greta JOHANSSON	SWE
1920	Stefanie CLAUSEN	DAN
1924	Caroline SMITH	USA
1928	Elizabeth BECKER PINKSTON	USA
1932	Dorothy POYNTON	USA
1936	Dorothy POYNTON-HILL	USA
1948	Victoria DRAVES	USA
1952	Patricia McCORMICK	USA
1956	Patricia McCORMICK	USA
1960	Ingrid KRÄMER	GER
1964	Lesley BUSH	USA
1968	Milena DUCHKOVA	CZE
1972	Ulrika KNAPE	SWE
1976	YYelena VOITSEKHOVSKAIA	SOV
1980	Martina JÄSCHKE	GDR
1984	ZHOU Jihong	CHN
1988	XU Yanmei	CHN
1992	FU Mingxia	CHN
1996	FU Mingxia	CHN
2000	Laura WILKINSON	USA

SYNCHRONISED SPRINGBOARD (3m)

2000	RUS	

SYNCHRONISED PLATFORM (10m)

2000	CHN	

EQUESTRIAN

GRAND PRIX (JUMPING)

1900	Aimé HAEGEMAN	BEL
1912	Jean CARIOU	FRA
1924	Alphonse GEMUSEUS	SUI
1928	Frantisek VENTURA	CZE
1932	Takeichi NISHI	JAP
1936	Kurt HASSE	GER
1948	Humberto MARILES	MEX
1952	Pierre JONQUÈRES D'ORIOLA	FRA
1956	Hans-Günter WINKLER	GER
1960	Raimondo D'INZEO	ITA
1964	Pierre JONQUÈRES D'ORIOLA	FRA
1968	William STEINKRAUS	USA
1972	Graziano MANCINELLI	ITA
1976	Alwin SCHOCKEMÖHLE	GER
1980	Jan KOWALCZYK	POL
1984	Joe FARGIS	USA
1988	Pierre DURAND	FRA
1992	Ludger BEERBAUM	GER
1996	Ulrich KIRCHHOFF	GER
2000	Jeroen DUBBELDAM	HOL

GRAND PRIX (JUMPING)

TEAM

1912	SWE
1924	SWE
1928	ESP
1936	GER
1948	MEX
1952	GBR
1956	GER
1960	GER
1964	GER
1968	CAN
1972	GER
1976	FRA
1980	SOV
1984	USA
1988	GER
1992	HOL
1996	GER
2000	GER

THREE-DAY EVENT

1912	Axel NORDLANDER	SWE
1920	Helmer MOERNER	SWE
1924	Adolph VAN DER VOORT VAN ZIJP	HOL
1928	Charles PAHUD DE MORTANGES	HOL
1932	Charles PAHUD DE MORTANGES	HOL
1936	Ludwig STUBBENDORFF	GER
1948	Bernard CHEVALLIER	FRA
1952	Hans VON BLIXEN-FINECKE, Jr	SWE
1956	Petrus KASTENMAN	SWE
1960	Lawrence MORGAN	AUS
1964	Mauro CHECCOLI	ITA
1968	Jean-Jacques GUYON	FRA
1972	Richard MEADE	GBR
1976	Edmund COFFIN	USA
1980	Federico ROMAN	ITA
1984	Mark TODD	NZL
1988	Mark TODD	NZL
1992	Matthew RYAN	AUS
1996	Robert TAIT	NZL
2000	David O'CONNOR	USA

THREE-DAY EVENT, TEAM

1912	SWE
1920	SWE
1924	HOL
1928	HOL
1932	USA
1936	GER
1948	USA
1952	SWE
1956	GBR
1960	AUS
1964	ITA
1968	GBR
1972	GBR
1976	USA
1980	SOV
1984	USA
1988	GER
1992	AUS
1996	AUS
2000	AUS

GRAND PRIX (DRESSAGE)

1912	Carl BONDE	SWE
1924	Ernst LINDER	SWE
1928	Carl Friedrich VON LANGEN-PAROW	GER
1932	Xavier LESAGE	FRA
1936	Heinz POLLAY	GER
1948	Hans MOSER	SUI
1952	Henri SAINT CYR	SWE
1956	Henri SAINT CYR	SWE
1960	Serguei FILATOV	SOV
1964	Henri CHAMMARTIN	SUI
1968	Ivan KIZIMOV	SOV
1972	Liselott LINSENHOFF	GER
1976	Christine STÜCKELBERGER	SUI
1980	Elisabeth THEURER	AUT
1984	Reiner KLIMKE	GER
1988	Nicole UPHOFF	GER
1992	Nicole UPHOFF	GER
1996	Isabell WERTH	GER
2000	Anky VAN GRUNSVEN	HOL

GRAND PRIX (DRESSAGE) TEAM

1928	GER
1932	FRA
1936	GER
1948	FRA
1952	SWE
1956	SWE
1964	GER
1968	GER
1972	SOV
1976	GER
1980	SOV
1984	GER
1988	GER
1992	GER
1996	GER
2000	GER

HIGH JUMP

1900	Dominique MAXIMILIEN GARDÈRES	FRA

LONG JUMP

1900	Constant VAN LANGHENDONCK	BEL

MAIL COACH (FOUR IN HAND)

1900	Georges NAGELMACKERS	BEL

HACK AND HUNTER COMBINED (CHEVAUX DE SELLE)

1900	Napoléon MURAT	FRA

FIGURE RIDING, INDIVIDUAL

1900	T. BUCKAERT	BEL

FIGURE RIDING, TEAM

1900	BEL

FENCING (MEN)

FOIL

1896	Eugène-Henri GRAVELOTTE	FRA
1900	Émile COSTE	FRA
1904	Ramón FONST	CUB
1912	Nedo NADI	ITA
1920	Nedo NADI	ITA
1924	Roger DUCRET	FRA
1928	Lucien GAUDIN	FRA
1932	Gustavo MARZI	ITA
1936	Giulio GAUDINI	ITA
1948	Jehan BUHAN	FRA
1952	Christian D'ORIOLA	FRA
1956	Christian D'ORIOLA	FRA
1960	Viktor ZDANOVITCH	SOV
1964	Egon FRANKE	POL
1968	Ionel DRIMBA	ROM
1972	Witold WOYDA	POL
1976	Fabio DAL ZOTTO	ITA
1980	Vladimir SMIRNOV	SOV
1984	Mauro NUMA	ITA
1988	Stefano CERIONI	ITA
1992	Philippe OMNÈS	FRA
1996	Alessandro PUCCINI	ITA
2000	KIM Young-ho	KOR

FOIL FOR FENCING MASTERS

1896	Leonidas PYRGOS	GRE
1900	Lucien MÉRIGNAC	FRA

FOIL TEAM

1904	CUB/USA
1920	ITA
1924	FRA
1928	ITA
1932	FRA
1936	ITA
1948	FRA
1952	FRA
1956	ITA
1960	SOV
1964	SOV
1968	FRA
1972	POL
1976	GER
1980	FRA
1984	ITA
1988	SOV
1992	GER
1996	RUS
2000	FRA

ÉPÉE

1900	Ramón FONST	CUB
1904	Ramón FONST	CUB
1908	Gaston ALIBERT	FRA
1912	Paul ANSPACH	BEL
1920	Armand MASSARD	FRA
1924	Charles DELPORTE	BEL
1928	Lucien GAUDIN	FRA
1932	Giancarlo CORNAGGIA-MEDICI	ITA
1936	Franco RICCARDI	ITA
1948	Luigi CANTONE	ITA
1952	Edoardo MANGIAROTTI	ITA
1956	Carlo PAVESI	ITA
1960	Giuseppe DELFINO	ITA
1964	Grigori KRISS	SOV
1968	Gyözö KULCSÁR	HUN
1972	Csaba FENYVESI	HUN
1976	Alexander PUSCH	GER
1980	Johan HARMENBERG	SWE
1984	Philippe BOISSE	FRA
1988	Arnd SCHMITT	GER
1992	Éric SRECKI	FRA
1996	Aleksandr BEKETOV	RUS
2000	Pavel KOLOBKOV	RUS

ÉPÉE FOR FENCING MASTERS

1900	Albert AYAT	FRA

ÉPÉE FOR AMATEURS AND FENCING MASTERS

1900	Albert AYAT	FRA

ÉPÉE TEAM

1908	FRA
1912	BEL
1920	ITA
1924	FRA
1928	ITA
1932	FRA
1936	ITA
1948	FRA
1952	ITA
1956	ITA
1960	ITA
1964	HUN
1968	HUN
1972	HUN
1976	SWE
1980	FRA
1984	GER
1988	FRA
1992	GER
1996	ITA
2000	ITA

SABRE

1896	Ioannis GEORGIADIS	GRE
1900	Georges DE LA FALAISE	FRA
1904	Manuel DIAZ	CUB
1908	Jenö FUCHS	HUN
1912	Jenö FUCHS	HUN
1920	Nedo NADI	ITA
1924	Sándor PÓSTA	HUN
1928	Ödön TERSZTYÁNSZKY	HUN
1932	György PILLER	HUN
1936	Endre KABOS	HUN
1948	Aladár GEREVICH	HUN
1952	Pál KOVÁCS	HUN
1956	Rudolf KÁRPÁTI	HUN
1960	Rudolf KÁRPÁTI	HUN
1964	Tibor PÉZSA	HUN
1968	Jerzy PAWLOWSKI	POL
1972	Viktor SIDIAK	SOV
1976	Viktor KROVOPOUSKOV	SOV
1980	Viktor KROVOPOUSKOV	SOV
1984	Jean-François LAMOUR	FRA
1988	Jean-François LAMOUR	FRA
1992	Bence SZABÓ	HUN
1996	Stanislav POZDNIAKOV	RUS
2000	Mihai Claudio COVALIU	ROM

SABRE FOR FENCING MASTERS

1900	Antonio CONTE	ITA

SABRE TEAM

1908	HUN
1912	HUN
1920	ITA
1924	ITA
1928	HUN
1932	HUN
1936	HUN
1948	HUN
1952	HUN
1956	HUN
1960	HUN
1964	SOV
1968	SOV
1972	ITA
1976	SOV
1980	SOV
1984	ITA
1988	HUN
1992	SOV
1996	RUS
2000	RUS

SINGLE STICKS

1904	Albertson VAN ZO POST	USA

FENCING (WOMEN)

FOIL

1924	Ellen OSIIER	DAN
1928	Helene MAYER	GER
1932	Ellen PREIS	AUT
1936	Ilona ELEK	HUN
1948	Ilona ELEK	HUN
1952	Irene CAMBER	ITA
1956	Gillian SHEEN	GBR
1960	Heidi SCHMID	GER
1964	Ildiko UJLAKI-REJTÖ	HUN
1968	Yelena NOVIKOVA	SOV
1972	Antonella RAGNO-LONZI	ITA
1976	Ildiko SCHWARCZENBERGER	HUN
1980	Pascale TRINQUET	FRA
1984	LUAN Jujie	CHN
1988	Anja FICHTEL	GER
1992	Giovanna TRILLINI	ITA
1996	Laura BADEA	ROM
2000	Valentina VEZZALI	ITA

FOIL TEAM

1960	SOV
1964	HUN
1968	SOV
1972	SOV
1976	SOV

1980	FRA
1984	GER
1988	GER
1992	ITA
1996	ITA
2000	ITA

ÉPÉE

1996	Laura FLESSEL	FRA
2000	Timea NAGY	HUN

ÉPÉE TEAM

1996	FRA
2000	RUS

FIGURE SKATING (MEN)

1908	Ulrich SALCHOW	SWE
1920	Gillis GRAFSTRÖM	SWE

SPECIAL FIGURES

1908	Nikolai PANIN	RUS

FIGURE SKATING (WOMEN)

1908	Florence SYERS	GBR
1920	Magdalena JULIN-MAUROY	SWE

COUPLES

1908	Burger/Hübler	GER
1920	Jakobsson/Jakobsson	FIN

FOOTBALL (MEN)

1900	GBR
1904	CAN
1908	GBR
1912	GBR
1920	BEL
1924	URU
1928	URU
1936	ITA
1948	SWE
1952	HUN
1956	SOV
1960	YUG
1964	HUN
1968	HUN
1972	POL
1976	GDR
1980	CZE
1984	FRA
1988	SOV
1992	ESP
1996	NGA
2000	CAM

FOOTBALL (WOMEN)

1996	USA
2000	NOR

GOLF (MEN)

1900	Charles SANDS	USA
1904	George LYON	CAN

TEAM

1904	USA

GOLF (WOMEN)

1900	Margaret ABBOTT	USA

GYMNASTICS (MEN)

ALL-AROUND

1900	Gustave SANDRAS	FRA
1904	Julius LENHART	AUT
1908	Alberto BRAGLIA	ITA
1912	Alberto BRAGLIA	ITA
1920	Giorgio ZAMPORI	ITA
1924	Leon STUKELJ	YUG
1928	Georges MIEZ	SUI
1932	Romeo NERI	ITA
1936	Alfred SCHWARZMANN	GER
1948	Veikko HUHTANEN	FIN
1952	Viktor CHUKARIN	SOV
1956	Viktor CHUKARIN	SOV
1960	Boris CHAKHLIN	SOV
1964	Yukio ENDO	JAP
1968	Sawao KATO	JAP
1972	Sawao KATO	JAP
1976	Nikolai ANDRIANOV	SOV
1980	Aleksandr DITYATIN	SOV
1984	Koji GUSHIKEN	JAP
1988	Vladimir ARTEMOV	SOV
1992	Vitaly SCHERBO	BLR
1996	LI Xiaoshuang	CHN
2000	Aleksei NEMOV	RUS

HORIZONTAL BAR

1896	Hermann WEINGÄRTNER	GER
1904	Anton HEIDA	USA
	Edward HENNIG	USA
1924	Leon STUKELJ	YUG
1928	Georges MIEZ	SUI
1932	Dallas BIXLER	USA
1936	Aleksanteri SAARVALA	FIN
1948	Josef STALDER	SUI
1952	Jack GÜNTHARD	SUI
1956	Takashi ONO	JAP
1960	Takashi ONO	JAP
1964	Boris CHAKHLIN	SOV
1968	Akinori NAKAYAMA	JAP
	Mikhail VORONIN	SOV
1972	Mitsuo TSUKAHARA	JAP
1976	Mitsuo TSUKAHARA	JAP
1980	Stoyan DELTCHEV	BUL
1984	Shinji MORISUE	JAP
1988	Vladimir ARTEMOV	SOV
	Valery LIUKIN	SOV
1992	Trent DIMAS	USA
1996	Andreas WECKER	GER
2000	Aleksei NEMOV	RUS

FLOOR EXERCISE

1932	Istvan PELLE	HUN
1936	Georges MIEZ	SUI
1948	Ferenc PATAKI	HUN
1952	William THORESSON	SWE
1956	Valentin MURATOV	SOV
1960	Nobuyuki AIHARA	JAP
1964	Franco MENICHELLI	ITA
1968	Sawao KATO	JAP
1972	Nikolai ANDRIANOV	SOV
1976	Nikolai ANDRIANOV	SOV
1980	Roland BRÜCKNER	GDR
1984	LI Ning	CHN
1988	Serguei KHARKOV	SOV
1992	LI Xiaoshuang	CHN
1996	Ioannis MELISSANIDIS	GRE
2000	Igors VIHROVS	LET

PARALLEL BARS

1896	Alfred FLATOW	GER
1904	George EYSER	USA
1924	August GÜTTINGER	SUI
1928	Ladislav VACHA	CZE
1932	Romeo NERI	ITA
1936	Konrad FREY	GER
1948	Michael REUSCH	SUI
1952	Hans EUGSTER	SUI

1956	Viktor CHUKARIN	SOV
1960	Boris CHAKHLIN	SOV
1964	Yukio ENDO	JAP
1968	Akinori NAKAYAMA	JAP
1972	Sawao KATO	JAP
1976	Sawao KATO	JAP
1980	Aleksandr TKACHOV	SOV
1984	Bart CONNER	USA
1988	Vladimir ARTEMOV	SOV
1992	Vitaly SCHERBO	BLR
1996	Rustam CHAPIROV	UKR
2000	LI Xiaopeng	CHN

POMMEL HORSE

1896	Louis ZUTTER	SUI
1904	Anton HEIDA	USA
1924	Josef WILHELM	SUI
1928	Hermann HÄNGGI	SUI
1932	Istvan PELLE	HUN
1936	Konrad FREY	GER
1948	Paavo AALTONEN	FIN
	Veikko HUHTANEN	FIN
	Heikki SAVOLAINEN	FIN
1952	Viktor CHUKARIN	SOV
1956	Boris CHAKHLIN	SOV
1960	Eugen EKMAN	FIN
	Boris CHAKHLIN	SOV
1964	Miroslav CERAR	YUG
1968	Miroslav CERAR	YUG
1972	Viktor KLIMENKO	SOV
1976	Zoltan MAGYAR	HUN
1980	Zoltan MAGYAR	HUN
1984	LI Ning	CHN
	Peter VIDMAR	USA
1988	Dimitri BILOZERCHEV	SOV
	Zsolt BORKAI	HUN
	Lubomir GERASKOV	BUL
1992	PAE Gil-su	PRK
	Vitaly SCHERBO	BLR
1996	LI Donghua	SUI
2000	Marius URZICA	ROM

RINGS

1896	Ioannis MITROPOULOS	GRE
1904	Herman GLASS	USA
1924	Francesco MARTINO	ITA
1928	Leon STUKELJ	YUG
1932	George GULACK	USA
1936	Alois HUDEC	CZE
1948	Karl FREI	SUI
1952	Grant CHAGINIAN	SOV
1956	Albert AZARIAN	SOV
1960	Albert AZARIAN	SOV
1964	Takuji HAYATA	JAP
1968	Akinori NAKAYAMA	JAP
1972	Akinori NAKAYAMA	JAP
1976	Nikolai ANDRIANOV	SOV
1980	Aleksandr DITYATIN	SOV
1984	Koji GUSHIKEN	JAP
	LI Ning	CHN
1988	Holger BEHRENDT	GDR
	Dimitri BILOZERCHEV	SOV
1992	Vitaly SCHERBO	BLR
1996	Juri CHECHI	ITA
2000	Szilveszter CSOLLANY	HUN

HORSE VAULT

1896	Carl SCHUHMANN	GER
1904	George EYSER	USA
	Anton HEIDA	USA
1924	Frank KRIZ	USA
1928	Eugen MACK	SUI
1932	Savino GUGLIELMETTI	ITA
1936	Alfred SCHWARZMANN	GER
1948	Paavo AALTONEN	FIN
1952	Viktor CHUKARIN	SOV
1956	Helmut BANTZ	GER
	Valentin MURATOV	SOV
1960	Takashi ONO	JAP
	Boris CHAKHLIN	SOV
1964	Haruhiro YAMASHITA	JAP
1968	Mikhail VORONIN	SOV
1972	Klaus KÖSTE	GDR
1976	Nikolai ANDRIANOV	SOV
1980	Nikolai ANDRIANOV	SOV

1984	LOU Yun	CHN
1988	LOU Yun	CHN
1992	Vitaly SCHERBO	BLR
1996	Aleksei NEMOV	RUS
2000	Gervasio DEFERR	ESP

ROPE CLIMBING

1896	Nicolaos ANDRIAKOPOULOS	GRE
1904	George EYSER	USA
1924	Bedrich SUPCIK	CZE
1932	Raymond BASS	USA

FOUR-EVENT COMPETITION

1904	Anton HEIDA	USA

NINE-EVENT COMPETITION

1904	Adolf SPINNLER	SUI

FREE SYSTEM

1912	NOR
1920	DEN

SWEDISH SYSTEM

1912	SWE
1920	SWE

SIDEHORSE VAULT

1924	Albert SEGUIN	FRA

TUMBLING

1932	Rowland WOLFE	USA

CLUB SWINGING

1904	Edward HENNIG	USA
1932	George ROTH	USA

TEAM COMBINED EXERCISES

1904	USA
1908	SWE
1912	ITA
1920	ITA
1924	ITA
1928	SUI
1932	ITA
1936	GER
1948	FIN
1952	SOV
1956	SOV
1960	JAP
1964	JAP
1968	JAP
1972	JAP
1976	JAP
1980	SOV
1984	USA
1988	SOV
1992	SOV
1996	RUS
2000	CHN

GYMNASTICS (WOMEN)

ALL-AROUND

1952	Maria GOROKHOVSKAIA	SOV
1956	Larissa LATYNINA	SOV
1960	Larissa LATYNINA	SOV
1964	Vera CASLAVSKA	CZE
1968	Vera CASLAVSKA	CZE
1972	Ludmila TURICHTCHEVA	SOV
1976	Nadia COMANECI	ROM
1980	Yelena DAVIDOVA	SOV
1984	Mary Lou RETTON	USA
1988	Yelena CHUCHUNOVA	SOV
1992	Tatyana GUTSU	UKR
1996	Lilia PODKOPAIEVA	UKR
2000	Simona AMANAR	ROM

FLOOR EXERCISE

1952	Agnes KELETI	HUN
1956	Agnes KELETI	HUN
	Larissa LATYNINA	SOV
1960	Larissa LATYNINA	SOV
1964	Larissa LATYNINA	SOV
1968	Vera CASLAVSKA	CZE
	Larissa PETRIK	SOV
1972	Olga KORBUT	SOV
1976	Nelli KIM	SOV
1980	Nadia COMANECI	ROM
	Nelli KIM	SOV
1984	Ecaterina SZABO	ROM
1988	Daniela SILIVAS	ROM
1992	Lavinia MILOSOVICI	ROM
1996	Lilia PODKOPAIEVA	UKR
2000	Yelena ZAMOLODTCHIKOVA	RUS

BALANCE BEAM

1952	Margit KORONDI	HUN
1956	Agnes KELETI	HUN
1960	Polina ASTAKHOVA	SOV
1964	Polina ASTAKHOVA	SOV
1968	Vera CASLAVSKA	CZE
1972	Karin JANZ	GDR
1976	Nadia COMANECI	ROM
1980	Maxi GNAUCK	GDR
1984	Julianne McNAMARA	USA
	MA Yanhong	CHN
1988	Daniela SILIVAS	ROM
1992	LU Li	CHN
1996	Svetlana KHORKINA	RUS
2000	Svetlana KHORKINA	RUS
	POUTRE	
1952	Nina BOCHAROVA	SOV
1956	Agnes KELETI	HUN
1960	Eva BOSAKOVA (VECHTOVA)	CZE
1964	Vera CASLAVSKA	CZE
1968	Natalia KUCHINSKAIA	SOV
1972	Olga KORBUT	SOV
1976	Nadia COMANECI	ROM
1980	Nadia COMANECI	ROM
1984	Simona PAUCA	ROM
1988	Daniela SILIVAS	ROM
1992	Tatiana LYSENKO	UKR
1996	Shannon MILLER	USA
2000	LIU Xuan	CHN

HORSE VAULT

1952	Yekaterina KALINCHUK	SOV
1956	Larissa LATYNINA	SOV
1960	Marharyta NIKOLAIEVA	SOV
1964	Vera CASLAVSKA	CZE
1968	Vera CASLAVSKA	CZE
1972	Karin JANZ	GDR
1976	Nelli KIM	SOV
1980	Natalia CHAPOCHNIKOVA	SOV
1984	Ecaterina SZABO	ROM
1988	Svetlana BOGINSKAIA	SOV
1992	Lavinia MILOSOVICI	ROM
	Henrietta ONODI	HUN
1996	Simona AMANAR	ROM
2000	Yelena ZAMOLODTCHIKOVA	RUS

ALL-AROUND, TEAM

1928	HOL
1936	GER
1948	CZE
1952	SOV
1956	SOV
1960	SOV
1964	SOV
1968	SOV
1972	SOV
1976	SOV
1980	SOV
1984	ROM
1988	SOV
1992	SOV
1996	USA
2000	ROM

PORTABLE APPARATUS

1952	SWE
1956	HUN

RHYTHMIC GYMNASTICS (WOMEN)

1984	Lori FUNG	CAN
1988	Marina LOBACH	SOV
1992	Alexandra TIMOCHENKO	CEI
1996	Ekaterina SEREBRIANSKAIA	UKR
2000	Yulia BARSUKOVA	RUS

TEAM

1996	ESP
2000	RUS

HANDBALL MEN (TEAMS OF ELEVEN IN 1936)

1936	GER
1972	YUG
1976	SOV
1980	GDR
1984	YUG
1988	SOV
1992	SOV
1996	CRO
2000	RUS

HANDBALL (WOMEN)

1976	SOV
1980	SOV
1984	YUG
1988	KOR
1992	KOR
1996	DEN
2000	DEN

HOCKEY (MEN)

FIELD HOCKEY (MEN)

1908	GBR (ENGLAND)
1920	GBR
1928	IND
1932	IND
1936	IND
1948	IND
1952	IND
1956	IND
1960	PAK
1964	IND
1968	PAK
1972	GER
1976	NZL
1980	IND
1984	PAK
1988	GBR
1992	GER
1996	HOL
2000	HOL

FIELD HOCKEY (WOMEN)

1980	ZIM
1984	HOL
1988	AUS
1992	ESP
1996	AUS
2000	AUS

ICE HOCKEY

1920	CAN

JEU DE PAUME

1908	Jay GOULD	USA

JUDO (MEN)

EXTRA LIGHTWEIGHT (60kg)

1980	Thierry REY	FRA
1984	Shinji HOSOKAWA	JAP
1988	KIM jae-jup	KOR
1992	Nazim GUSEINOV	CEI
1996	Tadahiro NOMURA	JAP
2000	Tadahiro NOMURA	JAP

HALF LIGHTWEIGHT (66kg)

1980	Nikolai SOLODUKHIN	SOV
1984	Yoshiyuki MATSUOKA	JAP
1988	LEE Kyung-keun	KOR
1992	Rogério SAMPAIO	BRA
1996	Udo QUELLMALZ	GER
2000	Huseyin OZKAN	TUR

LIGHTWEIGHT (73kg)

1964	Takehide NAKATANI	JAP
1972	Takao KAWAGUCHI	JAP
1976	Héctor RODRIGUEZ	CUB
1980	Ezio GAMBA	ITA
1984	AHN Byeong-keun	KOR
1988	Marc ALEXANDRE	FRA
1992	Toshihiko KOGA	JAP
1996	Kenzo NAKAMURA	JAP
2000	Giuseppe MADDALONI	ITA

HALF MIDDLEWEIGHT 81kg

1972	Toyokazu NOMURA	JAP
1976	Vladimir NEVZOROV	SOV
1980	Shota KHABARELI	SOV
1984	Frank WIENEKE	GER
1988	Waldemar LEGIEN	POL
1992	Hidehiko YOSHIDA	JAP
1996	Djamel BOURAS	FRA
2000	Makoto TAKIMOTO	JAP

MIDDLEWEIGHT (90kg)

1964	Isao OKANO	JAP
1972	Shinobu SEKINE	JAP
1976	Isamu SONODA	JAP
1980	Jürg RÖTHLISBERGER	SUI
1984	Peter SEISENBACHER	AUT
1988	Peter SEISENBACHER	AUT
1992	Waldemar LEGIEN	POL
1996	JEON Ki-young	KOR
2000	Mark HUIZINGA	HOL

HALF HEAVYWEIGHT (100kg)

1972	Shota KOKOCHVILI	SOV
1976	Kazuhiro NINOMIYA	JAP
1980	Robert VAN DE WALLE	BEL
1984	HA Hyoung-zoo	KOR
1988	Aurélio MIGUEL	BRA
1992	Antal KOVÁCS	HUN
1996	Pawel NASTULA	POL
2000	Kosei INOUE	JAP

HEAVYWEIGHT + 100kg

1964	Isao INOKUMA	JAP
1972	Willem RUSKA	HOL
1976	Serguei NOVIKOV	SOV
1980	Angelo PARISI	FRA
1984	Hitoshi SAITO	JAP
1988	Hitoshi SAITO	JAP
1992	David KHAKHALEICHVILI	GEO
1996	David DOUILLET	FRA
2000	David DOUILLET	FRA

OPEN

1964	Antonius GEESINK	HOL
1972	Willem RUSKA	HOL
1976	Haruki UEMURA	JAP

1980	Dietmar LORENZ	GDR
1984	Yasuhiro YAMASHITA	JAP

JUDO (WOMEN)

EXTRA LIGHTWEIGHT (48kg)

1992	Cécile NOWAK	FRA
1996	KYE Sun-hi	PRK
2000	Ryoko TAMURA	JAP

HALF-LIGHTWEIGHT (52kg)

1992	Almudena MUNOZ	ESP
1996	Marie-Claire RESTOUX	FRA
2000	Legna VERDECIA	CUB

LIGHTWEIGHT (57kg)

1992	Miriam BLASCO	ESP
1996	Driulys GONZALES	CUB
2000	Isabel FERNANDEZ	ESP

HALF MIDDLEWEIGHT (63kg)

1992	Catherine FLEURY	FRA
1996	Yuko EMOTO	JAP
2000	Séverine VANDENHENDE	FRA

MIDDLEWEIGHT (70kg)

1992	Odalis REVÉ	CUB
1996	CHO Min-sun	KOR
2000	Sibelis VERANES	CUB

HALF-HEAVYWEIGHT (78kg)

1992	KIM Mi-jung	KOR
1996	Ulla WERBROUCK	BEL
2000	TANG Lin	CHN

HEAVYWEIGHT (+ 78kg)

1992	ZHUANG Xiaoyan	CHN
1996	SUN Fuming	CHN
2000	YAN Hua	CHN

LACROSSE

1904	CAN
1908	CAN

MODERN PENTATHLON

INDIVIDUAL

1912	Gösta LILLIEHÖÖK	SWE
1920	Gustaf DYRSSEN	SWE
1924	Bo LINDMAN	SWE
1928	Sven THOFELT	SWE
1932	Johan OXENSTIERNA	SWE
1936	Gotthardt HANDRICK	GER
1948	William GRUT	SWE
1952	Lars HALL	SWE
1956	Lars HALL	SWE
1960	Ferenc NEMETH	HUN
1964	Ferenc TÖRÖK	HUN
1968	Björn FERM	SWE
1972	Andras BALCZO	HUN
1976	Janusz PYCIAK-PECIAK	POL
1980	Anatoli STAROSTIN	SOV
1984	Daniele MASALA	ITA
1988	Janos MARTINEK	HUN
1992	Arkadiusz SKRZYPASZEK	POL
1996	Aleksandr PARYGIN	KAZ
2000	Dimitri SVATKOVSKI	RUS

TEAM

1952	HUN
1956	SOV
1960	HUN
1964	SOV
1968	HUN
1972	SOV

1976	GBR
1980	SOV
1984	ITA
1988	HUN

MOTOR BOATING

8m CLASS

1908	GBR

60-feet CLASS

1908	GBR

OPEN

1908	FRA

MOUNTAIN BIKING (MEN)

1996	Bart Jan BRENTJENS	HOL
2000	Miguel MARTINEZ	FRA

MOUNTAIN BIKING (WOMEN)

1996	Paola PEZZO	ITA
2000	Paola PEZZO	ITA

PELOTA BASQUE

1900	ESP

POLO

1900	GBR/USA/IRL
1908	GBR
1920	GBR
1924	ARG
1936	ARG

RACKETS

MEN'S SINGLES

1908	Evan NOEL	GBR

MEN'S DOUBLES

1908	GBR

ROQUE

1904	Charles JACOBUS	USA

RUGBY

1900	FRA
1908	AUS
1920	USA
1924	USA

SOFTBALL (WOMEN)

2000	USA

ROWING (MEN)

SINGLE SCULLS

1900	Henri BARRELET	FRA
1904	Frank GREER	USA
1908	Harry BLACKSTAFFE	GBR
1912	William KINNEAR	GBR
1920	John KELLY	USA
1924	Jack BERESFORD	GBR
1928	Henry PEARCE	AUS
1932	Henry PEARCE	AUS
1936	Gustav SCHÄFER	GER
1948	Mervyn WOOD	AUS
1952	Juri TIUKALOV	SOV
1956	Viatcheslav IVANOV	SOV
1960	Viatcheslav IVANOV	SOV
1964	Viatcheslav IVANOV	SOV
1968	Henri Jan WIENESE	NED
1972	Youri MALICHEV	SOV
1976	Pertti KARPPINEN	FIN
1980	Pertti KARPPINEN	FIN
1984	Pertti KARPPINEN	FIN
1988	Thomas LANGE	GDR
1992	Thomas LANGE	GER
1996	Xeno MÜLLER	SUI
2000	Robert WADDELL	NZL

COXLESS PAIRS

1904	USA
1908	GBR
1924	NED
1928	GER
1932	GBR
1936	GER
1948	GBR
1952	USA
1956	USA
1960	SOV
1964	CAN
1968	GDR
1972	GDR
1976	GDR
1980	GDR
1984	ROM
1988	GBR
1992	GBR
1996	GBR
2000	FRA

LIGHTWEIGHT DOUBLE SCULLS

1996	SUI
2000	POL

DOUBLES SCULLS

1904	USA
1920	USA
1924	USA
1928	USA
1932	USA
1936	GBR
1948	GBR
1952	ARG
1956	SOV
1960	CZE
1964	SOV
1968	SOV
1972	SOV
1976	NOR
1980	GDR
1984	USA
1988	NED
1992	AUS
1996	ITA
2000	SLO

LIGHTWEIGHT COXLESS FOURS

1996	DEN
2000	FRA

COXLESS FOURS

1904	USA
1908	GBR
1924	GBR
1928	GBR
1932	GBR
1936	GER
1948	ITA
1952	YUG
1956	CAN

1960	USA
1964	DEN
1968	GDR
1972	GDR
1976	GDR
1980	GDR
1984	NZL
1988	GDR
1992	AUS
1996	AUS
2000	GBR

COXLESS QUADRUPLE SCULLS

1976	GDR
1980	GDR
1984	GER
1988	ITA
1992	GER
1996	GER
2000	ITA

EIGHTS

1900	USA
1904	USA
1908	GBR
1912	GBR
1920	USA
1924	USA
1928	USA
1932	USA
1936	USA
1948	USA
1952	USA
1956	USA
1960	GER
1964	USA
1968	GER
1972	NZL
1976	GDR
1980	GDR
1984	CAN
1988	GER
1992	CAN
1996	NED
2000	GBR

COXED PAIRS

1900	NED
1920	ITA
1924	SUI
1928	SUI
1932	USA
1936	GER
1948	DEN
1952	FRA
1956	USA
1960	GER

COXED PAIRS

1964	USA
1968	ITA
1972	GDR
1976	GDR
1980	GDR
1984	ITA
1988	ITA
1992	GBR

COXED FOURS

1900	GER
	FRA
1912	GER
1920	SUI
1924	SUI
1928	ITA
1932	GER
1936	GER
1948	USA
1952	CZE
1956	ITA
1960	GER
1964	GER
1968	NZL

1972	GER
1976	SOV
1980	GDR
1984	GBR
1988	GDR
1992	ROM

COXED FOURS (INRIGGERS)

1912	DEN

ROWING (WOMEN)

SINGLE SCULLS

1976	Christine SCHEIBLICH	GDR
1980	Sanda TOMA	ROM
1984	Valeria ROSCA-RASILA	ROM
1988	Jutta BEHRENDT	GDR
1992	Elisabeta LIPA (OLENIUC)	ROM
1996	Ekaterina KHODOTOVICH	RUS
2000	Ekaterina KARSTEN (KHODOTOVITCH)	BLR

COXLESS PAIRS

1976	BUL
1980	GDR
1984	ROM
1988	ROM
1992	CAN
1996	AUS
2000	ROM

LIGHTWEIGHT DOUBLE SCULLS

1996	ROM
2000	ROM

DOUBLES SCULLS

1976	BUL
1980	SOV
1984	ROM
1988	GDR
1992	GER
1996	CAN
2000	GER

COXLESS FOURS

1992	CAN

COXLESS QUADRUPLE SCULLS

1976	GDR
1980	GDR
1984	ROM

COXLESS QUADRUPLE SCULLS

1988	GDR
1992	GER
1996	GER
2000	GER

COXED FOURS

1976	GDR
1980	GDR
1984	ROM
1988	GDR

EIGHTS

1976	GDR
1980	GDR
1984	USA
1988	GDR
1992	CAN
1996	ROM
2000	ROM

SAILING (MEN)

49ER

2000	FIN

INTERNATIONAL 470

1976	GER
1980	BRA
1984	ESP
1988	FRA
1992	ESP
1996	UKR
2000	AUS

LASER

1996	Robert SCHEIDT	BRA
2000	Ben AINSLIE	GBR

DRAGON

1948	NOR
1952	NOR
1956	SWE
1960	GRE
1964	DEN
1968	USA
1972	AUS

FINN

1920	HOL	
1924	Léon HUYBRECHTS	BEL
1928	Sven THORELL	SWE
1932	Jacques LEBRUN	FRA
1936	Daniel KAGCHELLAND	HOL
1948	Paul ELVSTROEM	DAN
1952	Paul ELVSTROEM	DAN
1956	Paul ELVSTROEM	DAN
1960	Paul ELVSTROEM	DAN
1964	Wilhelm KUHWEIDE	GER
1968	Valentin MANKIN	SOV
1972	Serge MAURY	FRA
1976	Jochen SCHÜMANN	GDR
1980	Esko RECHARDT	FIN
1984	Russell COUTTS	NZL
1988	José Luis DORESTE	ESP
1992	José VAN DER PLOEG	ESP
1996	Mateusz KUSZNIEREWICZ	POL
2000	Iain PERCY	GBR

FLYING DUTCHMAN

1960	NOR
1964	NZL
1968	GBR
1972	GBR
1976	GER
1980	ESP
1984	USA
1988	DEN
1992	ESP

SAILBOARD

1984	Stephan VAN DEN BERG	HOL
1988	Bruce KENDALL	NZL
1992	Franck DAVID	FRA
1996	Nikolaos KAKLAMANAKIS	GRE
2000	Christoph SIEBER	AUT

SOLING

1972	USA
1976	DEN
1980	DEN
1984	USA
1988	GDR
1992	DEN
1996	GER
2000	DEN

STAR

1932	USA

1936	GER
1948	USA
1952	ITA
1956	USA
1960	SOV
1964	BAH
1968	USA
1972	AUS
1980	SOV
1984	USA
1988	GBR
1992	USA
1996	BRA
2000	USA

SWALLOW

| 1948 | GBR |

TEMPEST

| 1972 | SOV |
| 1976 | SWE |

TORNADO

1976	GBR
1980	BRA
1984	NZL
1988	FRA
1992	FRA
1996	ESP
2000	AUT

0.5 TON CLASS

| 1900 | Pierre GERVAIS | FRA |

0.5-1 TON CLASS

| 1900 | GBR |

1-2 TON CLASS

| 1900 | Herma COMTE DE PORTUALES | SUI |

2-3 TON CLASS

| 1900 | William EXSHAW | GBR |

3-10 TON CLASS

| 1900 | GBR |

10-20 TON CLASS

| 1900 | FRA |

OPEN

| 1900 | GBR |

5.5m

1952	USA
1956	SWE
1960	USA
1964	AUS
1968	SWE

6m

1908	GBR
1912	FRA
1920	NOR
1924	NOR
1928	NOR
1932	SWE
1936	GBR
1948	USA
1952	USA

6.5m

| 1920 | HOL |
| | FRA |

7m

| 1908 | GBR |
| 1920 | GBR |

8m

1908	GBR
1912	NOR
1920	NOR
1924	NOR
1928	FRA
1932	USA
1936	ITA

10m

| 1912 | SWE |

12m

1908	GBR
1912	NOR
1956	NZL

30 SQUARE METRES

| 1920 | SWE |

40 SQUARE METRES

| 1920 | SWE |

6m (1907 RATING)

| 1920 | BEL |

8m (1907 RATING)

| 1920 | NOR |

10m (1907 RATING)

| 1920 | NOR |

12m (1907 RATING)

| 1920 | NOR |

6m (1919 RATING)

| 1920 | NOR |

7m (1919 RATING)

| 1920 | GBR |

8m (1919 RATING)

| 1920 | NOR |

10m (1919 RATING)

| 1920 | NOR |

12m (1919 RATING)

| 1920 | NOR |

CLASS 12 SQUARE METRES

| 1956 | NZL |

SAILING (WOMEN)

INTERNATIONAL 470

1988	USA
1992	ESP
1996	ESP
2000	AUS

EUROPE CLASS

1992	Linda ANDERSEN	NOR
1996	Kristine ROUG	DEN
2000	Shirley ROBERTSON	GBR

SAILBOARD

1992	Barbara KENDALL	NZL
1996	LEE Laishan	HKG
2000	Alessandra SENSINI	ITA

SHOOTING (MEN)

AIR RIFLE

1984	Philippe HÉBERLÉ	FRA
1988	Goran MAKSIMOVIC	YUG
1992	Youri FEDKIN	CEI
1996	Artem KHADJIBEKOV	RUS
2000	CAI Yalin	CHN

SMALL BORE RIFLE (THREE POSITIONS)

1952	Erling KONGSHAUG	NOR
1956	Anatoli BOGDANOV	SOV
1960	Viktor CHAMBURKIN	SOV
1964	Lones WIGGER	USA
1968	Bernd KLINGNER	GER
1972	John WRITER	USA
1976	Lance BASSHAM	USA
1980	Viktor VLASOV	SOV
1984	Malcolm COOPER	GBR
1988	Malcolm COOPER	GBR
1992	Grachia PETIKÏAN	CEI
1996	Jean-Pierre AMAT	FRA
2000	Rajmond DEBEVEC	SLO

AIR PISTOL

1988	Taniu KIRIAKOV	BUL
1992	WANG Yifu	CHN
1996	Roberto DI DONNA	ITA
2000	Franck DUMOULIN	FRA

FREE PISTOL (50M)

1896	Sumner PAINE	USA
1900	Karl RÖDERER	SUI
1908	Paul VAN ASBROECK	BEL
1912	Alfred LANE	USA
1920	Karl FREDERICK	USA
1936	Torsten ULLMAN	SWE
1948	Edwin VASQUEZ CAM	PER
1952	Huelet BENNER	USA
1956	Pentti LINNOSVUO	FIN
1960	Aleksei GUCHTCHIN	SOV
1964	Väjnö MARKKANEN	FIN
1968	Grigori KOSYK	SOV
1972	Ragnar SKANAKER	SWE
1976	Uwe POTTECK	GDR
1980	Aleksandr MELENTIEV	SOV
1984	XU Haifeng	CHN
1988	Sorin BABII	ROM
1992	Konstantin LUKACHIK	CEI
1996	Boris KOKOREV	RUS
2000	Taniu KIRIAKOV	BUL

RAPID FIRE PISTOL

1896	Ioannis FRANGOUDIS	GRE
1900	Maurice LARROUY	FRA
1912	Alfred LANE	USA
1920	Guilherme PARAENSE	BRA
1924	Henry BAILEY	USA
1932	Renzo MORIGI	ITA
1936	Cornelius VAN OYEN	GER
1948	Karoly TAKACS	HUN
1952	Karoly TAKACS	HUN
1956	Stefan PETRESCU	ROM
1960	William McMILLAN	USA
1964	Pentti LINNOSVUO	FIN
1968	Jozef ZAPEDZKI	POL
1972	Jozef ZAPEDZKI	POL
1976	Norbert KLAAR	GDR
1980	Corneliu ION	ROM
1984	Takeo KAMACHI	JAP
1988	Afanasi KUZMIN	SOV
1992	Ralf SCHUMANN	GER
1996	Ralf SCHUMANN	GER
2000	Serguei ALIFIRENKO	RUS

FREE PISTOL (50M) TEAM

| 1920 | USA |

RAPID FIRE PISTOL TEAM

1920	USA	

RUNNING TARGET

1972	Iakov ZELEZNIAK	SOV
1976	Aleksandr GAZOV	SOV
1980	Igor SOKOLOV	SOV
1984	LI Yuwei	CHN
1988	Tor HEIESTAD	NOR
1992	Michael JAKOSITS	GER
1996	YANG Ling	CHN
2000	YANG Ling	CHN

SMALL BORE RIFLE (PRONE)

1908	Arthur CARNELL	GBR
1912	Frederick HIRD	USA
1924	Pierre COQUELIN DE LISLE	FRA
1932	Bertil RÖNNMARK	SWE
1936	Willy RÖGEBERG	NOR
1948	Arthur COOK	USA
1952	Josif SARBU	ROM
1956	Gérald OUELLETTE	CAN
1960	Peter KOHNKE	GER
1964	Laszlo HAMMERL	HUN
1968	Jan KURKA	CZE
1972	LI Ho-jun	PRK
1976	Karlheinz SMIESZEK	GER
1980	Karoly VARGA	HUN
1984	Edward ETZEL	USA
1988	Miroslav VARGA	CZE
1992	LEE Eun-chul	KOR
1996	Christian KLEES	GER
2000	Jonas EDMAN	SWE

OLYMPIC TRAP SHOOTING

1900	Roger de BARBARIN	FRA
1908	Walter EWING	CAN
1912	James GRAHAM	USA
1920	Mark ARIE	USA
1924	Gyula HALASY	HUN
1952	George GÉNÉREUX	CAN
1956	Galliano ROSSINI	ITA
1960	Ion DUMITRESCU	ROM
1964	Ennio MATTARELLI	ITA
1968	John BRAITHWAITE	GBR
1972	Angelo SCALZONE	ITA
1976	Donald HALDEMAN	USA
1980	Luciano GIOVANNETTI	ITA
1984	Luciano GIOVANNETTI	ITA
1988	Dmitri MONAKOV	SOV
1992	Petr HRDLICKA	CZE
1996	Michael DIAMOND	AUS
2000	Michael DIAMOND	AUS

OLYMPIC TRAP SHOOTING
TEAM

1908	GBR	
1912	USA	
1920	USA	
1924	USA	

SKEET SHOOTING

1968	Evgueni PETROV	SOV
1972	Konrad WIRNHIER	GER
1976	Josef PANACEK	CZE
1980	Hans-Kjeld RASMUSSEN	DAN
1984	Matthew DRYKE	USA
1988	Axel WEGNER	GDR
1992	ZHANG Shan	CHN
1996	Ennio FALCO	ITA
2000	Mykola MILCHEV	UKR

DOUBLE TRAP

1996	Russel MARK	AUS
2000	Richard FAULDS	GBR

MILITARY REVOLVER 25m

1896	John PAINE	USA

MILITARY REVOLVER 50m, TEAM

1900	SUI	
1908	USA	
1912	USA	

DUELLING PISTOL 30m, TEAM

1912	SWE	

FREE RIFLE 300m (THREE POSITIONS)

1896	Georgios ORFANIDIS	GRE
1900	Emil KELLENBERGER	SUI
1908	Albert HELGERUD	NOR
1912	Paul COLAS	FRA
1920	Morris FISHER	USA
1948	Emil GRÜNIG	SUI
1952	Anatoli BOGDANOV	SOV
1956	Vassili BORISSOV	SOV
1960	Hubert HAMMERER	AUT
1964	Gary ANDERSON	USA
1968	Gary ANDERSON	USA
1972	Lones WIGGER	USA

FREE RIFLE 300m STANDING

1900	Lars JÖRGEN MADSEN	DAN

FREE RIFLE 300m à GENOU

1900	Konrad STÄHELI	SUI

FREE RIFLE 300m PRONE

1900	Achille PAROCHE	FRA

FREE RIFLE 1000 YARDS
TROIS POSITIONS

1908	Joshua MILLNER	GBR

FREE RIFLE 600m (THREE POSITIONS)

1924	Morris FISHER	USA

FREE RIFLE TEAM

1900	SUI	
1908	NOR	
1912	SWE	
1920	USA	
1924	USA	

FREE RIFLE 200m

1896	Pantelis KARASEVDAS	GRE

MILITARY RIFLE 300m

1912	Sandor PROKOP	HUN

MILITARY RIFLE 600m

1912	Paul COLAS	FRA

MILITARY RIFLE 300m PRONE

1920	Otto OLSEN	NOR

MILITARY RIFLE 300m STANDING

1920	Carl OSBURN	USA

MILITARY RIFLE 600m PRONE

1920	Carl Hugo JOHANNSSON	SWE

FREE RIFLE TEAM

1908	USA	
1912	USA	

FREE RIFLE
TEAM, 300m STANDING

1920	DEN	

FREE RIFLE
TEAM, 300m PRONE

1920	USA	

FREE RIFLE
TEAM, 600m PRONE

1920	USA	

FREE RIFLE
TEAM, 300 + 600m PRONE

1920	USA	

SMALL BORE RIFLE
MOVING TARGET

1908	John FLEMING	GBR

SMALL BORE RIFLE
DISAPPEARING TARGET

1908	William STYLES	GBR
1912	Vilhelm CARLBERG	SWE

SMALL BORE RIFLE
50m STANDING

1920	Lawrence NUESSLEIN	USA

SMALL BORE RIFLE
50 + 100 yards TEAM

1908	GBR	

SMALL BORE RIFLE
25m TEAM

1912	SWE	

SMALL BORE RIFLE
50m TEAM

1912	GBR	
1920	USA	

RUNNING DEER SHOOTING
SINGLE SHOT

1908	Oscar SWAHN	SWE
1912	Alfred SWAHN	SWE
1920	Otto OLSEN	NOR
1924	John BOLES	USA

RUNNING DEER SHOOTING
SINGLE SHOT, TEAM

1908	SWE	
1912	SWE	
1920	NOR	
1924	NOR	

RUNNING DEER SHOOTING
DOUBLE SHOT

1908	Walter WINANS	USA
1912	Ake LUNDEBERG	SWE
1920	Ole Andreas LILLOE-OLSEN	NOR
1924	Ole Andreas LILLOE-OLSEN	NOR

RUNNING DEER SHOOTING
DOUBLE SHOT, TEAM

1920	NOR	
1924	GBR	

RUNNING DEER SHOOTING
SINGLE AND DOUBLE SHOT

1952	John LARSEN	NOR

| 1956 | Vitali ROMANENKO | SOV | |

SHOOTING (WOMEN)

AIR RIFLE

1984	Karen SPURGIN	USA	
1988	Irina CHILOVA	SOV	
1992	YEO Kab-soon	KOR	
1996	Renata MAUER	POL	
2000	Nancy JOHNSON	USA	

CARABINE 3 x 20

1984	WU Xiaoxuan	CHN	
1988	Sylvia SPERBER	GER	
1992	Launi MEILI	USA	
1996	Alexandra IVOSEV	YUG	
2000	Renata MAUER-ROZANSKA	POL	

AIR PISTOL

1988	Jasna SEKARIC	YUG	
1992	Marina LOGVINENKO	CEI	
1996	Olga KLOCHNEVA	RUS	
2000	TAO Luna	CHN	

SPORT PISTOL

1984	Linda THOM	CAN	
1988	Nino SALUKVADZE	SOV	
1992	Marina LOGVINENKO	CEI	
1996	LI Duihong	CHN	
2000	Maria GROZDEVA	BUL	

OLYMPIC TRAP SHOOTING

| 2000 | Daina GUDZINEVICIUTE | LIT | |

SKEET SHOOTING

| 2000 | Zemfira MEFTAKHETDINOVA | AZE | |

DOUBLE TRAP

| 1996 | Kimberley RHODE | USA | |
| 2000 | Pia HANSEN | SWE | |

SHOOTING (LUTTE) A LA CORDE

1900	SWE/DEN	
1904	USA	
1908	GBR	
1912	SWE	
1920	GBR	

SWIMMING (MEN)

50 YARDS

| 1904 | Zoltan HALMAY | HUN | 28:0 |

50m

1988	Matthew 'Matt' BIONDI	USA	22.14
1992	Aleksandr POPOV	CEI	21.91
1996	Aleksandr POPOV	RUS	22.13
2000	Anthony ERVIN	USA	21.98
	Gary HALL	USA	21.98

100m

1896	Alfréd HAJOS	HUN	1.22:2
1904	Zoltan HALMAY	HUN	1:02.8
1908	Charles DANIELS	USA	1:05.6
1912	Duke Paoa KAHANAMOKU	USA	1:03.4
1920	Duke Paoa KAHANAMOKU	USA	1:00.4
1924	Johnny WEISSMULLER	USA	59.0
1928	Johnny WEISSMULLER	USA	58.6
1932	Yasuji MIYAZAKI	JAP	58.2
1936	Ferenc CSIK	HUN	57.6
1948	Walter RIS	USA	57.3
1952	Clarke SCHOLES	USA	57.4
1956	Jon HENRICKS	AUS	55.4
1960	John DEVITT	AUS	55.2

1964	Donald SCHOLLANDER	USA	53.4
1968	Michael WENDEN	AUS	52.2
1972	Mark SPITZ	USA	51.22
1976	James MONTGOMERY	USA	49.99
1980	Jörg WOITHE	GDR	50.40
1984	Ambrose GAINES	USA	49.80
1988	Matthew 'Matt' BIONDI	USA	48.63
1992	Aleksandr POPOV	RUS	49.02
1996	Aleksandr POPOV	RUS	48.74
2000	Pieter VAN DEN HOOGENBAND	HOL	48.30

100m FOR GREEK SAILORS

| 1896 | Ioannis MALOKINIS | GRE | 2:20.4 |

200m

1900	Frederick LANE	AUS	2:25.2
1904	Charles DANIELS	USA	2:44.2
1968	Michael WENDEN	AUS	1:55.2
1972	Mark SPITZ	USA	1:52.78
1976	Bruce FURNISS	USA	1:50.29
1980	Serguei KOPLIAKOV	SOV	1:49.81
1984	Michael GROSS	GER	1:47.44
1988	Duncan ARMSTRONG	AUS	1:47.25
1992	Evgueni SADOVYI	CEI	1:46.70
1996	Danyon LOADER	NZL	1:47.63
2000	Pieter VAN DEN HOOGENBAND	HOL	1:45.35
	400m (440 yards in 1904)		
1904	Charles DANIELS	USA	6:16.2
1908	Henry TAYLOR	GBR	5:36.8
1912	George HODGSON	CAN	5:24.4
1920	Norman ROSS	USA	5:26.8
1924	Johnny WEISSMULLER	USA	5:04.2
1928	Alberto ZORILLA	ARG	5:01.6
1932	Clarence CRABBE	USA	4:48.4
1936	Jack MEDICA	USA	4:44.5
1948	William SMITH	USA	4:41.0
1952	Jean BOITEUX	FRA	4:30.7
1956	Murray ROSE	AUS	4:27.3
1960	Murray ROSE	AUS	4:18.3
1964	Donald SCHOLLANDER	USA	4:12.2
1968	Mike BURTON	USA	4:09.0
1972	Bradford COOPER	AUS	4:00.27
1976	Brian GOODELL	USA	3:51.93
1980	Vladimir SALNIKOV	SOV	3:51.31
1984	George DiCARLO	USA	3:51.23
1988	Uwe DASSLER	GDR	3:46.95
1992	Evgueni SADOVYI	CEI	3:45.00
1996	Danyon LOADER	NZL	3:47.97
2000	Ian THORPE	AUS	3:40.59

500m

| 1896 | Paul NEUMANN | AUT | 8:12.6 |

880 YARDS

| 1904 | Emil RAUSCH | GER | 13:11.4 |

1000m

| 1900 | John Arthur JARVIS | GBR | 13:40.2 |

1200m

| 1896 | Alfréd HAJOS | HUN | 18:22.1 |

1500m (Mile in 1904)

1904	Emil RAUSH	GER	27:18.2
1908	Henry TAYLOR	GBR	22:48.4
1912	George HODGSON	CAN	22:00.0
1920	Norman ROSS	USA	22:23.2
1924	Andrew CHARLTON	AUS	20:06.6
1928	Arne BORG	SWE	19:51.8
1932	Kusuo KITAMURA	JAP	19:12.4
1936	Noboru TERADA	JAP	19:13.7
1948	James McLANE	USA	19:18.5
1952	Ford KONNO	USA	18:30.3
1956	Murray ROSE	AUS	17:58.9
1960	John KONRADS	AUS	17:19.6
1964	Robert WINDLE	AUS	17:01.7
1968	Mike BURTON	USA	16:38.9
1972	Mike BURTON	USA	15:52.58
1976	Brian GOODELL	USA	15:02.40
1980	Vladimir SALNIKOV	SOV	14:58.27
1984	Michael O'BRIEN	USA	15:05.20

1988	Vladimir SALNIKOV	SOV	15:00.40
1992	Kieren PERKINS	AUS	14:43.48
1996	Kieren PERKINS	AUS	14:56.40
2000	Grant HACKETT	AUS	14:48.33

4,000m

| 1900 | John Arthur JARVIS | GBR | 58:24.0 |

100m BACKSTROKE

1904	Walter BRACK	GER	1:16.8
1908	Arno BIEBERSTEIN	GER	1:24.6
1912	Harry HEBNER	USA	1:21.2
1920	Warren Paoa KEALOHA	USA	1:15.2
1924	Warren Paoa KEALOHA	USA	1:13.2
1928	George KOJAC	USA	1:08.2
1932	Masaji KIYOKAWA	JAP	1:08.6
1936	Adolf KIEFER	USA	1:05.9
1948	Allen STACK	USA	1:06.4
1952	Yoshinobu OYAKAWA	USA	1:05.4
1956	David THEILE	AUS	1:02.2
1960	David THEILE	AUS	1:01.9
1968	Roland MATTHES	GDR	58.7
1972	Roland MATTHES	GDR	56.58
1976	John NABER	USA	55.49
1980	Bengt BARON	SWE	56.53
1984	Rick CAREY	USA	55.79
1988	Daichi SUZUKI	JAP	55.05
1992	Mark TEWKSBURY	CAN	53.98
1996	Jeff ROUSE	USA	54.10
2000	Lenny KRAYZELBURG	USA	53.72

200m BACKSTROKE

1900	Ernst HOPPENBERG	GER	2:47.0
1964	Jed GRAEF	USA	2:10.3
1968	Roland MATTHES	GDR	2:09.6
1972	Roland MATTHES	GDR	2:02.82
1976	John NABER	USA	1:59.19
1980	Sandor WLADAR	HUN	2:01.93
1984	Rick CAREY	USA	2:00.23
1988	Igor POLIANSKI	SOV	1:59.37
1992	Martin LOPEZ-ZUBERO	ESP	1:58.47
1996	Brad BRIDGEWATER	USA	1:58.54
2000	Lenny KRAYZELBURG	USA	1:56.76

100m BREASTSTROKE

1968	Donald McKENZIE	USA	1:07.7
1972	Nobutaka TAGUCHI	JAP	1:04.94
1976	John HENCKEN	USA	1:03.11
1980	Duncan GOODHEW	GBR	1:03.44
1984	Steve LUNDQUIST	USA	1:01.65
1988	Adrian MOORHOUSE	GBR	1:02.04
1992	Nelson DIEBEL	USA	1:01.50
1996	Frederick DEBURGHGRAEVE	BEL	1:00.65
2000	Domenico FIORAVANTI	ITA	1:00.46

200m BREASTSTROKE

1908	Frederick HOLMAN	GBR	3:09.2
1912	Walter BATHE	GER	3:01.8
1920	Hakan MALMROTH	SWE	3:04.4
1924	Robert SKELTON	USA	2:56.6
1928	Yoshiyuki TSURUTA	JAP	2:48.8
1932	Yoshiyuki TSURUTA	JAP	2:45.4
1936	Tetsuo HAMURO	JAP	2:41.5
1948	Joseph VERDEUR	USA	2:39.3
1952	John DAVIES	AUS	2:34.4
1956	Masaru FURUKAWA	JAP	2:34.7
1960	William MULLIKEN	USA	2:37.4
1964	Ian O'BRIEN	AUS	2:27.8
1968	Felipe MUNOZ	MEX	2:28.7
1972	John HENCKEN	USA	2:21.55
1976	David WILKIE	GBR	2:15.11
1980	Robertas ZHULPA	SOV	2:15.85
1984	Victor DAVIS	CAN	2:13.34
1988	Jozsef SZABO	HUN	2:13.52
1992	Mike BARROWMAN	USA	2:10.16
1996	Norbert ROZSA	HUN	2:12.57
2000	Domenico FIORAVANTI	ITA	2:10.87

400m BREASTSTROKE

1904	Georg ZACHARIAS	GER	7:23.6
1912	Walter BATHE	GER	6:29.6
1920	Hakan MALMROTH	SWE	6:31.8

100m BUTTERFLY

1968	Douglas RUSSELL	USA	55.9
1972	Mark SPITZ	USA	54.27
1976	Matt VOGEL	USA	54.35
1980	Pär ARVIDSSON	SWE	54.92
1984	Michael GROSS	GER	53.08
1988	Anthony NESTY	SUR	53.00
1992	Pablo MORALES	USA	53.32
1996	Denis PANKRATOV	RUS	52.27
2000	Lars FROLANDER	SWE	52.00

200m BUTTERFLY

1956	William YORZYK	USA	2:19.3
1960	Michael TROY	USA	2:12.8
1964	Kevin BERRY	AUS	2:06.6
1968	Carl ROBIE	USA	2:08.7
1972	Mark SPITZ	USA	2:00.70
1976	Mike BRUNER	USA	1:59.23
1980	Serguei FESSENKO	SOV	1:59.76
1984	Jonathan SIEBEN	AUS	1:57.04
1988	Michael GROSS	GER	1:56.94
1992	Melvin STEWART	USA	1:56.26
1996	Denis PANKRATOV	RUS	1:56.51
2000	Tom MALCHOW	USA	1:55.35

200m MEDLEY

1968	Charles HICKCOX	USA	2:12.0
1972	Gunnar LARSSON	SWE	2:07.17
1984	Alex BAUMANN	CAN	2:01.42
1988	Tamas DARNYI	HUN	2:00.17
1992	Tamas DARNYI	HUN	2:00.76
1996	Attila CZENE	HUN	1:59.91
2000	Massimiliano ROSOLINO	ITA	1:58.98

400m MEDLEY

1964	Richard ROTH	USA	4:45.4
1968	Charles HICKCOX	USA	4:48.4
1972	Gunnar LARSSON	SWE	4:31.981
1976	Rod STRACHAN	USA	4:23.68
1980	Aleksandr SIDORENKO	SOV	4:22.89
1984	Alex BAUMANN	CAN	4:17.41
1988	Tamas DARNYI	HUN	4:14.75
1992	Tamas DARNYI	HUN	4:14.23
1996	Tom DOLAN	USA	4:14.90
2000	Tom DOLAN	USA	4:11.76

4x50m

1904	USA	2:04.6

4x100m

1964	USA	3:33.2
1968	USA	3:31.7
1972	USA	3:26.42
1984	USA	3:19.03
1988	USA	3:16.53
1992	USA	3:16.74
1996	USA	3:15.41
2000	AUS	3:13.67

4x200m

1908	GBR	10:55.6
1912	AUS/NZL	10:11.6
1920	USA	10:04.4
1924	USA	9:53.4
1928	USA	9:36.2
1932	JAP	8:58.4
1936	JAP	8:51.5
1948	USA	8:46.0
1952	USA	8:31.1
1956	AUS	8:23.6
1960	USA	8:10.2
1964	USA	7:52.1
1968	USA	7:52.3
1972	USA	7:35.78
1976	USA	7:23.22
1980	SOV	7:23.50
1984	USA	7:15.69
1988	USA	7:12.51
1992	SOV	7:11.95
1996	USA	7:14.84
2000	AUS	7:07.05

4x100m MEDLEY

1960	USA	4:05.4
1964	USA	3:58.4
1968	USA	3:54.9
1972	USA	3:48.16
1976	USA	3:42.22
1980	AUS	3:45.70
1984	USA	3:39.30
1988	USA	3:36.93
1992	USA	3:36.93
1996	USA	3:34.84
2000	USA	3:33':73

200m OBSTACLE RACE

1900	Frederick LANE	AUS	2:38.4

UNDERWATER SWIMMING

1900	Charles DE VENDEVILLE	FRA	188.4 pts

200m TEAM

1900	GER	32 pts

SWIMMING (WOMEN)

50m

1988	Kristin OTTO	GDR	25.49
1992	YANG Wenyi	CHN	24.79
1996	Amy VAN DYKEN	USA	24.87
2000	Inge DE BRUIJN	HOL	24.32

100m

1912	Fanny DURACK	AUS	1:22.2
1920	Ethelda BLEIBTREY	USA	1:13.6
1924	Ethel LACKIE	USA	1:12.4
1928	Albina OSIPOVITCH	USA	1:11.0
1932	Helene MADISON	USA	1:06.8
1936	Hendrika MASTENBROEK	HOL	1:05.9
1948	Greta ANDERSEN	DAN	1:06.3
1952	Katalin SZÖKE	HUN	1:06.8
1956	Dawn FRASER	AUS	1:02.0
1960	Dawn FRASER	AUS	1:01.2
1964	Dawn FRASER	AUS	59.5
1968	Jan HENNE	USA	1:00.0
1972	Sandra NEILSON	USA	58.59
1976	Kornelia ENDER	GDR	55.65
1980	Barbara KRAUSE	GDR	54.79
1984	Nancy HOGSHEAD	USA	55.92
1988	Kristin OTTO	GDR	54.93
1992	ZHUANG Yong	CHN	54.64
1996	LE Jingyi	CHN	54.50
2000	Inge DE BRUIJN	HOL	53.83

200m

1968	Deborah 'Debbie' MEYER	USA	2:10.5
1972	Shane GOULD	AUS	2:03.56
1976	Kornelia ENDER	GDR	1:59.26
1980	Barbara KRAUSE	GDR	1:58.33
1984	Mary WAYTE	USA	1:59.23
1988	Heike FRIEDRICH	GDR	1:57.65
1992	Nicole HAISLETT	USA	1:57.90
1996	Claudia POLL	CRI	1:58.16
2000	Susan O'NEILL	AUS	1:58.24

400m

1920	Ethelda BLEIBTREY	USA	4:34.0
1924	Martha NORELIUS	USA	6:02.2
1928	Martha NORELIUS	USA	5:42.8
1932	Helene MADISON	USA	5:28.5
1936	Hendrika MASTENBROEK	HOL	5:26.4
1948	Ann CURTIS	USA	5:17.8
1952	Valeria GYENGE	HUN	5:12.1
1956	Lorraine CRAPP	AUS	4:54.6
1960	Christine VON SALTZA	USA	4:50.6
1964	Virginia DUENKEL	USA	4:43.3
1968	Debbie MEYER	USA	4:31.8
1972	Shane GOULD	AUS	4:19.04
1976	Petra THÜMER	GDR	4:09.89
1980	Ines DIERS	GDR	4:08.76
1984	Tiffany COHEN	USA	4:07.10
1988	Janet EVANS	USA	4:03.85
1992	Dagmar HASE	GER	4:07.18
1996	Michelle SMITH	IRL	4:07.25
2000	Brooke BENNETT	USA	4:05.80

800m

1968	Deborah 'Debbie' MEYER	USA	9:24.0
1972	Keena ROTHHAMMER	USA	8:53.68
1976	Petra THÜMER	GDR	8:37.14
1980	Michelle FORD	AUS	8:28.90
1984	Tiffany COHEN	USA	8:24.95
1988	Janet EVANS	USA	8:20.20
1992	Janet EVANS	USA	8:25.52
1996	Brooke BENNETT	USA	8:27.89
2000	Brooke BENNETT	USA	8:19.67

100m BACKSTROKE

1924	Sybil BAUER	USA	1:23.2
1928	Maria BRAUN	HOL	1:22.0
1932	Eleanor HOLM	USA	1:19.4
1936	Nida SENFF	HOL	1:18.9
1948	Karen-Margrete HARUP	DAN	1:14.4
1952	Joan HARRISON	RSA	1:14.3
1956	Judith GRINHAM	GBR	1:12.9
1960	Lynn BURKE	USA	1:09.3
1964	Cathy FERGUSON	USA	1:07.7
1968	Kaye HALL	USA	1:06.2
1972	Melissa BELOTE	USA	1:05.78
1976	Ulrike RICHTER	GDR	1:01.83
1980	Rica REINISCH	GDR	1:00.86
1984	Theresa ANDREWS	USA	1:02.55
1988	Kristin OTTO	GDR	1:00.89
1992	Krisztina EGERSZEGI	HUN	1:00.68
1996	Beth BOTSFORD	USA	1:01.19
2000	Diana MOCANU	ROU	1:00.21

200m BACKSTROKE

1968	Lillian WATSON	USA	2:24.8
1972	Melissa BELOTE	USA	2:19.19
1976	Ulrike RICHTER	GDR	2:13.43
1980	Rica REINISCH	GDR	2:11.77
1984	Jolanda de ROVER	HOL	2:12.38
1988	Krisztina EGERSZEGI	HUN	2:09.29
1992	Krisztina EGERSZEGI	HUN	2:07.06
1996	Krisztina EGERSZEGI	HUN	2:07.83
2000	Diana MOCANU	ROU	2:08.16

100m BREASTSTROKE

1968	Djurdjica BJEDOV	YUG	1:15.8
1972	Catherine CARR	USA	1:13.58
1976	Hannelore ANKE	GDR	1:11.16
1980	Ute GEWENINGER	GDR	1:10.22
1984	Petra VAN STAVEREN	HOL	1:09.88
1988	Tania DANGALAKOVA (BOGOMILOVA)	BUL	1:07.95
1992	Yelena RUDKOVSKAIA	CEI	1:08.00
1996	Penelope HEYNS	RSA	1:07.73
2000	Megan QUANN	USA	1:07.05

200m BREASTSTROKE

1924	Lucy MORTON	GBR	3:33.2
1928	Hildegard SCHRADER	GER	3:12.6
1932	Clare DENNIS	AUS	3:06.3
1936	Hideko MAEHATA	JAP	3:03.6
1948	Nelly VAN VLIET	HOL	2:57.2
1952	Eva SZÉKELY	HUN	2:51.7
1956	Ursula HAPPE	GER	2:53.1
1960	Anita LONSBROUGH	GBR	2:49.5
1964	Galina PROZUMENCHTCHIKOVA	SOV	2:46.4
1968	Sharon WICHMAN	USA	2:44.4
1972	Beverly WHITFIELD	AUS	2:41.71
1976	Marina KOCHEVAIA	SOV	2:33.35
1980	Lina KACIUSYTÉ	SOV	2:29.54
1984	Anne OTTENBRITE	CAN	2:30.38
1988	Silke HÖRNER	GDR	2:26.71
1992	Kyoko IWASAKI	JAP	2:26.65
1996	Penelope HEYNS	RSA	2:25.41
2000	Agnes KOVACS	HUN	2:24.35

100m BUTTERFLY

1956	Shelley MANN	USA	1:11.0
1960	Carolyn SCHULER	USA	1:09.5
1964	Sharon STOUDER	USA	1:04.7
1968	Lynette McCLEMENTS	AUS	1:05.5

1972	Mayumi AOKI	JAP	1:03.34
1976	Kornelia ENDER	GDR	1:00.13
1980	Caren METSCHUCK	GDR	1:00.42
1984	Mary T. MEAGHER	USA	59.26
1988	Kristin OTTO	GDR	59.00
1992	QIAN Hong	CHN	58.62
1996	Amy VAN DYKEN	USA	59.13
2000	Inge DE BRUIJN	HOL	56.61

200m BUTTERFLY

1968	Ada KOK	HOL	2:24.7
1972	Karen THOTNTON (MOE)	USA	2:15.57
1976	Andrea POLLACK	GDR	2:11.41
1980	Ines GEISSLER	GDR	2:10.44
1984	Mary T. MEAGHER	USA	2:06.90
1988	Kathleen NORD	GDR	2:09.51
1992	Summer SANDERS	USA	2:08.67
1996	Susan O'NEILL	AUS	2:07.76
2000	Misty HYMAN	USA	2:05.88

200m MEDLEY

1968	Claudia KOLB	USA	2:24.7
1972	Shane GOULD	AUS	2:23.07
1984	Tracy CAULKINS	USA	2:12.64
1988	Daniela HUNGER	GDR	2:12.59
1992	LIN Li	CHN	2:11.65
1996	Michelle SMITH	IRL	2:13.93
2000	Yana KLOCHKOVA	UKR	2:10.68

400m MEDLEY

1964	Donna De VARONA	USA	5:18.7
1968	Claudia KOLB	USA	5:08.5
1972	Gail NEALL	AUS	5:02.97
1976	Ulrike TAUBER	GDR	4:42.77
1980	Petra SCHNEIDER	GDR	4:36.29
1984	Tracy CAULKINS	USA	4:39.24
1988	Janet EVANS	USA	4:37.76
1992	Krisztina EGERSZEGI	HUN	4:36.54
1996	Michelle SMITH	IRL	4:39.18
2000	Yana KLOCHKOVA	UKR	4:33.59

4x100m

1912	GBR		5:52.8
1920	USA		5:11.6
1924	USA		4:58.8
1928	USA		4:47.6
1932	USA		4:38.0
1936	HOL		4:36.0
1948	USA		4:29.2
1952	HUN		4:24.4
1956	AUS		4:17.1
1960	USA		4:08.9
1964	USA		4:03.8
1968	USA		4:02.5
1972	USA		3:55.19
1976	USA		3:44.82
1980	GDR	RDA	3:42.71
1984	USA		3:43.43
1988	GDR	RDA	3:40.63
1992	USA		3:39.46
1996	USA		3:39.29
2000	USA		3:36.61

4x200m

| 1996 | USA | | 7:59.87 |
| 2000 | USA | | 7:57.80 |

4x100m MEDLEY

1960	USA		4:41.1
1964	USA		4:33.9
1968	USA		4:28.3
1972	USA		4:20.75
1976	GDR	RDA	4:07.95
1980	GDR	RDA	4:06.67
1984	USA		4:08.34
1988	GDR	RDA	4:03.74
1992	USA		4:02.54
1996	USA		4:02.88
2000	USA		3:58.30

SYNCHRONISED SWIMMING

DUET

1984	USA
1988	CAN
1992	USA
2000	RUS

TEAM

| 1996 | USA |
| 2000 | RUS |

SOLO

1984	Tracie RUIZ	USA
1988	Carolyn WALDO	CAN
1992	Kristen BABB-SPRAGUE	USA

TABLE TENNIS (MEN)

SINGLES

1988	YOO Nam-kyu	KOR
1992	Jan-Ove WALDNER	SWE
1996	LIU Guoliang	CHN
2000	KONG Linghui	CHN

DOUBLES

1988	CHN
1992	CHN
1996	CHN
2000	CHN

TABLE TENNIS (WOMEN)

SINGLES

1988	CHEN Jing	TAI
1992	DENG Yaping	CHN
1996	DENG Yaping	CHN
2000	WANG Nan	CHN

DOUBLES

1988	KOR
1992	CHN
1996	CHN
2000	CHN

TAE-KWONDO (MEN)

FLYWEIGHT (58kg)

| 2000 | Mikhail MOUROUTSOS | GRE |

FEATHERWEIGHT (68kg)

| 2000 | Steven LOPEZ | USA |

WELTERWEIGHT (80kg)

| 2000 | Angel Valodia MATOS | CUB |

HEAVYWEIGHT (OVER 80kg)

| 2000 | KIM Kyong-hun | KOR |

TAE-KWONDO (WOMEN)

FLYWEIGHT (49kg)

| 2000 | Lauren BURNS | AUS |

FEATHERWEIGHT (57kg)

| 2000 | JUNG Jae-eun | KOR |

WELTERWEIGHT (67kg)

| 2000 | LEE Sun-hee | KOR |

HEAVYWEIGHT (OVER 67kg)

| 2000 | CHEN Zhong | CHN |

TENNIS (MEN)

SINGLES

1896	John BOLAND	GBR
1900	Hugh DOHERTY	GBR
1904	Beals WRIGHT	USA
1908	Josiah RITCHIE	GBR
1912	Charles WINSLOW	RSA
1920	Louis RAYMOND	RSA
1924	Vincent RICHARDS	USA
1988	Miloslav MECIR	CZE
1992	Marc ROSSET	SUI
1996	Andre AGASSI	USA
2000	Evgueni KAFELNIKOV	RUS

SINGLES (INDOOR COURT)

| 1908 | Arthur GORE | GBR |
| 1912 | André GOBERT | FRA |

DOUBLES

1896	GBR/ALL
1900	GBR
1904	USA
1908	GBR
1912	RSA
1920	GBR
1924	USA
1988	USA
1992	GER
1996	AUS
2000	AUS

DOUBLES (INDOOR COURT)

| 1908 | GBR |
| 1912 | FRA |

TENNIS (WOMEN)

SINGLES

1900	Charlotte COOPER	GBR
1908	Dorothea CHAMBERS	GBR
1912	Marguerite BROQUEDIS	FRA
1920	Suzanne LENGLEN	FRA
1924	Helen WILLS	USA
1988	Steffi GRAF	GER
1992	Jennifer CAPRIATI	USA
1996	Lindsay DAVENPORT	USA
2000	Venus WILLIAMS	USA

SINGLES (INDOOR COURT)

| 1908 | Gladys EASTLAKE-SMITH | GBR |
| 1912 | Edith HANNAM | GBR |

DOUBLES

1920	GBR
1924	USA
1988	USA
1992	USA
1996	USA
2000	USA

MIXED DOUBLES

1900	GBR
1912	GER
1920	FRA
1924	USA

MIXED DOUBLES (INDOOR COURT)

| 1912 | GBR |

TRAMPOLINE (MEN)

2000	Aleksandr MOSKALENKO	RUS

TRAMPOLINE (WOMEN)

2000	Irina KARAVAEVA	RUS

TRIATHLON (MEN)

2000	Simon WHITFIELD	CAN

TRIATHLON (WOMEN)

2000	Brigitte McMAHON	SUI

VOLLEYBALL (MEN)

1964	SOV
1968	SOV
1972	JAP
1976	POL
1980	SOV
1984	USA
1988	USA
1992	BRA
1996	HOL
2000	YUG

VOLLEYBALL (WOMEN)

1964	JAP
1968	SOV
1972	SOV
1976	JAP
1980	SOV
1984	CHN
1988	SOV
1992	CUB
1996	CUB
2000	CUB

BEACH VOLLEYBALL (MEN)

1996	USA
2000	USA

BEACH VOLLEYBALL (WOMEN)

1996	BRA
2000	AUS

WATER-POLO (MEN)

1900	GBR
1908	GBR
1912	GBR
1920	GBR/IRL
1924	FRA
1928	GER
1932	HUN
1936	HUN
1948	ITA
1952	HUN
1956	HUN
1960	ITA
1964	HUN
1968	YUG
1972	SOV
1976	HUN
1980	SOV
1984	YUG
1988	YUG
1992	ITA
1996	ESP
2000	HUN

WATER-POLO (WOMEN)

2000	AUS

WEIGHTLIFTING

FLYWEIGHT (54kg)

1972	Zygmunt SMALCERZ	POL
1976	Aleksandr VORONIN	SOV
1980	Kanybek OSMANALIEV	SOV
1984	ZENG Guoqiang	CHN
1988	Sevdalin MARINOV	BUL
1992	Ivan IVANOV	BUL
1996	Halil MUTLU	TUR

BANTAMWEIGHT (56kg)

1948	Joseph DI PIETRO	USA
1952	Ivan UDODOV	SOV
1956	Charles VINCI	USA
1960	Charles VINCI	USA
1964	Aleksei VAKHONIN	SOV
1968	Mohammad NASIRI	IRN
1972	Imre FÖLDI	HUN
1976	Norair NURIKIAN	BUL
1980	Daniel NÚÑEZ	CUB
1984	WU Shude	CHN
1988	Oksen MIRZOÏAN	SOV
1992	CHUN Byng-kwan	KOR
1996	TANG Ningsheng	CHN
2000	Halil MUTLU	TUR

FEATHERWEIGHT (60kg)

1920	François DE HAES	BEL
1924	Pierino GABETTI	ITA
1928	Franz ANDRYSEK	AUT
1932	Raymond SUVIGNY	FRA
1936	Anthony TERLAZZO	USA
1948	Mahmoud FAYAD	EGY
1952	Rafael CHIMISKIAN	SOV
1956	Isaac BERGER	USA
1960	Evgueni MINAEV	SOV
1964	Yoshinobu MIYAKE	JAP
1968	Yoshinobu MIYAKE	JAP
1972	Norair NURIKIAN	BUL
1976	Nikolai KOLESNIKOV	SOV
1980	Viktor MAZIN	SOV
1984	CHEN Weiqiang	CHN
1988	Naim SULEIMANOGLU	TUR
1992	Naim SULEIMANOGLU	TUR
1996	Naim SULEIMANOGLU	TUR
2000	Nikolai PECHALOV	CRO

LIGHTWEIGHT (67.5kg)

1920	Alfred NEULAND	EST
1924	Edmond DECOTTIGNIES	FRA
1928	Hans HAAS	AUT
1932	René DUVERGER	FRA
1936	Robert FEIN	AUT
1948	Ibrahim HASSAN SHAMS	EGY
1952	Tamio 'Tommy' KONO	USA
1956	Igor RYBAK	SOV
1960	Viktor BUCHUEV	SOV
1964	Waldemar BASZANOWSKI	POL
1968	Waldemar BASZANOWSKI	POL
1972	Mukharby KIRZINOV	SOV
1976	Pyotr KOROL	SOV
1980	Yanko RUSSEV	BUL
1984	YAO Jingyan	CHN
1988	Joachim KUNZ	GDR
1992	Israil MILITOSIAN	ARM
1996	ZHANG Xugang	CHN
2000	Galabin BOEVSKI	BUL

MIDDLEWEIGHT (75kg)

1920	Henri GANCE	FRA
1924	Carlo GALIMBERTI	ITA
1928	Roger FRANÇOIS	FRA
1932	Rudolf ISMAYR	GER
1936	Khadr SAYED EL TOUNI	EGY
1948	Frank SPELLMAN	USA
1952	Peter GEORGE	USA
1956	Fiodor BOGDANOVSKI	SOV
1960	Aleksandr KURINOV	SOV
1964	Hans ZDRAZILA	CZE
1968	Viktor KURENTSOV	SOV
1972	Yordan BIKOV	BUL
1976	Yordan MITKOV	BUL
1980	Assen ZLATEV	BUL
1984	Karl-Heinz RADSCHINSKY	GER
1988	Borislav GIDIKOV	BUL
1992	Fedor KASSAPU	MOL
1996	Pablo LARA	CUB
2000	ZHANG Xugang	CHN

LIGHT HEAVYWEIGHT (82.5kg)

1920	Ernest CADINE	FRA
1924	Charles RIGOULOT	FRA
1928	El SAYED MOHAMMED NOSSEIR	EGY
1932	Louis HOSTIN	FRA
1936	Louis HOSTIN	FRA
1948	Stanley STANCZYK	USA
1952	Trofim LOMAKIN	SOV
1956	Tamio "Tony" KONO	USA
1960	Ireneusz PALINSKI	POL
1964	Rudolf PLUKFELDER	SOV
1968	Boris SELITSKI	SOV
1972	Leif JENSSEN	NOR
1976	Valery CHARY	SOV
1980	Yurik VARDANIAN	SOV
1984	Petre BECHERU	ROM
1988	Israil ARSAMAKOV	SOV
1992	Pyrros DIMAS	GRE
1996	Pyrros DIMAS	GRE
2000	Pyrros DIMAS	GRE

MIDDLE HEAVYWEIGHT (90kg)

1952	Norbert SCHEMANSKY	USA
1956	Arkadi VOROBIEV	SOV
1960	Arkadi VOROBIEV	SOV
1964	Vladimir GOLOVANOV	SOV
1968	Kaarlo KANGASNIEMI	FIN
1972	Andon NIKOLOV	BUL
1976	David RIGERT	SOV
1980	Péter BACZAKÓ	HUN
1984	Nicu VLAD	ROM
1988	Anatoli KHRAPATI	SOV
1992	Kachi KAKIACHVILI	CEI
1996	Aleksei PETROV	RUS
2000	Akakios KAKIASVILIS	GRE

SUPER HEAVYWEIGHT (OPEN)

1896	Viggo JENSEN	DAN
1904	Perikles KAKOUSIS	GRE
1920	Filippo BOTTINO	ITA
1924	Giuseppe TONANI	ITA
1928	Josef STRASSBERGER	GER
1932	Jaroslav SKOBLA	CZE
1936	Josef MANGER	GER
1948	John DAVIS	USA
1952	John DAVIS	USA
1956	Paul ANDERSON	USA
1960	Juri VLASSOV	SOV
1964	Leonid JABOTINSKI	SOV
1968	Leonid JABOTINSKI	SOV
1972	Vassili ALEXEEV	SOV
1976	Vassili ALEXEEV	SOV
1980	Sultan RAKMANOV	SOV
1984	Dean LUKIN	AUS
1988	Aleksandr KURLOVITCH	SOV
1992	Aleksandr KURLOVITCH	CEI
1996	Andrei CHEMERKIN	RUS
2000	Hossein REZAZADEH	IRN

FIRST HEAVYWEIGHT 100kg

1980	Ota ZAREMBA	CZE
1984	Rolf MILSER	GER
1988	Pavel KUZNETSOV	SOV
1992	Viktor TREGUBOV	CEI
1996	Akakide KAKIASVILIS	GRE

HEAVYWEIGHT 105kg

1972	Jaan TALTS	SOV
1976	Juri ZAITSEV	SOV
1980	Leonid TARANENKO	SOV
1984	Norberto OBERBURGER	ITA
1988	Yuri ZAKHAREVICH	SOV
1992	Ronny WELLER	GER
1996	Timur TAIMAZOV	UKR
2000	Hossein TAVAKOLI	IRN

ONE-HAND LIFT

1896	Launceston ELLIOT	GBR

ALL-AROUND

1904	Oscar OSTHOFF	USA

WEIGHTLIFTING (WOMEN)

FLYWEIGHT (48kg)

2000	Izabela DRAGNEVA	BUL

FEATHWEIGHT (53kg)

2000	YANG Xia	CHN

LIGHTWEIGHT (58kg)

2000	Soraya JIMENEZ	MEX

MIDDLEWEIGHT (63kg)

2000	CHEN Xiaomin	CHN

LIGHT HEAVYWEIGHT (69kg)

2000	LIN Weining	CHN

HEAVYWEIGHT (75kg)

2000	Maria Isabel URRUTIA	COL

SUPER HEAVYWEIGHT (+75kg)

2000	DING Meiyuan	CHN

WRESTLING

GRECO-ROMAN WRESTLING
LIGHT FLYWEIGHT (48kg)

1972	Gheorghe BERCEANU	ROM
1976	Aleksei CHUMAKOV	SOV
1980	Saksylik UCHKEMPIROV	SOV
1984	Vincenzo MAENZA	ITA
1988	Vincenzo MAENZA	ITA
1992	Oleg KUTCHERENKO	CEI
1996	SIM Kwon-ho	KOR

FLYWEIGHT (54kg)

1948	Pietro LOMBARDI	ITA
1952	Boris GUREVICH	SOV
1956	Nikolai SOLOVIEV	SOV
1960	Dumitru PIRVULESCU	ROM
1964	Tsutomu HANAHARA	JAP
1968	Petar KIROV	BUL
1972	Petar KIROV	BUL
1976	Vitali KONSTANTINOV	SOV
1980	Vakhtang BLAGIDZE	SOV
1984	Atsuji MIYAHARA	JAP
1988	Jon RÖNNINGEN	NOR
1992	Jon RÖNNINGEN	NOR
1996	Armen NAZARIAN	ARM
2000	SIM Kwon-ho	KOR

BANTAMWEIGHT (57kg)

1924	Eduard PÜTSEP	EST
1928	Kurt LEUCHT	GER
1932	Jakob BRENDEL	GER
1936	Marton LÖRINCZ	HUN
1948	Kurt PETTERSEN	SWE
1952	Imre HOBACKSTROKE	HUN

1956	Konstantin VYRUPAEV	SOV
1960	Oleg KARAVAEV	SOV
1964	Masamitsu ICHIGUCHI	JAP
1968	Janos VARGA	HUN
1972	Rustem KAZAKOV	SOV
1976	Pertti UKKOLA	FIN
1980	Chamil SERIKOV	SOV
1984	Pasquale PASSARELLI	GER
1988	Andras SIKE	HUN
1992	AN Hang-bong	KOR
1996	Youri MELNICHENKO	KAZ
2000	Armen NAZARIAN	BUL

FEATHERWEIGHT (63kg)

1912	Kaarlo KOSKELO	FIN
1920	Oskar FRIMAN	FIN
1924	Kaarlo ANTTILA	FIN
1928	Voldemar VÄLI	EST
1932	Giovanni GOZZI	ITA
1936	Yasar ERKAN	TUR
1948	Mehmet OKTAV	TUR
1952	Yakiv PUNKIN	SOV
1956	Rauno MÄKINEN	FIN
1960	Muzahir SILLE	TUR
1964	Imre POLYAK	HUN
1968	Roman RURUA	SOV
1972	Georgi MARKOV	BUL
1976	Kazimierz LIPIEN	POL
1980	Stylianos MYGIAKIS	GRE
1984	KIM Weon-kee	KOR
1988	Kamandar MADZIDOV	SOV
1992	Akif PIRIM	TUR
1996	Wlodzimierz ZAWADZKI	POL
2000	Varteres SAMOURGACHEV	RUS

LIGHTWEIGHT (67kg)

1908	Enrico PORRO	ITA
1912	Eemil WÄRE	FIN
1920	Eemil WÄRE	FIN
1924	Oskar FRIMAN	FIN
1928	Lajos KERESZTES	HUN
1932	Erik MALMBERG	SWE
1936	Lauri KOSKELA	FIN
1948	Gustav FREIJ	SWE
1952	Chazam SAFIN	SOV
1956	Kyösti LEHTONEN	FIN
1960	Avtandil KORIDZE	SOV
1964	Kazim AYVAZ	TUR
1968	Munji MUMEMURA	JAP
1972	Chamil KIZAMUTDINOV	SOV
1976	Suren NALBANDIAN	SOV
1980	Stefan RUSU	ROM
1984	Vlado LISJAK	YUG
1988	Levon DZULFALAKIAN	SOV
1992	Attila REPKA	HUN
1996	Ryszard WOLNY	POL
2000	Filiberto AZCUY	CUB

WELTERWEIGHT (73kg)

1932	Ivar JOHANSSON	SWE
1936	Rudolf SVEDBERG	SWE
1948	Gösta ANDERSSON	SWE
1952	Miklos SZILVASI	HUN
1956	Mithat BAYRAK	TUR
1960	Mithat BAYRAK	TUR
1964	Anatoli KOLESOV	SOV
1968	Rudolf VESPER	GDR
1972	Vitezslav MACHA	CZE
1976	Anatoli BYKOV	SOV
1980	Ferenc KOCSIS	HUN
1984	Jouko SALOMÄKI	FIN
1988	KIM Young-nam	KOR
1992	Mnatsakan ISKANDARIAN	ARM
1996	Filiberto ASCUY	CUB
2000	Mourat KARDANOV	RUS

MIDDLEWEIGHT (85kg)

1906	Verner WECKMAN	FIN
1908	Fritiof MARTENSSON	SWE
1912	Claes JOHANSON	SWE
1920	Carl WESTERGREN	SWF
1924	Edvard WESTERLUND	FIN
1928	Väinö KOKKINEN	FIN
1932	Väinö KOKKINEN	FIN

1936	Ivar JOHANSSON	SWE
1948	Axel GRÖNBERG	SWE
1952	Axel GRÖNBERG	SWE
1956	Givi KARTOZIA	SOV
1960	Dimiter DOBREV	BUL
1964	Branislav SIMIC	YUG
1968	Lothar METZ	GER
1972	Csaba HEGEDÜS	HUN
1976	Momir PETKOVIC	YUG
1980	Gennadi KORBAN	SOV
1984	Ion DRAICA	ROM
1988	Mikhail MAMIACHVILI	SOV
1992	Péter FARKAS	HUN
1996	Hamza YERLIKAYA	TUR
2000	Hamza YERLIKAYA	TUR

LIGHT HEAVYWEIGHT (90kg)

1908	Verner WECKMAN	FIN
1912	Anders AHLGREN	SWE
1920	Claes JOHANSON	SWE
1924	Carl WESTERGREN	SWE
1928	Ibrahim MOUSTAFA	EGY
1932	Rudolf SVENSSON	SWE
1936	Axel CARDIER	SWE
1948	Karl-Erik NILSSON	SWE
1952	Kaelpo GRÖNDAHL	FIN
1956	Valentin NIKOLAEV	SOV
1960	Tevfik KIS	TUR
1964	Boyan RADEV	BUL
1968	Boyan RADEV	BUL
1972	Valery REZANTSEV	SOV
1976	Valery REZANTSEV	SOV
1980	Norbert NÖVENYI	HUN
1984	Steven FRASER	USA
1988	Atanas KOMCHEV	BUL
1992	Maik BULLMANN	GER
1996	Viatcheslav OLEINIK	UKR
2000	Mikael LJUNGBERG	SWE

HEAVYWEIGHT (100kg)

1972	Nicolae MARTINESCU	ROM
1976	Nikolai BALBOCHIN	SOV
1980	Georgi RAIKOV	BUL
1984	Vasile ANDREI	ROM
1988	Andrzej WRONSKI	POL
1992	Hector MILIAN	CUB
1996	Andrzej WRONSKI	POL

SUPER HEAVYWEIGHT 130kg

1896	Carl SCHUHMANN	GER
1908	Richard WEISZ	HUN
1912	Yrjö SAARELA	FIN
1920	Adolf LINDFORS	FIN
1924	Henri DEGLANE	FRA
1928	Rudolf SVENSSON	SWE
1932	Carl WESTERGREN	SWE
1936	Kristian PALUSALU	EST
1948	Ahmet KIRECCI	TUR
1952	Johannes KOTKAS	SOV
1956	Anatoli PARFENOV	SOV
1960	Iwan BOHDAN	SOV
1964	Istvan KOZMA	HUN
1968	Istvan KOZMA	HUN
1972	Anatoli ROCHIN	SOV
1976	Aleksandr KOLCHINSKI	SOV
1980	Aleksandr KOLCHINSKI	SOV
1984	Jeffrey BLATNICK	USA
1988	Aleksandr KARELIN	SOV
1992	Aleksandr KARELIN	RUS
1996	Aleksandr KARELIN	RUS
2000	Rulon GARDNER	USA

FREESTYLE WRESTLING

LIGHT FLYWEIGHT(48kg)

1904	Robert CURRY	USA
1972	Roman DMITRIEV	SOV
1976	Hassan ISSAEV	BUL
1980	Claudio POLLIO	ITA
1984	Robert WEAVER	USA
1988	Takashi KOBAYASHI	JAP
1992	KIM IL	PRK
1996	KIM IL	PRK